PENGUIN PLAYS

IN CELEBRATION THE CONTRACTOR
THE RESTORATION OF ARNOLD MIDDLETON
THE FARM

DAVID STOREY was born in 1933 and is the third son of a mine-worker. He was educated at the Queen Elizabeth School at Wakefield and the Slade School of Fine Art. He has had various jobs ranging from professional footballer to schoolteaching and showground tent-erecting. He is now both a novelist and dramatist.

Among his publications are *This Sporting Life*, which won the Macmillan Fiction Award in 1960 and was also filmed; *Flight into Camden*, which won the John Llewelyn Rhys Memorial Prize and also the Somerset Maugham Award in 1960; *Radcliffe*, and *Pasmore*, which won the Faber Memorial Prize in 1973. These were followed by *A Temporary Life*, *Edward* and *Saville*, which won the Booker Prize in 1976. His other plays include *The Changing Room*, which received the New York Drama Critics' Award for Best Play of the Year, *Life Class*, *Sisters* and *Early Days*. Many of David Storey's works are published in Penguin.

David Storey lives in London. He was married in 1956 and has four children.

DAVID STOREY

IN CELEBRATION

THE CONTRACTOR

THE RESTORATION
OF ARNOLD MIDDLETON

THE FARM

PENGUIN BOOKS

Penguin Books Ltd, Harmondsworth, Middlesex, England
Penguin Books, 625 Madison Avenue, New York, New York 10022, U.S.A.
Penguin Books Australia Ltd, Ringwood, Victoria, Australia
Penguin Books Canada Ltd, 2801 John Street, Markham, Ontario, Canada l.3R 1B4
Penguin Books (N.Z.) Ltd, 182 190 Wairau Road, Auckland 10, New Zealand

In Celebration
First published by Jonathan Cape 1969
Published in Penguin Books 1971
Reprinted in this collection 1982
Copyright © David Storey, 1969

The Contractor
First published by Jonathan Cape 1970
Published in Penguin Books 1971
Reprinted in this collection 1982
Copyright © David Storey, 1970

The Restoration of Arnold Middleton
First published 1970
Reprinted in this collection 1982
Copyright © David Storey, 1970

The Farm
First published by Jonathan Cape 1973
Published in Penguin Books 1982
Copyright © David Storey, 1973

Made and printed in Great Britain by
Richard Clay (The Chaucer Press) Ltd, Bungay, Suffolk
Set in Monophoto Ehrhardt

CONTENTS

IN CELEBRATION

To my mother and father

IN CELEBRATION

First presented at the Royal Court Theatre, London, on 22 April 1969, under the direction of Lindsay Anderson. The cast was as follows:

MR SHAW	Bill Owen
MRS SHAW	Constance Chapman
ANDREW	Alan Bates
COLIN	James Bolam
STEVEN	Brian Cox
MRS BURNETT	Gabrielle Daye
REARDON	Fulton Mackay

CHARACTERS

MR SHAW, a miner, aged 64
MRS SHAW, his wife, aged 60
ANDREW, aged 38 ⎫
COLIN,   aged 36 ⎬ their sons
STEVEN, aged 33 ⎭
MRS BURNETT, a neighbour, aged 60
REARDON, a neighbour, aged 68

ACT ONE

Scene One

A solid, heavily furnished living-room: a door on one side leads to the kitchen and the stairs, a door on the other side to the front door and the road. There is also a window and a fireplace. The furniture is heavy and provincial: a three-piece suite, a table and four chairs, and a sideboard. There are various cushions, photographs, and pictures, as well as several cowboy paperbacks. The atmosphere is one of sobriety, with no particularly distinguishing features, either of period or 'character'.

Mid-morning.

STEVEN *comes in carrying a battered brief-case. He's dressed in an overcoat: a man in his thirties.*

STEVEN: Dad? ... [*Looks round.*] Dad? [*He hears a sound. Puts his bag down. Rubs his hands against the cold. Wanders round the room, examining old, familiar objects. One or two he picks up, shakes his head, etc.*]

[SHAW *comes in from the stairs: small and stocky, he's just woken, and is dressed in trousers and shirt, the shirt unfastened, the trousers held up by braces.*]

Dad ...

SHAW: Steven ... You're early. I've scarcely woken up.

[*They shake hands.*]

... What time ... [*Looks round dazedly.*] ... I thought you weren't coming till this afternoon.

STEVEN: I got away early ...

SHAW: Aye, well ... How are you? You're looking all right. [SHAW *is a bit shy of his son.*]

STEVEN [*taking his coat off*]: So's yourself. A bit older ... a bit more weight to go with it.

SHAW: Oh, take no notice of me ... I only got back from work three or four hours ago. Nights. My age ... You'd think they'd give me summat else ... Your mother's out ...

13

STEVEN: Yes ... I met a woman down the road ... she told me ...

SHAW: Nowt they don't know round here ... Gone to buy herself a hat.

STEVEN: A hat ...

SHAW: For tonight. [*Looking round for his cigarettes.*] I can't tell you ... I've heard nothing else for the past fortnight. You'd think we'd come up with a few thousand ...

   [*Finds his cigarette packet on the mantelpiece: offers one to* STEVEN.]

No, you don't, do you? Common sense. I'm choked up to here ... [*Coughs as he lights his own.*] Coal-dust. It's a wonder I'm still alive.

STEVEN: I've heard that before.

SHAW: Aye. But you won't for much longer.

STEVEN: I've heard that before as well.

SHAW [*sighs*]: Aye ... Do you fancy a cup of tea? I'll just make one. [*Going.*] How's the family, then? ... Are they keeping well? [*Goes to the kitchen.*]

STEVEN [*talking through*]: All right ... Up and down ... Look at this ... I don't think ought's changed here since I was last up ...

SHAW [*reappearing*]: Family, lad. Family. There's nothing as important as that. A good wife: children. God's good grace. [*Looks briefly up.*] If you have good health and your family, you don't need anything else.

STEVEN: Aye ...

SHAW: Sixty-four years next month. If I haven't learnt that I've learnt nothing. [*Suddenly shows him his hand.*] Damn near lost me hand last week. Seven stitches.

STEVEN: You'll have to watch out.

SHAW: Watch out? My age ... You're joking. One more year, you know, then I'm finished. Pension me off. Fifty years, you know, I've been down that lot. That's what I've got to show. [*Holds up his hands.*]

STEVEN: Oh, and a bit more ...

SHAW: Nay, I can't grumble ... And how's your lot? How's Sheila? Best daughter-in-law I ever had.

STEVEN: She's all right.

SHAW: Four kiddies. There can't be ten months between them. I

don't know how they do it. I thought I was impetuous. There was
two or three years, you know, between you lot.

STEVEN: When are they getting up?

SHAW: I don't know. This afternoon. Colin's bringing Andrew up in
his car. They'll get here sometime, I suppose. Your mother hasn't
been able to sit down for two minutes. Up and down. You'll have to
toss up for who's sleeping where. One down here, two up yonder.
It'll be like old times. She's cleaned that floor a dozen times if she's
cleaned it once. And them windows ... it's a wonder there's any
glass left in. Almost polished them right through ... [*Looks out.*]
Nothing changed out there either, you can see. Houses ... houses
... houses ... as far as the eye can see ... That's the kettle ... Get
your jacket off. Make yourself at home ... Mind where you put
yourself. She's puffed up every cushion, straightened every chair.
It's like being in the army ... [*He goes out to the kitchen. Off*] How
long are you staying?

STEVEN: I'll have to get back tomorrow.

SHAW [*off*]: How's your work going?

STEVEN: All right.

SHAW [*popping in the door*]: I wish I got half of what you got, I can tell
you: and for doing twice as much. I wouldn't mind.

STEVEN: It's got its drawbacks.

SHAW: Drawbacks. It could draw back as far as it liked for me ...
Teaching. Good God ... Ay up. Ay up. She's here. Look out. Look
out. [*He goes back in the kitchen.*]

  [MRS BURNETT *comes in; a neighbour, in her early sixties.*]

MRS BURNETT: Thought I saw you, Steven ... How are you keeping,
love?

STEVEN: Hello, Mrs Burnett ... Well enough ...

MRS BURNETT: And how's your wife?

STEVEN: Oh, surviving.

MRS BURNETT: I know. I've heard ... They've shown me photographs, you know ...

SHAW [*off*]: Pretend she's not there. She'll go away. Just take no
notice.

MRS BURNETT: Doesn't mind me popping in. Always the same ...
And your kiddies?

STEVEN: Fine.

MRS BURNETT: Your mother never mentions them. But I know. It all goes on inside. She's that sort of woman.

STEVEN: She's out shopping.

MRS BURNETT: I saw her go. New hat. She's very excited about tonight. Where are you taking them?

STEVEN: Into town ... Colin's arranged something.

MRS BURNETT: Your Andrew and Colin not here, then, yet?

STEVEN: They're coming up by car.

MRS BURNETT: Eh. It's a lovely treat for them.

STEVEN: I hope so.

MRS BURNETT: Forty years. They'll not forget ...

SHAW [*coming with a tray and two pots*]: Yakking. Yakking. Yakking.

MRS BURNETT [*to* STEVEN]: He never lets you get a word in. Don't worry.

SHAW: Word in? I can hardly open me mouth ... [*To* STEVEN] Smells tea, you know, a mile off. The 'uman blood 'ound. She's never out of this house.

MRS BURNETT: He hasn't forgotten me, don't worry, after all these years.

SHAW: No. That's true.

MRS BURNETT: He doesn't let you forget, don't worry. He's out showing it across the backs whenever he has any news. You get tired of hearing it, I can tell you ...

SHAW: Tired? They spend all their day flat on their backs round here. They don't know what work is. As soon as their husband's gone off, out it comes: teapot, cushion behind their backs, feet up ...

MRS BURNETT: I know. I know. That's why you never have anything to eat and your houses are full up to the chimney with last week's washing.

SHAW: Last week's. Last bloody year's more likely. [*To* STEVEN] We've to bolt the door you know at times just to get a bit of peace.

MRS BURNETT [*to* STEVEN]: Never changes. All the years I've known him ... Last week he gave your mother a shock. [*Looking at* SHAW *concernedly*] Came in. White as a sheet. He was.

SHAW: Jumping up and down.

MRS BURNETT: They had me fetch the doctor.

SHAW [to STEVEN]: Heart ... [Taps his chest.]

MRS BURNETT [to STEVEN]: Don't worry. He didn't treat it lightly.

SHAW: 'Better take it easy. More rest.' I said: 'You must be joking. How would you take it easy if you had a ten-ton rock coming down on top of your head?'

STEVEN: What did he say?

SHAW: He laughed. They don't give a damn. Why should they? An old man. It's a wonder I wasn't dead years ago. She'll tell you...

MRS BURNETT: Go on ...

SHAW: And that's what he thought, an' all. You can see it in his eyes when he examines you.

STEVEN: I don't think that's right, somehow.

SHAW: Nay. I've no illusions. None ... I've had a good life. With a lovely woman. Can't ask for anything more ... Still ...

MRS BURNETT: Aye ... Well ... [Gazes at SHAW fondly.]

SHAW: Go on. Go on ... Get shut. [To STEVEN] Waiting for a cup of tea. Be here all day if she has the chance.

MRS BURNETT [to STEVEN]: I'll pop in later, love. Remember ... [Gesturing at SHAW behind his back] Pinch of salt. [Goes.]

SHAW: Pinch of bloody salt ... I'll pinch her bloody salt. Noses ten miles long round here ... She'll be out yakking it across the backs.

STEVEN: Aye. [Laughs.]

SHAW: We had a letter from Colin the other week. First one I can tell you for some time. He's moved his job. Works' liaison. A factory that big it'd take you a fortnight to walk right round it ... Cars ...

STEVEN: So I heard ...

SHAW: Offered to get us one. Brand new. Cut price.

STEVEN: You ought to take it.

SHAW: Nay, what would I do with a car? If you can't shove it, pedal it, or hang it on a wall, it's no use to me ... He has to argue, you know ...

STEVEN: Yes ...

SHAW: Whenever the workers – that's us – are going on strike, or feel they ought to, Colin's the one the management calls out to nego-tiate. He can charm the horns off a bloody cow, that lad. Been like it since I've known him. Industrial relations ... When he was lying on

17

that rug I little thought that that's where he'd end up. Industrial relations. A family with relatives like ours, an' all.

STEVEN: Aye ...

[*They laugh.*]

SHAW: Offered to buy us a house, you know. Probably will when we retire. If I'm daft enough to let him ...

STEVEN: It sounds like a good idea.

SHAW: If you're used to having money. As it is, I'm used to nowt. Still, times change. And people with it. Told me I ought to get out, you know. Retire now. He'd put up all the cash.

STEVEN: Why don't you?

SHAW: What? ... [*Gets up, wanders round.*] Andrew's another one, you know. Chucked up his job to be an artist! He's only forty, with two children to support, one of them nearly old enough to go to university. It takes some reckoning. A career as a solicitor, that he's worked at ... that *I* worked at. I've spent some hours, you know, working at that table with him: fractions, decimals, Latin ... Do you know I'd go down that pit some nights declining or declensing, I've forgotten which, Latin verbs ... I could have set up as a schoolmaster any time. Greek, algebra, physics, chemistry: the lot. It's a wonder I haven't taken a university degree myself.

STEVEN: I seem to remember ...

SHAW: Nay. You were the last, Steve, but by God, the best. There wasn't much I had to teach you. As for them: I had to shove it down their throats. Like trying to eat burnt porridge.

STEVEN: How's Andrew making his money, then?

SHAW: Don't ask me. One of the reasons he's coming up, I shouldn't wonder, is to see if he can borrow a bit. He's never been one to refuse a back-hander: that's why he was so good at law. He could make it fit any set of facts he wanted ... I remember him coming home when he was about thirteen and proving to me that God no longer existed. He's never looked back since then.

STEVEN: Why don't you take up Colin's offer? We could all chip in a bit.

SHAW: Aye, well ... [*Moves away.*]

STEVEN: What difference does one year make?

SHAW: I first went down the pit when I was fifteen, lad.

STEVEN: Yes.

SHAW: Forty-nine years. Half a century. One more now and it'll make it a round number.

STEVEN: Not worth risking your health for.

SHAW: No. Well . . . [*Gazes out of the window.*] Do you remember the war? I used to take one of you, out yonder . . .

STEVEN: Me.

SHAW: You? I believe it was. They hardly bombed here. Must have flown over and not thought we were worth it.

STEVEN: Made a mistake there.

SHAW: What? They made no mistakes about that. Miles of nothing, this place. Always has been, always will be. The only thing that ever came out of here was coal. And when that's gone, as it will be, there'll be even less. Row after row of empty houses, as far as the eye can see . . . It's starting . . . I pass them on the way to work. I stop sometimes and look in – holes in the roof, doors gone, windows . . . I knew the people who lived there . . . All this was moorland a hundred years ago. Sheep. And a bit of wood . . . When they come in a thousand years and dig it up they'll wonder what we made such a mess of it for . . . [*Gestures at the walls.*] Look at these foundations and think we all lived in little cells. Like goats.

STEVEN: We did. [*He laughs, gets up and pours himself some more tea.*]

SHAW: Aye . . . Here. Have a drop of something stronger. I got a bit in, in case . . .

STEVEN [*looks at the clock*]: A bit early.

SHAW: Save it till later. Don't worry. We'll have a grand time tonight. They'll have seen nothing like it round here for years . . . [*Watches him.*] How's your book going, then?

STEVEN: All right . . .

SHAW: If one of them was going to be famous, you know . . . I always thought it would be you.

STEVEN: Why's that? [*Laughs.*]

SHAW: Nay. I don't know. I suppose because you were so clever. [*Shy*] Don't tell me it's something you forget . . .

STEVEN: I think I must have done.

SHAW: Aye . . .

[STEVEN *glances away, across the room.*]

Here. Do you want a wash? ... I'll forget my own head one of these days.

STEVEN: I'll go up ... Have a look around ...

SHAW: Not much to see ... I can tell you that. Two rooms, back and front. [*Laughs.*]

[STEVEN *goes to the door.*]

If the water's not hot enough, give us a shout and I'll heat some up for you ... Won't take a minute.

STEVEN: Right ... [*He goes.*]

[SHAW *looks a little aimlessly about the room: picks up* STEVEN's *overcoat then his brief-case: looks round for somewhere to put them, then puts them down together in a chair. Looks at the fire, puts on a piece of coal, picks up bucket to take outside to fill ... There's the sound of the outer door shutting. He looks up, puts the bucket down quickly, and sits down in a chair.*

MRS SHAW *comes in, dressed from shopping: sixty years old, matronly, circumspect: some authority and composure.*]

MRS SHAW: There you are ... [*Puts her bag on the table.*]

SHAW [*pleasant*]: Nay, and where else would I be?

MRS SHAW: Have you had some tea, then? ... [*Looks at the tray on the table.*]

SHAW: Aye ... Aye ...

MRS SHAW: Two of you.

SHAW: Aye ... Mrs Burnett came in.

MRS SHAW: Did she? And you gave her some tea, then? [*Matter-of-fact, taking off her gloves and coat.*]

SHAW: Well, I thought I better ...

MRS SHAW: Oh, yes. And what's going on, then?

SHAW: Going on? ... Oh. Aye ... Steven's here. I forgot.

MRS SHAW: Forgot.

SHAW: Slipped me mind ... He's upstairs. Having a wash.

MRS SHAW: Having ... Did you give him a clean towel?

SHAW: Towel ... I forgot.

MRS SHAW: Honestly ...

SHAW: It's a wonder the entire street didn't tell you.

MRS SHAW: Well, they didn't. I suppose I've got to ask to find out. [*Picks up tray to take out.*]

[*Sounds of* STEVEN *returning.* MRS SHAW *looks quickly round the room.*]

SHAW: Don't worry. Nothing moved. Nothing shifted.

MRS SHAW: We could do with some more coal.

SHAW: Aye ... [*Gets up slowly.*]

    [MRS SHAW *has put the tray down again and goes to the curtains, pulling them back slightly, adjusting them needlessly until she knows* STEVEN *is in the room.*]

MRS SHAW: Well, then. And where have you been all this time?

STEVEN: Oh. About ...

    [*He comes to her and embraces her, rather shyly.*]

MRS SHAW: You're not looking too good, love.

STEVEN: The climate. I'm not used to it up here.

MRS SHAW: Aren't they looking after you?

STEVEN: They are. All right.

    [SHAW *has gone to the bucket, picked it up, watching them, smiling, then goes out.*]

MRS SHAW: Here. Let's have a look at you. You've put on a lot of weight. Or taken a lot off. I can't remember ... [*She laughs.*]

STEVEN: I forget myself.

MRS SHAW: Have you had some tea? I'll get you something to eat ...

STEVEN: There's no hurry ...

MRS SHAW: How's the family?

STEVEN: Oh. Well.

MRS SHAW: They'll need a lot of upkeep. How old's Roger? Three months? Patrick scarcely one and a quarter ...

STEVEN: I don't know. I've lost count.

MRS SHAW: Well, I don't know. There seems to be a lot of them. [*Collects tray again.*] I'll just put this away ... I hope your Dad hasn't been on too much.

STEVEN: No ... We were talking.

MRS SHAW: I think you'd do a lot of good, you know, while you're up there, if you persuaded him to come out of that pit. He's only another year ...

STEVEN: He's told me.

MRS SHAW: Pride. You've never seen anything like it. [*Hears him coming.*] I'll just take this out.

SHAW [*coming in with the bucket of coal*]: Now, then, my old china ...
[*Puts it down in the hearth.*] I'm good for lifting if I'm good for nowt
else. When I come again I think they'll make me into a donkey.
Reincarnation. It's stamped all over me from head to foot ...

STEVEN: You better be careful. Somebody might hear you.

SHAW: Oh, she knows me. Ought to. Well enough.

STEVEN: I meant up there. [*Points up.*]

SHAW: Oh ... He goes His own way. Nothing I say'll alter that. Don't
you think she's looking well?

STEVEN: Yes. I think so ...

SHAW: Forty years of married bliss ... It's left its mark. When she
walks down that street they step back, you know, to bow to her. If I
come back as a donkey she'll come back as a queen.

[MRS SHAW *comes back in.*]

We were just saying, love. You look a picture.

MRS SHAW: I know. And what of?

SHAW: Nay. You don't need me to tell you. She spends that long at the
mirror that when I go to look at it I still find her there – looking out.

[STEVEN *laughs.*]

MRS SHAW: He doesn't change, does he? You should see him skip in
the back and comb his hair when Mrs Burnett comes around.

SHAW: Mrs Burnett? I'd need to be down to the last woman on earth to
consider that ... As it is, love, I'm still up with the first. [*Puts his arm
round her shoulder, kissing her cheek: she moves her head back slightly
and moves away.*]

MRS SHAW: I tell you. He hasn't known where to put himself since
he's known you were coming ... I don't think, ever since you went to
university, he's known what to do with himself. And that's how
long ago?

SHAW: Fifteen years.

STEVEN: Longer ...

SHAW: Education, lad: you can't get anywhere without ... Look at
your mother. She left school at sixteen. Sixteen. That was almost
retiring age in those days. She's still got her certificate upstairs ...

STEVEN: I remember ...

SHAW: 'Proficiency in Domestic Science, Nature Study, and the
English Language.' All done out in copperplate script. 'Miss Helen

Swanson.' Her father was a pig-breeder, you know. Just outside town.

MRS SHAW: A small-holder ...

SHAW: A pig-breeder! He kept pigs. By go, you had to be in love to step in that house, I can tell you. [*He laughs.*]

MRS SHAW: Well. I've heard some things ...

SHAW: And she ends up marrying me. Never forgiven me, have you, love? ... Nay, lass, you know I love you. I married you all the same. [*He laughs and kisses her cheek.*]

MRS SHAW [*stepping back*]: I'll see about some food. [*To* STEVEN] Colin and Andrew are driving up together. They won't get here until this afternoon. I'll show you my hat later, love.

STEVEN: Ah ... Yes.

SHAW: Won't frighten us all, then, will it? Remember, we've got to walk down that street beside you. In public. I don't mind being seen with a woman ...

MRS SHAW: Well, then, in that case you needn't be ashamed.

SHAW: Ashamed? I've never been ashamed, love. Whatever you wear, my darling, I've never been – and I never will be – ashamed.

MRS SHAW: Well, then, in that case, we'll be all right.

[*She goes, smiling at* STEVEN.]

SHAW [*to* STEVEN]: Embarrassed, now. I might be a bit embarrassed. But I wouldn't be ashamed.

[*They laugh.*]

She's a good woman. A lady ... One of the very best. You know, no one's ever got the better of her.

STEVEN: I can imagine.

SHAW: Bit of a let-down, marrying me.

STEVEN: Oh, now. I wouldn't have thought so.

SHAW: Nay, lad. Never one to grumble ... [*Brightly*] Well, then ..
What's it like to be back home, Steve?

STEVEN: Home ...

SHAW: After all this time.

STEVEN: Well, I don't know, Dad ... Very much the same.

[*They laugh.*
Fade.]

23

Scene Two

Afternoon.

MRS SHAW *is straightening the room, putting chairs more certainly in their places, straightening ornaments, mirror, pictures.*

There's a knock, then a banging on the outside door: whistles, etc.

MRS SHAW: Oh ... [*Looks at herself in the mirror, goes off to the kitchen.*]

[*Bolts are drawn, locks turned.*]

[*Off*] Andrew ... There you are, then, love ...

ANDREW [*off*]: Been whistling half an hour ...

[*Sounds of embrace*]

On the lav, then, were you?

MRS SHAW [*off*]: I was not!

ANDREW [*off*]: By go ... There's a lot been put on round here ...

MRS SHAW [*off*]: Get on. Go on ...

[ANDREW *enters: a fierce, compelling-looking figure dressed in a fairly dishevelled raincoat.*]

ANDREW: Where is he? Where's he hiding? [*Calls.*] I'll be up there, old lad! [*To* MRS SHAW] Snoring off his head ... I'll go up and tip him out ...

MRS SHAW: You won't ...

ANDREW: What ... ?

MRS SHAW: He's out ... Went down to the pub. With Steven ...

ANDREW: Steven ...

MRS SHAW: After dinner ... I've been expecting them any minute ... Isn't Colin with you, then?

ANDREW: He's coming on behind. Don't worry ... [*Going round, inspecting room*] Steven's here, then, is he? Might have known ... First in. Last out.

MRS SHAW: Go on. Get on ...

ANDREW: Like a museum is this. Hasn't changed in five thousand years.

MRS SHAW: We've just had it decorated. A few months ago.

ANDREW: What with, then ... soot? [*Runs his hand over the wall.*]

MRS SHAW: I can see somebody hasn't changed. I can.

ANDREW]*picks up paperback*]: *Battle at Bloodstone Creek.* I used to marvel at that. My Dad's reading age hasn't risen beyond when he was ten years old.

MRS SHAW: We can't all be educated, .you know.

ANDREW: No. No. Thank God for that.

MRS SHAW: Where is Colin, anyway?

ANDREW: Parking his car. Got moved on by a policeman.

MRS SHAW: Not here?

ANDREW: No. No. In town. Never seen anything like it. Bigger than a bus. Antagonized them, I believe, no end. Dropped off to buy a packet of cigarettes. 'Can't park that here.' ... Police.

MRS SHAW: Police ...

ANDREW: Got to watch my step ... These days in particular.

MRS SHAW: I thought you were a lawyer.

ANDREW: Was, my dear. Was. Am no longer.

MRS SHAW: I don't know what Peggy thinks. She must be out of her mind, worrying. What are you living on?

ANDREW: On love, my dear. Love. Like everybody else. We've been married now, you know, for seventeen years. If we haven't got a bit of that in stock then we might as well not try.

MRS SHAW [*glances out*]: I've heard of living on love before. With Steven. Going to be a writer. And now look at him: four kiddies in as many years, and he looks older than any of you.

ANDREW: Ah well. Steven always was a difficult boy. An infant prodigy, if I remember rightly. What we did under duress he did by nature ...

MRS SHAW: At school they said they'd never seen anything like it.
   [ANDREW *looks across at her: she's gone to the window again, glancing out.*]
   Where is he, then? It's not outside.

ANDREW: End of the road. Gone to find a garage. Didn't want to risk it: leaving it outside.

MRS SHAW: I'm not surprised ... Nowadays ... I don't know ... [*Comes back.*] How are you living? ... What sort of pictures do you paint?

ANDREW: I know ... [*Prompting her, goading*]

MRS SHAW: What ...?

ANDREW: You think I paint young ladies.

MRS SHAW: What? [*Retreats.*]

ANDREW: Or better still – young men.

MRS SHAW: What ... ?

ANDREW [*pursuing her*]: Come on. Admit it ... You think I'm painting young ladies with no clothes on ... She thinks I gave up my career as one of the greatest solicitors in the land in order to peruse certain ladies without their clothes on.

MRS SHAW: I thought nothing of the sort.

ANDREW: Come on. Come on. [*Stalking her round the furniture*] You're as bad as Peggy. She thought the same.

MRS SHAW: I'm not surprised.

ANDREW: You see. I'm right ... Just see what it is I'm up against ... I really puzzled her.

MRS SHAW: What?

ANDREW: Puzzled. Abstract. Not a sign of human life.

MRS SHAW: What ... ? [*Looking around*]

ANDREW: Me picture ... Peggy ... Came home from me studio with it tucked underneath my arm. Thought she was going to see ... Well, I don't know what she thought she was going to see. She was half-blushing before I'd even put it down. She knew, you see, I'd had me eye on the wife of the chap, from whom I rent my studio, for some considerable time ... but ... lo and behold. Triangles.

MRS SHAW: Triangles?

ANDREW: Or very nearly. The fact is, I'm not very good ... Subtle indentations on either side. Bit here ... Bit there ... Each one a different colour ... the variations in which would almost deceive the eye ... beautiful. If you like triangles, that is ... Abstract.

MRS SHAW: Abstract?

ANDREW: Not a sign of human life.

MRS SHAW: Oh.

ANDREW: Just the first. After that: squares.

MRS SHAW: Squares ...

ANDREW: Rectangles. *Rhomboids*. Sometimes, even – nothing.

MRS SHAW: Nothing?

26

ANDREW: Well, I say nothing ... there'd be a little ... spot ... of something, here and there. A little red [*Paints it for her.*] ... cerulean ... touch of viridian ... trickle here ... lovely. Still ... old-fashioned.

MRS SHAW: Old-fashioned?

ANDREW: Absolutely. Don't use paint now, you know.

MRS SHAW: Oh, well ... [*Dismissing it, turning away*]

ANDREW: Plastic compounds. Plus: miscellaneous bric-à-brac picked up from the refuse dump outside the town. Got arrested once. Loitering with intent. Ran rings round them at the station. 'You better get a solicitor,' they said. 'I am a solicitor,' I said. 'Why, Mr Shaw,' they said, 'we didn't recognize you.' 'Artist now, mate,' I said. 'Don't you forget it.'

MRS SHAW: I can't understand why you gave it up. After all the years you spent studying. It seems a terrible waste. You were never interested in art before.

ANDREW: No ... I'm not now, either.

MRS SHAW: Well, then ... It's not as if you were independent. There's Peter and Jack. It'll be years before they're financially independent.

ANDREW: I don't know so much. I'm thinking of sending them out to support me. I don't think, paradoxical as it may seem, Mother, that I can, any longer, afford to educate my children.

MRS SHAW: Well ... I ... [*Gestures about her.*]

ANDREW: What is it?

MRS SHAW: I've said enough. You must know what you're doing. [*Goes to window again.*]

ANDREW [*picks up another paperback*]: *Phoenix Showdown*. He must get through these faster than he does a cigarette.

MRS SHAW: He brings them home from work. I don't know where he gets them from.

ANDREW: I hope you fumigate them before they come into the house?

MRS SHAW: Well. I've thought about it a time or two, I can tell you.

ANDREW: I bet ... No alien bodies in this house. That's always been our motto ... What was that subject ... ?

MRS SHAW: Subject?

ANDREW: You were always top in at school.

MRS SHAW: Domestic science.

ANDREW: No ... no ...

MRS SHAW: Human hygiene.

ANDREW: Human hygiene ... I remember you telling us when we were lads ... human hygiene ... the sort of vision those words created ...

MRS SHAW: It was an experimental class ... It was the first time it was ever taught in a school ...

ANDREW: And never looked back since ... No wonder we were so clean ... Came top, eh?

MRS SHAW: Well ...

ANDREW: Used to tell me friends about it at school ... human hygiene ... frightened them all to death. They thought ... well, I don't know what they thought ... Anyway. Never had any trouble with them after that.

[*They laugh.*]

MRS SHAW [*looking out*]: Now, look ... There he is. You see ... he must have walked for miles ... I don't know.

[*She goes to the kitchen.* ANDREW *picks up another book, drops it, looks round.*]

COLIN [*calls*]: Hello ... ? [*Comes in the other door: a professional man in his middle thirties, not smooth, firm, a bit rough. He's dressed in a Crombie overcoat.*]

ANDREW: Hello.

COLIN: What ... ?

ANDREW: I say: 'hello'.

COLIN: Oh ...

ANDREW: She thinks you're coming in the back.

COLIN: Mother ... [*Crossing to the kitchen*]

ANDREW: Did you park the car?

COLIN: Yes ...

MRS SHAW [*coming in*]: There you are! I thought ...

[*They embrace.*]

Well, love. It's been a long time ...

ANDREW: Trust him to come in the front. Only for royalty is that. Workers, you know, have to use the rear.

MRS SHAW [*to* COLIN]: Take no notice of him, Colin. He's in one of his moods.

ANDREW: Iconoclastic.

COLIN: What?

ANDREW: I'm iconoclastic ... I remember her looking it up when I was how old ... eleven or twelve ... 'I've got just the word for you, my lad,' she said, and got out her dictionary ... you know, her first prize for ...

COLIN: Hygiene.

ANDREW: You see! He remembers that ...

MRS SHAW: I don't remember looking ...

ANDREW: I didn't dare mention it for years. I went round, all that time, thinking it was some sort of sexual deviation.

MRS SHAW: Well, I don't remember that.

ANDREW: Iconoclastic ... The first girl I ever went out with. When I took her home and we'd got to her gate, moonshining, I said, 'I better warn you, before you start anything, I'm iconoclastic.' 'Oh,' she said, 'well, I better go in, then.' 'Yes,' I said, 'I think you should.'

COLIN: Three hours of that I've had in the car. You've heard about his painting?

[ANDREW *has picked up another paperback, reading it, still standing.*]

MRS SHAW: I have.

COLIN: The only reason he took it up was because they couldn't stand his conversation in his office any longer. There was nobody – no clients, no staff, no nothing – to listen to him at all.

MRS SHAW: He's got his father's nature right enough.

ANDREW: I think I must have. [*Indicating book*] I might take a few of these back with me.

[*Holds it out to* COLIN.]

Massacre in Wolf Canyon.

COLIN: Where is he, by the way? In bed?

ANDREW: At the pub.

MRS SHAW: He went with Steven for a drink. After lunch.

ANDREW: Lunch. [*Winks at* COLIN.] Used to be dinner in my day ...

MRS SHAW [*to* COLIN]: Is there anything I can get you?

COLIN: I could do with a cup of tea. I've walked for miles. Did he tell you about being stopped in town? Five minutes: it couldn't have been any longer.

MRS SHAW: I don't know. It makes your blood boil ... I don't know what it's coming to ... I don't. Not any more.

ANDREW: A police state.

COLIN: It is ... I've parked it down at Sugden's. Not safe to leave it parked out here.

MRS SHAW: Here. I'll make some tea, love ... There's your Dad, now. And Steven. I won't be a minute. [*Goes.*]

    [*There are sounds of arrival from the kitchen.*]

ANDREW: All right ... ? [*Nods amicably at* COLIN.]

COLIN: All right?

ANDREW: Tie straight ... buttons ... Little over to the left ... Smashing.

    [*He straightens* COLIN's *tie, coat, etc.*]

MRS SHAW [*off*]: You're back, then.

STEVEN [*off*]: In one piece.

SHAW [*off*]: Haven't been too long, I hope, my dear? [*Kiss.*]

MRS SHAW [*off*]: Colin and Andrew are here.

SHAW [*off*]: Are they? Are they? So we heard. [*Entering*] There you are, then ... Heard about your commotion. How are you, lad? How are you? [*He shakes their hands in turn.*]

COLIN: You're looking pretty well yourself.

ANDREW: Damned old wreck. How many have you had?

SHAW: Ay, now. I go down there for social reasons. Not for anything else.

ANDREW: Aye. We know ...

SHAW: Nay, I'm not the drinker in the house. She's in there, stoking up. [*Thumbs at the kitchen.*]

MRS SHAW [*off*]: Oh, don't worry. They know you of old.

SHAW [*calls*]: Are you making us some tea, then, love?

MRS SHAW [*off*]: I am. I won't be a minute.

SHAW: Heart of gold. Never stops working ... Was that your car that Mrs Burnett told us about? We've just come up with her. She saw it down the road.

ANDREW: They'll bury that woman in a glass coffin.

SHAW: Aye. If she couldn't look out she'd never step inside.

COLIN: Well then, Steve. How's your writing going?

STEVEN: Oh, all right.

COLIN: Me mother said in her last letter you were going to publish a book.

STEVEN: I was. Sort of.

COLIN: Well, then. I'll look forward to seeing it.

SHAW: Aye. He's got all the brains, has Steven.

ANDREW: And all the kiddies too.

SHAW: Aye! [*He laughs.*] Are you all right in there, love? [*Winks.*]

MRS SHAW [*off*]: I'm all right. Don't you worry.

SHAW: They ought to run tea in pipes round here. Instead of water.

COLIN: They'd make a fortune.

SHAW: Round here they would. [*Coughs.*] Slakes your throat, you know. Dust.

ANDREW: Sounds as though you've got half a ton of best nugget down there, Dad.

SHAW: I have. Don't worry. I shouldn't be surprised.

STEVEN: My mother keeps telling him. He ought to come out.

SHAW: Come out. When I come out of that pit they can't tell the difference between me and a lump of muck. Never get out of that. Don't worry.

COLIN: I'll go and see if my mother needs some help. [*Goes into kitchen.*]

ANDREW [*gestures grandly after him*]: Executive.

STEVEN: Nice bit of coat. [*Fingers it over a chair.*]

SHAW: You won't find one of them where I work, I can tell you.

ANDREW: I don't know. They tell me miners earn as much as dentists these days.

SHAW: What? At the bloody dogs they might. That's the only place they can.

ANDREW: I've even thought of going down myself.

SHAW: You've got a career you have. I spent half my life making sure none of you went down that pit.

ANDREW: I've always thought, you know, coal-mining was one of the few things I could really do. [*Looks at his hands.*] One of the few things, in reality, for which I'm ideally equipped. And yet, the one thing in life from which I'm actually excluded.

SHAW: You're ideally equipped to be a professional man. Or ought you want. But that place: an animal could do what I do. And I can tell you, most of them are.

ANDREW: Aye. You're right.

[*Snarls at* STEVEN, *then picks up one of the paperbacks.*]

Been studying your library.

STEVEN: One of the first things I ever remember was a picture in one of them. A cowboy with a hat out here and trousers flapping like wings, mounted on the back of a rearing horse. Somehow, it still sums it all up.

ANDREW: What?

STEVEN: Dunno ... Freedom.

[*Pause.*]

SHAW: They're nowt. They pass the time.

ANDREW: I bet you can't remember a single one ... What happens ... [*Consults the book.*] ... at Bloodstone Creek when Barry Hogan rides up and sees a light glinting from among the rocks?

SHAW: I couldn't tell you.

ANDREW: You're stunted. That's what you are.

SHAW: I am. It's a wonder I've grown one foot at all.

[*They laugh.*]

MRS SHAW [*returning*]: Here we are ... Colin's bringing it in ...

[COLIN *follows her with the tray.*]

ANDREW: He'd make a lovely mother.

SHAW: You want to watch him. Or he'll shove it right over your head.

ANDREW: Couldn't knock a fly off a rice pudding.

COLIN: Don't be too sure.

ANDREW: He'd negotiate with it first.

MRS SHAW [*to* STEVEN]: You're a quiet one, love. I hope you didn't let your Dad persuade you to have too much to drink.

STEVEN: No ...

SHAW: He doesn't say so much, but he doesn't miss ought do you, lad?

COLIN: How's your book going, then, Steve?

[COLIN *has put the tray on the table and* MRS SHAW *is pouring out the tea.*]

STEVEN: Oh, all right ... Well, not really. I've packed it in.

COLIN: Packed it in? Why, it's years ...

STEVEN: Aye.

SHAW: Why have you given it up, then, lad?

STEVEN: Not my cup of tea. [*Laughs.*] Stick to what I've got, I suppose.

SHAW: Aye ... [SHAW *watches him.*]

MRS SHAW: He's better off looking after his wife and family, not writing books ...

COLIN: What was it all about, then, Steve?

STEVEN: Oh ... [*Shrugs.*]

ANDREW: Modern society. To put it into words.

STEVEN: I don't know. [*Shrugs.*]

ANDREW: Indicating, without being too aggressive, how we'd all succumbed to the passivity of modern life, industrial discipline, and moral turpitude.

MRS SHAW: Don't mock him.

ANDREW: I'm not mocking him. [*Spreads out his hands.*] He let me read a bit of it once. What? Four years ago. He's been writing it nearly seven. I don't know why he's packed it in. I agree with every word.

SHAW: Agree with what?

ANDREW: I don't know ... his view of society. The modern world ...

SHAW: Nay, I can't make head nor tail of it ...

MRS SHAW: Here you are, love ... Come and get your tea.

MRS BURNETT [*popping in*]: Are you in, love? Or are you out?

SHAW: We're out ... Don't worry. We've had her in here afore.

MRS SHAW: We're in, love. Don't take any notice.

MRS BURNETT: He never changes, does he?

    [*To* COLIN, *putting out her hand*]

We hear all about you, now, you know.

COLIN: Not too much, I hope.

MRS BURNETT: No, no. Just the right things. What your father wants to tell us.

SHAW: Nay. Don't worry. I tell her nowt.

MRS BURNETT [*turning*]: How are you, Andrew? I hear you've given up your job.

ANDREW: Aye. That's right. If you've aught going round here, just let me know.

MRS BURNETT: Get on with you.

[*Laughs, digs him with her elbow.*]

That'll be the day, when he comes looking for a job round here.

ANDREW: It'll be sooner than you think. Don't worry. We're thinking of setting up in business.

MRS BURNETT: Business? What sort of business, then, is that?

ANDREW: Glass coffins.

MRS BURNETT: Glass coffins?

ANDREW: Or wooden ones. With little windows in. [*Shapes one.*]

MRS SHAW: Would you like a cup of tea, then, love?

MRS BURNETT: I wouldn't mind. I wouldn't say no ...

SHAW [*to himself*]: Like asking a dog if it wants a pittle.

MRS BURNETT: I remember Colin. Mischief Night ...

ANDREW: Mischief Night? What mischief then has Colin ever got into?

MRS BURNETT: He's shoved some crackers through my back door a time or two. I can tell you that.

COLIN: I think I did. She's right. [*Laughs.*]

MRS BURNETT: And drain-pipes. Right along this street ... And Steven.

MRS SHAW: Steven?

STEVEN: Aye. I think I must.

ANDREW: It's coming out. Good God! I wouldn't believe it.

COLIN [*to* STEVEN]: Rafts on the canal. I remember that.

STEVEN: Aye ...

COLIN: We shoved our Steven in a time or two. It's a wonder he wasn't drowned.

STEVEN: Aye ...

SHAW: What about them kites, then, eh? Six foot. Fly for miles. You'd see them floating across the town when you went out shopping. Me. Reardon ... We used to give the lads half a crown to go climbing for them when they broke away ... It took two men to hold them. The string ... It could cut clean through your hand.

MRS BURNETT: Aye. I remember those days right enough ... And now look at you. Children of your own. [*To* MRS SHAW] It must be a proud day, love, for both of you ... Forty years.

MRS SHAW: Aye ...

SHAW: We'd have waited until we'd been married fifty, only I didn't think either of us would have lasted that long.

MRS SHAW: Oh, now ...

SHAW: At least, I didn't think I would ... We thought we'd better get it in while we had the chance.

MRS SHAW: Nay, I don't think it's as bad as that, love.

SHAW: Forty years. A round number ... I'm near retiring – God willing ... what with one thing and another ... Their mother's going to be ... well, I won't say, now, exactly ... but a *certain age* next week.

MRS SHAW: I'll be sixty. I don't mind them knowing.

SHAW: She was a young lass of twenty when I married her. And in my eyes, she's been the same age ever since.

MRS SHAW: Oh, now. Don't let's exaggerate too much.

SHAW: You're as old as you feel, and that's how I'll always see you, love. [*Kisses her cheek.*]

MRS SHAW: Nay, I don't know. He says some funny things ...

MRS BURNETT: Did you get your new hat, then?

MRS SHAW: I did.

SHAW: We'll have to go without food for a fortnight, I can tell you that.

MRS BURNETT: Oh, you'll look lovely, love.

SHAW: She'll look a picture. And for me she can dress up in rags.

MRS SHAW: I could as well. He wouldn't know the difference.

SHAW: Nay, we've gone without, I know. Getting these three into the world, setting them up in life.

MRS BURNETT: They're a credit to you, love. They are.

SHAW: Aye. Moments like this you begin to think it was all worth while.

[*They laugh.*]

MRS SHAW: Oh, now ... Just look at the time.

SHAW: Aye. We shall have to be getting ready.

MRS BURNETT: 'The Excelsior Hotel'.

SHAW: That's the one.

MRS BURNETT [*to* COLIN]: They only finished it last year. Twelve storeys high.

SHAW: It costs you a pound just to take your coat off. If you sneeze it costs you a fiver. And if you ask for a glass of water you've to tip ten bob just to pour it out. I tell you, I'm in the wrong bloody business.

[*They laugh.*]

MRS BURNETT: Aye ... Well ... I'm only sorry your Jamey never lived to see it.

SHAW: Aye. Yes.

MRS BURNETT: He was a lovely lad. He was.

SHAW: We'd have been all right with four of them. We would.

MRS BURNETT: They wouldn't remember him.

SHAW: Aye. Well. You have your tribulations.

MRS BURNETT [to STEVEN]: Missed him, you did, by about three months ... And Colin here ...

MRS SHAW: He'd be almost two. Andrew here was nearly five ...

MRS BURNETT [to ANDREW]: Now, he could have been an artist. He could draw like a little angel. How old was he?

MRS SHAW: Seven when he died.

SHAW: He had a little book. His teacher sent it home. Drawings ... You wouldn't have known they hadn't been done by an artist. Shapes and colours ... There was one of three apples on a plate. You could almost pick them up ... Pneumonia ... They didn't have the protection against it, not in those days. Not like they have now ... I'd have cut off my right arm. I bloody would ... [*Sees* MRS SHAW's *expression.*] Aye ... Well ... [*Brightly.*] Right, then ... [*Claps his hands.*] Let's be ready. On with the dance.

MRS BURNETT: Aye. Well, I better be getting back ...

ANDREW: How are your lads, then, Mrs Burnett?

MRS BURNETT: Oh, well enough. Half a dozen kiddies. Not two minutes to come up and see their mother ... Still. That's how it is. [*To* MRS SHAW.] That's where you're lucky, love. Your lads come home. Don't disown you. Don't forget you as you're getting old.

SHAW: Aye. We've been damn lucky.

MRS BURNETT [to MRS SHAW]: If you drop your key off, love, I'll make sure your fire's in when you get back home.

MRS SHAW: Right, love ...

MRS BURNETT: Don't do anything I wouldn't do.

SHAW: That doesn't leave us with so bloody much.

MRS BURNETT [*to the others*]: Tara, love. I'm off before he starts. [*Goes.*]

COLIN: One of the best. She is.

ANDREW: One of the best what?

COLIN: Forget it ...

ANDREW: You should have heard him in the car. Talk about the Two Nations. The dignity of the manual labourer.

SHAW: Labourer?

COLIN: I should forget it.

ANDREW: Never ask an expatriate working-class man about his views on his former class. Do you know, when he left school and went to university, Colin was a card-carrying member of the C.P.

MRS SHAW [*clearing cups*]: C.P.? What's that?

STEVEN: A communist.

MRS SHAW: A communist!

ANDREW: To my mother, communist is synonymous with sex deviate, pervert, luster after young girls, defiler of young men.

MRS SHAW: I never said that ... I never knew you were a communist, Colin.

ANDREW: Neither did he. It only lasted a year. It gives him an aura of respectability now when he's negotiating with 'the men'.

COLIN: You'd go down well, I can tell you.

ANDREW: Down well what? I've gone down. You can't get much lower than where I am, mate.

SHAW: We're here to celebrate, not to have arguments. [*To* MRS SHAW] I remember when they were all at home. Arguments! It was like a debating palace. Your head got dizzy following each one.

MRS SHAW: Well, I'll get up and get changed. I suppose all you are ready?

COLIN: Yes ... Here, I'll take that. [*Indicating tray*]

MRS SHAW: No, no. I've got it, love ... Harry? [*Goes.*]

SHAW: Aye. I better put on my suit. They might throw me out if I go as I am. 'The Excelsior'. Do you know, the man on the door, dressed up like an admiral – that much braid and epaulets on that he knocks your eye out whenever he turns round – he used to work for me. Swore like a trooper and never washed his face from one Sunday to the next. There he is now, dressed up for a coronation, with a spot of scent behind his ears. 'Why!' I said to him when I last went past, 'You're like a bloody woman, Alf. Get off home and get some clothes on.' Do you know what he said? 'If you don't move on, my man, I'll have you physically removed.' 'Physically removed'!

ANDREW: Did you sock him one?

SHAW: Sock him? I wouldn't have muckied my hands.
[*They laugh.*]
Ay, look, you know. About Jamey ... I shouldn't talk about him too much. I know you didn't bring it up, but your mother, you know ... as you get older you start thinking about these things.

COLIN: What about them?

SHAW: Nay, look ... I've said enough. [*Listens. Then, loudly*] Right, then, lads. I'll go and get polished up.

ANDREW: Leave a bit of muck on, Dad. We won't know you without.

SHAW: Aye. Some hopes of that. [*Gestures up.*] I'll be given a thorough inspection ...

ANDREW: Hygiene ...

SHAW: Hygiene. You're right. [*Laughs.*] Right, then. I'll get up ... Think on ... [*Goes.*]

ANDREW [*cheerful*]: Well, then: this time tomorrow we'll all be back home.

COLIN: I should just lay off, you know. Just once. Give it a rest.

ANDREW: Are you going to negotiate with me or something, Colin?

COLIN: We're here to give them a good time. Something they'll remember. God alone knows they deserve it.

ANDREW: Aye. He's right. How about you, Steve? What're you so quiet about? [STEVEN *shrugs.*] Silent Steven. [*To* COLIN] They called him that at school.

COLIN: I've just thought. I'll have all that way to walk back to get the car.

STEVEN: Ring for a taxi.

COLIN: It's the same distance to the phone box, the other way.

ANDREW: You forget, don't you, what a primitive place this really is. Do you know, the other morning, we ran out of toothpaste at home, and there was all hell let loose with Pete – he's courting his head-girl at school – and I suddenly remembered: we never had toothpaste at home. Do you remember? We all used to clean our teeth with salt. [*Laughs.*] Three little piles on the draining board every morning, when we came down.

STEVEN: We never had any cakes either. Do you remember that? There was a jam tart, or one piece of a sponge roll, for tea on Sunday.

COLIN: And old Steve there used to stand at table because we only had four chairs.

ANDREW: I remember. Would you believe it.

[*They look round at the room.*]

Do you remember when old Shuffler came to see my Dad about my going to university?

STEVEN: Shuffler?

COLIN: He'd left by the time you'd got there.

ANDREW: Sixth form. Careers. Came here one night to talk to my Dad about 'the pros and cons' of going to university. Sat in a chair: we had it there. Put his hands out like this and . . . ping! Bloody springs shot out.

COLIN: Nearly dislocated his elbow!

[*They laugh.*]

ANDREW [*laughing*]: And my Dad . . . my Dad said to him . . . 'Would you mind not putting your hands on the arms, Mr Rushton? . . . The springs are coming out!'

[*They laugh.*]

COLIN: Bare floors. We had a piece of lino which my mother moved round each week, trying to fit the chairs over the holes and spaces.

STEVEN: Newspaper on the table for dinner . . .

ANDREW: Breakfast, supper and tea.

STEVEN: 'Don't read when you're eating.'

[*They laugh.*]

COLIN: Do you remember my mother cutting up newspapers into lengths and trying to roll them together like a proper toilet roll?

[*They laugh.*]

ANDREW: Obsessive man.

COLIN: After he came here Shuffler never talked to us again. Whenever we met in the school corridor he used to gaze at some point exactly six inches above your head. Talk about the pain of poverty. I still dream about that look. I do . . . I often wake up trying to convince him that we're not as poor as that any longer.

[*Pause.*]

ANDREW: That comes of going to a good school.

COLIN: Full of drapers' sons, minor bureaucrats, and the children of the professional classes.

ANDREW: My dear old Col: your children are the children of the professional classes.

COLIN: I have no children.

ANDREW: Good God. You haven't. I'd forgot.

STEVEN: Why have you never married, Colin?

COLIN: Don't know. Haven't had the time.

ANDREW: You're not ... er ... ? [*Quivers his hand.*]

COLIN: Don't think so.

ANDREW: I mean, if you are, for my mother's sake, I'd keep it under your hat.

COLIN: Oh, sure.

ANDREW [*to* STEVEN]: It's one thing my mother cannot stand. 'I don't mind a man being as promiscuous as he likes' – within reason, of course, and with the sole exception of my Dad – 'but the thought of one man going with another ...'

COLIN: I don't think we've quite come to that ... In any case, as far as marriage is concerned, I probably might have to.

ANDREW: You don't mean ... there's not some unfortunate lassie carrying an embryonic Colin in her tum ...

COLIN: No. It's just less embarrassing to *be* married than not to be.

ANDREW: I see. Well. As long as it's only that.

COLIN: Yes.

ANDREW: You know the real reason he's never married.

COLIN: No, I don't think he does.

ANDREW: Well. Never mind ... Forget it ...

STEVEN: In any case ...

ANDREW: Yes?

STEVEN: With all that money lying around, Colin, you ought to make some woman happy.

COLIN: Aye! [*Laughs.*]

    [ANDREW *watches* STEVEN *a moment. Then:*]

ANDREW: What's gone wrong, then, Steve?

STEVEN: I don't know what you mean there, Andy. [*Moves about the room, casual.*]

ANDREW: I mean ... I don't know what I mean.

COLIN [*to* STEVEN]: He's not sure what he means.

ANDREW: For one thing ... in your youth ... you were so contemptuous of the proven way.

COLIN: The proven way ...

ANDREW: Admittedly you were – for ever – silent. But even when at school – the school we have only a moment before described, fit only for the sons of Christ – and then only after the most rigorous scrutiny – your arrogance, your disdain ... your *contempt* – were there for everyone to see ... I know. I know. Actually I respected you – very much – because of that. Misplaced it may have been – contempt ... God knows: the educated sons of that school, Steve, deserved all the pity they could get. But you – just look at you. Where oh where has all that venom gone to? Where, for Christ's sake, Steve, is the spirit of revenge? [STEVEN *shrugs*.]

COLIN: Four hours of that I've had inside that car ... You should have heard him ... If you ever have a car don't ever let him in it. Two miles with him in the passenger seat and you'll drive it into the nearest wall.

ANDREW: Though in his case, of course, he's more appreciative of the cost.

COLIN: You know, your one grievous disability, Andy – if you don't mind me mentioning this – is not only have you never grown up, but you've never even put in the first preliminary effort.

ANDREW [*to* STEVEN]: 'Management' talk. His 'men's' talk is both more subtly obscene and more overtly gratuitous.

COLIN: I must say, it's come to a sorry bloody pitch. [*To* STEVEN] I could have got him a job years ago if he'd wanted. I could have even got him on the board; what with his gifts, his tongue, his golden sense of opportunity. He might even have done him a bit of good.

ANDREW: You are listening to a man whose life – believe it or not – is measured out in motor cars.

COLIN: In blood! In men! In progress!

ANDREW: Do you know what he told me on the way up here? Cigar in mouth. Gloved hands firmly on the wheel. 'The well-being of this nation is largely – if not wholly – dependent on maintaining a satisfactory level of exports from the motor industry.' The *nation*! ... If my bloody nation is largely dependent on that I'd rather crawl around on all fours with a pig-skin on my back and a bow and arrow in my bloody hand. I would.

COLIN: You probably might have to. [*Laughs pleasantly.*] Sooner than he thinks.

ANDREW: May God speed that day. [*Looks up.*] May God speed it.

COLIN: And that mind you after witnessing my poor old father's life. Crawling around – in pitch black, on his belly, his life hanging on the fall of a piece of rock – for fifty bloody years!

ANDREW: My father – *old friend* – has more dignity in his little finger than all you and your automated bloody factories could conjure up in a thousand years.

COLIN: Yes?

ANDREW: You know, I weep for you. To think you once lived here, under this roof. My brother. And you end up . . . Just look at you . . . Like this.

COLIN [*goes to the stairs*]: Are you ready, then, up there?

SHAW [*off*]: Nay, damn it all. We're trying to fasten your mother's dress.

MRS SHAW [*off*]: Don't worry, love. We won't be long.

[COLIN *goes to the kitchen: starts to wash as:*]

ANDREW: I'm not trying to disparage, Steve . . . your work. Your ideas . . . It's simply: I do not understand.

STEVEN: No.

ANDREW: What's happened to that re-vitalizing spirit? To the iconoclast, to use my mother's word.

STEVEN: I don't know.

ANDREW: Steve!

STEVEN: Look. There's no hard and fast rule. The world's as real as anything else: you don't . . . compromise yourself by taking a part in it.

ANDREW: No? . . . Not even with *this* world, Steve? [*Gestures through at* COLIN.]

STEVEN: No. It's not essential.

ANDREW: And that's why you look as sick as you do, because that's something you believe?

STEVEN: I look as sick as I do – if I do look sick – because I'm not a moralist like you. In the end, attitudes like you've described are easily adopted. All you have to do is throw over what's already there. You're like an evangelist. You both are. You forget there's another kind of temperament.

ANDREW: Well . . .

STEVEN: I don't know what the word for it is. [*Turns away.*]

ANDREW: Have you ever thought of taking up welfare work?

STEVEN: What?

ANDREW: The *all-surveying eye* – inherited – I haven't a shadow of a doubt – from my mother, but used, also I have no doubt, with greater circumspection – isn't this something you could put to better use than . . . advising on – what is it? – suitable post-graduate, post-everything pursuits?

STEVEN: I don't know.

ANDREW: But for the fact that I almost witnessed the event, I would find it difficult to believe that you came, as it were, of man and woman, Steve. Dearly as I would like, myself, to be an intellectual . . .

STEVEN [*to* COLIN]: Intellectual . . . [*Laughs.*]

ANDREW [*through to* COLIN]: Whenever one such passes me in the street, whenever I meet a man who describes himself as a humanist, a rationalist, a man of reason, something in my soul, something deep inside me, calls out – in pain, in protest. 'This man,' it tells me, 'is *obscene.*'

COLIN [*coming in, drying face*]: It seems there's an awful lot of obscenity in your life, Andy.

ANDREW [*to* STEVEN]: When you see a cancer it's no commendation of your powers of loving to fall on your knees and give it a damn great kiss.

COLIN [*to* STEVEN]: He'll kill us all off. He will. He really will.

ANDREW: We already are.

COLIN: What?

ANDREW: Dead. Zombies. Killed by good intentions, administered by the ones above. [*Gestures up.*] Corpses.

COLIN [*lightly*]: Good God . . . What's he on about, then, Steve?

STEVEN: I don't know . . . It's not worth arguing about. I remember, when he first started grammar school . . .

ANDREW: Minor public. It said that in the brochure . . . [*to* COLIN] My dad underlined it with black, colliery crayon.

STEVEN: He came home and devastated all of us – me certainly, without a shadow of a doubt – with all the reasons why it was no longer tenable – a belief in God. As if belief itself were a kind of property, like a limb, which you could put on or take off at will . . . Believe me: remove any part and all the rest goes with it. I don't even understand . . . You've lived here half your life – Reardon – Mrs Burnett – even Shuffler . . . What sort of vengeance do you have in mind?

ANDREW: Are you *listening* to what I said? [STEVEN *nods.*] . . . God knows, you were always the most serious of the three – and God knows, there were sufficient reasons for it . . .

COLIN: What *is* all this? What reasons? What God knows? . . . I must say, for somebody who doesn't believe in God he invokes Him an awful bloody lot . . . you know . . . Formative traits have always been an obsession with our Andrew: as if he were a function of them and nothing else . . .

ANDREW: All right . . . [*turns away.*]

COLIN: Good God. [*Takes his tie from his pocket and starts to put it on.*] Amazing.

ANDREW: When poor old Jamey died . . .

COLIN: I knew it!

ANDREW: When poor old Jamey died . . .

COLIN [*to* STEVEN]: Do we have to go through all this again?

STEVEN: Andrew has a new theory about his origins.

ANDREW: Not new. And not theoretical, either.

STEVEN: He's discovered . . . I told him. A little time ago now . . . that Jamey was born only three months after my mother got married.

COLIN [*putting on tie*]: Good Lord. [*Feels walls.*] No. No. Upright . . . Standing.

ANDREW: Can you imagine, for one moment, what went on during those six months' negotiations? Prior to the event.

COLIN: . . . Let me see.

ANDREW: This is something you should be particularly good at . . . I mean: first in human hygiene . . .

COLIN: Why does he go *on* about that?

ANDREW: English language, domestic science: didn't leave school until she was sixteen . . . religious . . . raised up by a petty farmer to higher things . . . ends up being laid – in a farm field – by a bloody collier . . . hygiene . . . never forgiven him, she hasn't . . . Dig coal he will till kingdom come. Never dig enough . . . Retribution.

COLIN: Do you know what I'd say to you?

ANDREW: What?

COLIN: Mind your own bleeding business.

ANDREW: Oh ... All right. [*Turns away.* COLIN *goes off.*] Poor old Jamey.

COLIN [*off*]: Poor old Jamey ...

ANDREW: Poor old Dad.

COLIN: Poor old Dad. [*Reappearing with waistcoat: and jacket – which he puts on a chair.*]

ANDREW: Well, that's it exactly.

COLIN: What?

ANDREW: Guilt. Subsequent moral rectitude. They fashioned Jamey – as a consequence – in the image of Jesus Christ.

COLIN: I can think of worse examples. [*Goes to mirror to check tie.*]

ANDREW: Yes?

COLIN: Well – I wouldn't wish to get too personal. [*Laughs.*]

ANDREW: No. No. On the other hand?

COLIN: On the other hand ...

ANDREW: Christ didn't take too kindly to Jamey. His was not, after all, a messianic role.

COLIN [*to* STEVEN]: 'When Mary said, "We have a son," her husband said, "Tell me another one."'

STEVEN: Andrew thinks Jamey died because he could never atone ...

COLIN: Atone? For what?

STEVEN: I don't know ... Whatever my mother felt ...

COLIN: He died of pneumonia, according to the certificate. I remember seeing it myself, years ago. [*Looks round for his jacket.*]

ANDREW: He died from a bout of galloping perfection.

COLIN: Did he?

ANDREW: Do you remember Jamey?

COLIN [*to* STEVEN]: Not really ... I was only two or three at the time ... [*Picks up his jacket and puts it on.*]

ANDREW: I was nearly five. I remember him very well. Sitting there ... drawing ... Or upstairs. Crying. They never beat us, you know. But him ... he was black and blue ... And like Steven there – but for his little bloody pictures – *silent as the tomb.* [*To* STEVEN] ... Come on.

45

COLIN: Come on? Come on what? Honestly, the way he dramatizes the slightest inflection. Black and blue. I don't remember that. And I remember my Dad landing *me* once or twice, I do ... [*To* STEVEN] And you.

　　[STEVEN *doesn't answer.*]

　　Well?

　　[STEVEN *shrugs.*]

ANDREW: Come on. Fair's fair. If Colin's going to whitewash everything, why not give him every chance?

STEVEN: It's nothing ...

ANDREW: Nothing ... ?

STEVEN [*shrugs*]: It's nothing.

ANDREW [*to* COLIN]: Years ago ...

STEVEN: Years ago ...

ANDREW: My Dad ...

STEVEN: My father ... it's really nothing ... [*Sees* ANDREW'*s look.*] ... He told me – shortly after Jamey died – my mother tried ...

COLIN: What?

ANDREW: To kill herself.

　　[STEVEN *turns away.*]

ANDREW: Oh, no. Fair's fair. Look. ... She was already six months gone with Steve ... sitting here ... on the floor ... hugging a knife ... when the old man staggers in through that very door ...

COLIN: Not drunk ... ?

ANDREW: From work ... You see, this doesn't interest him at all.

COLIN: Do you think, in all honesty, that it should? All right ... she tried to kill herself.

ANDREW: You already knew.

COLIN: Yes. That's right. I already knew ... She told me. ... Years ago. I can't remember.

ANDREW: Well, then. That's that.

COLIN: All right. She tried to kill herself.

ANDREW: And Steve.

COLIN: And Steve ... He wasn't even born.

ANDREW: No. No. He wasn't ... Waiting there, that's all ... *To be delivered* ... Just look at him ... Still waiting. Solemn ... Silent.

COLIN: All right. All right ... I mean ... poor bloody soul ... is it something I should bear with me, every second, every day? ... I mean ... are we supposed to be endlessly, perpetually measured by our bloody imperfections, by our more unfortunate bloody actions? ... Just what precisely are you after, Andy? Do you want somebody to hold your hand throughout your entire bloody life?

ANDREW: Ask Steve.

COLIN: What about 'ask Steve'? He's more bloody common sense. For Christ's sake. You really take the can.

ANDREW: Ask Steve ... [*To* STEVEN] To tell him ... Go on ... I mean, giving up his book isn't really what you'd think ... a sign of his growing up ... maturity. He actually has been having nightmares ... In true, I might add, evangelical style.

COLIN: Nightmares? What about?

ANDREW: Jamey ... He sees him – crying out ... trying to appease the immaculate conception. Trying to tell them it *wasn't his fault* ... Jamey in the wilderness, Jamey on a mountain top, Jamey at the window ... saying ... 'Even if you were first in human hygiene, and intended marrying someone smarter than my dad, it wasn't my fault. Please God, forgive me ... Please ... God forgive me, Ma! It's not my fault.'

[COLIN *looks at* STEVEN *who shakes his head.*]

COLIN: What's he on about?

ANDREW: He wrote me a letter recently, Steven. I say recently. Some months ago – and I apologize for taking over ... appropriating, his pre-natal, post-natal, pre-genetive feelings of contempt – I'm sorry, in fact if I appear to sit in judgement on his suffering, on his perpetual psychic silences ... but that sickness, I should add, is a disease of mine. His affliction, I can assure him, is not endemic to his solemn, silent nature, atrophied while inside my mother's remorseful tum ... Jamey's cry, I can assure him, comes from the family! ... not just from his own, sleeping, nocturnal soul ...

COLIN: What's he ... ?

ANDREW: Colin's trouble is that he can't put an engine inside his consternation and drive it off ... *Good old Col!* Something has actually struck home at last.

47

COLIN: Look ... I've had enough. Just pack it in. For Christ's sake ... Steve.

STEVEN: It's nothing. I wrote Andy a letter a few months back. A year ... Asking what he thought. Revenge, I'm afraid, is his only answer. And I understand his motives well enough ...

COLIN: Revenge? On what?

STEVEN: On them.

COLIN: On them ... For what?

STEVEN: I don't know ... Everything.

COLIN: I see ... Nothing less than that.

ANDREW: Projecting him into a world they didn't understand. Educating him for a society which existed wholly in their imaginations ... philistine, parasitic, opportunistic ... bred in ignorance, fed in ignorance ... dead – in ignorance.

STEVEN: Only, of course, his common sense – perhaps even his compassion – forbids him to say anything of the sort ... The most tedious thing about his social attitudes, his moral insights, is the perversity of their motives – that's something I've always felt before about these screaming revolutionaries ... but now ... I see more clearly what they're intended to appease.

ANDREW [to STEVEN]: We'll build a bloody statue to you yet. I'm warning you. We shall ... He thinks by some superb gesture of self-exorcism, powered and engendered by God knows what, he'll rid himself of all this. His dreams and nightmares ...

STEVEN [quietly]: No ...

ANDREW: Transcend it. Become ... manifest.

STEVEN: No ...

ANDREW: I think, you know, some suitable post should be found for Steven. [To COLIN] He'll do you out of a job, if you're not careful. Don't let him near your factory. He'll have everybody, unless you're very careful, consoling one another.

STEVEN: Yes. Well ...

ANDREW: You're like a man with one foot on either side of an ever-widening chasm. The kind of detachment – or even the kind of *involvement* – you're telling me about: very soon, as your looks suggest ... is going to rip you wide apart. You can't be *for* this crummy world and at the same time be for your own psychic ...

spiritual ... *moral* autonomy, any longer. It is now the season of the locusts, and if you have anything to save then save it. Grab it in both hands and run.

STEVEN: Yes ... well.

ANDREW: Well? Well, what?

STEVEN: Let's hope there aren't too many of you.

ANDREW: Too many?

STEVEN: Someone has to stay behind.

ANDREW: Behind? You're not behind. You're nowhere. You're *overrun*.

SHAW [*off*]: Well then ... Well, then ... Here I come ...

COLIN [*to* ANDREW]: Forget it. [*Calling*] Do you want a hand, or can you manage?

SHAW [*off*]: I don't damn well know ... ooh! [*Groans.*]

COLIN [*to* ANDREW]: Look. Just lay off ...

[ANDREW *begins to whistle a tune, wandering round the room, his hands in his pockets.*

SHAW *comes in, in his best suit, dark blue, and a little old-fashioned in cut. He carries his shoes in his hand.*]

SHAW: By go. These braces. They're like a straitjacket on your back ... Your mother won't be a minute. I had to hang around to give her a hand. Can't reach any of her buttons these days, you know. Oooh! [*Sits down to put on his shoes.*] Just look at that. [*Holds up a shoe.*] She's had me polishing that since a week last Sunday. If you shone a light on it it'd burn your eyes.

[*They laugh, looking at one another.*]

COLIN: Look ... I better fetch the car.

SHAW: Aye. I was thinking of that ... Can you wait till she comes down? She wants to make 'an entry'. She'll be another half an hour after that, doing her gloves up, getting her hair right. So you'll be all right.

COLIN: Aye. Well. There's no great hurry. We'll have a drive around.

SHAW: She'd like that. She's been on at me to get a car. At my age. I can't bloody see a lamp-post till it hits me in the face ... She's had a hard life. She's worked very hard. Kept this like a palace ... One woman in a house of men. She'd have given aught, you know, to have had a daughter. You know, somebody to talk to ... Ay up. Here. She's coming. [*He gets up to take up a casual pose by the fireplace, winking at the others.*]

MRS SHAW [*off*]: Are you ready?

SHAW: Aye. We're ready, love. We've been waiting here for hours.

MRS SHAW [*off*]: Ups! Won't be a minute.

SHAW [*to the others*]: Last-minute hitch.

[*They're standing now in their respective places round the room, facing the door.*]

MRS SHAW [*off*]: Are you ready, then?

COLIN: We're ready.

SHAW: Here she comes ...

[*Pause. Then* MRS SHAW *appears at the door. She wears a dignified blue costume, her coat folded neatly over her arm. In one hand is a pair of white gloves and a handbag. On her head is a matching blue hat, not ostentatious.*]

COLIN: Wow!

ANDREW: Lovely.

SHAW: Beautiful.

MRS SHAW: Do you like it?

STEVEN: It's very nice. I couldn't have done better myself. [*He embraces her.*]

COLIN: Super ... smashing. [*Embraces her.*]

SHAW: Here ... better give her a kiss an' all. [*Kisses her modestly on the cheek.*]

ANDREW: Well, then. Are we ready?

COLIN: I'll go fetch the car.

MRS SHAW: Nay, well, look ... Let's all walk down. It's only half a mile.

COLIN: Well ...

ANDREW: Do you feel up to it?

[SHAW *and* COLIN *laugh.*]

MRS SHAW: We've walked down that road together often enough in the past. Once more won't do us any hurt.

[COLIN *holds the coat and she puts it on.*]

[*To* SHAW] Can you lock the door?

SHAW: Aye. Aye ... I'll just get my coat. [*Goes.*]

COLIN: Have we to go in front, or do we follow on behind? [*Pulling on his own coat.*]

MRS SHAW: Well, I don't know.

COLIN: Here you are, then. [*Offers her his arm.*] We'll go in front. Show the flag.

MRS SHAW: Have you all got your coats?

STEVEN [*pulling his on*]: That's an old familiar question.

COLIN: Cleaned your shoes? Washed your faces? Ties straight? Got your handkerchief? Right, then: have you all got your coats?

[*They laugh.*]

SHAW [*returning, his coat on*]: All locked up. Ready.

COLIN [*leading* MRS SHAW *the other way*]: Nay, out of the front door today, Mother. Dad – bring up the rear.

[COLIN *goes with* MRS SHAW *on his arm.*]

SHAW: Bring up the rear, he says. Who's boss here, I'm thinking.

ANDREW: You and me, old lad. [*Puts his arm round* SHAW'*s shoulder.*] Come on, Steve ... We're not leaving you at home.

[ANDREW *and* SHAW *go.* STEVEN *remains a moment, buttoning his coat.*

He pauses: looks round.]

MRS SHAW [*off*]: Steven?

[*He looks round the room once more.*

Then, slowly, he moves to the door and goes, closing it behind him.

Curtain.]

ACT TWO

Scene One

Late evening.

    MRS BURNETT *comes in. She puts on the light, draws the curtains, looks in the kitchen, puts coal on the fire.*

    Unseen by her, REARDON *puts his head round the door: an elderly man dressed in a neat suit, dark, a handkerchief in the top pocket, with gloves and a walking cane: an Irish accent, dandyish but by no means effete. He watches* MRS BURNETT *a moment. Then:*

REARDON: *Aha!*

MRS BURNETT: Ooh! [*Jumps, startled.*]

REARDON: Thought I saw a light. Burglars!

MRS BURNETT: Burglars. They'll be catching you one of these nights.

REARDON: Reardon? The one-man vigilante? ... [*Hastily looks round.*] They haven't left a drop, have they, by any chance?

MRS BURNETT: They have not. And the key's in my possession for safe keeping. Not for letting strangers in and out.

REARDON [*with dignity*]: Harry Shaw and I have been the closest friends for over thirty-five years.

MRS BURNETT: I know. And never closer than when he's standing at a bar.

REARDON: One man, one round. That has always been my motto. And what little secrets have you been prying out?

    [REARDON *is moving round the room inspecting.*]

MRS BURNETT: None. Not any. I have more respect for people's privacy than that. [*Shifts chairs, etc., as she talks.*] I've been building up the fire. They'll be back soon, unless they're going to make a morning of it as well as half a night ... Now ... [*Gestures at him to stop prying.*]

REARDON: It's all right. It's all right. Didn't I meet them on the way down the street this evening? 'Good day,' says I, 'but that's a sight

52

for sore eyes. Three famous sons taking out their mother and dad.'
Are you sure . . . ? [*Gestures at the sideboard.*]

MRS BURNETT: If there was I wouldn't touch it. In all the years
they've left me with the key I've never once touched anything in
here, and I never shall.

REARDON: Harry Shaw and I have never allowed the perversity of
private property to come between us. 'What is mine is yours, and
what is yours is mine' has always been our motto.

MRS BURNETT: Well, the same doesn't go for Mrs Shaw, and she's
the one you have to make account to.

REARDON: That's true. There goes a woman before whom I shall
always remove my hat.

MRS BURNETT: I should think so, too.

REARDON: Behind every great man, now, you find a promising
woman.

MRS BURNETT: You do. Don't you forget it.

REARDON: Am I likely? The one deficiency in an otherwise phenomenal life. Your respect for the privileged classes does you credit,
Mrs Burnett.

MRS BURNETT: Privileged?

REARDON: When the aspirations of the working classes are to join the
lower middle, what do the Shaws do, but jump over a couple and
land right up there, at the very top.

MRS BURNETT: The top?

REARDON: I wouldn't pretend, now, that they'd be aristocrats,
within the one generation. But it wouldn't surprise me if one day, in
the not too distant future, a Shaw is found sitting in the House of
Lords, breathing down enlightenment on every side, a mind nur-
tured . . . formed, inspired, within these four walls. So is a beacon
lit, Mrs Burnett. And so are the great allowed to shed their light . . .
One of gin, one of sherry, one of soda water, and unless I am very
much mistaken, a damn great one of Scotch. [*Has opened the
sideboard cupboard door.*]

MRS BURNETT: I don't care whether there's a crate-ful. You're not
touching a single drop. [*She steps in and shuts the cupboard door.*] I
would have thought Mrs Reardon would have wanted you home in
bed hours ago.

REARDON: Mrs Reardon, alas, Mrs Burnett, has not wanted me home in bed, or anywhere else for that matter, for more years than you and I could count together.

MRS BURNETT: Well, I'm sure ...

REARDON: If my father had given me the opportunities that Mr Shaw has given to his sons, do you know where I would be now?

MRS BURNETT: I've no idea. It'd have a bar in it, I know that for sure.

REARDON: You're right. I would accumulate what little wealth my golden opportunities had provided and, splitting everything in half, I would retire ...

MRS BURNETT: Retire?

REARDON: To the west coast of my native land, the wildness of which is past description. And from where, so many years ago I've lost count, my old father, God rest his soul, first brought me, a mewling infant in my mother's impoverished arms.

MRS BURNETT: And half would be for what?

REARDON: Half would be for building a modest little cottage, hewn from the rock from which my forebears sprang, the homeland of my fathers – stretching back into the very mists of time, before Christ, before the great dynasties of Egypt and Crete and Persia ... those mist-shrouded, northern shores ... where the sun rises like a holy fire ...

MRS BURNETT: Well ...

[REARDON *stands for a moment, gazing out, abstracted, one arm raised.*]

And the other half for what?

REARDON: The other half ... ?

The other half, my dear. With that I shall build a deep, concrete, lead-lined, bomb-proof, a-tomic shelter.

MRS BURNETT: A shelter.

REARDON: Unlike Mr Shaw, I am past retiring age. Certain irregularities in the local office of the National Coal Board have allowed me to spend rather longer than legally I am entitled to in the colliery office, checking pay, attempting, in my own small way, to settle amicably the various disputes – soothing the manager's sorrow, the deputy's rage, appeasing whenever I could the miner's consternation ... I have seen two world wars and several minor ones, and not a little of my life's energies have been expended in avoiding each and every one: I have lived through the most calamitous half-century since time began and my instinct for war, for rivalry and destruction, is unparalleled, I would imagine, by almost anyone. I have a vision, Mrs Burnett, a presentiment ... of a holocaust so gigantic, so monumental in its proportions, that beside it all our little dreams and hopes, our sorrows, and our little aims and fears ... must count as nothing. Whether these are the sort of visions endemic to a man very close to retiring age – and to a pension it can only humiliate him to receive – or whether they are a definitive view of reality as we and our children shall eventually come to know it – I cannot say. All I can see before me, I must confess, are flames – flames, pillage, burning, terror.

MRS BURNETT: You've been drinking. That's what you've seen: the bottom of too many glasses.

REARDON: When I retire to my bomb-proof shelter, Mrs Burnett, I will – if you'll grant me the privilege – take you with me. While the flames roar around our pathetic heads I shall take comfort from your good-natured incomprehension and – who knows? – recognize in it maybe some hope and reassurance for the future. Only those who cannot – through their own intrinsic stupidity – appreciate that something calamitous is happening: only among those will I feel really safe.

MRS BURNETT: There they are. You see. [*Lifts curtain to look out.*] I don't know what they're going to think to find somebody else in here ...

REARDON: I shall retire, Mrs Burnett. And who knows? A few moments later I might quite easily pop in my head as if I were, in a manner of speaking, passing by, on my way home, to my dear wife ... In all my life I have never been an embarrassment to anyone ... No. No ... and, if I can only manage it now, I never shall. [*He goes off with a little bow, through the kitchen.*]

    [*Noises of Shaws off:* MRS BURNETT *makes a last quick inspection. The door from the front opens.* ANDREW *comes in.*]

ANDREW [*calling back*]: No, no. It's Mrs Burnett. All safe. Come in ... [*To* MRS BURNETT] They thought they were being raided.

SHAW [*entering*]: What did I tell you? ... By, that's lovely and warm.

MRS BURNETT: I thought it might be going out ...

SHAW: Aye ... aye.

MRS BURNETT: Have you had a nice time?

SHAW: Grand! Grand! Lovely ... Couldn't have been better.

[MRS SHAW *comes in on* STEVEN'S *arm.*]

We have to hold her up. Got us nearly arrested.

MRS SHAW: Hold me up! I'm quite all right ... [*To* MRS BURNETT] It was very good of you, love. I appreciate it. That's a lovely fire.

MRS BURNETT: I've put the key on the sideboard.

SHAW: Nay, don't rush off yet. We're having a celebration, you know. Still got a drop put by.

MRS BURNETT: Well ...

SHAW [*to* MRS BURNETT]: Best night of my life! 'Excelsior'! Seen nothing like it. We had that many waiters running round the table you couldn't see the food ... [*Belches.*]

MRS SHAW: Oh, now ...

SHAW: That's right, love. You sit down.

[MRS SHAW *is helped to a chair.*]

MRS SHAW: Oh ... [*To* MRS BURNETT] It's been lovely.

MRS BURNETT: Ey, I'm glad ...

MRS SHAW: The view ... All the walls are made of glass. On the top floor, the restaurant. You can see right over the town.

SHAW: From the muck-heap at one end to the muck-heap at the other.

MRS SHAW: It wasn't like that at all ... You can see the moors from up there. Miles. Sweeping away. And rocks ... When the sun set you could see the light – glinting on a stream ... well, it must have been miles away.

STEVEN: Yes. That's right.

MRS SHAW: Beautiful. You'd have liked it ... When it got dark all the lights came on. You could see right up the valley ... Lines of lights. Little clusters ... And a train. Just like a snake ... winding in and out ... I don't know. We've lived here all our lives and I've never seen it like that.

SHAW: We've skint our Colin. [*To* ANDREW] Isn't that right?

ANDREW: Aye! [*Laughs.*]

SHAW: He won't come up here again in a hurry, I can tell you. Champagne? He's even got a bottle in the car. [*Takes* MRS

56

BURNETT's *arm*.] We tipped the doorman. Should have seen his face. Remember Alf Dyson? He worked with me. Face as black as a Christmas pudding. Never washed. 'Here you are, my man,' I said, and doffed him a five pound note. Our Colin's. You should have seen him. Nearly dropped his medals in the road.

[*They laugh*.]

I bet there isn't a bottle left in that place. What's he up to?

[ANDREW *has been looking in the cupboards*.]

ANDREW: Trying to find it.

SHAW: Here. In here, old lad. A bit of space left for a drop more.

MRS SHAW: Not for me, thanks.

SHAW: Mrs Burnett. You'll have the first. We'll have another toast.

MRS BURNETT: Oh, well ...

[REARDON *puts his head in from the door leading to the front*.]

REARDON: Did I hear ... 'Toast'?

SHAW: Why! ... Look what's here! Look what's here!

[REARDON *comes in, followed by* COLIN.]

COLIN: Found him skulking about outside ...

REARDON: Just passing by. Saw a light. Thought: by jove, burglars! Apprehend ...

SHAW: Nothing of the kind. [*To the others*] He can smell a drop of Scotch a mile off. We once went walking on the moors ... this is just after I was married ...

ANDREW: Already running off ...

SHAW: Nay. Nay. I was always going for walks ...

REARDON: He was.

SHAW: Got lost ... Should have seen us. Moorland stretching round on every side.

REARDON: It was. Those were the great days of our life.

SHAW [*indicating* REARDON]: 'Reardon. Which way is it to the nearest pub?'

[*They laugh*.]

He turns this way ... [*Turns*] Then that. [*Turns*] Then he says, 'Harry. This is the road we want.'

[*They laugh*.]

REARDON: I did.

SHAW: And it was. Over the next rise and there we were.

REARDON: 'The Flying Horse'.

SHAW: 'The Flying Horse'! You're right!

REARDON: Never forget a name like that.

SHAW: No. No. Me neither. Not them sort, any road.

[*They've been pouring out the drinks and passing them round.*]
Should have seen our Andrew.

REARDON: What's that?

MRS SHAW: Oh, better not ...

SHAW: Half-way through the meal – restaurant full of people.

REARDON: Captains of industry, Harry.

SHAW: They were. They were. You're right. Mill-owners. Engineer-
ing managers. Leaders of our imports ... exports. Never done a
day's work in their bloody lives ... He gets up and goes round to
every table.

MRS BURNETT: What?

SHAW: 'I'd like you to know,' he says, 'that *that* lady and *that*
gentleman, sitting over there, is – my mother and – my Dad. The
finest mother and the finest father you ever saw.'

MRS BURNETT: He said that?

SHAW: At every table. Went round the entire place.

MRS SHAW: He did. I didn't know where to put myself.

SHAW: 'If you'd like to do something which, in years to come, you'll
be able to recount to your grandchildren, with pride, with a feeling
of achievement, then get up, off your backsides, go over there, and
shake them by the hand.'

MRS BURNETT: He did that?

MRS SHAW: I thought they'd throw us out.

SHAW: Throw us out? ... They couldn't afford it. [*Indicating* COLIN]
Tipped the waiter two fivers when we went in ...

MRS SHAW: Head-waiter ...

SHAW: Head-waiter. 'Keep an eye on us, will you?' An eye! For that
I'd have kept both bloody feet and a half a dozen hands.

[*They laugh.*]

MRS SHAW: Now, now. Just go careful. [*To* MRS BURNETT] He
hasn't been very discreet with some of his jokes.

SHAW: Nay, when I have a good time I have one. No shilly-shallying
about. I know how to enjoy myself, I do.

REARDON: That's right. I can vouch for it now. As long as I care to remember.

ANDREW: A toast then ...

COLIN: A toast ...

ANDREW: Are you totted up, Steve?

STEVEN: Yes. I'm fine.

ANDREW: To the finest mother and the finest Dad that these three sons have ever had.

[*They laugh.*]

To the finest mother and the finest Dad.

ALL [*but* MRS SHAW]: To the finest mother and the finest Dad.

[*They drink.*]

ANDREW [*to* SHAW]: Nay, you don't say it, you daft nut.

SHAW: What ... ?

[*They laugh.*]

COLIN: It's you we're toasting.

REARDON: Never lost the opportunity to take a glass.

SHAW: No. He's right. I never have ... To the best wife, my darling, in the land.

REARDON: Aye.

SHAW: The best wife that any man could have.

ALL: The best wife!

[*They drink.*]

REARDON: To the best family in the land.

ALL: The best family in the land.

[*They drink.*]

SHAW: To the best neighbours that a man could wish to have.

ALL: The best neighbours!

[*They drink.*]

SHAW: I've damn well run out.

REARDON: Now, then. Allow me, if you don't mind, to put that immediately to rights. [*Offers bottle round.*]

MRS BURNETT: No, no. I think I've had enough.

STEVEN: No, no. I'm all right.

[*The others take a refill.* MRS SHAW *shakes her head.*]

SHAW: We'll soon get through this. Come this time tomorrow ...

REARDON: Plenty more where this came from, I'm thinking.

SHAW: Aye. Aye. The sky's the limit!

REARDON: Like the old days, Harry.

SHAW: Like the old days, Jim. You're right. There wasn't a bar we didn't turn upside down in those days.

MRS SHAW: The terror of the town.

SHAW: We were. We were ... Didn't know Jim here was once a professional fighter.

STEVEN: No.

ANDREW: I don't believe I did.

REARDON: For four consecutive weeks it lasted.

[*They laugh.*]

SHAW: Jim's trouble – shall I tell you? ... Never done a day's hard work in all his bloody life. Licking envelopes, filling in forms, wage-packets: dangling round the manager's back pocket.

REARDON: Ah, now, any damn fool can wield a pick and shovel. Takes a man with brains to get paid for sitting on his backside. Ask your sons, Harry.

SHAW: He's right. He's right. I'll tell you something now ... Do you know how high it is where I work? [*He looks round.*]

[*They shake their heads.*]

SHAW: Thirteen inches.

COLIN: It can't be.

SHAW: Thirteen inches. [*Stoops and measures it off the floor with his hand.*]

REARDON: He's right. The Rawcliffe seam.

SHAW: Thirteen inches. If I as much as cough, the whole damn roof'll come down on top of me. Two hundred yards of rock above, and the centre of the earth beneath. Why, you're nothing but a piece of stone yourself, propped up between one bit and the next. You lie with your belly shoved up against your throat.

MRS SHAW: Oh, now. We've just had our dinner ...

SHAW: They don't believe me, you know. I've often thought I ought to take her down, just once, in all these years, for her to see what it's like.

MRS SHAW: I've heard enough, without having to find out.

SHAW: Nay, you can't know what it's like unless you've been down ...
And not even then. It takes a few years of going down before you get

a glimmer ... You get a view of life you don't get anywhere else. You really get a feeling of what God's good protection means. [*Coughs.*] I tell you, if you stuck a pin in me you wouldn't get any blood: a little pile of coal-dust'd be all you'd see run out.

    [*They laugh.*]

MRS SHAW: He ought to come out. While he's got two arms, and two legs. And a head to go with it.

SHAW: Nay, they don't understand. You have some pride. Damn it all. You can't just come out and leave it. What's it all add up to?

MRS SHAW: Fifty years of good fortune. How many men have you seen maimed? And killed.

SHAW: Aye. Well. I shan't get morbid. Not at this hour of the night. Mrs Burnett: another drop!

MRS BURNETT: I ought to be going ... One last one, then.

REARDON: She has a great gift for it, I saw it at a glance.

MRS BURNETT: Once at Christmas. That's the only time I try ... and on an occasion like this, of course.

REARDON: My dear lady ... [*Fills her glass.*] Steven: your father tells me you have a learned text on the way as well.

STEVEN: Had. It's on the way, I'm afraid, no longer.

REARDON: Ah, now, artistic endeavour. It's open to a great many disappointments.

STEVEN: Well, it was nothing as ambitious as that.

REARDON: And what was your subject, Steven? If you don't mind me asking.

STEVEN: I'm not sure myself.

ANDREW: It was a summing up, Mr Reardon, of society as it is today.

REARDON: Society today? And is society today any different from society yesterday?

STEVEN: I suspect not. In any case ...

REARDON [*encouraging*]: No, no. Despite appearances to the contrary, I have a student's curiosity about the world. How it came to be; what it is; and in what manner it will die out.

MRS BURNETT: Believes we're going to be bombed to death. Going to build himself a shelter.

REARDON: Well, well. A figure of speech.

MRS BURNETT: No, no. He said a shelter. Wanted me to come in it with him.

ANDREW: Mr Reardon!

MRS SHAW: Where? Not round here, I hope.

REARDON: No. No. A figure of speech. A figure of speech entirely.

SHAW: Do you remember the shelters during the war, then, Jim?

REARDON: Do I not? ... A certain one I recollect of a remarkable construction. [*To the others*] The largest hole you ever saw.

SHAW: These lads: they won't remember it.

ANDREW: Remember it? We dug the bloody thing.

SHAW: Went down ... what was it? Fourteen feet. [*To* MRS BURNETT] Should have seen it.

ANDREW: You're forgetting, now. She did.

SHAW: 'Course. 'Course. Forgetting. Opened it first night of bombing to let her in ... Swam around, then, didn't you, love?

MRS BURNETT: I nearly drowned! Calls himself a miner ...

SHAW: Nay, ladies first. Alus been my motto ... [*Laughs.*] Whole place was full of water ... By go ... Freetened of being bombed to death and you end up being drowned. [*Laughs.*]

[MRS SHAW *has begun to hum the hymn tune 'Aberystwyth' quietly to herself.*]

REARDON: It was truly a miner's work of art. But for the fact that it was always full of water, it would have been of incalculable benefit to us all. As it was ...

MRS BURNETT: Spent all the time in the cupboard underneath the stairs.

REARDON: We did. Many a happy hour have I spent playing cards by the light of a single candle while the drone of German bombers came, hour after hour, from overhead.

SHAW: I used to carry Steven out. To watch the rockets. They came over sometimes in threes.

REARDON: I remember.

SHAW: You could see the flames from their exhausts ... used to rattle ... [*Indicating* STEVEN] He took it all to heart. Tried to tell him – you could tell when they were going to land ... Engines cut out. Silent ... Hell of an explosion.

REARDON [*to* MRS BURNETT]: No warning, now, the next time. Liquefaction will be the order of the day.

SHAW: Aye. It doesn't bear thinking of.

REARDON: No. No. Thank God we've reached the twilight.

SHAW: In one piece.

REARDON: In one piece. You're right.

[*They're silent.*

MRS SHAW *humming, then at the third line:*]

MRS SHAW [*sings quietly*]:

> While the tempest still is high:
> Hide me, O my Saviour, hide,
> Till the storm of life is past;
> Safe into the haven guide,
> O receive my soul at last.

[COLIN, ANDREW *and* STEVEN *exchange looks,* ANDREW *turning away to hide his laugh.*]

MRS SHAW [*sings*]: Other refuge have I none ...

[REARDON *starts, then* SHAW, *to sing too.*]

> Hangs my helpless soul on Thee;
> Leave, ah! Leave me not alone,
> Still support and comfort me ...

[MRS BURNETT *has started to sing too, they sing strongly. At the last* ANDREW, *then* COLIN *and* STEVEN, *join in.*]

> All my trust on Thee is stay'd,
> All my help from Thee I bring;
> Cover my defenceless head
> With the shadow of Thy wing.

[MRS SHAW *carries on humming the tune.*]

COLIN [*to* ANDREW]: Remember Sunday School?

ANDREW: 'Crusaders'. I was in 'St Andrew's', appropriately enough ... He was in 'St Peter's' ... each saint, you see, had a different pew.

COLIN: A different banner to each group.

ANDREW: St Peter was a fish. Eye-balls like damn great saucers.

COLIN: St Francis a bird ...

ANDREW: One leg, and a beak like a damn great parrot.

COLIN: He was no artist, that's for sure, who painted those.

ANDREW: No ... Jamey, now. He'd have gone down like a bomb.

COLIN: Jamey ...

MRS BURNETT: He would. [*To* REARDON] We were just saying earlier on ...

SHAW [*to* REARDON]: Do you remember the night he died?

REARDON: I do. I shall never forget ...

SHAW [*indicating* REARDON]: Woke him up ... knocking at his door.

REARDON: Aye ... he did.

SHAW: We were just lying there in bed ... couldn't sleep ... could we, love? ... then suddenly on the wall, just above the bed, three damn great crashes ... Like a fist ...

MRS SHAW: Bigger ...

SHAW: Bigger. Like a damn great giant ... Shook the house ... Tell you, frightened us to bloody death. Went to Jim's ... he sat with us ...

REARDON: The rest of the night.

SHAW: I've never been able to make that out. There were you two ... [*Indicating* COLIN *and* ANDREW] Never heard it ...

MRS SHAW: Slept right through ...

SHAW: I could never make that out. Three blows. Just like that ... The only two who heard it. [*Indicating himself and* MRS SHAW. *To* ANDREW] He died, you know, without any warning ... caught a chill one night ... dead by the next morning. Couldn't believe it ... I'd have given aught to have saved that lad ... Asked Him a time or two to take me in his place ... willed them rocks, I have, to fall on my bloody head ... He was a lovely lad ... I'd have given bloody aught. Still. [*Sees* MRS SHAW's *look.*] Aye. Well, then ...

MRS SHAW: I shall have to go to bed. I'm sorry. But I'm nearly asleep sitting here ... All this excitement.

MRS BURNETT: Aye. Look at the time ... I only came across to make up the fire. I've left the light on, the door open.

SHAW: Never mind, love. A damn good job you made of it.

REARDON: Shall I escort you across the way?

MRS BURNETT: No, no, I'll manage on my own, if you don't mind. I'll see you all tomorrow. [*To* MRS SHAW] I'm glad you've had a good night, love.

MRS SHAW: Yes. Thanks, love. I'll see you tomorrow ... all being well.

MRS BURNETT: All being well. Sleep tight ... I'll let myself out. [*She goes.*]

REARDON: Ah, well. I better be off, too. My wife will be thinking I've run away at last. After all these years, now, I don't wish to raise her hopes unduly.

MRS SHAW: Oh, now. Get on ...

[*He goes to the door.*]

REARDON: I shall pop in, if I may, in the morning, and say my farewells.

ANDREW: Aye. We'll have one more before we go.

REARDON: Now there's a promise I'll not forget ... Good night. And may sweet dreams illuminate your slumbers.

[*They laugh, call 'good night', and he goes.*]

MRS SHAW [*cheerful*]: It's been a lovely night. It has ... But if I stay up any longer ... Do you know where you're all sleeping?

COLIN: Don't worry. We'll toss up ... Good night, Mother. God bless ... [*Embracing her*]

MRS SHAW: Good night, love ... it's been a lovely night, it has ... [*To* STEVEN] Good night, love ... [*To* ANDREW] Good night, love ...

[*They kiss her cheek in turn.*]

See you in the morning ... You don't mind me going off?

COLIN: No. No. You get your rest.

SHAW: I'll be up in a jiffy, love. Shan't be long.

MRS SHAW: Good night, then. And thank you all again.

COLIN, ANDREW: Good night ...

[*She goes.*]

SHAW: Aye ... She's enjoyed tonight. She has ... Wouldn't have sung that hymn if she hadn't!

[*They laugh.*]

[*To* COLIN] Nay, you take it from me, lad. That's the best night she's ever had ...

ANDREW [*to* COLIN]: Heads I sleep upstairs, tails you sleep down here.

COLIN: Right ...

[ANDREW *tosses a coin.*]

ANDREW: Tails ... You sleep down here ... [*To* STEVEN] Heads I sleep up, tails you sleep down ...

COLIN: Ay ... wait a minute!

[*They laugh.*]

65

ANDREW: The destiny of fifteen thousand men rests in his hands, and you can fiddle him with a penny.

[*They laugh,* SHAW *turning to the mantelpiece, and taking down a box of matches.*]

COLIN: It's late. That's the only reason.

ANDREW: God bless our motor industry, and all who crucify themselves inside her.

SHAW: Here. Shortest match sleeps down. [*Holds three between his fingers, the ends concealed.*] ... Steve ...

STEVEN [*takes one*]: Not me.

COLIN [*takes one*]: ... Me.

[*They laugh.*]

STEVEN: Ah, bad luck.

ANDREW: I hope, for the nation's sake, you have better luck at work.

COLIN: Oh, it won't be so bad. [*Trying the settee*] Fine.

SHAW: Ah, well. A damn fine night. You can have it all. A car, money, a big house ... They're nowt. A family like this. That's all that counts.

ANDREW: You can tell he's enjoyed himself.

SHAW: I have. I have. Tonight's meant more to me than ought.

[COLIN *yawns, stretches.*]

Ah, well. I'll leave you to it ... this time tomorrow I'll be back down. Nights ... It's one I'll remember. I want you to know that. You've made me and your mother very proud.

COLIN: ... Nothing of it. We'll be back again this time next year, don't worry.

SHAW: Nay, I might damn well hold you to that as well ... Good night. And God bless you ... [*To* STEVEN *as he passes* SHAW *on the way to the stairs*] You're coming up?

STEVEN: Aye ... [*Goes.*]

SHAW [*watches him, then*]: Is Steve all right?

COLIN: What?

SHAW: I don't know ... He's not looked very well.

COLIN: Oh, he's all right ... [*Looks to* ANDREW.]

ANDREW: Aye.

SHAW: He works too hard. He's always put too much into whatever he did.

COLIN: He'll be all right.

SHAW: Aye. Right. Well ... I'll get off. Good night again.

COLIN: Good night, Dad.

ANDREW: Good night.

SHAW: Don't make a noise, will you? Your mother sleeps very light ...
Good night. [*Goes.*]

ANDREW: A fiver.

COLIN [*pause*]: What?

ANDREW: Me bed.

COLIN: You're joking.

ANDREW: I'm not. [*Feels the sofa.*] Ugh. Iron. They've had this
twenty years.

COLIN: They haven't. I bought it for them only last year.

ANDREW: Terrible taste.

COLIN: It was their taste. My money. I'm not going to tell them what
to buy.

ANDREW: Rest of the furniture, too?

COLIN: Just about.

ANDREW: What about it?

COLIN: Not likely.

ANDREW: You stingy sod. The money you earn, no dependants. And
you won't give up five quid for a decent bed.

COLIN: It's not that. It's just a feeling of repugnance.

ANDREW: Repugnance?

COLIN: My brother selling me his bed – well, not even his – for five
pounds.

ANDREW: Course, you could go in the car. But then ... you might get
run over.

COLIN: Or back to 'The Excelsior'. Don't worry. I know your
mentality. The fact is, for me, it's a privilege sleeping in this house.

ANDREW: A privilege? Here ... are you all right?

COLIN: Look. I honour what my mother and father have done. And I
don't give a sod for your bloody family analysis ...

ANDREW: Four pounds ten.

COLIN: No.

ANDREW: All right. A sacrifice. Four.

COLIN: Nothing. I'm sleeping here.

ANDREW [*watching him*]: High-pressure meetings tomorrow morning.

COLIN: I have, as a matter of fact. Tomorrow afternoon.

ANDREW: I don't know how they've managed without you. [*Looks at the clock.*] Must be what? . . . ten hours since they last saw you . . . You're not getting undressed, are you?

COLIN: Not entirely. No. [*Begins to take off his shoes, jacket and waistcoat.*]

ANDREW: You know. I just can't make this out . . . Only two years ago, it seems, you were running in through that door with little short trousers and a snotty nose.

COLIN: I'm tired. I've got to drive back and work tomorrow.

ANDREW: Yes, well. You're a busy man . . . I suppose you have a secretarial assistant.

COLIN: Yes . . .

ANDREW: Don't you ever . . . you know, feel you could make some progress with her?

COLIN: She happens to be a man.

ANDREW: A man!

COLIN: The assistance I require is not the kind that you imagine. There are any amount of women pushing typewriters.

ANDREW: I see . . . On second thoughts, I might be safer upstairs.

COLIN: Good. I'm glad. Good night.

ANDREW: Shall I put out the light?

COLIN: If you don't mind. I'll be very grateful.

ANDREW: And . . . er . . . I won't say anything to Mum.

COLIN: Look. Hop it. Scarper. Knock off.

ANDREW: I'm going . . . [*Puts out the light; goes.*]

[COLIN *settles on the settee beneath a blanket.*

A moment later ANDREW *reappears.*]

COLIN: Is anything the matter?

ANDREW: Forgot to say good night.

COLIN: *Good night!*

ANDREW: Three quid.

COLIN: *Good night!*

ANDREW: Two.

COLIN: *Good night!*

ANDREW: Ah, well. I hope it kills you . . . [*Goes: comes back in.*] I hope, when you come to negotiate tomorrow afternoon, you can't even *sit down*!

COLIN: Good.

ANDREW: One pound ten.

COLIN: For Christ's sake!

ANDREW: Right . . . I'm going. [*Goes.*]

[COLIN *settles down again, turns one way then another, settles down.*

After a while ANDREW *comes back, in shirt sleeves.*]

ANDREW: Psst . . .

COLIN: Wha . . .

ANDREW: Are you asleep?

COLIN: For Christ's sake.

[ANDREW *puts on the light.*]

COLIN: Oh! . . . God! [*Shields his eyes, half-rising.*]

ANDREW: It's Steven.

COLIN: What . . . ?

ANDREW: He's at it again.

COLIN: What . . . ?

ANDREW: Crying.

COLIN: Oh, Christ.

ANDREW: In his sleep.

COLIN: Oh, God . . . [*Gets up.*] What's the matter with him.

ANDREW: How do I know?

COLIN: Can't you wake him?

ANDREW: I don't know . . . All right. I suppose I'll have to.

COLIN: Look . . . He may have drunk too much.

ANDREW: You must be joking.

COLIN: It could be anything. Indigestion . . .

ANDREW: Indigestion?

COLIN: Anything . . .

ANDREW: All right. You go. If you're so bloody efficient. [*Sits down on settee.*] Perhaps you can negotiate some suitable compromise . . . Let's say . . . a whimper.

COLIN [*goes to stair*]: I can't hear anything . . .

ANDREW: No. Probably not.

COLIN: Look. Is this something you've just ... What're you doing?

ANDREW: Well, I can't sleep up there with that row going on. [*He's taken* COLIN'S *place on the settee, lying down.*] It's yours. For nothing.

COLIN: Look here ... God. There's somebody getting up. [*Listens at the door.*]

ANDREW: It'll be Steven ...

COLIN: No ... [*Listens*] My Dad ... Oh, Christ.

ANDREW: Better go up.

[COLIN *listens at the door leading to the stairs.*]

It's not so bad here after all. I was wrong ... [*Eases himself, covering himself more surely with the blanket.*] ... Bit more on the fire, and we'll be all right.

COLIN: Oh, Christ.

ANDREW: What?

COLIN [*coming across*]: He's coming down.

ANDREW: Better get the cards out. Be here all night ... Where's that Scotch?

COLIN: Look, you better get up off there ...

SHAW [*coming in, blindly, in trousers and shirt*]: What's going on, then?

ANDREW: What ... Colin's just off to bed. I've swapped him. Need a spot of oil. Hear those springs? Christ ...

SHAW: There's Steven ...

ANDREW: Steven? [*Looks around.*]

SHAW: Upstairs, in bed.

ANDREW: What ... ?

SHAW: I've just been in.

ANDREW: Sleeping. Wind ...

SHAW: Well ... I've never heard a noise like it ...

ANDREW [*matter-of-fact*]: Look here, Col. You better go up and have a look.

COLIN: What ... ?

ANDREW [*getting up*]: All right. I'll go. [*To* SHAW] What did he say?

SHAW: Nothing ...

ANDREW: Right ... Well. [*Nods at* COLIN.] Soon settle that. Can't have him saying nothing ... Right ... Well ... Off we go. [*Looks round then goes.*]

70

COLIN: Do you fancy another drink?

SHAW: I couldn't touch another. I couldn't ... I was ... look. I was fast asleep and I thought it was a cat. Then I thought it was in here ... then ... [*Listens.*] I don't know ... If your mother hears ... I've shut her door.

COLIN: He could be just dreaming.

SHAW: He was awake. His eyes were open. When I leaned over him he shook his head. [*Looks up. Listens.*] He never cried as a baby ... Did you know that? ... The only time he ever cried was once ... I better go up.

COLIN: Right ... look ... All right. No. Look ... We'll both go up ...

SHAW: Don't make a noise ...

[SHAW *has gone to the door: as he goes out, and* COLIN *makes to follow him, he pauses.*]

Oh ... He's coming ... [*Comes back in.*] He's coming ...

COLIN: Who?

[ANDREW *comes in.*]

SHAW: What's he say?

ANDREW: Dreaming ... nothing ... right as rain. [*Looks round.*] Better have another drop. Knock us all out together.

SHAW: He's been working too damned hard. I know. I could see it when he first came. He's always been so conscientious.

ANDREW: He's coming down ... Dressing-gown. Would you believe it? Brought it in his little bag ... Show you he's all right. Dreaming. Wind. Nothing to worry about. [*To* COLIN] That *steak Diane* ... I almost made a complaint when I first saw it. Did you see him put it in the pan?

COLIN: No ...

ANDREW: Damn faded colour. Set light to it before you could have a proper look. Chopped onions and mushrooms on top of it ... I bet they'd had that in for weeks waiting for somebody like us ... uneducated. Inexperienced.

[SHAW *is looking towards the stairs.*]

ANDREW: What was yours?

COLIN: Tartare ... Steak.

ANDREW: I'd have thought that was very fresh ... Going by the colour. Blood red.

COLIN: Yes ...
> [STEVEN *has appeared. He's wearing a dressing-gown, his trousers underneath.*]

ANDREW: Steve's was the rump, wasn't it?

COLIN: Sirloin ...

ANDREW: Sirloin ... Could easily have been that. I wouldn't have minded having another look at those carrots. The way he served them from the pot ...

COLIN [*holding his stomach*]: All right ...
> [STEVEN *has sat down.*]

SHAW: Are you all right, Steve?

STEVEN: Yes.

SHAW: I mean, nay lad ... if there's anything the matter.

STEVEN: No.

SHAW: It's not Sheila is it?

STEVEN: No. No. [*Shakes his head.*]

ANDREW: Sirloin ... If we'd all had steak tartare like Colin ... trust him to have all the luck.

SHAW: Nay, look ... I don't know ... Your mother'd be that unhappy to see you upset ...

ANDREW: She would.

SHAW: You're not ill? ... I mean ...

STEVEN: No ... [*He shakes his head.*]

SHAW: Well ... It could be tonight ... All that excitement. I mean, well, it's been a very emotional evening for all of us.

COLIN: It has ... What with that.

ANDREW: ... And the *steak Diane*.

COLIN [*to* ANDREW]: Look. I think we've had enough.

ANDREW: Yes. [*Walks about, hands in pockets, whistling quietly to himself.*

> STEVEN *sits as if abstracted.*

To COLIN.] Better watch it.

COLIN: What?

ANDREW: Watch it.

COLIN: Look. I've just about had enough ... His systematic ... bloody ... disparagement ... of every ... bleeding thing .. inside this house ...

SHAW: I don't know what's going on, you know, but you better keep your voices down. I'm not having your mother woken up. If you have any arguments you can save them till tomorrow ... outside, any time. But not down here. I've asked you that.

ANDREW: Why not? What's she to be protected from?

SHAW: What?

ANDREW: I mean ... that ... Goddess, we have up there.

SHAW: What?

COLIN [to SHAW]: Take no notice of him. He's drunk. He doesn't know what he's saying.

ANDREW: He'd know of course. The supreme bloody sycophant. The professional bloody paster-over-er. The smoother-downer. The shoddy, fifth-rate, sycophantic whore ...

SHAW: Look ... look ... you better get out ...

ANDREW: Get out? I've never been in.

SHAW: What ... ?

ANDREW: This family.

COLIN: Oh God.

SHAW: What ... ?

ANDREW: Look. [Points to STEVEN.] Tears! What the hell is he crying for?

COLIN: You better get out. Go on. I'll bloody turn you out myself.

ANDREW: Dad. Wise up. You've enshrined that woman in so much adoration that she's well-nigh invisible to you as well as to everybody else.

SHAW: What ... ?

ANDREW: You owe her *nothing*. What're you trying to pay off?

SHAW: What ... ? [Stands, blinded, in the centre of the room.]

COLIN [to ANDREW]: I think you better go. Go on. I'll give you the keys. You can drive to the hotel.

ANDREW: I've no money on me.

COLIN: ... [Hunts round for his coat.]

ANDREW: Aye ... Aye ... [Watches COLIN get the notes out. Then, as he offers them] Are you actually aware ... I mean, of what you're doing?

COLIN: I am.

ANDREW: I mean, can you actually detach yourself a moment –

73

perverse as such an action well might be – and actually see what it is you're doing?

COLIN: I'm protecting ...

ANDREW: Protecting? You're protecting nothing. [*To* SHAW] He's the one you ought to kick out. And that one with him, up yonder ... The one that's made us so bloody clean and whole.

SHAW: What ... ?

COLIN [*to* SHAW]: Leave him. It's envy. It's jealousy. Listen to nothing he has to say.

ANDREW: No, no. He's right. Listen to nothing that I have to say. Instead ... [*Gestures at* STEVEN] Fasten your eyes on that.

SHAW: If ... What ... ? [*Holds his head.*]

COLIN: Dad ... [*Takes* SHAW's *shoulder.*]

ANDREW: Come on, Steve. You're not deaf. You've heard it. What is it, seething around inside that head, that causes you and ... *look* ... my dad, to cry?

[STEVEN *stands up. He gazes before him a moment, distracted.*]
No, no. No rush. No hurry. Come on ... What's eating out your mind?

COLIN: Shut up.

STEVEN: I've ... [*Shakes his head.*]

SHAW: Look ... Steve ...

[SHAW *goes to* STEVEN. *He puts his arm round him, as much for his own support as* STEVEN's.]
You mustn't lad ... You mustn't ... Nay. All I ever had ...

COLIN [*to* ANDREW]: God. I'll bloody kill you for this.

SHAW: Nay ... every night ... Look, Steve ...

ANDREW: I hope she's listening. [*Looks up*] I hope you're listening ... I hope in all sincerity she can hear ... Her sons, her abject bloody lover ... commend their bloody souls to thee.

COLIN: For Christ's sake.

[SHAW *has turned away, lost.*]

ANDREW: Dad. Dad. Forty years ... what chance have we ever had with *that!* ... Steve ... Steve ... Tell him.

COLIN: I'll bloody kill you for this! I will! I'll bloody kill you!

ANDREW: Let's negotiate a settlement, Col ... Forty years of my father's life for a lady like my mother, conscientious, devout of

74

temperament, overtly religious ... sincere ... for getting her with child at the age of eighteen, nineteen, twenty ... I've forgotten which ... on the back of which imprudence we have been borne all our lives, labouring to atone for her sexuality ... labouring to atone for ... what? Labouring to atone ... When I think of all the books I've had to read. When I think of all the facts I've had to learn. The texts I've had to study. The exams I've had to ... with that vision held perpetually before me; a home, a car, a wife ... a child ... a rug that didn't have holes in, a pocket that never leaked ... I even married a Rector's daughter! For Christ's sake: how *good* could I become? The edifice of my life – of *his* life – built up on that ... We – *we* – are the inheritors of nothing ... totems ... while all the time the Godhead ... slumbers overhead.

STEVEN: My mother ...

ANDREW: What?

[STEVEN *has shaken his head.*]

COLIN: You blame them for that ... ?

ANDREW: Blame? Blame? ... Blame ... Good God. No blame. No bloody nothing.

STEVEN: No ... [*He shakes his head.*] No.

ANDREW: ... What is it, Dad? What image did you have ... crawling around down there at night ... panting, bleeding, blackened ... What world was it you were hoping we'd inherit?

COLIN: Shurrup. For Christ's sake, shurrup.

ANDREW: These aren't your sons, old man ... I don't know what you see here ... But these are nothing ... less than nothing ... has-beens, wash-outs, semblances ... a pathetic vision of a better life ...

COLIN: I think you've said enough.

ANDREW: Enough? Life measured out in motor-cars ... I'll put one on your tomb ... I hope tomorrow you have a damn great strike. And I hope they come along and ask you to negotiate. I hope they make you Chancellor, or Prime Minister. And I hope it gives you something to do, fills in your time, infects your life with a certain feeling of significance and meaning ... for if it doesn't, I hold out for you, Colin, *brother*, no hope of any kind at all. Steve! ...

[*No answer.*]

Dad? ... Fast asleep ...

[SHAW *sits dazed across the room.*]

Why not ... Steve? Nothing. I'll go on up, then. Cheerio. [*He goes to the stairs, and goes.*]

COLIN: My God ...

[*They're silent for a moment.*]

Dad? ... It's all right ... [*He goes across to him.*] Dad?

SHAW: Aye ...

COLIN: It's all right ... It's all right.

SHAW: Aye ...

COLIN: Are you listening? ... Dad!

SHAW: Aye ... It's ... [*Shakes his head.*]

COLIN: Look. It's okay ... Are you listening?

SHAW: Nay ... whatever's happened? ... I don't know.

STEVEN: Dad?

SHAW: I'd do ought for you lads. You know that.

COLIN: Aye. We do.

SHAW: I don't know ...

COLIN: Trust the Shaws ... Not two minutes together – and out it comes ... Fists all over the place.

SHAW: I'll never forgive him for that. You know. I won't ...

STEVEN: Dad ... Don't.

SHAW: Nay, lad. He took advantage of us ... If your mother ever got to hear, it'd tear her in two.

STEVEN: Dad ... Leave it.

SHAW: Aye ... I know. You do too much, Steven. You've got to live your life as well as work. There's Sheila. Your family ... I can tell you, I know what too much work does to a man.

STEVEN: Yes ... Well, Dad ... You go to bed.

SHAW: I could sleep down here ...

STEVEN: Now what for? ... You go up. Go on ... No. Look. I'm all right ...

SHAW: Nay ... I don't know ... Are you going up?

STEVEN: I am. In a minute ... Go on ...

SHAW: I shouldn't sleep with him up yonder.

STEVEN: Dad: he was upset as well ...

SHAW: I should stay with Colin. Let him lie up there alone.

STEVEN: Go on, now ... you get off.

COLIN: Aye ... Go on, Dad. We'll be all right.

SHAW: I hope to God she's not awake ...

COLIN: She won't be. Don't worry.

SHAW: In the morning ...

COLIN: Don't worry. We'll have that troublemaker out.

SHAW: Aye ... Right ... He said some things ...

COLIN: Go on, now ...

SHAW: Aye. Well ... Good night, lads.

COLIN: Good night, Dad.

SHAW: Aye ... Well ... Good night ... [*He turns and goes.*]

COLIN [*sighs; then, to* STEVEN]: Do you want a drink?

STEVEN: No ... [*Shakes his head.*]

COLIN: I'll have one. I'll have two, I think. [*He's gone to pour it out.*] Christ. Thanks for small mercies ... [STEVEN *looks up.*] My dad. Didn't understand a word.

STEVEN: No ... He's like a child.

COLIN: Andrew? ... Say that again.

[COLIN *watches* STEVEN *for a while, uncertain of his mood. Then:*]

STEVEN: The funny thing is ... [*He laughs.*] The funny thing is that he [*gestures up*] raised us to better things which, in his heart – my Dad – he despises even more than Andrew ... I mean, his work actually has significance for him ... while the work he's educated us to do ... is nothing ... at the best a pastime, at the worst a sort of soulless stirring of the pot ... Honestly, what hope have any of us got?

COLIN: I think I'll have another.

STEVEN: What actually do you do with it, Colin?

COLIN: What ...

STEVEN: I mean, this feeling of disfigurement.

COLIN: Disfigurement?

STEVEN: I mean ... this crushing, bloody sense of injury ... inflicted, as he says, by wholly innocent hands.

COLIN: Well, I don't ...

STEVEN: No. Well ... I better get up.

COLIN: Do you ... I mean, have you had any medical advice?

STEVEN: Advice?

COLIN: About your ...

STEVEN: No ... Well ...

COLIN: Shouldn't you get some sort of guidance? I mean, Christ, there's any amount of stuff nowadays.

STEVEN: Yep ...

COLIN: Christ, if we all thought like that maniac up yonder – we'd all be what?

STEVEN: Artists, most likely.

COLIN: Sure. [*Laughs.*] And I can just see the sort of art ...

STEVEN: Aye. Well, I better get up.

COLIN: First thing in the morning – we must get him out.

STEVEN: Yep ... Right ... I'll say good night.

COLIN: Are you okay, then ... ?

STEVEN: Sure ... Right ... I'll see you.

COLIN: Good night, Steve, then ...

STEVEN: Aye ... Good night. [*Goes.*]

> [COLIN *gazes after him a moment; then he glances round. He picks up the blanket, the glass, puts out the light. He goes to sit in a chair by the fire, wraps the blanket about him. He drinks from the glass, empties it, then sits gazing at the fire.*
> *Slow fade.*]

Scene Two

Morning.

> COLIN *is sleeping in the chair, his head fallen on one side. There's the sound of activity in the kitchen, plates, cups, etc.*
>
> *After a moment* MRS SHAW *comes in, dressed, from the kitchen. She goes to the window, opens the curtains.*

COLIN: Oh ... Oh! ... [*Eases himself stiffly in the chair, wakening.*]

MRS SHAW: Did I wake you, love? I've made the breakfast ... If we don't eat it it'll all get cold.

COLIN: Yes ... Aye. [*Stretches.*]

MRS SHAW: Did you sleep all right?

COLIN: Yes. Fine ...

MRS SHAW: What was the matter with the couch?

COLIN: Oh ... I ... dropped off here.

MRS SHAW: I thought it'd be either you or Steven. Trust Andrew. Snoring his head off in bed.

COLIN: Aye. [*Rubs his hair. Gets up. Stretches his stiff body.*]

MRS SHAW: Fire's still going from last night. We were up that late. What time do you have to be leaving?

COLIN: Oh, pretty soon. Straight after breakfast ... Sleep all right?

MRS SHAW: Like a top. It was a lovely night. Thank you. [*Kisses his cheek in passing.*] I'll just fetch it through. [*Goes.*]

COLIN [*looks out of the window*]: Rain ... Looks like it.

MRS SHAW [*off*]: We don't get much else this time of the year.

COLIN [*talking through*]: You know, you ought to get my dad to retire. He'll listen to you. Not to us ... I can get you a house on the coast, a cottage or a bungalow. You'd have no extra work to do.

MRS SHAW [*re-entering with the tray*]: Nay, I've tried. Work for your father, well, it's something he doesn't seem able to do without.

COLIN: Even then, I think you could persuade him. There must be some inducement he'll listen to.

MRS SHAW: He's not going to come out of that pit until they carry him out, and then he'd go back at the first chance. I don't know ... He's been a good man. But I don't know: in some things he's been very simple.

COLIN: Aye ... [*Turns away and starts to get dressed, i.e. tie, waistcoat, shoes, jacket.*]

MRS SHAW: I'll go and call them down. Andrew'll sleep all day, if I remember.

COLIN: Aye ...

[*She goes.*]

MRS SHAW [*off*]: Dad ... Steven!

SHAW [*off*]: I'm coming.

MRS SHAW [*off*]: Can you knock up the others? Tell them it's getting cold.

SHAW [*off*]: Aye ... Aye ... I will.

MRS SHAW [*reappearing*]: Well, then. That's that ... What time do you want to be off by?

COLIN: Oh, as soon as that one up there is ready.

MRS SHAW: Are you taking him back with you?

COLIN: I suppose I'll have to.

MRS SHAW: He's wrecking his career. I suppose you realize that? ...
Still. They're old enough to look after their own affairs at his age ...
He was always wild.

COLIN: Yes ...

MRS SHAW: I don't know. He took it very badly ...

COLIN: What? ...

MRS SHAW: When Jamey died. He was five years old – Andrew. We
put him out with Mr Reardon, you know, when Steven was born.

COLIN: Why was that?

MRS SHAW: Nay, love. To save me the work ... Saved my life, you
did, you know. We kept you at home. You were only two. [Kisses his
head.] I don't know where we'd have been without ... I don't think
he's ever forgiven me.

COLIN: What? ...

MRS SHAW: Andrew ... He was away six weeks. He used to come to
the door, crying, you know. I don't know ... I tried to tell him. If
he'd have been here we'd have had a terrible time. What with your
Dad at work, Steven ... Jamey ...

COLIN: Aye, well. We all have our problems, love.

MRS SHAW: We have ... As you get older you find more and more that
these things somehow work out.

COLIN: Aye. That's right ...

MRS SHAW [she goes to the stairs. Calls]: Dad! It's getting cold ...
I'll have to tip it away in a minute.

SHAW [off]: Aye ... We're coming.

MRS SHAW [to COLIN]: Well, we better be getting ours.

COLIN: Yes.

MRS SHAW: And how's your work going?

COLIN: Oh. Very well ... As a matter of fact ...

MRS SHAW: Yes ...

COLIN: Well, I didn't want to tell you about it ... until I was more
certain ...

MRS SHAW: Now ... you'll have to. Come on ...

COLIN: Nay, well ... [Scratches his head.]

MRS SHAW: Come on. We'll have it out of you ...

COLIN: Well, it's not finally settled ... But fairly soon, now ...

MRS SHAW: Come on!

COLIN: I might be getting married.

MRS SHAW: Well!

COLIN: It's not all been agreed yet. But it's ... sort of on the cards.

MRS SHAW: Well!

COLIN: So ...

MRS SHAW: Here. Let me give you a kiss, love. [*She comes round the table and kisses his cheek.*] Well, then ... Congratulations ... I knew something was up!

COLIN: Up?

MRS SHAW: Oh, your mood. I could tell. On top of things ... Well, then. And what's she do?

COLIN: A dentist.

MRS SHAW: A dentist!

COLIN: I'll bring her up ... You can have a look. Better still – you can come down. Show you round the factory.

MRS SHAW: Well, then ... [*Watches him, pleased.*] Have you told your Dad?

COLIN: No ... No one yet.

MRS SHAW: Honestly. If you'd have told us last night! I am pleased ... After all these years.

COLIN: Yep.

MRS SHAW: Going to take the plunge ... I thought you'd never get to it. [*She laughs.*] ... Oh!

   [SHAW *appears.*]

I thought you'd gone to work or something.

SHAW: No, no. Just waking them lot upstairs.

MRS SHAW: We've just got some news to tell you ... Are you feeling all right?

SHAW: Yes. What news?

MRS SHAW: Nay. You've to be in a proper mood to hear it. [*To* COLIN] I told you he'd drunk too much last night.

SHAW: I am in a proper mood ... [*Looking at* COLIN.]

COLIN: I was telling my mother ... I might be getting married. Fairly soon.

MRS SHAW [*to* COLIN]: Fairly soon ...

SHAW: Aye. Well. That's very good.

   [*Pause.*]

MRS SHAW: Aren't you going to say more than that?

SHAW: Nay, well. I'm very pleased.

MRS SHAW: Well, if that's all you have to say.

SHAW: No. Well ... Congratulations, lad. [*Shakes his hand formally.*] It's a grand thing, I can see that.

MRS SHAW: Well, you don't have to tell us ... Here ... there's your breakfast ... [*Pleasant.*]

SHAW: Nay ... I didn't sleep too well last night ... Nay, I'm pleased, Colin ... When are we going to see her?

COLIN: I was just saying ... I might bring her up. Or you could come down ...

SHAW: Aye ...

[ANDREW's *cheerful whistling off.*]

MRS SHAW: Wait till the others hear ... That'll wake them up. [*Laughs.*]

[ANDREW *comes in.*]

ANDREW: Morning. Morning. Morning. And a lovely day it is.

MRS SHAW: It is. He's right for once.

ANDREW: I am ... And how's my old mater this morning? Apple of my eye.

MRS SHAW: I'm very well, thank you. [ANDREW *kisses her cheek with a loud embrace.*]

ANDREW: Been dreaming about you, I have.

MRS SHAW: I hope something pleasant for a change.

ANDREW: Oh, very pleasant. Very. [*To* COLIN] And how are you, old chap, today?

COLIN: All right.

MRS SHAW: He's just given us some very wonderful news. That's how well he's feeling.

ANDREW: He's not ... Good God ... he can't be ... For one minute there I thought he might be pregnant.

MRS SHAW: He's getting married. Fairly soon. That's all he's got to say.

ANDREW: Oh ... Look at this. Dried up ... Tea cold. [*Examines the breakfast.*]

MRS SHAW: Is that all you've got to say?

ANDREW: Well done. Poor sod. Oh, dear. Whatever it is that's recommended.

MRS SHAW: Well, I must say.

SHAW: Nay, mother. Just leave them to it.

ANDREW: That's right. Settle it up among ourselves.

[MRS SHAW *starts to take the teapot to the kitchen.*]

No, no. It's hot enough. No, no. Really, I assure ... I was merely pulling your leg. And ... er ... [*To* COLIN] When's this happy event going to take place, Col?

COLIN: It hasn't been announced yet.

ANDREW: She hasn't started suing you yet?

COLIN: No: merely that it hasn't been announced.

ANDREW: I hope she's one of us, Col. I mean, not one of them ...

MRS SHAW: A dentist.

ANDREW: A dentist! By God. [*To* SHAW] I knew he'd marry a sadist. Formative experience: can't beat it. Every time ... this tastes very nice ... Good job you came up with the goods, Col. My mother was beginning to get worried. [*To* SHAW] Thought he might be one of those ... [*Quivers his hand.*]

MRS SHAW: I thought nothing of the kind.

ANDREW: Must have thought something ... I mean, all that time, you couldn't have thought nothing.

MRS SHAW [*reasonably*]: I thought he was taking his time.

ANDREW: Taking his time. He's been through half a dozen motor cars while we've been waiting ... thought he'd given up the human race ... look well if he'd fathered a string of shooting brakes, or a line of two-tone limousines, as it is ... well done. Come up to scratch.

MRS SHAW [*to* COLIN]: What did I tell you? Same as usual.

ANDREW [*to* MRS SHAW]: What did you tell him?

MRS SHAW: Well, nothing, exactly. Except we might have expected something like that.

ANDREW: Oh, might you? I'm as predictable as that?

SHAW: Now look. Let's just have our breakfast ... I'll just give Steven another shout.

MRS SHAW: Nay, you don't have to defend him. He's always been old enough to look after himself.

ANDREW: I have. She's right. Ever since I was turned out I've been able to look after myself.

MRS SHAW: You weren't turned out.

83

ANDREW: No. No. Brought back into the fold, now. I remember. [*Embraces her.*] Here's Steve, now, looking as bright as a Christmas penny ...

[STEVEN *has come in from the stairs.*]

MRS SHAW: Good morning, love. How are you?

STEVEN: Well ... Thanks.

ANDREW: Aren't you going to give your mother a birthday kiss? Forty-first year of marital bliss we're moving into.

MRS SHAW: He's got out of the bed the wrong side this morning.

ANDREW: I have. Same every day. Without exception.

[STEVEN *embraces* MRS SHAW.]

Well, then. That's that. Colin's got an announcement to make.

STEVEN: What's that?

ANDREW: Nothing calamitous. Don't worry ... Not for us at least, it isn't.

MRS SHAW: He's trying to say – I don't know whether you can tell – that Colin is going to get married.

STEVEN: Oh.

ANDREW: Galvanized him into action. Look.

STEVEN [*to* COLIN]: Congratulations.

COLIN: Thanks.

MRS SHAW: Well, I don't know. What's got into you this morning?

ANDREW: I think it's the atmosphere up here ... Industrial pollution. It's noticeable the moment you step off that train.

SHAW [*to* ANDREW]: Look ... what ... when ... ?

COLIN: We'll be going in a few minutes.

MRS SHAW: Oh, now. As quickly as that?

ANDREW: That's all right ... Important meetings. The destiny of the nation ... Steve and I can prop our feet up a little longer. Keep things ticking over.

COLIN: I thought you were coming back with me.

ANDREW: Well, I am. But I'm not leaving at this hour. Damn it all. I've only just got up. If you were an artist you'd understand these things.

COLIN [*looking at his watch*]: Well, I'm going pretty soon. If you want a lift you better hurry.

ANDREW: The arrogance of the man. S'what comes with property and

position. No, no ... I'll probably hitch one instead. Haven't done it,
I must confess, for some considerable time, and it is some distance.
Nevertheless, I think – speaking, of course, entirely as an artist – the
insecurity might do me good.

COLIN: Yes ... well.

MRS SHAW: For me you can stay all day. You know that. We see so
little of you ...

ANDREW: You're very kind. And we appreciate it, don't we, lads?
[*No answer.*]

MRS SHAW: Well, I don't know. You've all got up all right ... Next
time we have one of these I'll see you don't drink as much, for one
thing ... Aren't you going to have anything, Steve?

STEVEN: No ... I ...This tea is fine.

MRS SHAW: Well, if that's all you're eating, then, I can start clearing
this away.

ANDREW: Yes. Yes. I think that might be in order.
[MRS SHAW *waits.*]

STEVEN: Oh ... Sorry, I'll give you a hand.

MRS SHAW: Thanks, love.

COLIN: Here ... I'll take that.

ANDREW [*to* COLIN]: Give 'em a good wash will you, while you're at it.
You never know, the experience might come in handy. A dentist ...
[*to* SHAW] You know, I always thought that they were men.
[COLIN *and* STEVEN *clear the table into the kitchen.*]

SHAW: Well, I better be getting my work things out.

MRS SHAW: Work things! What on earth's the matter? You're not
going to work for ... what? Ten hours.

SHAW: Aye ... Well ...

MRS SHAW: The way you're looking I think you ought to stay home
another day. In bed. I've told you. Once you start, you just don't
know how much you're drinking.

SHAW: Aye, well, I've played one night. I can't play another.

ANDREW: I think it'd be better, Dad, if you retired altogether.

SHAW: What?

ANDREW: My mother was saying before. It doesn't do anyone any
good, this endless digging, digging, digging ... What're you trying
to dig out anyway?

SHAW: What ... ?

COLIN [*reappearing*]: Look ...

ANDREW: No, no. I was just asking. For his own good, Colin, as it were.

SHAW: I'm not trying to dig out anything.

ANDREW: No, no. I mean, you'd be silly if you were, wouldn't you? I mean, there's nothing down there, is there, but lumps of bloody coal.

SHAW [*to* MRS SHAW]: Look ... I'll go up and get dressed.

ANDREW: You are dressed.

COLIN: It's time I was leaving ...

MRS SHAW: What on earth ... ?

ANDREW: The trouble is, Mother, you see ...

SHAW: That's enough!

ANDREW: We had an argument last night. After you'd gone to bed. One of the usual Shaw domestic tourneys: nothing to get excited about. You were probably too replenished to hear our little contretemps, but one or two people here, unless I'm severely mistaken, got very worked up indeed.

[STEVEN *has come to stand in the door from the kitchen.*]

MRS SHAW: Oh. And what was all that about?

COLIN:⎫ You needn't ...
SHAW: ⎭ It wasn't ...

ANDREW: Well, you'll be very pleased to hear, Ma ... [*Waits, looking round*] ... politics.

MRS SHAW: Well, I know he gets very worked up about that.

ANDREW: Oh, he does. I mean, I suppose, with all our years of experience, we ought to be ready for it. But no: stick a pig. We'll never change.

MRS SHAW: It's a good job I wasn't there ... I'd still have fallen asleep.

ANDREW: You would. You would. It's true. Nid-nod.

MRS SHAW: I would have thought, in any case, you were all on the same side. Your background, and the experience you've had ... [*She's finishing off the table, putting the cloth away, etc.*]

ANDREW: Oh, it's true. We are. It's just that Steven, unbeknown to us, as it were, had some very unusual opinions to express ... I mean, that caught us unprepared.

MRS SHAW [*laughs*]: Oh, and what opinions were those, then, Steve?
   [*He stands in the doorway and shakes his head.*]
   Well, if you don't want me to know ...

ANDREW: No, no. Come on, Steve. I mean, it's all over. We've settled,
   as it were, the issues out of hand ... What opinions were they?

MRS SHAW: Nay, love. If you don't want me to hear, that's quite all
   right. I'm broad-minded enough, I think, for most things.

ANDREW: That's what she says.

STEVEN [*to* ANDREW]: Look ... I appreciated what you said. Last
   night.
   [*As* SHAW *begins to intervene:* 'Look ...']
   No, Dad ... [*To* ANDREW] But judgements, in certain situations,
   come very easily to hand.

ANDREW: You've got to make a decision sometime, Steve.

STEVEN: I've made my decision.

ANDREW: Decision! Steve!

STEVEN: I've *made* my decision. You, of course, can ignore it. If you
   like ... But actually, I've made it.
   [ANDREW *gazes at him for a while.*
      MRS SHAW *stands watching them, puzzled, smiling.*]

ANDREW: I too, then, have a choice?

STEVEN: Yes ...
   [ANDREW *weighs his hand, as if he holds the handle of a sword.*]

ANDREW: Vengeance ... is mine, then.

STEVEN: Yes ...

ANDREW: Saith the Lord.

STEVEN: I don't want you doing any damage here.

ANDREW: Here?

STEVEN: I don't want you doing any harm.

ANDREW: Harm. [*Looks slowly round the room, his gaze finally coming
   to rest on* MRS SHAW.]
   [*The others are rigid, silent: she still gazes at him, smiling, puzzled.
      He smiles at her. Then:*]

ANDREW: Is it true ... your father was a breeder ...

MRS SHAW: A breeder?

ANDREW: Of livestock ... And the like?

MRS SHAW: Well, he had a few ...

SHAW: Look ... Here ...

ANDREW: I seem to remember ... Kept in little pens.

MRS SHAW: That's right ... [*Smiling.*]

ANDREW: Pigs ... I remember you telling us, often. Not dirty animals at all, unless their environment was allowed to become polluted.

MRS SHAW: Yes ... That's right.

ANDREW: Kept them very clean.

MRS SHAW: He did ... He looked after them very well.

ANDREW: Habit.

MRS SHAW: What?

ANDREW: I say. A habit ... cultivated by his daughter.

MRS SHAW: Well, I ... [*Looks to the others, smiling.*]

COLIN: Look ...

ANDREW: S'all right ... S'all right. S'all right ... No harm ... no harm ... [*To* COLIN] Would you mind?

COLIN: What ...

ANDREW: Warming up the engine ...

COLIN: What ... [STEVEN *gestures at him.*]

STEVEN: Go on, then, Col ... Go on.

MRS SHAW: Well ... I don't know ... I've always said we were a funny family.

[COLIN, *a wild look round, then goes.*]

ANDREW: Funny. I think we are. By any standard. A family of comedians. Clowns. Excruciating tricks. Everything, for your amusement, Ma ...

MRS SHAW: Well, I'm not sure we're as good as that.

ANDREW: Oh, I think we are. Don't underrate us. Ask my Dad. The strongest here ... Take all the weight. The lightest climb to the very top, and there ... take all the praise. Acknowledgement ... adulation ...

MRS SHAW: Well, drink's done *him* no harm at all.

ANDREW: The harm that I was done, was done a very long time ago indeed.

MRS SHAW: He's nearly as bad as he was last night.

ANDREW: I am bad. I am ...

STEVEN: Andy ...

ANDREW: Do you remember when I used to cry outside that door ... 'Let me in! Let me in!'

MRS SHAW: Oh, now ...

ANDREW: Why wasn't it ever opened? *Why?*

STEVEN: Andy ...

ANDREW: Why wasn't it ever opened, Steve?

STEVEN: *Andy* ...

ANDREW [*shouts*]: Why wasn't it ever opened, Steve?

[ANDREW *gazes at* STEVEN. *Then he goes slowly to* MRS SHAW.]

ANDREW [*to* MRS SHAW]: Shall we dance?

MRS SHAW: Well, I ... [*Laughs as he puts out his arms.*] Honestly, I don't know what we're coming to ...

ANDREW: Salvation. I can feel it in my bones.

[ANDREW *has started dancing with* MRS SHAW *who is laughing, flushed.*]

MRS BURNETT [*popping in her head*]: Well, then. All up. I thought I'd have to come round and ring a bell.

MRS SHAW: You've come just at the right moment, love, I think! [*Disengaging herself.*]

MRS BURNETT: Has he been to bed? Or is he on his way?

ANDREW: We're on our way. About to take our leave. The others, as you can see, are somewhat overwhelmed. Events have caught up with them so to speak. While I ... well, I'm afraid that I too have been overrun. Encapsulated. Caught well before my time ...

MRS BURNETT: Well, I don't know ...

MRS SHAW: Well, I don't either. It's some joke of theirs left over from last night.

MRS BURNETT: If you want a bit of fun you know what house to come to! [*Laughs.*]

REARDON [*appearing*]: Hello. Hello. Hello. What's this? What's this? What's this? Signs of departure. Sounds of festivity and laughter ... Colin warming up his aeroplane outside ...

SHAW: Aye. Come in, lad. Come in.

ANDREW: Just leaving. About to take our leave.

REARDON: So I see ... So I see ...

STEVEN: Look. I'll just pop up.

MRS SHAW: All right, love ... I'm sorry you're going now, so soon.

[*To* MRS BURNETT] They've all got work to go to ... except Andrew here, of course.

89

ANDREW: Always the sole exception ... Compassion. I can feel it in my bones.

REARDON: Men of the world. What a place they have to go to.

MRS BURNETT: They have. They have. You're right.

REARDON: Brimful of opportunity ... Round them on every side ... Wish I had my time over again, Harry.

SHAW: Aye.

REARDON: The journey to the stars! What a damn fine future lies before them.

SHAW: Aye.

COLIN [*coming in, wiping hands on a cloth*]: Well, then. All set ... A car like that. You'd think you'd have no trouble ...

SHAW: Aye.

COLIN [*sees* ANDREW]: Yes. Well, then ... If you're ready.

ANDREW: Steven is on his way. Packing his few things together.

COLIN: Right, then ... Well. I'm sorry it's been so short, Mother.

MRS SHAW: So am I, love. Maybe when you bring your ...

COLIN: Aye. Well. Tell them when I've gone, love.

MRS SHAW [*laughing*]: Oh, all right, then ... And maybe when *he* retires we'll be able to arrange something better.

ANDREW: Aye. Let's hope so. Keep my eye open, Dad, I shall.

MRS SHAW: Well, good-bye, love. [*Embraces* COLIN.] And I'm very pleased about you-know-what.

COLIN: Aye. Well. Good-bye, Mother ... 'Bye, Dad. [*Shakes* SHAW's *hand.*]

SHAW: Aye. Good-bye, lad ... And congratulations.

ANDREW: Look after them, Mr Reardon. They're very precious. Keep your eye on them, you know. [*To* MRS BURNETT] He kept an eye on me once, you know, when I was a little lad. Never looked back since then.

REARDON: Nay, I wouldn't claim any credit for that. [*Laughs.*] I'll watch them.

ANDREW: Good-bye, then, Mother. Let's have a kiss.

[*They embrace.*]

MRS SHAW: Good-bye, love. And a bit less of that joking.

ANDREW: Aye. Aye. I promise that ... Good-bye, Dad ... Remember, now, when you're down that pit. Dig one out for me.

SHAW: Aye.

[ANDREW *has taken his father's hand.*]

ANDREW: Remember, now.

SHAW: Aye. I'll remember. [*Holds his hand a moment longer, gazing at him.*]

ANDREW: Right, then ... Best be off.

[STEVEN *has come on* ... ANDREW *turns away and he and* COLIN *start saying good-bye to* REARDON *and* MRS BURNETT.]

STEVEN: Good-bye, Mother.

MRS SHAW: Good-bye, love. And take care.

STEVEN: Aye. I will.

[*They embrace.*]

MRS SHAW: You'll remember, now?

STEVEN: Aye. I will ... 'Bye, Dad.

SHAW: 'Bye, lad. [*Takes his hand.*]

STEVEN: Here ... give you a kiss, an' all, shall I ...

[*Kisses his father's cheek, then embraces him. They're silent a moment.*]

ANDREW: Well, then. Off we get.

STEVEN: 'Bye, Mrs Burnett ... Keep your eye on them.

MRS BURNETT: I will, love. Don't you fret. [*Shakes his hand.*]

STEVEN: Mr Reardon ...

REARDON: Aye. Remember. Future of the nation in your hands ...
[*They shake.*]

STEVEN: Aye ... I'll try.

MRS SHAW: And he's got four of his own to remind him.

[*They laugh.*]

COLIN: Right, then ...

STEVEN: After you.

COLIN: No, no. Youngest first. Always shall be.

STEVEN: Good-bye, then ...

SHAW: Good-bye, lad. Good-bye ... We'll see you off.

REARDON: Aye ...

[STEVEN *goes.*]

ANDREW [*to* COLIN]: After you, old pal ... First time I've seen him without a shave.

[*They laugh.*]

COLIN: Aye ... Right. [*Goes.*]

SHAW [*to* MRS SHAW]: Are you coming out, love?

MRS SHAW: No, no ... You go. I'll see them off from here.

REARDON: Aye. We'll give them a shove. They'll need it.

SHAW: Aye ... Come on. These city lads'll need a spot of muscle.

REARDON: Aye!

[*They go.*

Laughter and shouts off: 'Make way! Make way! ... Here he comes ...'

MRS SHAW *is left alone. She goes to the window, gazes out. Watches, moving back one of the curtains, slightly. She gets out a handkerchief, then wipes her eyes. Blows her nose.*

Shouts from outside: she puts her handkerchief down and waves. After a while the shouting dies.

Silent. She gazes out a moment longer, then lets the curtain fall. She straightens it, turns back to the room. Abstracted, she straightens a cushion, etc.

After a moment SHAW *comes back in, slow.*]

SHAW: Well, then ... that's that, eh?

MRS SHAW: Yes ...

SHAW: Did you enjoy it, love?

MRS SHAW: I did. Yes ... And you?

SHAW: Aye ... Aye.

MRS SHAW: They never change.

SHAW: Aye.

MRS SHAW: What was all that about, then?

SHAW: Nay, search me, love ... Now then. Where do you want me? Here. Look. Let me give you a start. [*Goes to help her.*]

[*Light slowly fades.*]

THE CONTRACTOR

For Kate

THE CONTRACTOR

First presented at the Royal Court Theatre, London, on 20 October 1969, under the direction of Lindsay Anderson. The cast was as follows:

KAY	Philip Stone
MARSHALL	Jim Norton
EWBANK	Bill Owen
FITZPATRICK	T. P. McKenna
BENNETT	Norman Jones
PAUL	Martin Shaw
CLAIRE	Judy Liebert
GLENDENNING	John Antrobus
OLD EWBANK	Billy Russell
MAURICE	Christopher Coll
OLD MRS EWBANK	Adele Strong
MRS EWBANK	Constance Chapman

CHARACTERS

KAY, foreman
MARSHALL, workman
EWBANK, the contractor
FITZPATRICK, workman
BENNETT, workman
PAUL, Ewbank's son
CLAIRE, Ewbank's daughter
GLENDENNING, workman
OLD EWBANK
MAURICE, Claire's fiancé
OLD MRS EWBANK
MRS EWBANK

ACT ONE

The stage is set with three tent poles for a marquee, twenty or thirty foot high, down the centre of the stage at right angles to the audience. The poles should be solid and permanently fixed, the ropes supporting them, from the top, running off into the wings. Each pole is equipped with the necessary pulley blocks and ropes, the latter fastened off near the base as the play begins. Two ridge poles, to be used for the muslin, are set between the poles.

Early morning. KAY *enters. He's a big man, hard, in his forties, dressed in working trousers and a jacket, not at all scruffy. He's smoking, just off the lorry, and comes in looking round with a professional eye at the scene, at the poles. He tests one of the ropes, checks another, casual, in no hurry.*

MARSHALL *follows him in a moment later. He's a thin, rather lightweight Irishman, pleasant, easy-going, with no great appetite for work. He's dressed in overalls, well-worn, from age rather than use. He's stretching as he enters, from the ride: arms, legs, back.*

MARSHALL: You put these up yesterday, then, Mr Kay?

[KAY *doesn't answer, going on with his inspection, smoking.*]

[*Calling off*] Aye, Fitzpatrick. If you're bringing in your snap can you bring mine with you?

[MARSHALL *rubs his hands together against a chilly morning, slaps his shoulders, etc.*]

God, This time of the morning. It shouldn't be allowed.

KAY [*indifferent*]: Aye.

[EWBANK *has entered. He's a solid, well-built man, broad rather than tall, stocky. He's wearing a suit, which is plain, workman-like and chunky; someone probably who doesn't take easily to wearing clothes, reflecting, perhaps, the feeling of a man who has never really found his proper station in life. The jacket of his coat is open as if it's been put on in a rush.*]

EWBANK: You've got here, then.

KAY [*looking up*]: Morning, Mr Ewbank.

EWBANK: Morning. God Christ. It's bloody afternoon.

KAY: We had some trouble ...

EWBANK [to MARSHALL]: Look ... look ... look. Mind where you put your bloody feet.

MARSHALL: To God ... [Moves them in a hurry.]

EWBANK: That's grass, is that. God Christ, just look at it. [He presses down a divot.]

KAY: It must have been from yesterday ...

> [FITZPATRICK enters as EWBANK busies himself with looking around and pressing down a further divot.
>
> FITZPATRICK is eating a sandwich and in addition to his own bag of food is carrying MARSHALL's, an old army shoulder bag.
>
> FITZPATRICK is a hard, shrewd Irishman, independent.]

FITZPATRICK: Is that a ton of lead you have in there, Marshy, or the latest of your mother's buns?

> [He slings the bag to MARSHALL who misses it.]

He couldn't nick a tail off a chocolate mouse.

MARSHALL: Nor a cold off a wet morning!

> [They both laugh.]

FITZPATRICK [catching sight of EWBANK]: Oh, good Christ. Good morning. How are you? Good day. Good night ... [Mumbles on through a ritual of touching forelock, bowing, etc.]

EWBANK: Mind where you put your feet, Fitzpatrick, or I'll have them bloody well cut off.

FITZPATRICK: Aaaah! [Steps one way then another. To MARSHALL] As long as it's my feet only he's after.

> [They both laugh.]

EWBANK: I came down here ... Are these all you've got? [Indicating men.]

KAY [calling off]: Bennett!

EWBANK: I've never known such a damn place for eating.

> [MARSHALL as well as FITZPATRICK is eating a sandwich.]

MARSHALL: It's me breakfast ... I haven't eaten a thing all night.

FITZPATRICK: Nor drunk a drop of anything, either.

MARSHALL: Now would I do a thing like that? ... Eating, now, is a different matter.

> [They both laugh. BENNETT has come in carrying a ridge pole on his shoulder.

BENNETT *is a fairly anonymous person, prefers to be inconspicuous, that is, without being overlooked. He'll do whatever is
asked of him, no more and occasionally, if he's sure it'll cause no
trouble, a little less. His hair is neatly combed and he wears the
trousers of an overall and a clean shirt. He, too, as he enters, carrying
the ridge pole, has a sandwich in his mouth and, over his other
shoulder, a food bag; in his arms he carries the muslin ropes.*]

BENNETT [*through sandwich*]: Quick! Quick! I'm going to drop it ...

EWBANK: Damn and blast it, man, look where you're walking ...

BENNETT: Quick! Quick! It's going on my toes ... [*He puts the ridge
pole down between the first two vertical poles, groaning and then
holding his back as he straightens: evidently the root of all his problems.*] Oooooooh ...! I should never ... Oooooooh! [*Holds his back
with both hands.*] Rheumatism. Have you ever had anything like it?

EWBANK: Aye. Often.

BENNETT: You have?

EWBANK: When anybody mentions bloody work. I've seen it. Don't
worry.

BENNETT: That's right. This place is full of skivers. Just look at that.
[*Looks up at the house.*] It's a damn sight warmer in the cab.

EWBANK: I came down, Kay ... Just look at this. [EWBANK *has
examined where he's laid the ridge pole. Now he presses in another
divot.*]

FITZPATRICK: That's a lovely house you have there, Mr Ewbank.
[*Gestures off.*]

MARSHALL: Beautiful ... ! Beautiful.

EWBANK: And I'll bloody well keep it that way if I've half a chance.

FITZPATRICK [*to* MARSHALL]: He wouldn't be letting us in there,
now, that's for sure. To warm up by the fire.

MARSHALL: Toes and fingers ...

FITZPATRICK: Toes and fingers.
    [*They laugh.*]

MARSHALL: Just look, to God. [*Holds up his fingers.*] They're drop-
ing off.

EWBANK: I came down to give you all a warning. Before you start.
That house, now, is full of people.

MARSHALL [*looks up*]: People ...

EWBANK: Relatives of mine. It overlooks the lawn.

FITZPATRICK: It does. It does. [*To* MARSHALL] How long's he had it?

EWBANK: And I don't want you, Fitzpatrick, up to your usual habits. Piddling all over the place, for one thing, whenever you feel like it. And language. I'd appreciate it very much, Kay, if you saw to it that they watched their tongues.

KAY: Aye. Right.

FITZPATRICK: You do that, Kay.

EWBANK: And for another thing, Kay: this lawn.

[PAUL *comes in.*]

FITZPATRICK: Don't tell me, now. [*Stoops: examines grass.*] He has.

MARSHALL: Numbered every blade.

FITZPATRICK: Lettered every scratch.

EWBANK: Right. I think you know what's what.

PAUL [*to* KAY, *etc.*]: Morning ... Anything I can do ... ?

[PAUL, EWBANK'*s son, is a bit slighter in build than his father, feckless, a little uncoordinated, perhaps. He's dressed in a shirt and slacks, the former unbuttoned and showing an apparent indifference to the chill of the morning. His initial attitude, deliberately implanted, is that of a loafer. His hands are buried in his trouser pockets and a cigarette hangs, largely unattended, from the corner of his mouth. His manner is a conscious foil to his father's briskness. He has no particular refinement of accent.*]

EWBANK: Aye. You can keep out of the bloody way. Have you had your breakfast?

PAUL: I don't believe ... [*Thinks.*] No. I'm positive. I haven't. [*As he talks he drifts over to the poles, examines them, without taking his hands from his pockets, nods to the men, etc., wandering round.*]

EWBANK: You can come in then for that. Kay, I don't think you've met my son?

KAY: No ...

EWBANK: If he gets in the road kick him out of it. It's the only thing he'll understand. Same goes for the rest of the family, too. Get it up. Get it finished. And get away.

KAY [*to* MEN]: Right ... Let's have the other ridge ...

MARSHALL: Fitzpatrick ... I reckon it's up to you and me.

KAY [*to* BENNETT]: Side poles ...

[*They go,* MARSHALL *and* FITZPATRICK *still eating.*]

PAUL: I don't mind giving a hand.

EWBANK: Aye, I know what sort of hand that that'll be.

PAUL: I'm very good at this sort of stuff. Though I say it myself. [*Takes his hands leisurely from his pockets and, still smoking, stoops and lifts the ridge pole a few inches off the ground. Then he puts it back down.*] There, then. What did you think to that?

EWBANK: Bloody astonishing. I'd forgotten you'd got hands on inside them pockets.

PAUL: There's quite a lot of things I've got you haven't seen. I don't know. Some of them might surprise you.

EWBANK [*to* KAY]: Surprises. I live from one minute to the next.
[*He laughs.* KAY *gives no expression.*
There are frantic wolf-whistles off.
CLAIRE, EWBANK's *daughter, comes in. Slightly younger than* PAUL, *easy-going yet never anxious to be imposed upon. She's wearing jeans and a sweater which show a regard for practicality rather than fashion. Pleasant. Acts tough.*]

CLAIRE: They've started, then.

EWBANK: That's right. They have. Just about.

CLAIRE: How long'll they take? [*Looks at poles, ropes.*]

EWBANK: All day and a bit beyond if you can't keep clear. Now come on. Get in. This's no place here for you ... The lucky bride, Kay.

KAY: How d'you do? [*Laying out the muslin ropes.*]

EWBANK: How many lasses have you got, Kay?

KAY: Four.

EWBANK: Four! To God. One is well enough for me.
[EWBANK *puts his arm affectionately about her shoulder.*]
One of each, and they've skint me afore I'm fifty.

PAUL: I don't know. There's still a bit to go.

EWBANK: Aye. So they say. So they tell me.

CLAIRE [*to* KAY]: If there's anything you want just let us know. In the house, I mean.

KAY: Right ...

PAUL [*stooped, hands in pockets*]: And if you want an extra hand .

KAY: Aye.

CLAIRE: Yours truly ... [*Laughs, indicating* PAUL.]

PAUL [*to* CLAIRE]: They don't believe me. I'm bloody good at this.

EWBANK: Don't worry. If Kay wants any help he knows where to look for it . . . [*To* KAY] I'll leave you to it. I'll pop back in half an hour.

KAY: Aye. All right.

PAUL [*to* CLAIRE]: D'you wanna fag?

CLAIRE: No thanks . . .

PAUL: Me last one. [*Coughs heavily, to amuse her.*]

EWBANK [*going, confidential to* KAY]: I don't mind so much about the piddling. It's just with the house. I have me mother here, you know. And my old man.

KAY: Aye. I understand.

EWBANK: You've got to be able to look out of your own front window, Kay. You understand?

KAY: I'll keep an eye on them.

EWBANK [*looking round*]: A grand day for it. No wind. A bit of sun . . .

KAY: Aye . . .

EWBANK [*going, arm round* CLAIRE]: Well, lass, how're you feeling?

CLAIRE: Champion.

EWBANK [*pleased*]: Champion, is it?

CLAIRE: Aye. That's right.

[*They go.* CLAIRE *laughing,* PAUL *slouching along with deliberate affectation behind, casting a glowering look at* KAY, *coughing, before he finally goes.*

During their departure other sounds have started up outside from MARSHALL *and* FITZPATRICK.]

MARSHALL: ⎫ Hup, three. Hup, three. Hup, three. Hup, hup, hup
　　　　　　⎬ . . . two, three, four. Hup, hup, hup, hup.
FITZPATRICK: ⎭ Hup . . . two, three, four. Hup, hup, hup, hup.

[*They enter carrying a ridge pole between then on their shoulders. It's quite light, but they make a routine of it, as if on parade, each carrying at the same time a sandwich in their free hand.*]

MARSHALL: Four, five, six . . .

FITZPATRICK: Left, left, left . . .

MARSHALL [*to* KAY]: Is that Ewbank's daughter, then?

KAY: That's right.

FITZPATRICK: Good Christ . . .

MARSHALL: Aye, now . . .

ACT ONE

FITZPATRICK: How could something as beautiful as that come out of something so repulsive?

[MARSHALL *laughs. They've put the pole down between the uprights.*]

KAY [*going*]: All right, then. Let's have the canvas off ... [*Goes.*]

FITZPATRICK: Nay, steady on, Kay. I've just done a spot of work. It's freezing. Let's have a little look around. Now, then ... There's the town, from which, earlier in the day, unless I'm mistaken, we ascended. Covered, I'm sad to say ... [*Stopps to peer at it more closely*] by a cloud of smoke.

MARSHALL: Impenetrable. [*Eating his sandwich.*]

FITZPATRICK: Not a spot of anything ... [*Eating too.*]

MARSHALL: On a clear day though ...

FITZPATRICK: Oh, the view, Marshy, is magnificent. Quite worth the effort, I'd imagine, of coming all the way up here to work.

[BENNET *has come in, dropping down a quantity of side poles.*]

BENNETT: Is that Ewbank's son, then?

FITZPATRICK: Is that his daughter?

[*They laugh.* KAY *has returned, bringing in a quantity of side poles which he lays down.*]

Who's she getting married to, then? [*To* KAY.]

KAY: I've no idea. [*Goes off.*]

FITZPATRICK: A university man if ever I saw one. [*Still eating his sandwich.*]

BENNETT: Who's that, Fitzie? [*He's shackling the muslin ropes to the muslin ridges.*]

FITZPATRICK: The son.

MARSHALL: The mark of an educated man.

FITZPATRICK: Unlike his bloody old man.

[*They laugh.*

KAY *comes back with more side poles.*]

An intellectual. [*Taps the side of his head knowingly.*] You can tell it at a glance.

MARSHALL: Never done a day's work in his life.

[*They laugh.*]

BENNETT: A house like that, and you don't need to do any work ...

MARSHALL: Built up from what ... ?

FITZPATRICK: The money he never paid us ...

BENNETT: And a damn sight more besides.

FITZPATRICK [*gestures*]:

>   The windows bright with our sweat
>   The concrete moistened by our sorrows.

MARSHALL: Did you get that out of the paper?

FITZPATRICK: I did.

KAY: Bloody eating. I've never seen such a place for food. Where's
Glendenning? [*Checks* BENNETT'*s shackling of the muslin ridges.*]

BENNETT: He's fastening up the gates.

FITZPATRICK [*imitating, suddenly, a wild and vicious man*]: 'Will you
keep the gate shut, damn you! Haven't I enough trouble in here
wid'out you letting more in besides?'

MARSHALL: Is that what he said? [*Looks up at house.*]

FITZPATRICK: That's right, Kay, isn't it?

[KAY *doesn't answer but goes on working.*]

No sooner got the poles up than he comes tearing across the lawn,
the dogs yapping at his heels. 'Who the hell left that damn gate
open?' I thought he'd fire him on the spot.

MARSHALL: No such damn luck, I'm thinking.

FITZPATRICK: No: no such damn luck. You're right.

[*They laugh. The tone of this, directed as much at* KAY *as at anyone
else, is that of a casual effort to fill in time, to smoke, eat, etc.*]

BENNETT: He's not a man to provocate.

[*They laugh.*]

KAY: He's a man to come back down here in half an hour. Come on.
Come on ... Glendenning, where the *hell* are you going with that?

[GLENDENNING *is perhaps in his early twenties, a good-natured,
stammering half-wit. He wears overalls, well-worn but scrupulously
clean, and considerably too large for him. A big pair of boots stick out
from underneath; something, altogether, of a caricature of a workman. He has entered, carrying a fourteen-pound sledgehammer over
one shoulder, and several marquee stakes over the other, crossing over
the stage towards the other side.*]

GLENDENNING: I ... I ... I ... I ... I ... I ...

MARSHALL [*sings to the tune of* '*Down Mexico Way*']: Ay, yi, yi, yi ...
Ay, yi, yi, yi!

GLENDENNING: I . . . I . . . I . . . I'm going to n . . . n . . . n . . . *nnnnn* . . . knock in some . . . *sssss* . . . stakes.

BENNETT: Stakes!

FITZPATRICK: Stakes, bejesus.

KAY [*matter-of-fact*]: You bloody idiot.

GLENDENNING: W . . . wwww . . . what?

MARSHALL: He said: 'You bloody idiot.'

GLENDENNING: Wa . . .

BENNETT: The stakes, man. The stakes.

[GLENDENNING *looks at the stakes. He gazes at them for a while.*]

GLENDENNING: W . . . wwww . . . what?

KAY [*going, casual*]: Fitzpatrick. Bennett . . . Come on, now. Come on. [*Goes.*]

FITZPATRICK: You don't knock stakes in here.

MARSHALL: You don't at all.

GLENDENNING: What? [*He looks up at the poles.*]

BENNETT: Not in Mr Ewbank's lawn.

MARSHALL: No, no.

FITZPATRICK: He's planted this, he has, with special grass. [*Gestures at house.*] You've to step over it . . . like walking on a cloud. Here, now. Here. Look at this . . .

[FITZPATRICK *tiptoes to and fro so that* GLENDENNING *might see.*]

KAY [*off*]: Fitzpatrick . . .

FITZPATRICK: Come on, now. Let's see you do it.

MARSHALL [*indicating house*]: If you can't do it, you know, he'll not have you near the house.

FITZPATRICK [*doing it himself*]: Come on, now. Like this . . .

MARSHALL: Do you know what he'll do?

GLENDENNING [*uncomprehending*]: W . . . wwww . . . what?

MARSHALL: If he looks through his window and sees you walking about with stakes dangling from your arm?

[GLENDENNING *is uncertain, looking from one to the other. Then:*]

GLENDENNING: N . . . *nnnn* . . . no.

FITZPATRICK: He'll come out here . . .

BENNETT: And take that hammer . . .

MARSHALL: And drive one right through your ...

GLENDENNING: Oh!

[MARSHALL *has placed a forefinger to each of* GLENDENNING's *temples, pinning his head between.*]

FITZPATRICK: Come on, now. Let's see you do it.

MARSHALL: You have to pass the test!

BENNETT: If he's watching, he might just change his mind.

[FITZPATRICK, *with something of a gesture, poses on his toes.* GLENDENNING *looks at them, then up at the house.*]

FITZPATRICK: Up, now ... Higher.

GLENDENNING: I can't ...

MARSHALL: Oh, now. That's not so bad.

FITZPATRICK: He'll be very pleased with that.

[GLENDENNING *has scarcely raised his heels.*]

MARSHALL: He will. I haven't a doubt.

FITZPATRICK: That's the best piece of toe-walking I've seen in all my life.

BENNETT: For many a year.

MARSHALL: For many a year. You're right.

FITZPATRICK: Do you know, now, what I think he'll do ...

KAY [*off*]: Bennett ... !

MARSHALL: He'll come out here ...

[GLENDENNING *still poses, watching them.*]

BENNETT: 'Glendenning,' he'll say ...

FITZPATRICK: 'As a special favour to myself – to myself, mind – I'd be very grateful if you'd come down here each morning ...'

GLENDENNING: M ... mmmm ... morning.

MARSHALL: 'To my house ...'

FITZPATRICK: 'For it just so happens I've been looking for a man the very likes of you ...'

MARSHALL: 'A special person ...'

GLENDENNING: Sp ... sp ... sp ... sssss ... special.

BENNETT: 'For a job, that is, I have in mind ...'

FITZPATRICK: 'And for which it seems to me you have all the necessary qualifications.'

GLENDENNING: Aye!

MARSHALL: Aren't you going to ask him what it is, Glenny?

GLENDENNING: Aye!

FITZPATRICK: Do you see, now, all those little holes ...

GLENDENNING: Aye!

FITZPATRICK: Lying all over the grass ...

GLENDENNING: Aye!

FITZPATRICK: Each one, you know, has a little worm inside.

GLENDENNING: Aye!

FITZPATRICK: And every time it pops its head out ...

GLENDENNING: Aye!

FITZPATRICK: I want you to hit it. As hard as you can. With that. [*Indicates hammer.*]

    [*They laugh.* GLENDENNING, *not at all put out, gazes round at them with a broad smile, pleased.*

    KAY *comes back carrying first bag of canvas. He dumps it down.*]

KAY: Bennett. Let's have the canvas off. Fitzpatrick.

FITZPATRICK: Aye, aye, sir.

KAY: And easy with it as it comes. [*To* GLENDENNING] You better put those back, lad.

GLENDENNING: H ... hhh ... How're you going to k ... kkkk ... keep it up?

FITZPATRICK [*going*]: That's a very philosophical question ... [*He and* MARSHALL *go off, laughing.* MARSHALL, *a moment later, however, comes back.*]

MARSHALL: Ay, now. He didn't mention me at all. [*Put out, he potters with the ropes, checking them with no interest at all.*]

KAY [*patiently to* GLENDENNING]: Mr Ewbank, now – he's asked us to put no holes into his lawn. [*Presses lawn with his foot to demonstrate its quality.*]

GLENDENNING: Aye!

MARSHALL: We're going to float it up, Glenny. If we all stand here, now, and puff together ... I think we'll be all right.

KAY [*to* MARSHALL]: Come on. You can lift a piece with me ... [*As they go*] You want to leave Glendenning alone. Have you heard that, now?

MARSHALL: Me! Me? I've never even touched him ... [*To* FITZPATRICK *coming in*] Have you heard him, now? They're blaming me. Not a damn minute's rest here for anyone.

[FITZPATRICK *and* BENNETT *are carrying in the second bag of canvas.*]

FITZPATRICK: We've left the heaviest piece behind.

MARSHALL [*going*]: What?

FITZPATRICK: Couldn't shift it, man. Needs a great big feller like yourself.

MARSHALL: Oh, to God, now: every time.

[MARSHALL, *groaning, follows* KAY *out.* FITZPATRICK *and* BENNETT *dump the canvas on the first ridge pole.* GLENDENNING *watches, nodding, smiling.*]

BENNETT: We'll have some trouble here.

FITZPATRICK: What's that?

BENNETT: Running the guys back to the house.

FITZPATRICK: As a matter of topicality. And [*indicating* GLENDENNING] between ourselves. What are we going to fasten them to?

[*They're unlacing the bag, getting the canvas out, obviously familiar with the job.* KAY *and* MARSHALL *return with the third bag of canvas, for the rear end of the tent.*]

BENNETT: You remember yesterday?

FITZPATRICK: Do I not?

BENNETT: After we'd put the poles up and you'd gone back to the yard?

FITZPATRICK: I do. Work for me, Benny, at least, had finished.

BENNETT: He had Kay and myself knocking stakes into ... Can you guess?

FITZPATRICK [*looks round. Then*]: I can not.

BENNETT: The beds.

FITZPATRICK: The beds.

BENNETT: Each one disguised, very nearly, as a flower.

FITZPATRICK: The cunning bastard.

BENNETT: Do you remember the time ... ? [*Spreading the canvas.*]

FITZPATRICK: I do.

BENNETT: When he made us put up that marquee in a gale at Arsham?

MARSHALL [*spreading out the second bag of canvas with* GLENDENNING]: The time it blew away?

FITZPATRICK: 'Come back! Come back wid' you! Come back!'
   [*They laugh.*]

MARSHALL: He's a very funny feller.

FITZPATRICK: He's amusing, right enough.

KAY: Get it out. Get it out.

FITZPATRICK: What? Right here?
   [*They laugh.* BENNETT *and* FITZPATRICK *have spread out the canvas, neatly, either side of the ridge pole.*
   MARSHALL *and* GLENDENNING *are doing the same.* KAY *is shackling and spreading the third piece.*
   Gradually, in spite of their chatter, the pace of work has begun to assert itself.]

MARSHALL [*to* GLENDENNING]: No, this way, boy. This way.

BENNETT: Have you noticed?

FITZPATRICK: What? What? What?

BENNETT: New. All of it. [*Indicating canvas, which is clean and white.*]

KAY: He's had the canvas specially made.

MARSHALL: He has. You're right.

FITZPATRICK: Just look now at this stitching. Beautiful.

MARSHALL [*to* GLENDENNING]: We'd never get a tent like that, Glenny, if you or I were wed.

BENNETT: And how long have you been married?

MARSHALL: Married? Longer than you can count.
   [BENNETT *laughs disbelievingly.*]

FITZPATRICK [*falteringly*]: W...w...w...One...T...t...t... Two.
   [*They laugh.*
   They've begun to attach the rings, fastened to the necks of the canvas, round the poles. They're secured with a bolt, like a collar. The collar itself is then shackled to the pulley rope above and the ridge pole underneath. The guys they fasten off to the 'pegs' in the wings.]

BENNETT: Been a bachelor, he has, all his life.

MARSHALL: I have not.

FITZPATRICK: A Protestant agnostic, Marshy. [*Indicating* MARSHALL]

MARSHALL: That I am ...

FITZPATRICK: Of mixed parentage, and of a lineage so obscure it'd defy a mouse to unravel it – has been married three times already.

MARSHALL: That I have.

FITZPATRICK: Once to a lady bus-conductor.

MARSHALL: That's right.

FITZPATRICK: Once to a greengrocer's right-hand assistant.

MARSHALL: That is correct.

FITZPATRICK: And once, would you believe it, to a nun.

MARSHALL: She was not.

FITZPATRICK: I could have sworn you said she worked in a convent.

MARSHALL: I did. But she wasn't a nun.

FITZPATRICK: Good God. I hate to think what it is, now, you've been up to.

MARSHALL: She worked inside. In the kitchens.

FITZPATRICK: In the kitchens. No wonder, to God, he's so fond of food.

MARSHALL: I am! Eatin', now, is one of life's greatest pleasures!
[*They laugh.* FITZPATRICK *has been fastening off the guys; so has* GLENDENNING. *The others are working at the shackles at the foot of the poles.*

OLD EWBANK *has come on. In his late sixties, wearing a tweed suit: gnarled. An old artisan. He wanders across absent-mindedly, lighting his pipe.*]

OLD EWBANK: Have you seen an old piece of rope lying around? . . . About this length.

MARSHALL: What?

OLD EWBANK: Here. About this thick. [*Makes a circle thumb and finger which he adjusts with some care.*]

MARSHALL: No, no. I don't think I have . . .

OLD EWBANK: Water? You couldn't rot it if you tried.

MARSHALL: Oh . . .

OLD EWBANK: No damn stamina. Resilience: nothing. [*He walks off.*]

FITZPATRICK: And who the hell was that?

MARSHALL: I've no idea. [*Laughs.*]

FITZPATRICK: Well, now. This is the funniest place I've ever seen.

KAY: Right, then . . . let's have it up.

FITZPATRICK: Up?

MARSHALL: Up.

FITZPATRICK: Glenny, now – that's you he means.

[*They laugh.*]

KAY: Right, then. Shoulder height ... fasten off.

[*Between them, having spread out the canvas – two middle pieces and an end – they haul it up to shoulder height, the sections fastened together by the collars.*

They fasten the ropes off, through holes in the base of the tent poles, and begin to lace the sheets of canvas together.

MARSHALL *sings, begins to whistle, then:*]

FITZPATRICK: There was this place, now ... where was it? ... where this feller came in with a little can.

BENNETT: A can?

FITZPATRICK: A can. Full of ... where were we?

MARSHALL: Full of pennies.

FITZPATRICK: Pennies. Asked Ewbank if he could give him one.

[*They laugh.*]

Miles from anywhere ... wanders up ...

MARSHALL: 'Have you got one, then, mister?' ... shakes his can.

FITZPATRICK: Ewbank ...

MARSHALL: Should have seen him.

FITZPATRICK: Green to purple vertigo in fifteen bloody seconds.

[*They laugh.*]

Picks up a hammer ... 'Here, then ...'

MARSHALL: Fifty bloody stakes.

FITZPATRICK: Shoves them in his hand ... 'Here, now. There's a penny ... knock them in, and I'll pop one in your can.'

[*They laugh.*

They're all lacing now, except FITZPATRICK *who has threaded the muslin rope through the loop hanging from the downstage ridge pole.*]

GLENDENNING [*lacing*]: If my d ... d ... d ... daughter ...

MARSHALL: Aye, aye, aye. What's that?

GLENDENNING: If my d ... d ... d ... daughter ...

FITZPATRICK: If his daughter. I never knew you had a daughter, Glenny ...

MARSHALL: Nor even a mother.

FITZPATRICK: Nor even a dad.

[*They laugh.*]

BENNETT: Where did you find her, Glenny?

FITZPATRICK: In your wage packet on a Friday night.

[*They laugh.*]

MARSHALL: If you had a daughter, Glenny?

GLENDENNING: I'd like her go ... g ... get m ... m ... *mmmm* ... married ... in one of these.

MARSHALL: You would?

GLENDENNING: Aye!

FITZPATRICK: On top, Glenny, or underneath?

[*They laugh.*]

BENNETT: Wearing it, Glenny? [*Showing him*] Or underneath?

GLENDENNING [*uncertain*]: Aye ...

FITZPATRICK: Ah, well. One day, Glenny.

GLENDENNING: Aye. [*He smiles shyly.*] Aye.

[FITZPATRICK *takes his place at the lacing.*]

KAY: Glendenning ... [*Calls* GLENDENNING *over to take his place.*] Get on with it, Bennett. [*Going.*]

BENNETT: It's always me. Always me. Did you notice that? It's always me he's after.

[KAY *has gone off.*]

FITZPATRICK [*lacing*]: Kay, you know, is a married man.

[*They look off as they work.*]

MARSHALL: He is?

FITZPATRICK: He has four daughters, each one of them a bit bigger than himself.

BENNETT: D'you hear that, Glenny? There might be one of them in there for you.

GLENDENNING: Ah ... I w.w ... w.w ... w.w ... wouldn't want one of Kay's lasses.

MARSHALL: Which one would you like, Glenny?

GLENDENNING: I w ... w ... wouldn't mind the one they have in theer. [*Gestures at house.*]

[*They laugh.* GLENDENNING *is very pleased.*]

BENNETT: She's already spoken for is that, Glenny.

FITZPATRICK: Though I'm thinking if she hasn't set eyes on Glenny here she might very well change her mind.

[*They laugh.*]

GLENDENNING [*carried away*]: Th . . . th . . . th . . . there's many a slip twi . . . twi . . . twi . . . twixt c . . . c . . . c . . . cup and l . . . l . . . l . . . l . . . lip!

BENNETT: There is, lad. There is.

MARSHALL: Now then, where have I put me rubber hammer? [*Looking anxiously round.*] Me hammer, Glenny. And me glass nails.

GLENDENNING: Sh . . . sh . . . sh . . . shall I look in the cab?

MARSHALL: Aye. Aye, you do that. I'll be in a fix without –

BENNETT: Glass hammer in the cab, Glenny. And rubber nails in the back.

[GLENDENNING *goes.*]

FITZPATRICK: Aye, now. That's a sight that'd turn a donkey round. [KAY *has come in with a huge bag of walling on his shoulder. Tips it down at one side. With him, too, he's brought the four quarter guys.*]

KAY: Come on. Come on. Haven't you finished yet? Where's Glendenning wandering off to?

MARSHALL: He's fallen in love, Kay.

FITZPATRICK: With the lady of the house.

[*They laugh.*]

MARSHALL: She was only a tentman's daughter
But she knew how to pull on a guy.

KAY: Glendenning: come on, here!

[GLENDENNING *has come back on.*]

MARSHALL: Ay, now. Ay, now. I believe he hasn't found it.

BENNETT: Did you get it, Glenny?

FITZPATRICK: Don't tell me I'll have to do without.

[GLENDENNING *laughs, indicating he's seen the joke.*]

MARSHALL: Here I am now, stuck waiting. Can't move another step without.

[GLENDENNING *shakes his head, still laughing, swaying from side to side, his hands hanging, clenched, before him.*]

KAY: Get all the guys fastened off, Glendenning.

[*They go on lacing up the canvas which is done by threading loops from one side through eyelets on the other.*

KAY *positions and fastens on the quarter guys.*]

FITZPATRICK: Ay, now. I'm dying for a smoke.

MARSHALL: Do you think they're watching from the windows? [*Looking at the house.*]

FITZPATRICK: Do I not?

MARSHALL: Toes and fingers.

FITZPATRICK: Toes and fingers.

KAY: *Glendenning!*

BENNETT: Bloody cold. Just look. [*Shakes his fingers.*]

> [GLENDENNING *is still standing there, swaying, grinning. The men turn round to look.*
>
> > BENNETT *has finished his lacing and has gone over to finish* GLENDENNING's.]

KAY: What the *hell*, Glendenning, do you think you're doing?

> [GLENDENNING *still grins.*]

MARSHALL: Ay, Glenny, lad, you don't want to get the old feller upset.

GLENDENNING [*pleased*]: I w.w.w ... w.w.w ... w.w.w ...

BENNETT: Nay, Glenny ...

GLENDENNING: You're nnn ... nnnn ... not going to trick mmmm ... mmmm ... me again!

KAY: I said fasten off the ropes.

GLENDENNING: You're mmmm ... going to mmmm ... blow it up. Mmmmm ... Marshall told me.

KAY: God Christ.

> [KAY *unlaces the walling bag, forestage. He turns away in disgust. The others laugh, more to themselves in order not to provoke* KAY *unduly.*]

Bloody lunatics. It'll be the day in this place when they hire a bloody man.

MARSHALL: Now, Glenny. You've got Mr Kay upset.

> [GLENDENNING *nods, smiling broadly.*]

FITZPATRICK: Nay, nay, Glenny, lad. No joking. Mr Kay wants you to examine all the ropes. The stakes are hidden in the flower beds. Just see if they're fastened on ... One little rope now round each petal.

> [*They laugh.* GLENDENNING *smiles confidently, pleased, · still swaying, his hands clenched before him.*]

KAY: You see how it ends up, Fitzpatrick. Rubber nails. Glass hammers.

MARSHALL: Nay, fair's fair. Glass nails it was.

FITZPATRICK: And a rubber shaft.

[*They laugh.*]

KAY: You go, Marshall. You started it.

MARSHALL: What?

[*The men laugh as* MARSHALL *sets off to fasten on the guys.*] There's only one person does any work round here. [*To* GLENDENNING] Can't you see? Stuck in front of you. Geee ...! [*Smacks his hand against his own forehead.*]

[*The men laugh,* FITZPATRICK *doubled up.*]

KAY [*indicating lacing*]: Pull it tight. Pull it tight.

FITZPATRICK [*to* MARSHALL]: Pull it tight, Marshy.

MARSHALL: Pull it tight I shall.

[BENNETT *laughs.*

They've begun to put in the side poles now: one at each corner of the tent, and four more at the 'quarters', i.e. at the point where the laced edges meet. On to these quarter poles they fasten the quarter guys, already clipped to the 'pegs' by KAY.]

FITZPATRICK: Have you seen his wife?

[BENNETT *looks round.* FITZPATRICK *gestures at the house.*] Ewbank's.

BENNETT: Don't think I have.

[MARSHALL *laughs.*]

FITZPATRICK: If I had a wife like that I wouldn't spend my time, now, making tents.

BENNETT: No?

MARSHALL: Concrete shelters, I should think more likely.

[*They laugh.*]

FITZPATRICK: What do you say, Kay?

KAY [*putting in the downstage corner pole –* FITZPATRICK *is putting in the other*]: Either way, one wife, after a couple of years, is very much like another.

FITZPATRICK: Is that so, now. Is that a fact?

KAY: It is.

FITZPATRICK: You're seen old Ewbank's wife, then, Marshy?

MARSHALL: What? What? Where's that? [*Looking quickly round.*]

[*They laugh.*]

FITZPATRICK: Bloody nig-nog, man.

MARSHALL: Oh. Aye.

FITZPATRICK: You don't think much to her, Marshy?

MARSHALL: Do I not? [*Laughs.*]

FITZPATRICK: Seen better, have you, Marshy?

MARSHALL: Seen better? I should think I have.

BENNETT: And where would that be, Marshy?

MARSHALL: Around, I think. Around.

BENNETT: Around? Around where, then, Marshall?

MARSHALL: One or two places I have in mind.
[*They laugh.*]

BENNETT: The places Marshall hangs around I'd be surprised if you'd find a woman there at all.

FITZPATRICK: Is that a fact, now, Benny. I'm not so sure of that.

MARSHALL: Won't find Bennett there, now: that's for sure.

FITZPATRICK: Find Bennett some places I wouldn't care to mention.
[*They laugh.*]
Seen him one night ... now, where was it? ... taking out his dog.

MARSHALL: A dog!

FITZPATRICK: Fine little mongrel ... Black and white, now ...

MARSHALL: Wags its tail.

FITZPATRICK: Wags its tail, you're right.

KAY: Right, then ... are you ready? Let's have you underneath.
[*The canvas has been stood up now around the edges and the men have started scrambling underneath, moving on all fours to get to the ropes by the poles.*]

FITZPATRICK [*underneath*]: Ay, get off! Get off!
[*There are cries and laughs as they horse around.*]

BENNETT [*underneath*]: What're you doing ...

MARSHALL [*underneath*]: Aaaah!

FITZPATRICK [*underneath*]: Get off! Get off!

BENNETT [*underneath*]: Give over!
[*A burst of laughter.*]

KAY [*underneath*]: Are you ready?

MARSHALL [*underneath*]: Aaaah!

KAY [*underneath*]: Are you ready?

MARSHALL [*underneath*]: Aaaaaaaah! [*A great scream from* MARSHALL.]

FITZPATRICK [*underneath*]: Okay. We're ready, Kay.

MARSHALL [*underneath*]: Aaah. Get off!

KAY [*underneath*]: Right. Glendenning. Have you got hold of a rope?

GLENDENNING [*underneath*]: I ... I ... I ... I ... I've mmmm ... got one!

FITZPATRICK [*underneath*]: It's not a rope he's got hold of, Mr Kay.
    [*A burst of laughter from underneath.*]

KAY [*underneath*]: Are you right? Then pull together.

BENNETT [*underneath*]: Pull together!
    [*Another burst of laughter.*]

KAY [*underneath*]: Heave ... Heave ... Heave!
    [FITZPATRICK *and* MARSHALL *pull together at one pole:*
    '*Heave! Heave! Heave!*'
        GLENDENNING *and* BENNETT *pull together at the second pole:*
    '*Heave! Heave! Heave!*'
        KAY *pulls alone at the nearest pole, one rope in either hand.*]

FITZPATRICK [*underneath*]: Don't pull too hard, now, Glenny.

MARSHALL [*underneath*]: You might do yourself an hurt.
    [*They laugh, pulling up.*
        *Slowly the canvas is drawn up to the top of the poles and the men
    come into view.*]

KAY: All right. Get in your side poles and tighten up your quarter guys.
    [*The ropes are fastened off: threaded through holes in the pole for
    that purpose, then knotted, the men going to put in the side poles as
    they finish, hoisting up the edges of the tent.*]

MARSHALL: Rubber poles, Glenny. Make sure they bend.
    [*Demonstrates.*]

GLENDENNING: Aye! [GLENDENNING *laughs, fitting in the poles like
    everyone else.*]
    [FITZPATRICK *at one point, as he goes past, grabs*
        GLENDENNING's *backside, off-hand, whistling.*]
    Aaaah!

BENNETT: Keep at it, Glenny.

MARSHALL: Never knew you were fond of animals, then, Bennett.

FITZPATRICK: Don't think he is, to tell the truth.

MARSHALL: Persecution.

FITZPATRICK: Persecution.

KAY: All right. All right. Just get 'em in.

FITZPATRICK: Get 'em in, there, Marshy.

MARSHALL: Get 'em in, I shall.

[KAY *has started 'dressing-off' the ropes, i.e. wrapping them off, naval fashion, around the foot of the poles.*]

FITZPATRICK [*sings*]: It's that man again ... It's that man again. [*Whispers urgently to* GLENDENNING.] Glenny! Glenny! Glenny! [*Gestures to* GLENDENNING: *approaching danger, trouble, watch it, careful ... burlesque. Whistles shrill, toneless tune.*]

[EWBANK *has come in. Stands there, watching, intent.*]

[*Sings drunkenly as he works*] 'I was staggering home one night ...'

MARSHALL [*sings*]: 'As sober as a newt ...'

FITZPATRICK: 'When I should see a sight
                       You'd think was rather cute ...'

[MARSHALL *joins in the chorus.*]

MARSHALL: '*White* elephants, *pink* elephants,
                   Hanging on the wall ...
                   O ... oooo ... oh, what a palaver,
                   Fifty-one feet tall ...'

EWBANK [*to* BENNETT]: That's not some bloody field you're digging up. Just look at this here. Go steady, man! Go steady! Kay! [*Presses in divot.*]

KAY: Right ... [*Dressing downstage pole.*]

EWBANK [*to* MARSHALL]: Walling. Walling! God Christ. They stand about as if they were paying *you*!

KAY: Aye ... Walling.

EWBANK [*to* GLENDENNING]: And look! Look! Look! Look! Look! Look! Look! Look! Look! Don't walk around as if you were at home. God damn and blast. Just look at this ...!

GLENDENNING: I'm ... I'm ... I'm ... I'm ... I'm ...

EWBANK: That's all right, then.

[*The men have begun to hang the walling, hooking it up on the rope that underlies and is sewn into the lower edge of the canvas.*]

That's nice bit of canvas, Kay.

KAY: It is. [*Nods, looking up at it.*]

EWBANK: They don't make them like that no more. [*Gestures at tent.*]

'Least, not if I can help it. [*Laughs at his own humour*.] It'd be too damn expensive.

KAY: Aye. It would.

EWBANK [*pleased, contemplating*]: Would you believe it?

KAY: Aye?

EWBANK: It's the first time I've hired a bit of my own tenting. It'll go down in the books you know. Pay meself with one hand what I tek out with the other.

KAY: Aye! [*Laughs dutifully*.]

EWBANK: I'll never do it again. Never. Never have to.

KAY: No. Well. It's worth making a splash.

EWBANK: Splash? By God, this is a bloody thunderclap! It's not just the tent I'm paying for. God, Christ. I wish it was. No. No. [*To men*] Hang it! Hang it! Hang it! Hang it! *Hook it up!* That's what they're there for. [*To* KAY] Three or four hundred people here. Bloody string orchestra. Waiters. Chef. I could buy four marquees with what I've laid out here . . . Ah, well. That's another matter. [*Looks round, examining canvas*.] Let's hope it keeps fine. Have you got the lining?

KAY: It's on the truck . . .

EWBANK: No marks on it, Kay. And no marks on this either. [*Indicates canvas*.] Four lasses, eh?

KAY: Aye . . .

EWBANK: They'll cost you a packet. If I had four I'd set 'em to work and retire. [*Laughs. Wanders round, examining*.] Four. And I can't even manage one. And none of 'em married?

KAY: No, no. They're still at school.

EWBANK: By God. If you had the benefit of my experience you'd never set a lass at school. God Christ, they're only good for one damn thing. And for that you don't have to read a book.

KAY [*laughing*]: Aye.

EWBANK: You've kept your eye on them relieving themselves, have you?

KAY: Aye. They've been all right.

EWBANK: I don't give a damn myself. I've told you that already. But I can't have the old lady looking out of the window and not knowing where to put herself. [*To* MARSHALL] Leave that side alone. You want it open to bring the floor in. [*To* KAY] I noticed on the truck, Kay. That floor costs a bloody fortune. When you put it on you want to load it near the front. If a bit drops off it's done. That's a lovely bit of sewing. [*Looking up*] Look at that seam. [*Reads.*] 'Made by F. Ewbank to commemorate the wedding of his daughter Claire.' My wife chose it.

KAY: The tent?

EWBANK: The bloody name. Paul. That's another of her choices . . .

BENNETT: Shall we get the battens in, Kay?

KAY: Aye. Start fetching them in. And watch the walling.

   [*The men, as they finish off the walling, leaving the one side open, go off to fetch in the battens which they begin to lay out on the floor.*

     BENNETT *has raised the muslin ridges a few inches, fastening them off to enable the battens to go underneath. The ropes for raising these are threaded by* FITZPATRICK *and* BENNETT *before the canvas is raised.*

     CLAIRE *has come in. Wanders round.* FITZPATRICK *whistles a tune.*]

EWBANK: Do you know how many tents we have out this week?

KAY: Quite a lot, I know.

EWBANK: Thirty-four. And that's just about the lot. If the wind gets under this we'll have some trouble. It blows like a bloody hurricane up here.

KAY: It's a lovely view.

EWBANK: Aye. It is. Whenever you can see it. At one time, do you know, there was nothing in that valley but a farm, a mill, and half a dozen houses. And what're you doing out here you wouldn't be better doing somewhere else?

   [CLAIRE *has been wandering round the edges of the tent, looking around, slow . . . only now has she been noticed by* EWBANK.]

CLAIRE: They're coming out to have a look. [*To* KAY] See how you're getting on.

EWBANK: We're all right. We don't need no helpers. [*Looks off.*]

CLAIRE [*to* KAY]: Best to keep him on his toes.

KAY [*laughs*]: Aye. [KAY *is dressing the second pole.*]

EWBANK: They don't need any supervision. Not with Kay. How long've you been with me? Three years. That's about as long as anybody in this place. They don't stay long. I employ anybody here, you know. Anybody who'll work. Miners who've coughed their lungs up, fitters who've lost their fingers, madmen who've run away from home. [*Laughs.*]

[*As the men go in and out they gaze over at* CLAIRE, FITZPATRICK *still whistling his tune whenever he appears.*]

They don't mind. They know me. They can soon get shut. I've the biggest turnover of manual labour in this town. I take on all those that nobody else'll employ. See that? [*He indicates the inscription on the tent.*]

CLAIRE: You'll look well if we put it off.

EWBANK: Put it off? You'll not get this chance again. Not from me. Not from him either. [*He thumbs off, to* KAY.] She's marrying a bloody aristocrat, Kay. He's so refined if it wasn't for his britches he'd be invisible.

CLAIRE: Not like somebody else we know ...

EWBANK: Oh, she doesn't mind. Frank by name and frank by nature. If they don't like it they soon get shut. Have you ever seen a straight line, Bennett?

BENNETT: A straight line?

EWBANK: Well I have, man, and that's not one of them. [*He indicates the rows of battens they're laying across the floor.*] By ... ! Just look at this. Grass. Grass. Fitzpatrick!

FITZPATRICK: Yes, sir.

EWBANK: Don't bloody well sir me or I'll fetch you one round your ear. I'm not too old. Rest them ... *rest* them ... gently. [*To* KAY *and* CLAIRE] The trouble I take. What for? I might as well be shoving up a circus. [*Then, looking up at the tent*] I'm going to like this tent. Do you know? I'm going to like it, very much.

[PAUL *has come in and had a look around, hands in pockets.*]

PAUL [*to* EWBANK]: Do you know. For one minute there, I thought I'd come in to find you working.

EWBANK: I am working.

PAUL: I heard you. From the house.

EWBANK: My work's done here. I'm a bloody artisan, I am. Not a worker. [*To* KAY] He's never believed that, Kay. And he's a ... Well, I don't know what he is. He's supposed to be a summat.

PAUL [*to* KAY]: I'm a drain on his pocket for one thing. He must have told you that.

EWBANK: Aye. For one thing. And as for another ... Aye, well. Least said, soonest mended. [*To* MARSHALL] Have you got that level? I don't want no ups and downs.

PAUL [*to* CLAIRE]: How are you feeling?

CLAIRE: All right. [*Laughs.*]

PAUL: I don't know. [*Thumbs at* EWBANK *behind his back then looks up at the tent.*]

CLAIRE: It's going to be very nice.

PAUL: Lovely.

CLAIRE [*gesturing at tent*]: Why, what's the matter with it?

PAUL: Nothing.

CLAIRE: Nothing.

PAUL [*broadly*]: We don't get married every day.

CLAIRE: Let's all thank God for that.

PAUL [*to* KAY]: I'll give you a hand if you like.

KAY: Well, I don't know ...

PAUL [*broadly*]: I've done it before. I know a bit about it. [*Gestures at* EWBANK.] When I was younger he used to let me help him, for half a crown an hour. Did the work of three men. Quite a saving.

KAY: I reckon it must have been at that.

PAUL: Well, then. Let's set about it. [*He goes, joining the men fetching in the battens.*]

EWBANK [*to* KAY]: I'm off in. I'll leave you to it before the rest of 'em arrive. [*Gestures at house.*] Is there ought you want while I'm at it?

KAY: No, no. We'll be all right.

EWBANK [*to* CLAIRE]: Working under t'boss's eye. They none of them like it.

CLAIRE: That's going to be the floor, then.

EWBANK: That's right. This time tomorrow you'll be dancing over it light as a feather.

CLAIRE: Let's hope you're right.

EWBANK: Nay, damn it all. I wish I had my time over again, I do. [*To* KAY] I'm off in, then. [*To* CLAIRE] Are you coming with me?

CLAIRE: I think I better.

EWBANK [*to* KAY]: Here, come with me, lad. I'll show you what I mean with that bloody load ... [*Going*]

> [KAY *glances round then follows* EWBANK *who goes out with his arm absent-mindedly round* CLAIRE's *shoulders.*]
>
> PAUL *has come in with his battens: he's followed by* GLENDENNING, *laying them side by side.*]

PAUL [*to* GLENDENNING]: What's your name, then?

GLENDENNING: G ... G ... G ... G ... Glenny!

FITZPATRICK: That's Glenny.

MARSHALL: He's a bit soft in the head.

GLENDENNING: I ... I ... I ... I ... Aye. I am. [*He laughs.*]

BENNETT: Takes all sorts to make a world.

PAUL: That's right. It does. What do you think of this one, then? [*Indicates tent.*]

> [BENNETT *has started to bring in the sections of polished floor, beginning to lay them on the battens.*]

FITZPATRICK: A bit of all right, boy.

MARSHALL: Your old man can make a tent when he wants to.

PAUL: That's right. He can.

FITZPATRICK: There's not many of them around these days.

PAUL: What's that?

FITZPATRICK: Butterflies with caps on.

> [*They laugh.*]

PAUL [*to* GLENDENNING]: Will you give us a lift with that?

GLENDENNING: Aye. Aye! I will.

PAUL: Do you like working here, Glenny?

GLENDENNING: I ... I ... I ... Aye!

PAUL: Yes?

GLENDENNING: Aye ... I ... I ... I ...

MARSHALL [*sings*]: Ay, yi, yi, yi ... Ay, yi, yi, yi ...

GLENDENNING: I ... I ... I couldn't nnnnnn ... get a job anywhere else.

PAUL: There's not many places.

GLENDENNING: They w ... w ... w ... won't have you if you're o ... o ... off your head.

PAUL: Are you off your head?

GLENDENNING: Aye! [*Laughs pleasantly.*]

FITZPATRICK: You'd never have believed it.
[*They laugh.*]
GLENDENNING [*to* PAUL]: W . . . w . . . w . . . what do you d . . . d . . . d
. . . do, then?
PAUL: Me?
GLENDENNING: F . . . f . . . f . . . for a living.
PAUL: Well, I'm a sort of a . . . No, no. I'm a kind of . . . I don't do
anything at all as a matter of fact.
GLENDENNING: Oh, aye!
PAUL: You fancy a bit of that, do you?
GLENDENNING: Aye! [*Laughs.*]
[MAURICE *comes in.*]
PAUL: Ah, well, Glenny. Each one to his trade.
GLENDENNING: I . . . I . . . I . . . I . . . I'd like to give it a g . . . g . . . g . . .
go, though! [*Laughs.*]
PAUL: Aye, well. That's a privilege few of us can afford, Glenny.
[MAURICE *has come in while they're working, wandering round
until he comes to* PAUL.
MAURICE *wears a jacket and flannels, a bit crumpled. He's tall,
perhaps with a moustache: fairly ordinary and straightforward.*]
FITZPATRICK: Can we do anything then, to help?
MAURICE: Oh, I belong here as well. [*To* PAUL, *casual*] I thought I
better warn you. There's your Grandad on his way.
PAUL [*carrying on working*]: Aye. [*He's bringing in and laying sections of
polished floor.*]
MAURICE: Have you seen her anywhere around?
PAUL: She was here just now. A few minutes ago.
MAURICE: This is where all the do-dah's going to be?
PAUL: Seems so.
MAURICE: I can't see why we couldn't have had it in the house.
PAUL: He says there wasn't room.
MAURICE: There seems plenty room to me.
PAUL: You know Frank.
MAURICE: By name and nature.
[*They laugh.*]
I suppose it means a lot to him.
PAUL: A bit of his own tenting over his head.

MAURICE: I suppose it does. You haven't got a fag, have you?

PAUL: I'm working. [*To* MARSHALL] Have you got a fag to spare?

MARSHALL: Me? No. Never. [*Scandalized, he turns to* BENNETT.]

BENNETT [*instant*]: No. Not one at all.

FITZPATRICK: Here. Have one of mine.

PAUL: This's the blushing bridegroom.

FITZPATRICK: I thought as much.

MAURICE [*lights up from* FITZPATRICK]: I'll fetch you one out of the house if you'll hang on.

FITZPATRICK: S'all right. Just put it on me wages.

   [*They laugh.*]

MAURICE: Good God. [*Coughs.*]

FITZPATRICK: S'all right. I make them up meself. Good Irish baccy, there is, wrapped up in that.

MARSHALL: Swept up, that is, from some of the best bar-rooms in the town.

   [*They laugh, still working.*]

FITZPATRICK: No, no, now. He's having you on.

MAURICE: Let's hope you're right. [*To* PAUL] If I didn't feel so exhausted I'd have given you a hand.

PAUL: I know the feeling.

MAURICE: I don't know. What are we supposed to do in here, for instance?

PAUL [*shrugs*]: Dance around. Look jolly.

MAURICE [*surreptitiously putting out cigarette*]: It's a lot of fuss.

PAUL: It may never happen again. You might be lucky.

MAURICE: Aye. Let's hope you're right ... What's the matter with him?

   [*While they've been talking,* GLENDENNING *has gone out and returned carrying his fourteen-pound sledgehammer, proudly, over his shoulder.*

   Now, smiling, he marches up and down for PAUL'*s benefit.*]

PAUL: He's a ... Well done, Glenny.

GLENDENNING [*pleased*]: Aye!

   [KAY *has returned; with him are* OLD EWBANK *and* OLD MRS EWBANK, *in her sixties, a small, practical, homely person.*]

OLD MRS E. [*to* KAY]: If we're in the way just let us know ...

KAY: No, no. It's all right by me.

FITZPATRICK [*calling to* GLENDENNING]: Hup, two, three, four ... Right a ... a ... a ... a ... about – *turn*! By God. They ought to make him a bloody general.

OLD MRS E.: You're having a look as well, Maurice?

MAURICE: Surveying the scene of battle.

OLD MRS E.: Oh, now. Get on.

MAURICE: Best to take precautions.

[PAUL *drifts back to work.*]

OLD MRS E.: We're having a struggle – now he's seen the tent – to keep him retired. [*Indicating* OLD EWBANK *whose arm she holds.*]

OLD EWBANK: What?

OLD MRS E. [*shouting*]: We have a struggle keeping you retired.

OLD EWBANK [*to* MAURICE]: Good God. I am. We've never had this damn fuss before.

OLD MRS E.: It'll sink in, don't worry.

FITZPATRICK [*in background*]: Hup, two, three, four ... Hup, two, three, four ... Lee ... eeeeft wheeee – eeeeeeel!

KAY: Glendenning, for Christ's sake. Put that hammer down.

MARSHALL: You want to watch how you speak to him, Kay. Or he'll fetch you one with that right over the head.

[*Nudges* PAUL.]

KAY [*to* GLENDENNING]: Come on. Come on, now. Let's have this floor down.

[*Gently,* KAY *takes the hammer from him. Smiling, pleased,* GLENDENNING *joins the others.*]

FITZPATRICK: The army's the place for you, Glenny, all right.

MARSHALL: Frighten the bloody enemy to death.

[OLD EWBANK *has crossed to* BENNETT, *who is working assiduously at the floor, and continues to do so.*]

OLD EWBANK: You know what I used to be?

BENNETT: What? [*Looks up startled.*]

OLD EWBANK: Rope-maker. [*Pauses for effect.*] You see all the ropes that hold up this tent?

BENNETT: What? Aye ... [*Looks up.*]

OLD EWBANK: I made 'em!

BENNETT: That's very good.

OLD EWBANK: No. No. Not for good. The ones I made're all worn out. Started making tents in my old age. Passed it on.

BENNETT [*working*]: Ah. Yes.

OLD EWBANK: You haven't seen the old man?

BENNETT: Old man?

OLD EWBANK: The gaffer. [*Waits for* BENNETT *to nod, mystified.*] That's my son. He owns all this now. He made it.

BENNETT: Aye?

OLD EWBANK: The tent.

BENNETT: Aye ...

OLD EWBANK [*suddenly*]: Ropes. That's my trade. Nowt like it.

PAUL [*calling*]: I should get him out of here, Gran. Something's likely to fall on his head.

[*A section of floor, in fact, has narrowly missed* OLD EWBANK's *head.*]

OLD MRS E.: I will. I will ... I never knew you were employed here, Paul.

PAUL: I don't know ... Got to find your natural level, Gran.

OLD MRS E.: I've heard that before, I think, somewhere else —

PAUL: Aye. I believe you have. [*Laughs.*]

OLD EWBANK [*to* BENNETT]: The best education money can buy. That's my grandson. Oxford. Cambridge. University College. All the rest. Ask him about anything and he'll come up with an answer.

BENNETT: Oh. Aye ...

OLD EWBANK: Not got his father's skill.

FITZPATRICK [*joining in*]: No?

OLD EWBANK: Sure? I am. He couldn't thread a needle. Have you seen the way that canvas is cut? [*To* OLD MRS EWBANK] ... What is it?

KAY: Come on, Fitzpatrick. Let's see you stuck in.

OLD EWBANK: I've come up for the wedding. Otherwise I wouldn't be here.

BENNETT: Ah, yes.

OLD MRS E. [*to* OLD EWBANK]: It'll soon be time for dinner.

OLD EWBANK: I'll what?

OLD MRS E. [*shouting*]: Dinner.

OLD EWBANK: Good God, we've only just got up.

[*They go out slowly,* OLD MRS EWBANK *taking his arm.*]

FITZPATRICK: A fine old man.

MARSHALL: One of the great old-timers.

BENNETT [*to* PAUL]: He has a very high opinion of yourself.

PAUL: Has he? I know the thing you mean.

[*They laugh.*]

MAURICE [*to* PAUL]: I'll be off then. See you in the house. [MAURICE *goes.*] Thanks for the cigarette.

FITZPATRICK: Not at all. [*To* PAUL] A college man.

PAUL: Yes?

FITZPATRICK: Yourself. I could see it at a glance.

PAUL: Well, then. That's pretty good.

FITZPATRICK: I've always fancied that, you know, myself. Books. Study. A pile of muffins by the fire.

MARSHALL: A pile of what?

[*They laugh.*]

FITZPATRICK: And the bridegroom feller. The one that's such a great one with the cigarettes.

[*They laugh.*]

PAUL: A doctor.

FITZPATRICK: A doctor! By God.

MARSHALL: Fitzie's always fancied himself as that.

FITZPATRICK: Aye. The stethoscope is my natural weapon. There's not many a thing, now, that I couldn't find with that.

[*They laugh.*

Most of the floor is now in, though GLENDENNING *and* KAY *could still be bringing in the last,* BENNETT, MARSHALL, FITZPATRICK *and* PAUL *going round fitting the polished sections into place, on top of the battens.*]

And your sister's been a nurse?

PAUL: That's right.

FITZPATRICK: Ah, yes. A hospital, now. You can't go wrong with that.

PAUL: And yourself?

FITZPATRICK: Me? Why, I'm like the rest of them.

MARSHALL: An honest working-man.

FITZPATRICK: That's right.

MARSHALL: Born and bred in Ireland!

FITZPATRICK: Like every one before me.

PAUL: And ... [*Indicating* MARSHALL.]

MARSHALL: Marshall.

FITZPATRICK: It's the funniest Irish name I've ever heard.

MARSHALL: My mother was a decent Irish woman.

FITZPATRICK: That's not what she told him, now, when she met his grand old man.

    [*They laugh.*]

BENNETT [*at a gesture from* PAUL]: Oh, I'm good old English stock.

MARSHALL: Stock, did he say?

FITZPATRICK: English born, English bred:

                Long in the leg, and thick in the head.

    [*They laugh.*]

BENNETT: Done a bit of everything.

MARSHALL: He has. And everybody, too.

    [*They laugh.*]

BENNETT: And I end up in a place like this.

PAUL: Why's that?

BENNETT: I don't know.

MARSHALL: He likes the fresh air: coming through the windows.

BENNETT: Fresh air. [*Laughs.*] You get fresh air all right, inside that cab.

MARSHALL: Empire-builders! That's us!

    [*They laugh.*

      The floor now is laid, smooth squares of parquet that slot together over the battens.

      The men pause, resting.]

BENNETT [*tousles* GLENDENNING's *hair*]: How's old Glenny? He's the only one of us that doesn't hold a grudge.

GLENDENNING: Ay ... ay ... Aye! [*Laughs.*]

BENNETT: Glass hammers and rubber nails. All day long. Never remembers.

MARSHALL: Does it in his sleep I shouldn't wonder.

GLENDENNING: I ... I ... I ... Aye! I do!

MARSHALL: Nearly caught him this morning sticking stakes in your dad's green grass.

FITZPATRICK: Aye. We did. That'd have put the kibosh on it, Glenny!

BENNETT: He's a good lad at knocking in stakes. You should see him with that hammer. Isn't that right, Glenny?

GLENDENNING: Aye! [*Laughs.*]

MARSHALL: Hits it once in every four.

FITZPATRICK: Damn great pit you find, with a little stake sticking up inside.

BENNETT: He's a good lad.

KAY [*coming back*]: Have you finished off that flooring? Bennett. Fitzpatrick. Can you carry in the lining?

FITZPATRICK: Nay, steady on, Kay. We've had no snap for hours.

KAY [*getting watch out*]: Get the lining in, then you can have it. Best get it under cover, then we'll be all right.

FITZPATRICK: Ah, come on, Glenny ...

MARSHALL: And where's he been the last half hour?

FITZPATRICK: Tipping it back, no doubt, with number one ... [*Mimes drinking.*]

 [*They laugh.* KAY *takes no notice.*]

KAY: Marshall. Come on. Let's have you ... [*As* PAUL *makes to follow*] There's your mother looking for you outside ...

 [*From outside come* FITZPATRICK, MARSHALL, *etc., saying,* 'Morning ... Good morning', *and* MRS EWBANK's *pleasant reply,* 'Morning ...'

  MRS EWBANK *comes in as men leave: a pleasant, practical-looking woman in her middle forties, not smart but certainly not dowdy.*]

PAUL: We were just fetching in the lining ...

MRS EWBANK [*looking round*]: I thought I'd just pop out ... Don't worry. I won't get in the way. It's not often I see one of your father's tents go up.

PAUL: No ... I suppose not.

MRS EWBANK: It's going to look very grand.

PAUL: So they say.

MRS EWBANK: How have they been getting on? [*Indicating the men who've gone outside*]

PAUL: All right.

MRS EWBANK: This wood ... [*Walking over the floor*] A few years back one man got a splinter in his hand, left it unattended ...

PAUL: Turned septic ...

MRS EWBANK [*looks up*]: He had to have one of his fingers off.

PAUL: Dangerous job.

MRS EWBANK: Yes.

[*She walks on after a moment, looking round. Sees inscription overhead, on the canvas.*]

I didn't know he'd written that.

PAUL: All done by stencils.

MRS EWBANK: Is that it? [*Gazes up at it.*]

PAUL: Takes it all to heart.

MRS EWBANK: Yes. He does. [*Pause*] Why? Don't you like it? [*Casual, pleasant.*]

PAUL: I don't know. [*Shrugs, laughs.*] I suppose I do ... Frank by name ... [*Imitates* EWBANK's *voice.*]

MRS EWBANK: But not by nature.

PAUL: No?

MRS EWBANK: No.

[*From outside come the voices of the men.*]

FITZPATRICK [*off*]: To you ... [*Sing-song*]

MARSHALL [*off*]: To me ...

FITZPATRICK [*off*]: From me ...

MARSHALL [*off*]: From you ...

FITZPATRICK [*off*]: Here you are, Glenny ... Ooooops! [*Laughter off.*]

MRS EWBANK: Is there anything we can get them?

PAUL: Probably a pot of tea would go down very well. [*Pause.*]

MRS EWBANK: Are you going off, then?

PAUL: Off?

MRS EWBANK: When all this is over.

PAUL: Suppose so.

MRS EWBANK: Where to?

PAUL: Don't know ...

[*Pause.*]

MRS EWBANK: Suppose you'll let us know.

PAUL: Yep.

MRS EWBANK: Well, then ... I'll see about the tea.

PAUL: Don't worry ... [*Holds up his hands.*]

MRS EWBANK: No, no. [*She smiles.*]

[*She goes out as the men come in, bringing three bags of muslin with them.*]

FITZPATRICK [*off*]: I knew a man called Glenny
              Who went to spend a penny:
              He got inside,
              And tried and tried –
              But found he hadn't any. [*Entering*]

[*The men burst into laughter, putting down the bags,* GLENDENNING *smiling, pleased.*]

MARSHALL: There was a man Fitzpatrick ...

FITZPATRICK: He wouldn't know a poem if he saw one.

MARSHALL: Who sat on an egg to hatch it:
              He sat and sat,

BENNETT: And sh ... at and sh ... at.

MARSHALL: But found he hadn't cracked it.

[*They laugh among themselves,* KAY *coming in last.*]

KAY: Right, then ... You can break it up.

FITZPATRICK [*to* PAUL]: Kay, you know, is a very conscientious man. Always does as he's told. Keeps strictly to instructions.

KAY: It's a damn good job there's somebody here to do something.

[*They're going.*]

MARSHALL: It's right. It's right. Value for money is his motto.

FITZPATRICK [*arm round* GLENDENNING *as they go*]: Grub at last, Glenny.

GLENDENNING: Aye!

FITZPATRICK [*winking to* PAUL]: You'll see the bloody sparks fly now.

[*They go, leaving* PAUL *alone.*
    Their laughter and shouts fade outside.]

[*off*]: Here, Glenny. Have a snap at that!

[*Laughter.*
    It grows silent.
    PAUL *stands gazing round at the interior, grows abstracted. Sits on bag of muslin, arms resting on knees.*

Begins to whistle quietly to himself: a slow, rather melancholy tune.

After a while lights slowly fade.

Curtain.]

The muslin is being taped to the muslin ridges which have been raised to shoulder height. Most of the muslin now has been taped, and most of it has been laced – in the same manner as the canvas before it.

The men work minus GLENDENNING *and* KAY.

FITZPATRICK: Do you know. I never fasten one of these without thinking of my mother.

[MARSHALL *and* BENNETT *laugh.*]

MARSHALL: Why's that, Fitzie?

FITZPATRICK: I don't know. I don't know. I'd go a long way, now, to find that out.

[KAY *has come in.*]

KAY: All right, then. Let's have it out.

FITZPATRICK: Out?

MARSHALL: Out.

FITZPATRICK: Out we shall.

[*They draw the muslin out on either side: a thin drape in green, yellow, and white, each band of colour is perhaps two feet or eighteen inches in width: the seams are ruched.*

There are three pieces in all, corresponding to the three pieces of canvas: one piece between each of the three poles (1 and 2) and the end piece (3) at the back of the stage.

Having laid it out across the floor the men go back to complete the lacing.]

MARSHALL [*looking round*]: Where's Glenny, then? He's taking a long time to take them cups back.

FITZPATRICK: When you give Glenny a job he likes, he gives it his full attention.

[*They laugh.*]

KAY: I wish I could say the same for yourself. Now get on with your lacing.

[FITZPATRICK *glances at* MARSHALL. *They laugh.*]

MARSHALL: Kay. It's lovely stuff. It is. It is . . . Made too, if I'm not mistaken, specially for the occasion.

FITZPATRICK: I remember the first day I came here, now, to work. At the beginning of the summer.

MARSHALL [*looking at the sky*]: It's damn near the end of it now.

FITZPATRICK: Except in the army, I'd never seen a tent before.

BENNETT: Aye!

FITZPATRICK: We were driven out of the town, on one of the trucks ... Up the valley, past a lot of trees and hills. And suddenly ... looking down ... this field. Full of tents. White canvas, everywhere you looked.

MARSHALL: Big as a balloon.

FITZPATRICK: Big as an elephant ... Aye.

[*They work for a moment in silence. Then:*]

When we got down here, and we got out of the cab ...

MARSHALL: One of the favourites ... Not riding on the back.

FITZPATRICK: I stood there, looking up at them and thinking, 'It's a damn great pity it is, to take them down at all.'

MARSHALL: I remember that day very well. Almost four hours before he did a stroke of work himself.

[*They laugh.*]

KAY: Fitzpatrick, get on with your bloody lacing.

[MARSHALL *and* FITZPATRICK *exchange glances, then laugh.*]

MARSHALL: Four daughters!

[*They laugh.*

FITZPATRICK *has begun to sing as he works.*]

MARSHALL: Where were you working, then, Kay, before you came to Ewbank's?

KAY: I was working.

BENNETT: Kay was in the nick. Isn't that right?

[KAY *doesn't answer.*]

MARSHALL: Well, I never knew that. Is that right, then?

BENNETT: It is.

[FITZPATRICK *stops singing.*]

FITZPATRICK: In the lock-up, Kay, were you?

[KAY *doesn't answer but continues lacing.*]

MARSHALL: And what was he in for? If that's not the wrong thing to ask.

BENNETT: I don't know. You better ask him.

[MARSHALL *laughs.*]

FITZPATRICK: Come on, now, Kay. What did they put you in for?

KAY: Get on with your lacing.

MARSHALL: Ah, come on, now, Kay. Aren't you going to give us a clue?

FITZPATRICK: Was it animal, vegetable, or mineral?

[*They laugh.*]

KAY: I was sent up ...

MARSHALL: Aye?

KAY: For not minding my own business. [*Factual: goes on working without being distracted.*]

FITZPATRICK: Is that a fact? [*To the others*] God damn it: we deserve to be put inside an' all.

[*They laugh.*]

MARSHALL: Kay ... you ... me ... Glenny.

[*Following* KAY's *lead, they hook the corners and quarters of the muslin up, in the same fashion as the canvas was first raised on the 'quarter' and corner side poles. It hangs in a great loop now across the flooring.*]

FITZPATRICK: Ah, it's a great life if you can afford it.

MARSHALL: And what, now, is that?

FITZPATRICK: A wife ... home ... children.

MARSHALL: Hot chocolate.

FITZPATRICK: Hot chocolate.

MARSHALL: Toes ...

FITZPATRICK: Toes ...

MARSHALL: Fingers.

FITZPATRICK: Fingers.

KAY: All right, then ... Let's have it up.

[*The men have scrambled underneath, the muslin billowing as they reach the ropes.*]

Are you ready?

BENNETT: Ready ...

MARSHALL: Ready, Mr Kay.

FITZPATRICK: Ready, Mr Kay; you're right.

[*They laugh.*]

KAY: Right, then ... together.

[*They haul up the muslin, fastening it off.*]

MARSHALL: *Christopher!* Just look at that!

[GLENDENNING *has come in, looking pleased, standing to one side and eating, so that they all might see, a very large bun.*

As they turn to look across he smiles dazedly at them, eating.]

FITZPATRICK: Eating on the job, Mr Kay! Mr Kay! Glendenning here is eating a big fat bun.

BENNETT: Did you nick it from the house, Glenny?

GLENDENNING: No ... n ... n ... no. [*He shakes his head.*]

FITZPATRICK: Then where ... then what ... then what*ever* have you done with ours, Glenny?

[GLENDENNING *happily shakes his head.*]

MARSHALL: He's eaten it!

[GLENDENNING, *happy, dazed, smiling, still eating, shakes his head again.*]

BENNETT: I don't understand, Glenny. Do you mean to say, the lady of the house ...

MARSHALL: Herself ...

BENNETT: Gave you a bun? And didn't give us one – as well?

GLENDENNING: I ... I ... I ... Aye! [*Nods happily, putting the last large fragment into his mouth.*]

[*The men start taping up the muslin to the sides of the tent. It's hung in such a way that it hangs slightly, billowing in, a soft lining to the tent.*]

FITZPATRICK: Well, I'll be damned. I will.

[GLENDENNING *nods at them, smiling.*]

MARSHALL: And not a bite to share between us.

KAY: Glendenning, make yourself useful. Pick up the bags.

[GLENDENNING *still gazes at them, smiling.*]

Glendenning. Have you heard?

GLENDENNING: Aye! [*Happily goes to work.*]

FITZPATRICK: Well, I'll be damned. I *will* be damned. All this time I've been thinking: Glenny is a friend of mine. If I have *one* friend in this big wide world, it's Glenny. All the rest I can do without.

GLENDENNING: I ... I ... I ... Aye!

MARSHALL: It's a great and terrible disappointment. I shall never get over this. I shan't. [MARSHALL *gets out his handkerchief, dabs his eyes, wipes his nose ...*]

FITZPATRICK: Aye. This really is the end. For sure.

KAY: Keep your folds even. Space it out. Space it.

MARSHALL: Work your fingers to the bone. Break your back. Crack your head. And out there, all the time, Glenny is cramming his face with buns. It's more than anyone could stand.

[GLENDENNING *is pleased with all this, no more so than with* MARSHALL'*s attempts at crying: he watches, smiling, anxious for them to go on.*]

KAY [*going*]: Bennett ... Give me a hand in with the furniture.

BENNETT: I think Kay's greatest disappointment in life – *prison sentence apart* – is for him not to see me working – hard. [*Follows* KAY *out.*

FITZPATRICK *signals* MARSHALL.]

FITZPATRICK: By God, and I could have done with that bun, Marshy. My stomach's trembling here from lack of food.

GLENDENNING [*laughing*]: Aye!

MARSHALL: When I get a bun myself – *which I shall* – not a crumb of it will I give away.

FITZPATRICK: No, no. Not a drop.

MARSHALL: At least, not to a *certain person* whom I shall not go to the trouble of puttin' a name.

[KAY *and* BENNETT *come back in carrying white metalwork chairs and tables.*]

FITZPATRICK: No, no. That's a fact.

MARSHALL: The one I have in mind has cream on.

KAY [*to* BENNETT]: Come on. Let's have some more inside.

BENNETT: Bloody hell ... [*Groans to himself.*]

[KAY *and* BENNET *go out.*]

FITZPATRICK: With a strawberry on top.

MARSHALL: And thick jam inside.

FITZPATRICK: With a touch of apricot.

MARSHALL: About as big as a Christmas pud. [*Shapes it.*]

[GLENDENNING, *as he listens, loses his smile. For a while he watches them concernedly then, slowly, he turns away.*]

FITZPATRICK: Aye. Aye. I know just the shop. They sell them by the score. God, it takes half an hour to get through one of them.

MARSHALL: And that, mind you, is just the start.

FITZPATRICK: Aye. Aye. The rate we work, the money we earn, we s'll have enough for half a dozen.

MARSHALL: I can just see it, sitting there. Waiting to be eaten up.

BENNETT [*coming in with* KAY, *with another table*]: Oh, now you're not letting them get on top? [*To* GLENDENNING.]

[GLENDENNING *is still turned away, slowly picking pieces up*.]

MARSHALL: Ah, Fitzie, now. Just look.

FITZPATRICK: He's . . . Why? . . . [*Stepping round so that he can look in* GLENDENNING's *face*] You're not wishing, now, that you'd given us a bit of that?

[KAY *and* BENNETT *go out again*.]

MARSHALL: He's wishing now he'd broken off a bit. Perhaps, even, as much as half.

FITZPATRICK: Or more.

MARSHALL: Or more. Come on, now, Glenny . . . I was pulling your leg.

[GLENDENNING *is immobilized, standing now with his head hanging down*.]

FITZPATRICK: Why, you've gone and made the feller roar.

MARSHALL: I have?

FITZPATRICK: There are tears streaming from his eyes.

MARSHALL: And nose.

FITZPATRICK: And nose.

BENNETT [*carrying in a tin of polish and rag*]: You want to leave the lad alone.

[GLENDENNING *has begun to shake his head slightly, turned away, wiping his eyes and sobbing*.]

KAY [*coming in with another table*]: Look out. Look out. He's here.

FITZPATRICK: Kay is ever such a conscientious feller. It just shows the benefits, now, of being put inside. [*Going*.]

[*They laugh*.

FITZPATRICK *goes*.]

BENNETT [*crossing to* GLENDENNING]: Ah, now, Glenny. Don't take it so much to heart.

[GLENDENNING *shakes his head. He goes*.

MARSHALL *laughs*.]

You want to leave him alone!

MARSHALL: Jump on your bloody head. [*Faces up to him, then darts away, laughing*.]

[EWBANK *has come in behind them, watching them*.]

EWBANK: *Get your boots off that bloody floor!* God Christ. Just look at him. Studs and half a ton of earth sliding about on top of it.

[BENNETT *is standing at the centre of the polished floor.*]

Get your boots off, off, off, off, off, off, if you're going to stand on it.

KAY: Bennett. We'll work this side. You work that. [*Indicating* BENNETT *should take his boots off.*] ·

BENNETT: Me?

[*It's evident, though not too much, that* EWBANK *has had a drop.*]

MARSHALL: His socks are full of holes, Kay.

FITZPATRICK [*entering with polish*]: He hasn't got no socks.

[*They laugh, starting to polish.*]

MARSHALL: If he takes his boots off in here there'll not be one of us left alive.

EWBANK [*swaying slightly*]: I take it that that lining's not been hung right yet.

KAY: No. No.

BENNETT: Bloody hell... [*He's begun to take his boots off, sitting on the polished floor.*]

[FITZPATRICK *has begun to sing, drunkenly.* GLENDENNING *has come back in.*]

FITZPATRICK: We hash a good night to ... night ...

MARSHALL: We'll have a good one to ... morrow ...

FITZPATRICK: We hash a few drops to ... night ...

MARSHALL: We'll have a few more to ... morrow ...

EWBANK [*head craning back*]: Aye. That's going to look very nice.

[EWBANK *has become aware of* GLENDENNING, *walking, drooped, at a snail's pace.*]

KAY: They've been having him on ...

EWBANK: Ay, ay, ay ... Do you hear that, now. Do you hear?

FITZPATRICK: Aye. Aye. [*Ruffling* GLENDENNING's *hair*] You're all right, aren't you?

EWBANK: I'm not having you tormenting that lad. A bloody half-wit. You ought to have more common sense.

MARSHALL: Aye. Aye. We should.

EWBANK [*has tripped up*]: God damn and blast ... Glendenning. Give me a hand with this. [*Picks up the bag he's tripped over.*]

KAY: What's the *matter* with Fitzpatrick?

[FITZPATRICK *is doubled up, laughing.*]

MARSHALL: It's the smell. Bennett, for God's sake.

BENNETT: My feet are all right.

KAY: What?

BENNETT: I wash them. Every night.

MARSHALL: Soap and water.

FITZPATRICK: Soap and water.

[EWBANK *has sent* GLENDENNING *out.*]

MARSHALL: You could make a collander of his socks. Just look at them. Bennett, don't you have a wife?

KAY [*to* FITZPATRICK]: If you find it so damn funny no doubt you'll tolerate your own.

MARSHALL: No. No. Don't ask him that. I'd rather be annihilated by Bennett than by Fitzpatrick. [*Looks up to the sky.*] If it has to come, O Lord, let it not be at the feet of my friend, Fitzpatrick.

EWBANK: Just watch that floor. Watch it. It's a precious thing is that. [*To* KAY] I've sent Glendenning down to the shop.

FITZPATRICK [*to* MARSHALL, *polishing*]: I hope, not for another tot.

EWBANK: What's that?

FITZPATRICK: I say: he's about the only decent one we've got.

MARSHALL: I hope to God it's nothing lethal: matches or a packet of cigarettes.

[MARSHALL *and* FITZPATRICK *laugh, polishing.*]

EWBANK: Have you levelled off that floor?

BENNETT: We have.

[MARSHALL *and* FITZPATRICK *have begun to sing the drinking song in quiet voices.*]

PAUL: I've had me snap. I've had me rest. Now. Where would you like me? [PAUL *has come in, in shirt-sleeves hanging loosely down, his hands deep in his pockets, standing in the door, stooping slightly.*]

EWBANK [*looking up*]: There's nowt in here for you, lad.

PAUL: I don't mind. I'll give a hand.

EWBANK: There's no need.

PAUL: No, no. I understand. Nevertheless . . . I'll do whatever it is I'm able.

[*He goes to dress the muslin ropes on the main poles.*]

EWBANK: Marshall. Fetch in the walling. You can start hanging that.

[MARSHALL *gets up and goes out.*]

[*To* KAY] Keep that evenly spaced there, Kay.

KAY: Aye. We'll have it straight. Don't worry. [*Arranging muslin*]
   [EWBANK *stands gazing round, a little helpless.*]

EWBANK: Aye, well ... [*looks at his watch*]. I'll look in again in a few
   minutes. I shan't be long. [EWBANK *goes.*

   MARSHALL *comes in with the sack containing the muslin walling.*]

BENNETT [*working with his back to the door*]: Has he gone?

MARSHALL: You can breathe again, feller. [*To* PAUL] No disrespect,
   mind, to you at all.

PAUL: No. No. None at all.

FITZPATRICK: What're you going to be at the wedding, then?

PAUL: Oh, I don't know ...

FITZPATRICK [*cheerful*]: Not the best man, then?

PAUL: I might well be that.
   [*They laugh.*]

FITZPATRICK: What did you study at the school, then?

PAUL: Nothing much.

MARSHALL: Nothing much, to God. You better not tell him that.
   [*Gestures at house.*]
      [*They laugh.*

      MARSHALL *has got out the muslin walling and starts to hang it.*]

FITZPATRICK [*loud*]: I've always fancied myself, you know, as a
   criminal lawyer ...

MARSHALL: He's very good at that. Knows it from the inside ...
   [*They laugh.*]

FITZPATRICK: No, no. I'm too old now, to go to school, and too damn
   poor to bother.

MARSHALL: But then, you know ... Talking of criminality ...

FITZPATRICK: That's right ...

MARSHALL [*to* PAUL]: You were probably not aware that you were
   working in the presence of one such man himself.

FITZPATRICK: You are. I bet you didn't know it.

MARSHALL: A fair-minded, decent feller like yourself, coming in
   here, hoping to find himself among his equals. Only to discover,
   behind his back, that one of *them* had crept in unnoticed.

PAUL [*laughing*]: And who's that?

FITZPATRICK: Why, none other than – himself. [*Gestures at* KAY.]

BENNETT: I wish you'd pay a bit more attention to this here. Just look at the bloody floor. [*Polishing*]

FITZPATRICK: Attention, now. Attention.

KAY [*to* BENNETT]: Watch that walling ... Fitzpatrick. I hope you're going to rub that floor. [KAY *goes to dress one of the remaining muslin ropes.*]

BENNETT: Oh, God. My bloody back. [*To* PAUL] Have you ever suffered from rheumatism?

PAUL: I don't think I have.

BENNETT: One of the worst diseases known to man.

FITZPATRICK: Bloody indolence, more likely.

BENNETT: What's that?

FITZPATRICK: I say, you get it all the time.

BENNETT: I do. [*Holds his back, groans.*] God.

FITZPATRICK [*to* PAUL]: On the other hand, what we haven't discovered – and speaking purely as a man familiar with nothing but his own profession –

[MARSHALL *snorts.*]

is, what crime this person, this man, who has inveigled himself into our presence, what crime it is precisely, that he's committed.

MARSHALL: I hope it was nothing indecent to do with little girls.

FITZPATRICK: Good God. Crimes of that nature I cannot stand.

MARSHALL: I can't bear to read a word about them in the papers.

FITZPATRICK: I sincerely hope – I sincerely hope, Marshall – that it's nothing I'd be afraid to mention to me mother.

[*They laugh.*]

Come on, now, Kay. Between these four walls – or three and a half to be exact – what manner of crime was it that you committed? Were you driven to it by the pressures of the world; or is it simply that you're a rotten *sod*?

[*They laugh.*]

Kay is a very hard man. You'll get nothing out of him. He didn't suffer all that, you know, in vain. [*Friendly*] Isn't that right, Kay?

[KAY, *unmoved until now, has gone on with his work, not even looking up.*

Now, however, he pauses.He looks up very slowly. Then:]

KAY: And what sort of suffering have you done, Fitzpatrick?

FITZPATRICK: Suffering? By God. I'm suffering every day.

[MARSHALL *laughs, snorting.*]

MARSHALL: All day. Seven days a week. Fifty-two weeks in the year.

KAY: Aye. Between one bottle and another. One bar-room and the next.

FITZPATRICK: Me? I hope you heard all that. I wouldn't touch a drop of liquor.

[MARSHALL *snorts again.*]

I mean, dropping no names, Kay, and all that there and that, aspersions of that nature would be better cast in a different direction altogether.

[FITZPATRICK *gestures at the house.*]

KAY: Some people have a grievance. And some of them haven't.

FITZPATRICK: And what is that supposed to mean?

[KAY *looks at* PAUL, *then looks away.*

The others look at PAUL.]

PAUL: Don't mind me. I'm easy.

KAY: Bennett. Mind that walling.

FITZPATRICK: Are you frightened of telling us something, Kay?

KAY: If you want to work, Fitzpatrick, work. If not, the best thing you can do is to clear off altogether. [KAY *returns to hang and arrange muslin walling.*]

FITZPATRICK: Ay. Ay, now. Those are very strong words. [*To* MARSHALL] Very strong words indeed.

MARSHALL: If it wasn't for the fact that no trade union would have us . . .

FITZPATRICK: I'd repeat that to the man in charge.

MARSHALL: The top official.

FITZPATRICK: Right away.

MARSHALL: Intimidation . . .

FITZPATRICK: Suppression of the right to labour.

KAY: You wouldn't know a piece of work, Fitzpatrick, if you saw it. The bloody lot of you . . . [*Gestures at the house.*] Poor sod.

[GLENDENNING *has come in, eating a bar of chocolate.*]

FITZPATRICK: Now, then. Now, then. Now, then. What have we got here?

MARSHALL: Come on, now, Glenny. Are you going to let us have a bit of that?

BENNETT: What is it you're eating, Glenny?

GLENDENNING: O ... O ... O ... O ... Oh, a bit of stuff.

FITZPATRICK: A bit of stuff, is it?

GLENDENNING: Ch ... ch ... ch ... ch ... ch ... ch ...

MARSHALL: And have you brought us some of it back?

GLENDENNING: I ... I ... I ... I ... I ... I ...

MARSHALL [*sings*]: Ay, yi, yi, yi ... Ay, yi, yi, yi ...

BENNETT: You have, then?

GLENDENNING: Aye!

FITZPATRICK: Chocolate!

[GLENDENNING, *happy, hands out pieces of chocolate, breaking them from the bar.*]

BENNETT: Ah, he's a good lad is Glenny.

FITZPATRICK: I hope he's washed his hands.

[*They laugh.*]

KAY: You better get on with a bit of the walling, Glendenning. [*Looks over at* PAUL.]

MARSHALL: Currying a bit of favour, Kay.

FITZPATRICK: Don't give him any of your sweets, Glenny.

MARSHALL: And don't get too near.

[*They laugh.*

GLENDENNING *starts hanging the muslin wall.*

In the doorway CLAIRE *and* MAURICE *have appeared. They stand on the threshold, looking in. They make some comment to one another and laugh as they watch* PAUL *working, dressing the muslin ropes.*]

MAURICE: Are you enjoying yourself, man?

PAUL: What? [*Looks up.*] I don't know. [*Stands up from the floor where he's been kneeling.*] I've no idea.

MAURICE [*to* CLAIRE]: It comes naturally to hand.

CLAIRE [*indicating drapes*]: Shouldn't that be a bit higher?

PAUL: Probably. You want to try?

CLAIRE: I was asking.

PAUL: Jolly good.

MAURICE: She's a bloody authority, man.

KAY: Marshall. Over here.

FITZPATRICK: Watch it, Marshy. Watch it.

MARSHALL: Don't worry, now. I shall.

[*They laugh.* KAY *and* MARSHALL *adjust the muslin.*]

FITZPATRICK: And what's it like, then, to be the happy couple? The blushing bride and the handsome groom?

MAURICE: All right, I suppose.

FITZPATRICK: I was never married myself.

[MARSHALL *snorts.*]

I could never find the time.

[MARSHALL *snorts again.*]

MAURICE: No. It is a bit of a problem.

FITZPATRICK [*to* CLAIRE]: On the other hand, I could never find a lady, as beautiful as yourself, who'd be glad enough to have me.

BENNETT [*calling*]: I'd take no notice of Fitzpatrick. He has a tongue where his brains belong.

FITZPATRICK: I have. It's true. I suffer from over-stimulation. [*To* MAURICE] Have you got a fag?

MAURICE: I have. [*Brings out a case.*]

FITZPATRICK: Now. That makes a pleasant change. [*Takes one.*] I won't smoke it at the present. I'm not allowed. [*Indicates* KAY *with sly gestures.*] But I assure you: I'll enjoy it all the same.

MARSHALL: All the greater, now, for saving it till after.

[FITZPATRICK *laughs and goes back to work.*]

GLENDENNING: Ha ... Ha ... Ha ... Ha ... Ha ... Ha ... Have you seen ... mmmmmmmmmm ... Mister Ewbank?

MAURICE: Wh ... what?

CLAIRE [*to* MAURICE]: My dad. [*To* GLENDENNING] No ... We haven't.

GLENDENNING: I ... I ... I ... I ... I ... I ... I ...

MARSHALL [*sings*]: Ay, yi, yi, yi ... Ay, yi, yi, yi ...

GLENDENNING: I ... I ... I ... I've got some ... mmmmmmm ... tobacco for him.

CLAIRE: I'll give it to him if you like.

GLENDENNING: I ... I ... I ...

MARSHALL: [*sings*]: Ay, yi, yi, yi ... Ay, yi, yi, yi ...

GLENDENNING: I ... I ... I'll give it to him.

PAUL: There's not much more now to do.

[OLD EWBANK *has come in with a short piece of rope and wanders round the back of the tent.*]

148

CLAIRE: I don't know. There's a lot of stuff in the house. He says he wants it bringing out. He's left it a bit late if you ask me.

[PAUL, *having gone back to his work after the last exchange, has got up and crossed over again to* CLAIRE.]

Still. A bit of improvisation might go a long way in here.

PAUL: That's right ...

FITZPATRICK: I heard that. I heard that. A woman who improvises is never to be trusted.

BENNETT [*calling*]: And what sort of woman would you trust, Fitzpatrick? [BENNETT *is polishing the floor where he's kneeling with a rag.*]

FITZPATRICK: Why, Benny, one very much, I think, like you.

[*They all laugh, but for* BENNETT.]

OLD EWBANK: Am I in the way? What? Sitting about in the house.

[*He looks vaguely about him, spots* MARSHALL *and goes over.*]

Here. Now that's a bit of the rope I made.

MARSHALL: Oh. That's ... [*Polishing*]

OLD EWBANK: All by hand. Up and down a rope walk. You wind it up at one end and come up along it with a shuttle. Like this. You can walk up to twenty or thirty miles a day.

MARSHALL: That's a fine bit of rope.

OLD EWBANK: They don't make them like that no more. Machines. A hand-made rope is a bit of the past. [*Gestures up blindly.*] All these: machines.

MARSHALL: Still, they do their job.

[MRS EWBANK *has come in.*]

OLD EWBANK: Good God, man. I've had one all my life. It's my wife who got me to retire. I'd be in here I can tell you if I had a chance.

MRS EWBANK [*to* CLAIRE *and* MAURICE]: I've been looking for him all over ... Have you finished in here, Paul?

PAUL: Me personally? Or them in general?

MRS EWBANK: You personally, I think.

PAUL: I'm not sure. I'm standing here, I believe, waiting for instructions.

MRS EWBANK: As long as you're not in the way.

PAUL: I think I've been able to lend a little hand.

MRS EWBANK [*to* CLAIRE]: Will he be all right in here? [*Gesturing at* OLD EWBANK]

MAURICE: He'll be all right. Don't worry.

OLD EWBANK: Good God ... Now what does she want?

[EWBANK *has appeared, oblivious it seems of all of them, carrying two long boxes, five or six feet tall, which will be used to enclose the bottom of the poles. He walks to the centre and puts them down. Over his shoulder are three further lengths of muslin which he'll use to drape the poles, and in his coat pocket is a hammer.*

His mood is one of self-absorption.]

EWBANK: Get out of the bloody way ... God Christ ... Walking all over the bloody floor. God damn and blast. Just look at his bloody boots.

MRS EWBANK [*to* CLAIRE]: I'll go in, and make some tea. Keep out of trouble. [*She goes.*

EWBANK's *remarks are directed to no one person in particular.*]

OLD EWBANK: Poor? Damn it all, I've never owed a penny to any man!

EWBANK: Put some bloody bags down. Bags. Kay. Get them off here and get it covered. Marshall. Fetch in that other box outside.

[MARSHALL, *after a good look round at* FITZPATRICK, *does so.*

The others begin to cover the floor with the discarded muslin and tent bags.]

OLD EWBANK: When I was sixteen I was working eighteen hours a day.

[FITZPATRICK, *softly, has begun to sing his drinking song.*]

BENNETT: God, look. I've got a splinter in my foot. [*Examines it, sitting on the floor.*]

EWBANK [*to* KAY]: If you've got it covered you can't do any harm. Where have I put it? [*Hunts round for his hammer, finding it in his pocket.*] What's he doing in here? [*Seeing* OLD EWBANK]

CLAIRE: He's come to show them his rope.

EWBANK: Rope ... There's a ladder out there, Fitzpatrick.

[MARSHALL *has come in with the third box which he places by the third tent pole.* FITZPATRICK *goes to fetch the ladder.*]

[*Calling after him*] And don't put it down until I tell you. [*To* KAY] Have these been fastened off? [*Indicating poles.*]

KAY: Aye. We've just been doing that.

OLD EWBANK: What's he on about? I'll damn well clip his ear.

MARSHALL [*low to* BENNETT]: I wish he bloody would.

EWBANK: What's that? [*Blindly.*]

MARSHALL: I say. It's very soft, this wood.

EWBANK: Keep your fingers off it!

[MARSHALL, *working on the floor, draws his hand away.* PAUL, BENNETT, MARSHALL, *and* GLENDENNING *are working on the floor.*]

OLD EWBANK: When I was twenty-four I earned thirteen shillings a week.

CLAIRE: Come on, Grandad ... [*Goes to take his arm.*]

OLD EWBANK: I was married when I was nineteen. Three died. Four survived.

[FITZPATRICK *has come in with the ladder.*]

PAUL: Do you want a hand? [*To* CLAIRE]

MAURICE: We'll manage.

[OLD EWBANK, CLAIRE, *and* MAURICE *go.*]

FITZPATRICK: Now, then. Where would you want it?

EWBANK: Here, now. Put it down on that ... Gently.

[*He has put a bag at the foot of the first pole and* FITZPATRICK *brings the ladder to rest against it.*]

GLENDENNING: I ... I ... I ... I ... I ... I ... I ...

MARSHALL [*sings*]: Ay, yi, yi, yi ... Ay, yi, yi, yi ...

[GLENDENNING *has come up to* EWBANK *with the tin of tobacco.*]

EWBANK [*to* FITZPATRICK *as he manoeuvres the ladder*]: Gently, gently. God Christ, do you want to drive it through the floor! Gently!

GLENDENNING: I ... I ... I ... I ...

EWBANK: What? What? What? [*He's busy getting the muslin drapery ready to take up the ladder.*]

BENNETT: He's brought you your tobacco, Mr Ewbank.

EWBANK: What? ... Oh. [*Pauses. Then takes it.*] Aye. You're a good lad.

GLENDENNING: I ... I ... I ... I ...

EWBANK: Did you buy yourself some chocolate?

GLENDENNING: Aye.

[MARSHALL *whistles 'Down Mexico Way' refrain.*]

EWBANK [*to* FITZPATRICK]: Hold it. Hold it. Hold it. Hold it. God damn and blast ... [EWBANK *has turned to the ladder and begun to mount it, hammer in one hand, drapery in the other.*

All the men now, but for GLENDENNING, *and* FITZPATRICK, *who is holding the ladder, are working, watching* EWBANK *at the same time.*]

FITZPATRICK [*sings*]: Somebody has had a tipple ...
                    Somebody has had a drop ...

PAUL: I think we've had enough of that

FITZPATRICK: What ... ?

PAUL: I think we've had enough of it.

FITZPATRICK: I was just ... [*To* MARSHALL] I have a very melodious voice.

   [BENNETT *snorts.*]

MARSHALL: He has. It's right.

   [FITZPATRICK *shrugs.*

      PAUL *goes back to work.*

      FITZPATRICK, *so the others can see, sings silently, mouthing the words hugely.*]

KAY: All right, Fitzpatrick. You've had your laugh.

EWBANK [*above*]: Hold it. God damn and blast.

FITZPATRICK: No hands! [*Stands with his arms out, one foot pressed against the foot of the ladder.*]

KAY: Get that bloody floor rubbed up. Glendenning, do you hear?

GLENDENNING: Aye!

   [FITZPATRICK *looks up to where* EWBANK *is tacking the muslin, draping it round the pole.*]

MARSHALL: Go on. Go on. It'll be over in a flash.

   [*They laugh.*]

EWBANK: I'm coming down ... [*Finishing.*]

PAUL [*having crossed over*]: Here. I'll hold it.

   [FITZPATRICK *hesitates.*]

 I'll hold it.

   [PAUL *takes the ladder from* FITZPATRICK *who shrugs.*

      EWBANK *comes down the last rungs.*

      FITZPATRICK *has gone off, picking up bags, clearing the mess.*]

EWBANK [*to* PAUL]: If you want summat to do you can fetch the flowers in from outside. Fitzpatrick, I thought I told you to hold this. Carry it over. [*Indicating the next pole.*]

FITZPATRICK [*to* PAUL, *taking it*]: Do as the old lad says.

PAUL: I'll hold it. I don't mind. [*To* EWBANK.]

EWBANK: Do you think I don't know what goes on. I've got eyes in my backside I have …

FITZPATRICK: He has. I've seen them.

EWBANK: I miss nowt here. Don't worry. Bennett. Fasten the box round this last pole …

[PAUL *watches him cross to the next pole where* FITZPATRICK *is setting up the ladder. Then he turns and goes.* BENNETT *has begun to fasten the box round the first pole, the end of the muslin, draped round the pole, hung inside. One side of the box is hinged, like a door, and round the top fits a kind of round collar or tray, hinged too so that it can fit round the pole.*]

[*Mounting the ladder and beginning to hang the second drape*] Glendenning, help to bring in those flowers. Marshall …

MARSHALL: Yes, sir!

EWBANK: When you've got your boots off start at that end polishing the floor.

FITZPATRICK: Good God. It's come at last.

MARSHALL: My boots?

FITZPATRICK: He can't mean it.

EWBANK: Get on with it. Get on … [*To* FITZPATRICK] Hold that ladder!

[MARSHALL *takes off his boots and begins, at the farthest end, with a mop and duster, to polish the floor.*]

Thousands on his education … Bloody flowers. Six bob an hour.

[KAY *is finishing off the floor and then adjusts the drapes round the walls.*

PAUL *has begun to carry in the flowers, arranging them round the box that* BENNETT *has fastened.*]

FITZPATRICK [*to* EWBANK]: Can you see up there all right?

EWBANK: I can see, all right. Don't worry.

FITZPATRICK: Which pair, now, is it that you're using?

[MARSHALL, BENNETT, *and* FITZPATRICK *laugh.*]

EWBANK: Hold it, now. I'm coming down … Bennett. Let's have the other box round here. God damn and blast. I can see somebody's feet marks from up here. Kay, just watch it . . . Boots. Boots. Boots, man. Boots. [*As he reaches the ground*] Here, Fitzpatrick. You take it. Hammer. Tacks. Drape. Have it up on that last pole.

FITZPATRICK: Me?

[MARSHALL *has begun to laugh, giggling.*]

EWBANK: I'm not talking to the bloody floor?

FITZPATRICK: No . . .

EWBANK: Right, then. Get on with it. [*To* KAY] I'm not so bloody silly as I look.

MARSHALL: No, no. He's probably right, at that.

EWBANK: What's that?

MARSHALL [*indicating floor where he's polishing*]: I say, there's a hell of a shine, on that.

EWBANK [*to* KAY]: You'll find the tables out there. The chairs as well.

KAY [*going*]: Glendenning. Here, give me a hand.

EWBANK [*looking up at the interior*]: I shall never do it again. I shan't. Never . . .

[BENNETT *is fastening the box and its collar round the second pole.*

FITZPATRICK *has carried the ladder over to the third pole and begun to climb it, tacking up the drape.*

OLD MRS EWBANK *comes in carrying a pot plant with a splendid flower.*

PAUL *is arranging the flowers now round the second pole as* BENNETT *finishes the box.*

MARSHALL *polishes the floor, starting the farthest end and now working towards the middle, leaving it clear behind him. The whole interior now has slowly fallen into shape, a gentle radiance coming through the drapes.*

KAY *and* GLENDENNING *have begun to bring in the rest of the white, wrought-iron tables: they're small and neat, with chairs to match. They set them round the edge of the floor.*]

OLD MRS E.: Where shall I put it?

FITZPATRICK [*calling down*]: The lady here . . . wants to know where you'd like her to put it.

PAUL: Here. I'll take it.

OLD MRS E. [*admiring the flowers*]: It's very nice.

PAUL: Yes. Just about.

OLD MRS E.: He has a great flair with flowers.

EWBANK: What?

OLD MRS E.: Paul.

EWBANK: Aye. [*To* BENNETT] I'll finish that. You can get out now and start loading the truck.

MARSHALL [*calling*]: He's going to put his boots on.

FITZPATRICK [*calling*]: What?

MARSHALL: He's going to put his boots on.

FITZPATRICK: Thank God for that. [*Wafts his nose.*] The atmosphere up here is damn near revolting.

EWBANK: Marshall, finish off that floor. I want you out of here now, as quick as you can.

MARSHALL: It'll be over in a jiffy ... [*Polishing.*]

[EWBANK *himself has taken the box over to the last post.*]

EWBANK: Come on. Come on, Fitzpatrick. I could have fastened up half a dozen.

FITZPATRICK: I'm coming. I'm coming. Now clear the decks.

MARSHALL: Steady as she goes.

FITZPATRICK: Steady as she goes. You're right. [*He comes down, and starts to take the ladder out.*

EWBANK *begins to fasten on the box.*]

OLD MRS E. [*to* PAUL]: I'll give you a hand. If you like. [*She helps to arrange the flowers.*] Was your Grandad in here?

PAUL: With his bit of rope.

EWBANK: He'll bloody hang himself with it one of these days. [*To the* MEN] Come on. Come on.

[OLD MRS EWBANK *gestures in the direction of* EWBANK *and* PAUL *nods his head.*]

OLD MRS E.: There are some more in the house to come across I think.

PAUL [*still arranging*]: It's all right. I'll fetch them. There's no hurry.

OLD MRS E.: No, no. I'd like to help ... [*She goes out.*]

[FITZPATRICK *has come back after taking out the ladder. He begins to take out odds and ends, setting chairs, winking at* MARSHALL *who is still polishing, making him laugh.*]

EWBANK [*to* KAY]: You've fastened off them guys, I take it. [*Indicating outside*]

KAY: Aye. Aye. They're all right. We're nearly ready for off.

EWBANK: You've got to watch every damn thing yourself in this place, Kay. If you don't, not one . . . not one do you ever get done . . . Who the hell's that shouting? [*To* FITZPATRICK] Get out of here, now. Go on. Clear off.

[KAY *collects bags from floor and goes.*]

FITZPATRICK: Have we finished?

EWBANK: Finished? You were finished long ago. You want to think yourself damn lucky there's somebody here'll employ you.

FITZPATRICK: Oh, I do. I do. Those are lovely flowers.

EWBANK: Get out. Go on. Clear off. Marshall, you clear off with him.

MARSHALL: Thank the Lord for that. [*Going*] It's been a hard day, now. It has.

[*The whole place now has been cleared: the floor shining, the men crossing it on tip-toe. The white tables and chairs have been set round the sides, bowls of flowers put on them,* PAUL *completing this and arranging flowers round the last of the three poles as* EWBANK *finishes fastening the box.*

Gradually the whole place is cleared, leaving, finally, EWBANK *and* PAUL *alone.*]

EWBANK: I said arrange them, lad. Not plant them.

PAUL: That's all right. Don't worry. None of these'll grow.

EWBANK [*looking up at awning*]: It's not straight even now. . . . I don't know. All that damn care and trouble.

PAUL: Don't worry.

EWBANK: What . . . ? [EWBANK *is suddenly aware that he and* PAUL *are alone.*] Aye. Well . . .

[*They both fall silent.*

For some little while PAUL *works quietly at the flowers,* EWBANK *standing in the centre of the tent, still.*

KAY *suddenly comes in.*]

KAY: I've checked on all the guys. Slacked them off for the night . . . [*He glances at them both, he himself still standing in the door.*] The truck's loaded . . . I'll get them back down, then. To the yard.

EWBANK: Aye.

KAY: Well, then. I'll say good night.

EWBANK: That's right.

PAUL: See you.

KAY: Aye. Right, then . . . [KAY *nods and goes.*
　Silence. Then:]
EWBANK: Do you ever fancy this job?
　[PAUL *looks up.*
　　EWBANK *gestures at the tent.*]
　This.
　[PAUL *looks round. Then, after a moment, he shakes his head.*]
　Aye. Well . . . I'm not surprised. [*Briskly*] Not much thanks you get
　for it.
PAUL: No.
EWBANK: Aye. Well . . . [*Pause. Then:*]
　[FITZPATRICK *pops his head in.* MARSHALL *is just behind him.*]
FITZPATRICK: I'll say good night then. Looks a picture.
MARSHALL: Wouldn't mind living here meself.
FITZPATRICK: You should see his bloody room.
MARSHALL: An hovel.
FITZPATRICK: Pig-sty.
MARSHALL: It is. He's right.
BENNETT [*popping in behind*]: We'll say good night, then, er . . . er.
EWBANK: Aye. Right-o.
FITZPATRICK: Right, then. Let's be off.
MARSHALL: Good luck tomorrow.
EWBANK: Aye.
FITZPATRICK [*going*]: They'll need it, now, all right.
　[*They go.*]
MARSHALL [*off*]: Come on, now, Glenny . . .
GLENDENNING [*off*]: Aye!
　[GLENDENNING *appears in doorway.*]
　G . . . g . . . g . . . g . . . g . . .
EWBANK: Aye. Good night, lad. I'll see you at the yard tomorrow.
GLENDENNING: I . . . I . . . I . . . I . . . I . . . I . . .
MARSHALL [*sings off*]: Ay, yi, yi, yi . . . Ay, yi, yi, yi.
EWBANK: Aye. Thanks for the tobacco.
GLENDENNING: Mmmmmmmmmmm . . . [*Can't get it out.*]
PAUL: Bye, Glenny. [PAUL *gets up now from the flowers.*]
GLENDENNING: See you . . . mmmmmm . . . d-day after tomorrow!
PAUL: Aye. That's right.

GLENDENNING [*gesturing at tent:*] I ... I ... I ... I ... I ...

MARSHALL [*sings off*]: Ay, yi, yi, yi ... Ay, yi, yi, yi ...

GLENDENNING: Lovely.

PAUL: Aye ...

GLENDENNING: W ... w ... w ... well ... [*Nods and grins at them.*]

FITZPATRICK [*off*]: Come on, Glenny. We're going to be here all night.

MARSHALL [*off*]: Spends forty-eight hours, does Glenny, saying good morning.

EWBANK: Get off, lad. Or they'll be gone without you.

GLENDENNING: Aye! [*He smiles at them, then goes.*

    EWBANK *and* PAUL *stand silently in the tent. Vaguely they look around.*]

EWBANK: You know. You mustn't mind them ... [*Gestures off.*]

PAUL: Oh ... [*Realizing*] No.

EWBANK: They've a mind for nowt, you know.

PAUL: Yes ... [*Nods.*]

EWBANK: It'll not happen again, you know ...

    [PAUL *looks up at him.*

    EWBANK *gestures round.*]

  This.

PAUL: There'll not be the chance.

EWBANK: Too bloody old to start again.

PAUL: Aye.

EWBANK: Ah ... well, then ...

    [*Pause.*]

PAUL: Aye ... Well ... I'll go and fetch some flowers.

    [PAUL *goes.*

    EWBANK *stands gazing at the tent.*

    He leans up after a moment against one of the boxes, his arm stretched to it, contemplative.

    OLD MRS EWBANK *comes in quietly, unnoticed, carrying a plant. She puts it in place, regards it.*

    Then, seeing EWBANK, *she looks up.*]

OLD MRS E.: Oh ... It's lovely.

EWBANK: Aye.

    [MRS EWBANK *has come in, admiring.*]

OLD MRS E.: It's finished, love. D'you like it?

MRS EWBANK [*nods, coming farther in*]: Well, then ... They should be pleased. [*To* EWBANK]

EWBANK: Aye.

OLD MRS E.: I'll ... There are one or two more to fetch in.

    [EWBANK *nods.*

       OLD MRS EWBANK *goes.*]

MRS EWBANK: Have the men gone?

EWBANK: That's right.

    [MRS EWBANK *comes farther in, looking round.*]

MRS EWBANK: Is it what you were hoping for?

EWBANK: Hoping?

MRS EWBANK [*pause*]: He's done the flowers well ...

EWBANK [*looking up at the tent*]: Come today. Gone tomorrow.

MRS EWBANK [*watches him. Then:*] Ah, well.

EWBANK: Aye ...

    [CLAIRE *and* MAURICE *appear at the door after a moment, looking in together.*]

MAURICE: Can we come in? Is it all right to enter?

EWBANK: Aye. That's what it's for.

MRS EWBANK: Come in ...

CLAIRE: It's lovely. [*Slides across the floor in a vague dance.*] Super. [*To* MAURICE] What do you think?

MAURICE [*standing in the centre, gazing up*]: Lovely.

MRS EWBANK [*to both*]: Well ... I'm glad you like it.

CLAIRE: Course we do. Why not?

MRS EWBANK: Tell your Dad. Not me.

CLAIRE: 'Thanks, old man,' she said.

EWBANK: Aye.

MAURICE: Lovely.

    [PAUL *has come in quietly at the back with flowers.*

       OLD EWBANK *comes in carrying a piece of rope, entering quite confidently, only then, as he reaches the centre, looking round, aware that it isn't as it was before.*

       OLD MRS EWBANK *has come in after him.*]

OLD EWBANK: Where are they? I've brought him another bit to look at.

MRS EWBANK: They've gone.

PAUL: On the lorry.

OLD EWBANK: I damn well would. It's not often you get the chance.

MAURICE: Wanna dance?

CLAIRE: Sure. [*Holds out her hands.*]

MRS EWBANK: Do you think you should ...

CLAIRE: Why not? [*Laughing*]

MRS EWBANK: I don't know ... [*Laughs.*] I'm not sure.

MAURICE: 'S bad luck.

CLAIRE: Luck never came into it.

[*She laughs and dances tentatively with* MAURICE *round the floor.*]

CLAIRE: Aren't you going to give your mother a dance, Paul?

PAUL: I don't know ... If she wants one.

[MRS EWBANK *shrugs, pleased.*]

MRS EWBANK: I don't mind. If you think you can manage ... [*She laughs.*]

PAUL: Mind me hands. Black. [*Holds them up.*]

[*He holds her tentatively, and they dance round with some pleasure.*]

OLD EWBANK: I've never seen ought like it. Can you turn up the sound?

OLD MRS E. [*crossing to him*]: There isn't any. Here ... Sit down.

[*They sit at one of the tables.*]

MAURICE: Ought to break out a few drinks. What? Celebrate.

MRS EWBANK: Oh, there's plenty enough time for that.

CLAIRE: In any case. We're not hitched.

MAURICE: Not yet.

MRS EWBANK: Oh, now. Don't let's start on that.

CLAIRE [*gestures at tent*]: If only for this we have no option.

[*They laugh.*]

PAUL: Do you want to dance with my mother, Dad?

EWBANK: Aye. I'll give her a dance. Why not?

[EWBANK *takes* MRS EWBANK *firmly.*
They begin to dance, whirling round in an old-fashioned waltz.
MAURICE *and* CLAIRE *have stopped dancing to watch.*
EWBANK *and* MRS EWBANK *dance round the whole tent.*
EWBANK's *dancing is heavy, firm, and implacable, entirely characteristic of himself.*]

MRS EWBANK: Wow! Wow! Not so fast.

MAURICE: I'd say ... He was a drop or two ahead of us.

CLAIRE [*puts her finger to her lips, shaking her head*]: Aye, now. That's enough.

MAURICE: Go on, Dad. Let 'em have it.

[EWBANK *and* MRS EWBANK *dance on.*]

EWBANK [*stopping*]: Theer now.

MRS EWBANK: Oh. Goodness. [*Holds her head, pulls back her hair.*] Am I still in one piece? [*To* CLAIRE. *She staggers, laughing.*] Oh, dear. I'm spinning.

OLD EWBANK: If I had my time o'er again, I'd burn the bloody lot.

PAUL: What's that?

OLD EWBANK: Machines. It's never too late. Bloody burn them, and that's that.

CLAIRE: If he's like this now, what's he going to be like tomorrow?

OLD EWBANK [*holding rope*]: A bit of pressure, and they come to pieces in your hand.

OLD MRS E.: I'll take him in and let him lie down.

EWBANK: Aye ... He needs looking after.

EWBANK: I worked thirty or forty hours a day.

OLD MRS E.: He means at week-ends.

OLD EWBANK [*going*]: What? If I'd had any more I'd have given him a bit ...

OLD MRS E.: Oh, well. We might find a piece or two you've forgotten.

OLD EWBANK: By God. They are. One glance and they damn well come apart.

[*They go.*

EWBANK *sits.*

Silence.]

MRS EWBANK: Well, then ...

[*Pause. Then:*]

PAUL: I'll go in and wash up. [*Looking at his hands.*]

MAURICE: Yes. Well, I better be getting home ...

CLAIRE: I'll get your things.

MAURICE [*to* MRS EWBANK]: I'll see you later. This evening.

MRS EWBANK: Yes. Later on.

[*They go.*]

CLAIRE: And tonight, try and stay ...
MAURICE: What?
CLAIRE: Sober.
    [EWBANK *and* MRS EWBANK *are left alone.*
        They are silent. Then:]
MRS EWBANK: Well. All ready.
EWBANK: Aye.
    [*They are silent. Then:*]
MRS EWBANK: Are you coming in?
    [EWBANK *looks up.*]
    Spend your last evening with your daughter.
EWBANK: Aye ... [*He looks up at the finished tent.*]
MRS EWBANK: We'll manage.
EWBANK: Aye. We'll make a damn good job of it. [*Half-laughs.*] ...
We will.
MRS EWBANK: Well, then. [*Going*] Aren't you coming? [*Goes.*]
    [EWBANK *gazes round, picks up the old piece of rope* OLD
    EWBANK *has left. Gazes round. Rises. Goes.*
    Slowly the light fades.
    Curtain.]

ACT THREE

Early morning.

The tent has suffered a great deal. Part of the muslin drapery hangs loosely down. Similarly, parts of the lining round the walls hang down in loose folds, unhooked, or on the floor. Part of the dance floor itself has been removed, other parts uprooted and left in loose slabs: chairs have been upturned, tables left lying on their sides. Bottles lie here and there on the floor, along with discarded napkins, streamers, tablecloths, paper-wrapping. Most of the flowers have gone and the few that remain have been dragged out of position, ready to be disposed of.

GLENDENNING [*heard*]: I ... I ... I ... I ... I ...

MARSHALL [*heard, sings*]: Ay, yi, yi, yi ... Ay, yi, yi, yi.

FITZPATRICK [*heard*]: Wakey-wakey!

BENNETT [*heard*]: Not a word ...

    [FITZPATRICK *trips and falls into the door, regaining his balance as he stumbles into the tent.*]

FITZPATRICK: Good grief and God help us ... Et cetera and all that ...

    [BENNETT *has come in behind him after a few moments. He too stands dazed, looking round.*]

GLENDENNING [*heard*]: I ... I ... I ... I ...

MARSHALL [*heard, sings*]: Ay, yi, yi, yi ... Ay, yi, yi, yi.

FITZPATRICK: Somebody's been enjoying themselves. I'd say, at a very quick guess ... [*Picks up a bottle, examines it, finds it empty, puts it down.*] At a very quick guess indeed, I'd say there was nothing left.

BENNETT: There's not a lot left here for us to do, Fitzie ...

FITZPATRICK: There's not. There's not ... Just look at that. [*Indicates some damage.*]

    [KAY *has come in the other side, lifting the walling and stooping underneath.*]

[*Calling off*] Come in here, Marshy, old man. This should impress you all right.

KAY: Mind the floor ... Don't step on any glass.

MARSHALL [*appearing*]: Good God. And may the saints preserve us.

FITZPATRICK: More empty bottles, Marshy, than even you can count.

MARSHALL: And me not a drinking man, either.

FITZPATRICK [*laughs*]: No. No. And you not a drinking man at all.

MARSHALL: That's a rare old sight indeed. [*Picks up a bottle.*]

FITZPATRICK: And not a drop to have.

MARSHALL: I wouldn't at all, now, like to be the one to foot the bill.
    [*He puts the bottle down and, like* FITZPATRICK, *drifts around the interior inspecting the bottles.*
    GLENDENNING *has come in, eating a sandwich.*]

GLENDENNING: Th ... th ... th ... th ... that's a good old ... mmmmm ... mmmmess.

KAY: You better start on the bottles, Fitzpatrick.
    [MARSHALL *roars with laughter.*]

FITZPATRICK: And what's so funny about that?

MARSHALL [*to* KAY]: Ah, now, if they'd sent him down to yonder ... [*Thumbs down.*] That'd be just the job they'd find.

FITZPATRICK [*picking up bottles*]: Empty ... empty ... every one.

KAY: Marshall. You help him. And with the mess as well.
    [FITZPATRICK *roars with laughter.*]
    Bennett ... [*Indicates tables.*] Glendenning ... [*Indicates chairs.*]

GLENDENNING: I ... I ... I ... Aye!

MARSHALL: Don't you ever get tired of eatin', Glenny?

FITZPATRICK [*holding bottle to light*]: And where now, do you think, is the happy bride? [*He drinks off the dregs, grimaces, holds his stomach.*]

BENNETT: Not here, for one. That's sure.

MARSHALL: I don't know. Might find half a dozen under the table, if this place is any indication to go by at all.

BENNETT: God. God. But it's freezing.

MARSHALL [*holding bottle up, gazing at it*]: Ice.

GLENDENNING: I ... I ... I ... I ...

MARSHALL [*sings*]: Ay, yi, yi, yi ... Ay, yi, yi, yi ...

GLENDENNING: I ... I ... I ... I ... Ice!

FITZPATRICK: In summer, Glenny.

BENNETT: It's damn near autumn now.

MARSHALL: What?

GLENDENNING: Aye!

MARSHALL [*drinking dregs*]: To God! It's glass! [*Spits out.*]
　　[FITZPATRICK *laughs.*
　　　　GLENDENNING *and* BENNETT *laugh.*]

FITZPATRICK: You mad Patrick. You'll never learn.

MARSHALL: It's glass. God damn it! I've nearly cut meself to
　　death!

FITZPATRICK: A bloody booby-trap. [*Doubles up with laughter at*
　　MARSHALL's *discomposure.*] Watch out!

KAY: I said take it outside.

BENNETT: That stuff'll poison you.

KAY: Glendenning, *chairs.*

GLENDENNING [*happy*]: Aye!

FITZPATRICK: And what, now, do you think of that?

BENNETT: What is it?

FITZPATRICK: A lady's undergarment, or I'm a frog. [*Holds up a*
　　piece of muslin.]

KAY: It is not. [*Looks up at lining.*]

BENNETT: It's off the lining. Some madman has torn it down.

MARSHALL: He'll go through the tent top. When he sees all this.

FITZPATRICK: God damn and blast.

KAY: What is it?
　　[FITZPATRICK *looks frantically about him.*]

FITZPATRICK: Me hammer. Me hammer ... I've lost it. [*To*
　　GLENDENNING] God damn it. Will you go find it in the cab?

GLENDENNING: Aye! [GLENDENNING *immediately puts down the*
　　chair he's carrying, nods, and goes quickly outside.]

BENNETT: You want to leave him alone ...

MARSHALL: What?

BENNETT: Glendenning.

MARSHALL: Ah, now. Go jump on your bloody head.

BENNETT [*backs down*]: God. It's freezing. [*Shivers.*]
　　[*They continue working.* KAY *has begun to take down the muslin*
　　walls.]

KAY: Marshall, will you bring in the muslin bags.

MARSHALL: Aye. Aye. [*To* BENNETT] It's me today. Fitzpatrick, no doubt it'll be you tomorrow.

FITZPATRICK [*looking round again*]: Good God, you know, but this is a bloody mess.

BENNETT: Aye. Aye ...

[MARSHALL *comes back in with the bags.*]

FITZPATRICK [*to* KAY]: Have you seen Ewbank this morning?

KAY: I have not. [*Still working.*]

MARSHALL: Steady. Steady. Might find him underneath all that. [*Indicates floor.*]

FITZPATRICK: No. No. Up! He's not there at all.

[GLENDENNING *has come back in.*]

KAY: You better keep your boots off just the same. Marshall ...

[*Indicates* MARSHALL *to help him with the muslin walling: wrap it and put it in the bags.*

BENNETT *has started sweeping the paper streamers and debris off the floor.*

GLENDENNING *has resumed work as though nothing has happened, picking up the chairs, carrying them out, expressionless, not looking up.*]

MARSHALL: Ay, now. And where's that hammer? Here's Fitzpatrick waiting to have a smash.

FITZPATRICK: I am. I am. That's right.

BENNETT: You want to leave him alone, Fitzpatrick.

MARSHALL [*innocent*]: Was I intending any harm? [*Indicating* GLENDENNING] He wouldn't know what to do without us.

FITZPATRICK: Have you noticed how – of recent times, I'm speaking – Bennett has grown quite dictatorial in his habits? [*Starts taking up the floor.*]

MARSHALL: He has.

FITZPATRICK: Censorious, if I didn't know him better.

MARSHALL: Censorious is the word.

FITZPATRICK: And we all know, now, the reason for it.

MARSHALL: Reason? Is there a reason, too, for that? [*Gazing up.*]

FITZPATRICK: It's explained, Benny, is it not, easily enough?

[BENNETT *goes on working.* KAY *looks up briefly then continues.*]

MARSHALL: Now, now. You'll have to tell us all the rest.

FITZPATRICK: Benny, here is the one you ought to ask.

[BENNETT *glances up at* FITZPATRICK, *then continues with his work.*

GLENDENNING *comes and goes with the remaining chairs and tables and the odd bits of rubbish.*]

MARSHALL: No, no. We're going to get nothing out of that.

KAY: Fitzpatrick ... [*Indicates he get on with his work.*]

[FITZPATRICK *gets on, clearing the rest of the rubbish, bottles, etc., then starting on the floor.*]

FITZPATRICK: It's quite easy to explain, nevertheless, and though I might well be wrong in detail, the whole mass, as it were, is reasonably correct.

MARSHALL: Go on. Go on, I'm listening. Kay, have you opened up an ear? Would you mind, Glenny, now, if you left the room?

GLENDENNING: Aye!

FITZPATRICK: His wife left him for another man.

MARSHALL: She did!

FITZPATRICK: She did.

MARSHALL: As long as it wasn't for another woman.

[MARSHALL *and* FITZPATRICK *laugh.*]

To God. And whoever would have thought of that? A man with a face like that ...

FITZPATRICK: And figure.

MARSHALL: And figure.

FITZPATRICK: And boots.

MARSHALL: And boots.

FITZPATRICK: Socks.

MARSHALL: Socks.

FITZPATRICK: Teeth. [*Showing his*]

MARSHALL: Teeth. [*Showing his*]

FITZPATRICK: Smiling ... [*Smiles.*]

MARSHALL: Smiling ...

BENNETT: Your mouth's going to open too wide one of these days, Fitzpatrick.

FITZPATRICK: It'll be all the easier to let the truth come flying out.

BENNETT: And for me to put my fist inside it.

FITZPATRICK: Since when has a man like me let a man like you put his fist inside my mouth?
[MARSHALL *laughs.*
   BENNETT *tenses but doesn't answer.*]
KAY: Fitzpatrick, get out, and load the truck outside.
FITZPATRICK: On my own? God damn it. I'm only human.
MARSHALL: Almost.
FITZPATRICK: Almost. [*Going*] It's a hard bloody life is this: walk the straight and narrow and you end up working by yourself. [*He goes.*]
MARSHALL: Well. Well. Now there's a thing. [*Tuts away to himself.*] Revelations.
BENNETT: And it's not only Fitzpatrick.
MARSHALL: Not only what?
BENNETT: Who'll feel the end of this. [*Holds up his fist.*]
MARSHALL: What? What? . . . You're not thinking . . . You can't mean it?
   [BENNETT *gazes steadily at him, obviously unable to carry out his threat, then turns and goes back to his work.*]
Good God. He can.
   [FITZPATRICK *can be heard singing outside.*
      Silence for a moment inside the tent.]
Do you think now . . .
   [BENNETT *looks up threateningly.*]
[*Spreading his arms*] We'd get anything back on the bottles.
   [*They go back to work.*
      FITZPATRICK *pops his head in.*]
FITZPATRICK: I can hear Mr Ewbank singing.
KAY: Singing . . . ?
FITZPATRICK: Round the back side of the house . . . [*Pops out.*]
MARSHALL: There's a blue sky around the corner.
FITZPATRICK [*listens*]: Beautiful.
MARSHALL: Like a bird . . .
FITZPATRICK: Like a bird.
KAY: Fitzpatrick . . .
FITZPATRICK [*indicating house*]: Must be in a great good humour.
MARSHALL: Great good humour: I think you're right.
FITZPATRICK: Tucked up warm and cosy.

MARSHALL: Warm and cosy.

FITZPATRICK: Shaving.

MARSHALL: Mirror ...

FITZPATRICK: Hot water.

MARSHALL: Fingers ...

FITZPATRICK: Toes.

KAY: Fitzpatrick!

FITZPATRICK: All right. All right. [FITZPATRICK *goes.*

    BENNETT *has started taking up the floor;* GLENDENNING *takes the pieces out.*

    KAY *is detaching the muslin roof from the walls, letting it fall to the centre of the tent, where it hangs like a sail.*

    MARSHALL *himself now has started on the floor.*]

MARSHALL: How many hours, now, Glenny, do you sleep at night?

GLENDENNING: Aye!

MARSHALL: And how many hours is that? [*To* KAY] I don't think Glenny sleeps at all. Like a damn great owl, sitting there, his eyes wide open.

GLENDENNING: Aye! [*He watches them, pleased, then takes out floor.*]

BENNETT: I never need more than six or seven.

MARSHALL: Six or seven ... ?

BENNETT: Hours.

MARSHALL: Hours ... I thought ... Ah, well. But then ...

BENNETT: What's that? [*Genially*]

MARSHALL: A separated man ... You can never sleep long, on your own, in a single bed.

    [BENNETT *seems about to turn on him.*]

    [*To* KAY] It's true, then, Kay. They put a man like you inside.

FITZPATRICK [*popping back*]: There's many a better man been put in with him.

MARSHALL: There has. There has ... Still singing?

FITZPATRICK [*shakes head, picks up piece of flooring*]: Having, I think, a little rest.

MARSHALL: Recuperation. No sound of breathing? No shouts? No cries.

FITZPATRICK: Not a bird. Not a twitter.

MARSHALL: Resting then. No doubt. A damn great house like that . . .

FITZPATRICK: He's worked hard now, Marshy, for every penny he's got.

MARSHALL: He has. You're right. And we as well, now, have worked a damn sight harder.

[FITZPATRICK *laughs, taking up more of the dance floor.*]

MARSHALL: It looks to me like a damn great orgy . . .

KAY: What's that?

FITZPATRICK: He pricked his ears at that.

MARSHALL: I shouldn't wonder. Just look at that. Scratches . . .

BENNETT: That's made with glass.

MARSHALL: Glass? I'd have sworn it was somebody's fingers . . . Dragged out. Protesting to the last.

[*They laugh.* BENNETT *and* GLENDENNING *carry out pieces. Then:*]

If you ask me, they're both heading hard for trouble.

FITZPATRICK: Who?

MARSHALL: The bridegroom and the bride.

[*They're both taking up the floor, waiting for* BENNETT *to return.*]

FITZPATRICK: Oh, now. What makes you feel like that?

MARSHALL [*as* BENNETT *returns*]: Experience, man. Marriage, as an institution – in my opinion – is all washed out. Finished . . . Kaput.

FITZPATRICK [*towards* BENNETT]: Ah, now. There speaks a know-ledgeable man.

MARSHALL: I do. I am.

KAY: All right, now. Let's have it down. [KAY *has now released the muslin roof from the sides of the tent and it hangs in a single drape down the centre of the tent.*

FITZPATRICK *goes on clearing the floor; the others go to the ropes to lower the muslin.*]

FITZPATRICK: Bus-conductor . . .

MARSHALL: Rose nearly to inspector, but for her sex, Fitzpatrick.

FITZPATRICK: But for our sex, Marshy, and we'd all rise to something else. Greengrocer's right-hand assistant. Nun . . .

MARSHALL: Baked apple-pie. [*Lowering*]

FITZPATRICK: Is that a fact?

MARSHALL: So many apples in, they nearly tore the crust apart.

FITZPATRICK: Good God. Glenny! I hope you're listening.

GLENDENNING: Aye!

FITZPATRICK: I wonder if old Benny's was a cook? [*He goes, carrying the floor.*

The muslin now is lowered. BENNETT *looks up wildly, then he goes on with the others untaping the muslin from the ridges and unlacing it at the seams.*]

MARSHALL [*untaping*]: I knew a man once. Came home from work one afternoon ... Been let off early — an act of charity — by the boss ...

BENNETT: Aye?

MARSHALL: Found his wife in bed with another man.

[BENNETT *looks across.*]

KAY: Be careful where you let it fall.

MARSHALL: Comes in. Finds no dinner. Goes upstairs. Commotion ... Opens door ...

FITZPATRICK [*returning*]: And Bob's your uncle.

MARSHALL: No. No. You weren't the one I had in mind at all.

[*They laugh.*]

KAY [*to* FITZPATRICK]: Side poles ...

FITZPATRICK: Good God ... I was getting used, now, to trotting off outside.

MARSHALL: Aren't you going to let me finish my story?

FITZPATRICK: Hung up a notice.

MARSHALL: What?

FITZPATRICK: Hung up a notice: DO NOT DISTURB, outside.

[FITZPATRICK *and* MARSHALL *laugh.*]

KAY: All right, now. All right. Let's have it in the bags.

[*The men start to pack the three separated pieces of muslin lining.* FITZPATRICK *has started to remove the side poles.*]

MARSHALL: I've been badly suited, I have, in the matter of fidelity.

FITZPATRICK: Easy come ...

MARSHALL: That's what they say.

KAY: Careful ... gently.

[MARSHALL *and* FITZPATRICK *laugh.*]

BENNETT: I've told you, Fitzpatrick. That's the last chance you'll have.

FITZPATRICK: That's what I said …

MARSHALL: She didn't believe me.

[MARSHALL *and* FITZPATRICK *laugh.*]

GLENDENNING: I … I … I … I … I …

MARSHALL [*sings*]: Ay, yi, yi, yi … Ay, yi, yi, yi …

[GLENDENNING *takes out the bagged muslin.*

BENNETT *is now releasing the ropes from the muslin ridges.*]

FITZPATRICK: A faithful wife …

MARSHALL: Is like a stone round your neck …

FITZPATRICK: No decent man would be seen without it.

[FITZPATRICK *and* MARSHALL *laugh.*]

KAY: Fitzpatrick. Shut your mouth.

FITZPATRICK: It's Bennett …

BENNETT: You've had your chance, Fitzpatrick.

MARSHALL: You've had your chance, Fitzpatrick.

FITZPATRICK: That's what she said.

[MARSHALL *and* FITZPATRICK *laugh.*]

KAY [*to* MARSHALL]: If you call that work, you better get yourself another job.

MARSHALL [*horrified*]: Another!

FITZPATRICK: God. That's the worst thing I've ever heard.

[MARSHALL *shakes his head, clearing out either ear with his little finger.*]

KAY: Marshall … Fitzpatrick … [*Indicates the floor.*] Bennett …

[*The men start taking up the rest of the floor.*]

MARSHALL: Trade unions.

FITZPATRICK: What?

MARSHALL: Trade unions.

[BENNETT *looks up, then continues taking out the floor with* GLENDENNING *as* MARSHALL *and* FITZPATRICK *lift it.*]

FITZPATRICK: That's an interesting proposition.

MARSHALL: It is.

FITZPATRICK: Why certain people …

MARSHALL: Who shall be nameless …

FITZPATRICK: Come seeking employment …

MARSHALL: Of all places ...

FITZPATRICK: At Mr Ewbank's place itself.

MARSHALL: Aye.

FITZPATRICK: Tenting contractor ...

MARSHALL: For all outside ...

FITZPATRICK: And inside occasions.

    [*They laugh.*]

  [*Direct to* MARSHALL] Some of course ...

MARSHALL: Have no alternative ... No. No. They haven't. That's right.

FITZPATRICK: In a manner of speaking, they have no choice.

MARSHALL: No, no. That's right. They can't be blamed.

FITZPATRICK: While on the other hand ...

MARSHALL: You're right. You're right.

FITZPATRICK: Some of them ...

MARSHALL: You're right.

FITZPATRICK: Come here because they're bone idle.

MARSHALL: Like myself you mean.

FITZPATRICK: Like yourself. On the other hand ...

MARSHALL: Aye ...

FITZPATRICK: There are those ...

MARSHALL: Aye ...

FITZPATRICK: Who have it in them to rise to higher things.

MARSHALL: Higher things. They have.

FITZPATRICK: Who have, within them, Marshy, the capacity to get on.

MARSHALL: They have. They have. You're right.

FITZPATRICK: But who, suddenly – through some calamity on the domestic front ...

MARSHALL: The domestic front ...

FITZPATRICK: In a manner of speaking ...

MARSHALL: In a manner of speaking. That's right.

FITZPATRICK: Lose ...

MARSHALL: Lose.

FITZPATRICK: All interest in carrying on.

MARSHALL: They do. They do. You're right.

FITZPATRICK: Some terrible calamity overwhelms them ...

MARSHALL: ... on the domestic front ...

FITZPATRICK: And up, into the wide blue yonder ... all pride and initiative: gone.

MARSHALL: Aye ... Vanished.

BENNETT: I'm not above using this, Fitzpatrick!

   [BENNETT *has come in and has wrapped one of the muslin ropes: now he threatens* FITZPATRICK *with the shackle end.*]

FITZPATRICK: No, no. Each man to his tools I've always said.

MARSHALL [*to* FITZPATRICK]: A tradesman from his tools should never be divided.

BENNETT: I'll kill you. I bloody will!

KAY: That's enough, Fitzpatrick.

FITZPATRICK: I was merely ascertainin' the truth of the matter, Kay.

MARSHALL [*to* FITZPATRICK]: What's a man's life worth if it's comprised of nothing but untruths and lies?

FITZPATRICK: What is it now, indeed?

KAY: And what's so remarkable about your life, Fitzpatrick?

FITZPATRICK: Remarkable?

KAY: That it gives you the right to go poking so often into other people's.

   [GLENDENNING *has come in slowly.*]

   A loud-mouth. A wet-rag. That doesn't do a crumb of work unless he's driven to it. [KAY *has crossed slowly over to* FITZPATRICK.]

FITZPATRICK: Loud-mouth, now, I might be. And bone-idle.

   [MARSHALL *snorts.*]

   But I'm the only one round here who hasn't anything to hide.

KAY: Are you, now. Then you're very lucky. You're a very lucky man, Fitzpatrick. If you don't mind me saying so.

FITZPATRICK: No. I don't mind. I probably am. You're right.

   [MARSHALL *laughs.*]

KAY [*unruffled*]: And you think that, then, has some virtue.

FITZPATRICK: Aye. I think it probably has. Meaning no disrespect whatsoever [*indicating* BENNETT], it was Bennett who pointed out the fact with which, until then, we were unacquainted. Namely that you, Kay, yourself, had been in clink. So what ... ?

MARSHALL: Some of my best friends are criminals.

FITZPATRICK: What I can't abide is a man who can point his finger at other people but can't bear the same one to be pointed at himself.

KAY: Some people, Fitzpatrick, have injuries that go deeper than you imagine.

MARSHALL: Oh, very nice. [*Applauds discreetly.*] He got that from a book.

FITZPATRICK: I mean, glass houses, Kay. Glass houses. There's not one now you can't see here. Just by turning round.

[MARSHALL *turns round.*]

KAY: That's very fine, Fitzpatrick.

MARSHALL: It is. I agree with that myself.

KAY: Do you put a price on anything, Fitzpatrick?

FITZPATRICK: I don't know. I put a price on the work I do here. Minimal it may be, but I do put a price on that.

MARSHALL: Come on now, then. Let's get back to work. [*Rubs his hands.*]

FITZPATRICK: And one other thing. A little more civility might have been more becoming.

MARSHALL: It would.

FITZPATRICK: We're not just here, now, to be pushed around.

KAY: It looks to me, Fitzpatrick, that you've come here – this morning like any other – to cause trouble wherever you can ...

FITZPATRICK [*looking at* BENNETT]: If a man puts his fist in my face I'll be damned if he doesn't get one back. Wherever that man might come from.

BENNETT: And you think that's something to admire, Fitzpatrick?

FITZPATRICK: No. No. It's not admiration at all I'm after.

[MARSHALL *laughs.*]

KAY: I think you better get home, Fitzpatrick.

FITZPATRICK: What?

KAY: I think you better get off. Come into the office at the end of the week and you'll get whatever you're owed.

[*Silence. Then:*]

FITZPATRICK: Huh. [*Looks round for his jacket.*] Do you mean that?

KAY: I do.

[FITZPATRICK *goes to his jacket. He slowly pulls it on.*]

FITZPATRICK [*to* MARSHALL]: Are you coming?

MARSHALL: Well, now ... If there's one of us to be out of work ... better that the other sticks to what he can.

FITZPATRICK [*bitterly*]: Aye. I suppose you're right. [*He goes to the door.*]

It's amazing, you know ... the way he surrounds himself with cripples. [*Gestures at the house.*]

KAY: Cripples?

FITZPATRICK: Yourself ... Bennett ... Glenny ... Marshall ...

MARSHALL: Fitzpatrick ...

FITZPATRICK: And lastly, of course, myself. It qualifies, I suppose, the nature ... of his warm and understanding heart. Ah, well. You can tell him one thing for nothing. The road up yonder is a harder climb than that. [*Thumbs upwards.*] I'll say good-bye. May God go with you, and treat you more kindly than Himself. [*Taps GLENDENNING on the shoulder as he goes.*] Watch it, Glenny. One day, mind ... [*Gestures hammer with his hand.*]

GLENDENNING: Aye! [*Laughs.*]

[*As he goes to the door* EWBANK *comes in.*]

EWBANK: And where the hell do you think you're going to? God Christ. Just look at the time. Knocking off and they've only been here half an hour.

FITZPATRICK: I've been fired.

EWBANK: Don't be so bloody silly. Get on with this bloody walling ... God damn and blast. Just look. Covered in bloody muck. *Marshall ... !* [*Gestures at* MARSHALL *to get on with the floor.*] Fitzpatrick ... let's have it up. [*Indicates floor.*]

[*Slowly they go back to their tasks.* KAY *alone doesn't look up.*] Kay, let's have these battens out ... Good God. We're going to be here all night.

KAY: Bennett ...

MARSHALL: The couple got off to a happy start, then, Mr Ewbank.

EWBANK: What? ...

MARSHALL: The happy ...

EWBANK: Mind your own bloody business. Bennett, I don't call that working. [*To* MARSHALL] How the hell would you know that?

MARSHALL: I ... Me ... We ...

FITZPATRICK: Ah, but a great day. Celebratin' ...

EWBANK: I'll celebrate my boot up your bloody backside, Fitzpatrick. That's what I'll do . . . God Christ. God Christ. They come in here and start telling you what sort of night you've had . . .

KAY: Bennett, over here . . .

[*They work, silent, taking out the battens and the last of the floor.* EWBANK *grunts, groans, murmurs to himself.*

They watch him, glancing at one another, as they work. Then:]

MARSHALL: Married life. There's nothing like it. You can't beat it. Though I do say so myself.

EWBANK: Lift it. Lift it. God Christ, they think you live here, you know, like they do at home . . .

MARSHALL: They do. They do. That's right. A bloody pigsty. He knows.

EWBANK: Flat on their backs all night. And flat on their bellies all day long to go with it . . .

MARSHALL: He was sacked, nevertheless, Mr Ewbank. Demoted.

EWBANK: There's been nobody sacked from this firm since the day it first began. God Christ, Kay, I've heard some bloody tales in my time, but that one takes the can.

FITZPATRICK: Ah, it's a great life if you can afford it.

MARSHALL: And what, now, is that?

FITZPATRICK: A wife. Home . . . children.

GLENDENNING: I . . . I . . . I . . . I . . . I . . . I . . . I . . .

MARSHALL: Hot chocolate by the fire.

FITZPATRICK: Hot chocolate by the fire.

GLENDENNING: I . . . I . . . I . . . I . . . I . . . I . . .

[EWBANK *mumbles and groans to himself, unnoticing, then:*]

EWBANK: If you took my advice, Kay, you'd bloody well get shut . . .

KAY: What . . .

EWBANK: Four lasses. Good God. You ought to have more common sense . . . A man your age: you ought to have more bloody common sense . . . God Christ.

GLENDENNING: I . . . I . . . I . . . I . . .

EWBANK: That's all right, then . . .

[*The men take out the battens.* KAY *is working, loosening them.*]

God. Bloody orchestra. Kay, you should have seen it. Dressed up like a cockatoo. There'll be some of them stretched out still, out yonder. I shouldn't be surprised. God Christ. You've seen nowt like it.

FITZPATRICK: Had a damn fine time, did you, an' all?

EWBANK: Who's asking you?

FITZPATRICK: I thought ...

MARSHALL: Married life. You can't beat it.

EWBANK [*to* KAY]: Made me speech standing on the bridegroom's table ... Just look at that. [*Gestures at the ground.*]

MARSHALL: On the other hand, Mr Kay here has been telling us how he's been to prison. Enjoyed the experience, he said, no end ... Regaling us you know with all the sordid details.

EWBANK: Tipped half a bottle over some chap's head ... Bloody waiters. Chef ... If you can't for one day in your life enjoy it.

FITZPATRICK: And not left a drop of the damn good stuff for us.

EWBANK: What's that?

FITZPATRICK: I say, Kay here isn't one to make a fuss.

EWBANK: By God, bloody embezzlement. That'd make 'em shift, Kay. Four lasses.

MARSHALL: Embezzlement?

EWBANK: By God. There's nowt for him to embezzle here. [*Laughs.*] Ay bloody hell. You need a firework up your arse. Just look at that ... Get on. Get on. Here, I'll give you a lift myself.

FITZPATRICK: Embezzlement. Now there's a wonder.

MARSHALL: And all the time now ...

FITZPATRICK: One of us.

MARSHALL: Hiding his light beneath a bushel.

FITZPATRICK: Along, that is, with the cash from someone else's tub.

[MARSHALL *and* FITZPATRICK *laugh.*]

EWBANK: What's that?

MARSHALL: I say, your son's not out to help us, then, this morning.

EWBANK: No. He's not.

FITZPATRICK: Ah. It's a great life if you can mix it.

EWBANK: He's off on his bloody travels.

MARSHALL: Travels?

FITZPATRICK: Abroad, is that?

EWBANK: I wouldn't know if you told me ... He's never in one place two minutes running.

FITZPATRICK: Ah, travelling. A great broadener of the mind.

EWBANK: A great emptier of the pocket, if you ask me, more likely.

[OLD EWBANK *has come in at the back*.]

FITZPATRICK: Don't worry. One day he'll settle down.

EWBANK: Will he? That's your opinion, Fitzpatrick?

FITZPATRICK: Modern times, Mr Ewbank. The up-and-coming generation.

EWBANK: Aye, well. They can up and come all right . . . You can start loading that bloody lorry, Kay. Let's have 'em out.

FITZPATRICK: The world of the imagination . . .

EWBANK: Is that what it is, Fitzpatrick?

FITZPATRICK: The ferment of ideas.

EWBANK: If he'd ferment something out of it we shouldn't be so bad.

MARSHALL: Like a damn good liquor . . .

FITZPATRICK: Like a damn good Scotch. You're right.

[*They go, taking the last of the battens with them.* BENNETT *remains, starting to strip the ropes on the centre poles.*

After a while, as OLD EWBANK *talks,* MARSHALL *and* GLENDENNING *return to wrap the walling, laying it out on the ground at the back of the tent and folding it, seam on seam.*]

OLD EWBANK [*to* BENNETT]: Did I show you that rope the other day?

BENNETT: What? I don't . . .

OLD EWBANK: In the house. I keep it there.

BENNETT: Aye. I think I saw it . . .

OLD EWBANK: Four hundred feet some days. By hand.

BENNETT: Aye . . .

OLD EWBANK: What? You saw nothing like it.

BENNETT: Aye. That's quite a lot.

OLD EWBANK: Horses? Damn it all. Sheep-nets . . . Fishing boats . . . Dogger Bank. Iceland. Scapa Flow . . . *Greenland*. You'll find bits of rope I made, you know, floating under the North Pole. Good God. A piece of rope in those days . . .

BENNETT [*still working*]: Aye . . .

OLD EWBANK: Balloons? Do you know once they used it on an airship. Bigger than a house. Damn it all. You could go anywhere with a bit of rope. [*Suddenly confidential*] I know. Don't you let these people mislead you.

BENNETT: Ah, well. I better get on with this.

OLD EWBANK: They haven't the strength to stand up. A bit of an ache and they're dashing for a pill and a sup from a bottle. They haven't the appetite, you know, for work ... There's one sat out there now, on the back of the lorry, eating a damn great cake. I've never seen so many people sitting down, eating ... Have I showed you my rope?

BENNETT: Aye.

OLD EWBANK: Twelve? Eighteen. Sometimes twenty hours a day. Good God, you'd no time to sit eating. When I married my wife I never used to see her but one day in four.

MARSHALL: Those were the days, Benny, right enough!

OLD EWBANK [*turning to* MARSHALL]: Steam? By God, there was!

[EWBANK *has returned, followed by* KAY.

FITZPATRICK *has already come back and is laying out the walling.*]

EWBANK: Come on, now. Let's have it folded.

OLD EWBANK: I can't stop now. I'm just going for my walk.

[OLD MRS EWBANK *has come in.*]

Got used to it, you know. Used to walk twenty or thirty miles a day. It'd take ten miles walking to make a hundred foot of rope.

OLD MRS E.: I've been looking for you all over. Do you realize you haven't got on any socks? [*To* EWBANK] Has he been here long?

EWBANK: He's just arrived. He'll be all right.

OLD MRS E. [*reprovingly*]: He's been out walking. He'll catch his death of cold.

MARSHALL: He's a fine old man, missis.

OLD MRS E.: He needs looking after. That's a fact.

OLD EWBANK [*to* BENNETT]: One day in four. Five if I worked over.

OLD MRS E. [*looking around*]: It's amazing how soon they disappear ... [*To* EWBANK] We're off in half an hour.

EWBANK: I'll come and see you ...

OLD MRS E.: Aye ... Well, I'll take him in. Get him dressed. [*Shouts in* OLD EWBANK's *ear.*] I'll take you in!

OLD EWBANK: What? We've only just started.

OLD MRS E. [*going, her arm in* OLD EWBANK's]: He still thinks we're having the party.

OLD EWBANK: God damn and blast. When you tied a knot it'd take you a fortnight to unravel it.

[*They go.*]

EWBANK: Get packing this walling up ... Let's have it out.

[*They start to pack the walling. The others are removing the last side poles.*]

FITZPATRICK: The lucky couple are on their travels, then?

EWBANK: Aye. Aye, that's right ... Shan't see them again for a damn long time.

FITZPATRICK: A doctor ...

EWBANK: Aye.

FITZPATRICK: The medical profession. It's a fine thing, to have a vocation in life.

EWBANK: And what's one of them when you've got it at home?

FITZPATRICK: Why, I'd say Kay, here, was a vocated man.

MARSHALL: That's right.

FITZPATRICK: An air of dedication.

EWBANK: Dedication ... He knows which side his bread's buttered on. Isn't that right, Kay? So's all the rest of them, an' all.

FITZPATRICK: Aye. We're all pragmatists at heart.

EWBANK: Pragmatists, is it? Bone bloody idle. There's nobody else round here'd employ any one of you as far as I can make out.

MARSHALL: Ah, now. That's a fact ...

FITZPATRICK: The debris of society ... That's us.

EWBANK: Watch that bloody lacing ...

[MARSHALL *and* GLENDENNING *are lacing the bag of walling;* BENNETT *goes to relieve* GLENDENNING.]

BENNETT: Here, let me have it ...

[*He and* MARSHALL *carry it out.* FITZPATRICK *follows them, taking side poles;* GLENDENNING, *after glancing round, goes out after them.*

PAUL *has come in as the last of the work is being done; now he comes down the tent, casual. He wears a coat.*]

PAUL: Well, then, I'm off.

EWBANK: By God, then ... Look at this.

PAUL: All up ... all finished.

KAY: Just about.

EWBANK: Crawled out of his bloody hole ... [*To* KAY, *who's now taking off the quarter guys*] Seen him last night ... wouldn't believe it ... Comes up here, you know, for the bloody booze ... nowt else ...

PAUL: That's it. Just about.

EWBANK: By God. Nomads, Kay, that's us ... Tenting ... First tent I ever had, you know, caught fire ... went up ... should have seen it ... Went up ... [*Pauses, abstracted.*] Off, then, are you?

PAUL: That's right.

EWBANK: Aye ... [*Gazes at him.*] Back up, I suppose, when you need some money.

PAUL: Manage by meself.

EWBANK: Aye ... Still to see it.

PAUL: Alus a first time.

EWBANK: Aye ... can just imagine.

PAUL: Well, then ...

    [*Pause, gazing over at one another.*

        FITZPATRICK *comes in, followed by the others.* GLENDENNING *carries a little sack with which he goes round, picking up litter from the grass.*]

FITZPATRICK: So you're leaving us behind.

PAUL: Aye. That's right.

FITZPATRICK: A wandering spirit. I know the feeling well ...

PAUL [*laughs*]: I can imagine.

FITZPATRICK: Aye. I'm a born traveller. Circumstances alone conspire against it.

MARSHALL: On the Dublin to Liverpool express.

    [*They laugh.*]

FITZPATRICK [*to* BENNETT]: Being a single man, I know the temptations very well.

MARSHALL: You don't know where you're off to, then?

PAUL: Oh ... [*Shrugs.*]

FITZPATRICK: I'll give you one piece of sound advice.

    [PAUL *looks up.*]

For nothing now. If you're ever tempted, at any time, to marry ...

MARSHALL: Don't.

FITZPATRICK: Not until you're far too old.

MARSHALL: Not until you're far too old.

PAUL: I'll try and remember that ... Good-bye, Glenny.

GLENDENNING: I ... I ... I ... Aye! [*Nods his head.*]

PAUL: See you some time.

GLENDENNING: Aye!

PAUL: Well, then ... [*Looks over at* EWBANK.]

EWBANK: Aye. I'll walk with you to the house . . . [*To* KAY] When you let it down keep it clean. No bits and pieces . . .

KAY: Right . . .

[EWBANK *goes with* PAUL, *who waves to the others and they call out as he goes.*]

FITZPATRICK: They had a great time then, last night.

MARSHALL: Aye. You can tell it by his manner.

[*They laugh.*]

FITZPATRICK: It's a great feeling. [*Stretches.*]

MARSHALL: What's that?

FITZPATRICK: To feel reinstated.

[MARSHALL *laughs.*]

KAY: You can get the rest of this out now . . . [*Indicating remaining flooring*] And start loading the truck.

FITZPATRICK: Aye, aye, sir! [*To* MARSHALL] See that?

MARSHALL: It's a great man who knows his place.

FITZPATRICK: You're right, Marshy. It is that.

[*They take out the last side poles, and any remaining pieces.*

KAY *and* BENNETT *work alone, untying the laced edges of the canvas, prior to taking it down. The edges of the canvas are supported now only by the four corner side poles.*

BENNETT, *aware suddenly that he and* KAY *are alone, wanders over to the view of the valley.*]

BENNETT: It's amazing, isn't it. The number of chimneys they can put into a place the size of that.

KAY [*unlacing canvas*]: Aye.

BENNETT: They'll soon be gone.

KAY: What's that?

BENNETT: Central heating. They don't need chimneys, you know, for that.

KAY: Aye.

BENNETT: Just roofs you'll see.

KAY: And aerials.

BENNETT: Aerials?

KAY: Television.

BENNETT: Oh, aye . . . You can just see a car. Going up the other side. Sun shining on its window . . . Look . . . Gone.

KAY: I shouldn't let Fitzpatrick worry you.

BENNETT: No.

KAY: Gets under your skin. [*Watching him.*]

BENNETT: Aye ... Well, I suppose you have to laugh.

KAY: Aye. [*Nods.*]

BENNETT: The thing is ... I suppose one day, I'll bloody kill him.

KAY: Aye.

> [*They laugh.*
>   *The others start coming back.*]

KAY [*as* FITZPATRICK *and* MARSHALL *come in*]: Right, then. Let's have it down.

> [*They go to the poles,* FITZPATRICK *rubbing his hands, spitting on them.*]

FITZPATRICK: Nice to know, now, that we're speaking.

MARSHALL: Ah, Kay's not the one to hold a grudge ... A spot in jail would do us all the world of good.

FITZPATRICK [*fingering canvas*]: Damn fine stuff ...

> [*They take the ropes.*]

FITZPATRICK: Easy come. Easy go.

MARSHALL [*lowering rope*]: Benny, now: his old man ...

> [FITZPATRICK *and* MARSHALL *laugh.*]

ALL: Ready!

KAY: Right, then ... Let's have it down.

> [*They've taken the ropes holding the canvas, and take the ends outside the tent, at each of the 'quarters'. At* KAY's *signal they release the hitches holding the ropes at the foot of the poles and the canvas slowly descends. As it comes down they rip the lacing, working towards the centre poles, separating the three pieces of canvas.*
>   *Then, as the men unshackle the canvas:*]

GLENDENNING: I ... I ... I ... If I had a ... had a ... had a ... had a son ...

FITZPATRICK: Aye? Aye? What's that?

GLENDENNING: If I ... I ... I ... I ... had a lad I w ... w ... w ... wouldn't have him w ... w ... w ... wandering off.

BENNETT: What's that, Glenny?

GLENDENNING: I ... I ... I ... I ... I ...

MARSHALL [*sings*]: Ay, yi, yi, yi ... Ay, yi, yi, yi ...

GLENDENNING: I'd have him a ... a ... a ... at home.

FITZPATRICK: At home, would you?

GLENDENNING: W ... w ... w ... w ... working.

FITZPATRICK: Aye, well, lad. That day might come.

MARSHALL: Son and daughter, Glenny.

GLENDENNING: Aye!

FITZPATRICK: Though there's one thing, Glenny.

GLENDENNING: Aye!

FITZPATRICK: You'll have to stop 'em eating.

MARSHALL: Meal-times, now, and nothing else.

GLENDENNING: Aye!

[*The men have unshackled the canvas and now begin to fold it.*]

MARSHALL: A big fat cream bun, now ...

FITZPATRICK: Once every Christmas.

GLENDENNING: Aye!

MARSHALL: And the odd kiss at bedtime, Glenny, for the wife. [*Winking*]

GLENDENNING: Aye! [*Laughs, pleased.*]

FITZPATRICK: He'd make somebody a good husband would Glenny.

GLENDENNING: Aye!

MARSHALL: Either that, now, or a damn fine wife.

[*They laugh.*]

FITZPATRICK: I read in the paper once about this place where all the women live together ...

MARSHALL: I can just imagine that. I can ...

FITZPATRICK: And all the men in another place entirely ...

MARSHALL: And they pass over there ...

FITZPATRICK: That's right ...

MARSHALL: At night.

[*They laugh, wrapping the canvas.*]

FITZPATRICK: Had families like you have chickens ...

MARSHALL: Broilers ...

FITZPATRICK: Or those cows that never see the light.

MARSHALL: And all the man had to do was his day's work. The rest of the time was all his own.

KAY: Suit one or two people I could mention.

BENNETT: Suit one or two people here. You're right.

[KAY *and* BENNETT *laugh.*]

MARSHALL: Bennett, on the other hand, of course, is a different case entirely.

FITZPATRICK: 'Tirely.

BENNETT [to FITZPATRICK]: Aye ... They'd create a special post for you.

KAY: One to lean up against, I'm thinking.

BENNETT: Aye. One to lean up against ... you're right.

[KAY and BENNETT laugh.]

FITZPATRICK: Hey ...

MARSHALL: Hey, now ...

FITZPATRICK: There's a provocation.

KAY: That's right ... [To BENNETT] Without a bloody doubt.

[KAY and BENNETT laugh.

Behind them EWBANK has come back with a bottle and several glasses on a tray, together with several small pieces of wedding cake.]

EWBANK: Here, now. You've not finished. Get it off, now, and we'll have a drop of this ... Glenny. Fetch us in a table.

GLENDENNING: Aye! [He goes off.]

[FITZPATRICK and MARSHALL exchange looks; the men have begun to bag the canvas and lace it in the bags.]

KAY: What about the poles, now? [Looking up]

EWBANK: Leave them now for the other truck. They'll never fit on this one ... Now go damn careful with that. [Indicating canvas] By God, that was bloody quick.

[GLENDENNING has gone out and come back in with a white metalwork table.]

EWBANK: Mention food and you can't see him for dust.

MARSHALL: He's smelled that cake.

FITZPATRICK: He has.

EWBANK: Now off, lad. Let's see you working. It won't run away, don't worry. [He puts the tray on the table.] It'll still be here when you've finished.

BENNETT: It's a lovely view you have here, Mr Ewbank.

EWBANK: Aye. And it costs a tidy drop, an' all.

BENNETT: I never thought of that ... [Looking towards the house.]

EWBANK: There's no compensation, I can tell you, for being saddled with a lot of brass.

MARSHALL: Aye. Those of us without it have a great job remembering.

EWBANK: You're a damn sight better off without ... Ask Kay. He'll tell you. [*They laugh.*]

FITZPATRICK: Aye. Aye. We could ask him that.

BENNETT: Your lad's gone then, Mr Ewbank, on his travels?

EWBANK: Aye ... He has. His mother's wept bloody buckets. I don't know why. He'll be back again tomorrow.

FITZPATRICK: It's a great thing to have. The spirit of adventure.

EWBANK: There's only one spirit that I know of and you don't have to travel far for that.

[*They laugh.* EWBANK *remains impassive.*]

KAY: Come on, Fitzpatrick. Let's have a bit of carrying ...

EWBANK: Aye. Let's tidy up the lawn.

[*They carry the canvas out.*

GLENDENNING *returns with his bag and wanders round the lawn, picking up the pieces of paper streamers.*]

KAY: Well, then. I think that should do it.

EWBANK: Aye ... [*Looks round.*] Left a few damn marks.

KAY: I suppose it has to be reckoned.

EWBANK: Aye ... You pay a price for everything, Kay. Best not to look, then you never know whether you've got it, or you've gone without ... [*Calling off*] Put it straight, for Christ's sake. All that lot'll bloody well fall off. [*To* KAY] There's one thing, though ...

KAY: Aye?

EWBANK: Ah, well ... [*Uncertain for a moment. Then:*] I came out here, you know, this morning ... Saw it all ... Damn near broke my bloody heart ... You saw it. God. What a bloody mess ... Seen nowt like it. I haven't.

KAY: S'all made to be used.

EWBANK: Aye. You're right. Doesn't bear much reckoning. Best get on with it while you can.

KAY: Aye. [*Laughs.*]

EWBANK: Did you see much of my son?

KAY: No ... Not much.

EWBANK: What do you reckon to it, then? Do you know, I've lived all this time – and I know nowt about anything. Least ways, I've settled that. I've come to that conclusion. [*He laughs. Shakes his head.*] A bloody wanderer.

KAY [*watches him. Then*]: Your lad?

EWBANK: I've no idea at all. None. Do you know? ... Where he's off to. I don't think he has himself. His mother sits at home ... [*Shakes his head.*] The modern world, Kay. It's left you and me behind.

KAY: Aye. Well. It can't be helped.

[*They are silent a moment. Then:*]

EWBANK: Pathetic. [*He looks round.*] A lot of bloody misfits. You could put us all into a string bag, you know, and chuck us all away, and none'd be the wiser.

KAY [*laughs*]: Aye. I think you're right.

EWBANK: Aye. [*Laughs.*] Sunk without trace.

[MARSHALL *comes in, rubbing his hands.*]

MARSHALL: Ay, now. That's just the stuff you want ... [*To* GLENDENNING] Tickle your bloody tonsils.

GLENDENNING: Aye!

[*Follows* MARSHALL *over to the table.* BENNETT *also comes in.*]

EWBANK: Never changes. Tell 'em there's summat here needs shifting and you'll be bloody hollering all day long. Show 'em half a bottle and they'll knock you over where you stand.

KAY: Aye! [*He nods and laughs.*]

MARSHALL: Had a drop of this before we started and we'd have been over in half the time.

EWBANK: Aye. I know. Over the lawn, more likely. Stretched out, flat on your back. [*He's pouring a liberal portion into each glass.*]

FITZPATRICK [*coming in*]: A lot of holes you have in here ... [*Looking round*]

EWBANK: Aye. Well. It'll grow again. Come today. Gone tomorrow.

BENNETT: Everything in its season.

EWBANK: Aye. That's right ...

BENNETT: This time next year ...

MARSHALL: Bloody philosopher.

BENNETT: I had a lawn of my own once ... [*Pauses.*]

EWBANK: Here you are, then. Hand it round ...

[*They pass round the glasses and* EWBANK *holds out the plate with the cake.*]

FITZPATRICK: Nay, Glenny, lad ... This isn't for you.

MARSHALL: Make your ears drop off.

FITZPATRICK: Your tongue drop out.

MARSHALL: Black hairs sprout up all over.

GLENDENNING: Aye! [*Takes his glass.*]
    [*They laugh.*]

KAY: Here's to your good health, then.

MARSHALL: And the happy couple.

BENNETT: Aye, and the happy couple.

FITZPATRICK: And to ought else now that you have in mind. [*They laugh. Drink.*]

MARSHALL: By God. But that's a mighty drop of stuff.

FITZPATRICK: That'll curl your bloody whiskers.

BENNETT: Aye!

FITZPATRICK: Still all there, Glenny, are they?
    [*They laugh.*]

GLENDENNING: Aye!

MARSHALL: You better count them. We don't want you leaving, now, without.

GLENDENNING: Aye!

FITZPATRICK: He's a damn fine lad. [*Arm round* GLENDENNING'*s shoulder*]

MARSHALL: He is. He is. You're right.

BENNETT: And that's a lovely drop of cake, too, to go with it.

KAY: It is. It's very good.

GLENDENNING: I ... I ... I ... I ... I ...

FITZPATRICK: He's after another.
    [*They laugh.*]

EWBANK: Nay, lad. That'll have to do you.

KAY [*putting down his glass*]: Right, then. We better be getting off.

EWBANK: Aye. I'll be down to the yard later ... Make sure you've packed that load right, Kay.

KAY: Aye ... [*He goes.*]

EWBANK: Drive carefully. Drop nowt off.

FITZPATRICK [*setting down his glass with* BENNETT]: Ah, that was a damn fine drop. I won't say that I couldn't stand another ... But then, work's work.

EWBANK: Aye. And don't you forget it.

    [FITZPATRICK *goes*.]

MARSHALL: See you at the yard ... [*Sets down his glass*.]

EWBANK: Aye. Aye. That's right.

BENNETT: Thanks again, Mr Ewbank ...

EWBANK: ... nothing of it.

    [BENNETT *goes with a nod*.]

  Go on, Glenny. Get off, or they'll leave you here behind.

GLENDENNING: Aye!

EWBANK: Sithee. I've a bit extra for you. [*Takes a bit of cake from his pocket*.] E't it now when they're not looking, or they'll have it off you.

GLENDENNING: Aye!

EWBANK: Right, then. Off you go.

    [GLENDENNING *goes, eating.*

      EWBANK *is left alone.*]

FITZPATRICK [*off*]: Come on. Come on, now. My turn in the cab.

KAY [*off*]: On the back, Fitzpatrick.

FITZPATRICK [*off*]: Good God.

MARSHALL [*off*]: He'll be blown away.

BENNETT [*off*]: Some hopes of that.

MARSHALL [*off*]: Ay, now. There's no room for me up there.

KAY [*off*]: Are you right, then, Glenny ... ?

GLENDENNING [*off*]: Aye!

FITZPATRICK [*off*]: Here he is. He's here.

MARSHALL [*off: sings*]: Ay, yi, yi, yi ... Ay, yi, yi, yi ...

    [*Laughter. Dies away.*

     Silence.

      EWBANK *stands alone, gazing out from between the poles. Fastens the ropes hanging from the pulleys, almost absent-mindedly, abstracted. He gazes at view again.*

      After a while, MRS EWBANK *comes on. Silent a moment, looking round*.]

MRS EWBANK: They've gone, then.

EWBANK [*doesn't look up*]: Aye.

MRS EWBANK [*pause*]: You get used to the noise around you after a while.

EWBANK: Aye. You do.

[MRS EWBANK *gazes across at the view.*]

MRS EWBANK: Your mother and dad are leaving in a few minutes.

EWBANK: I'll come and see them off.

MRS EWBANK: He's lost his bit of rope.

EWBANK: I'll cut him off a bit. He'll never know the difference.

MRS EWBANK: ... All that smoke ... Like a carpet ... They had a drink, then.

EWBANK: Aye. Wet the baby's head ... [*Looks up at her expression.*] Well, I don't know, do I? These days ... one damn thing ...

[*Pause. Then:*]

Set an example there'll be no stopping. They'll be wanting a sup on every job from now on ... I don't know. [*Looks down at the view, standing beside her.*] You'd think you'd have something to show for it, wouldn't you. After all this time.

MRS EWBANK: Well, now ... [*Abstracted*]

EWBANK: I don't know ... [*Looks round. Then down at the lawn.*] Made a few marks in that.

MRS EWBANK: One or two ...

EWBANK [*shivers. Looks up*]: Autumn ...

MRS EWBANK [*abstracted*]: Still ... It's been a good summer.

EWBANK: Aye. Comes and goes.

MRS EWBANK: What ... ?

[*Pause.*]

EWBANK: Do you know that Kay was had up once for embezzlement?

MRS EWBANK: They've been had up for a lot of things. The men that work for you.

EWBANK: Aye ... Nobody else'll have 'em ... I must be bloody daft. Well. I suppose we better see the old uns off.

MRS EWBANK: Yes ...

EWBANK: I don't know ... What's to become of us, you reckon?

[MRS EWBANK *looks at him, smiles, then shakes her head.*]

Never do this again, you know.

MRS EWBANK: No ... [*She smiles.*]

EWBANK: Me heart wouldn't stand it.

MRS EWBANK: No ... [*She laughs.*]

OLD MRS E. [*off*]: Frank ... !

EWBANK: Aye, well. [*Half-laughs.*] That's summat.

    [*They turn slowly, arm in arm.*]

OLD MRS E. [*off*]: Frank ... !

EWBANK: S'all right. We're coming. [*To* MRS EWBANK] Well, then.
  We better go.

    [*They go.*

    The stage stands empty: bare poles, the ropes fastened off. The light
    fades slowly.

    Curtain.]

THE RESTORATION OF
ARNOLD MIDDLETON

THE RESTORATION OF ARNOLD MIDDLETON

First produced at the Traverse Theatre, Edinburgh, on 22 November 1966, under the direction of Gordon McDougall. The cast was as follows:

MRS EDIE ELLIS	June Watson
JOAN MIDDLETON	Marian Diamond
ARNOLD MIDDLETON	David Collings
JEFFREY HANSON	Paul Williamson
SHEILA O'CONNOR	Ann Holloway
MAUREEN WILKINSON	Rosemary McHale

Subsequently produced at the Royal Court Theatre, London, on 4 July 1967, under the direction of Robert Kidd. The cast was as follows:

MRS EDIE ELLIS	Noel Dyson
JOAN MIDDLETON	Eileen Atkins
ARNOLD MIDDLETON	John Shepherd
JEFFREY HANSON	Tenniel Evans
SHEILA O'CONNOR	Gillian Hills
MAUREEN WILKINSON	Andree Evans

CHARACTERS

MRS EDIE ELLIS
JOAN MIDDLETON
ARNOLD MIDDLETON
JEFFREY HANSON
SHEILA O'CONNOR
MAUREEN WILKINSON

ACT ONE

Scene One

A cosy, well-furnished, scrupulously clean living-room, equipped with dining table and chairs as well as a three-piece suite and sideboard.

Arranged round the room, on the walls and furniture, are various objects, mounted and in excellent state of preservation: a stuffed eagle, a sword, a ship, a model aeroplane, a model engine, etc., which may suggest the rudiments of a museum, but bereft of any specific human connotation. Over the mantelpiece hangs a Lee-Enfield rifle.

The centre of the room is dominated by a full-size suit of armour, standing in a pile of brown paper and string from which it has just emerged. A two-handed sword runs down from its hands.

Regarding this object with a mixture of amazement and distaste are two women: JOAN, *an attractive, good-humoured if tenacious-looking woman in her early thirties, and* MRS ELLIS, *her mother, a rather unconsciously sensual woman in her late fifties. Like her daughter, she is neatly and prettily dressed. They are also both wearing pinafores:* JOAN's *full,* MRS ELLIS's *petite and frilly and fastened around her waist.*

JOAN *has a label in her hand.*

MRS ELLIS: Well ...

They must have sent it here by mistake.

JOAN [*glancing at the label*]: It's the right address.

MRS ELLIS: But it should have gone to the school, surely? That's where he has all the others.

JOAN: The man said that he'd asked for it to be delivered here.

MRS ELLIS: Here? But why here? We've nowhere to keep it here. Whoever would want a thing like that in their house?

JOAN: Perhaps it's his idea of a joke. [*She looks round the room.*] At this rate we shan't be here at all soon.

MRS ELLIS: He must *mean* it to go to the school, Joan. Eventually. That's where all the others are. And he's had it sent here so we can see it.

JOAN: Well, it's strange if he has, because it's the only one I've seen. Queen Elizabeth, George V and all the rest. I'm the only person who hasn't been allowed in. 'Some other time. Some other time.' While any school child can go in and out as he pleases.

MRS ELLIS: I'm sure that's where this will end up. The history museum. Just you see.

JOAN: Clean the paper up, mother, will you? I'll put his tea on. [*Goes through into the kitchen; she treats her mother strictly, as she would a servant.*]

MRS ELLIS [*clearing up*]: Well, it's a surprise, and no mistake.

JOAN [*calling through*]: Have you got all the string? I don't want bits left lying about.

MRS ELLIS [*looking up at the armour as she stoops*]: Of course . . . it's as you say. His idea of a joke. [*She laughs uneasily.*]

JOAN [*reappearing with the teatray to set the table*]: Or an insult.

MRS ELLIS: Insult? It needs time to sink in. I can see now . . .

JOAN: Could you put it all in the kitchen. There's a piece of string.

[MRS ELLIS, *her arms full of brown paper, stoops down, retrieves the last morsel of string, and carries her load into the kitchen.*

JOAN *is setting the table: as she goes to the sideboard during this conversation to get the tablecloth she passes the armour one way, then changes her mind and goes the other, as though it were a person to be avoided.*]

MRS ELLIS [*calling through*]: Of course, if you were really stuck for somewhere to put it, you could keep it in the bedroom.

JOAN: In the bedroom!

MRS ELLIS [*calling through*]: No one would see it, would they?

JOAN: No one?

MRS ELLIS: Not in the bedroom.

JOAN: What about me?

MRS ELLIS [*reappearing*]: Well. I'm sure I don't want to quarrel about it.

JOAN [*lightly*]: Well, then, at least I'm glad of that.

MRS ELLIS: I do live here as well, Joan.

JOAN [*disregarding*]: Could you do the bread? [*Checks her watch with the clock.*] He'll have forgotten altogether that we're going out tonight.

MRS ELLIS: You're so inconsiderate, Joan.

JOAN: It would be different, wouldn't it, if he ever showed any interest in them. But he spreads them all over the place then never looks at them again. Accidentally move one and he comes down on you as though it were the house you'd shifted.

MRS ELLIS: Why can't you let it rest? He doesn't give you anything else to grumble about. You can't complain about him. Not really.

JOAN: He's never out of the damned house. [*She picks up one or two of the pieces.*] He puts on his coat, goes out to school, and leaves them like this. They're like spies. He never lets you rest. Everywhere you look there's some part of him watching and waiting. Even in the bathroom . . .

MRS ELLIS: It's just you, Joan, that.

JOAN: Two slices. That's enough. Well, it's not staying there.

MRS ELLIS: Where are you going to put it?

JOAN: Don't just stand there. [*She's taken hold of it, leaning it back, and with* MRS ELLIS *she drags it over to a built-in cupboard near the kitchen door.*] In the cupboard.

MRS ELLIS: In the cupboard! Do you think we should?

JOAN: It's obscene. Something like this in the house. It makes you feel terrible just to touch it . . . These houses weren't built for things like this. Mother: will you open the door?

[*They put it in the cupboard and* JOAN *hands out a few brushes, mops and an umbrella which she gives to* MRS ELLIS *before shutting the cupboard doors on the armour.*]

Put those in the kitchen, will you?

MRS ELLIS: Are you going to hide it from him?

JOAN: It'll do for now.

Why did he have to have it here? Aren't there enough people here already?

[MRS ELLIS *has gone to the kitchen.*

JOAN *goes to the door to talk in at her, instructionally.*]

No, in the cupboard, mother. There's his mother and father coming in two days' time. Can you imagine what *they* are going to think?

MRS ELLIS [*re-emerging*]: They'll hardly complain, Joan.

JOAN: Coming to somebody's house only to find out as you step through the door it's a museum. It's not a home it's an institution.

MRS ELLIS: They've never seen *either* of you all these years. They're hardly in a position to judge anybody.

JOAN: But that's just what they will do. They're just about total strangers, aren't they? Come to that, it's just as well they are.

MRS ELLIS: I don't know . . .

[JOAN *turns restlessly about the room*, MRS ELLIS *watching her concernedly*.]

If only you had something.

JOAN [*beginning to re-arrange the tea-table already scrupulously prepared by both of them*]: Had something what?

MRS ELLIS: An interest.

JOAN: Interest! I have an interest.

MRS ELLIS: You could go out to work, get a job. You're qualified to do any number of things.

JOAN: This is my house.

MRS ELLIS: I know it's your house, Joan.

JOAN: And it takes some looking after.

[MRS ELLIS *doesn't answer*.]

I run this as I want it.

MRS ELLIS: All I'm saying is I could run the house while you do something else.

[JOAN *sits down:* MRS ELLIS *begins to re-arrange the table now*.]

And there would be so much more coming in.

JOAN: And your widow's pension.

MRS ELLIS: I don't just mean money. But all those opportunities for other interests as well.

JOAN: You think, then, we'd all be better off if we each had an interest?

MRS ELLIS: What's life for if you can't have an interest?

JOAN [*examines her mother shrewdly*]: You know, mother, you're too much like me.

MRS ELLIS: People can laugh at interests, but it's like religion. He who laughs . . .

JOAN [*shouting*]: We've got an interest here already! *His!* It's scattered in every cranny of this building. You can't sit down without finding a stone 'with an interesting mark' on it, or a bit of wood that fell off Noah's ark, or a rotten old nail that dropped out of somebody's rotten old chariot. And just look at that thing. Standing behind that cupboard door listening to every word I say. It's not fair. It's not fair.

MRS ELLIS: Joan, I do my work here.

[*They are silent a moment. Then, contemplative:*]

JOAN: Do you remember once when you bought him a little statue – a man's head and shoulders? God only knows where his body had got to. And he accidentally knocked it off the sideboard and broke it?

MRS ELLIS: He was more concerned with my feelings than with the thing.

JOAN: He wanted to get rid of it.

MRS ELLIS: He did not.

JOAN: He wanted to get rid of it. It was the only thing that resembled a human being in the entire house.

MRS ELLIS: You've never understood him, Joan. You never have.

JOAN: And now he brings this thing. There's something strange about it. It's the first life-like thing he's ever had here. He usually keeps them all at school. [*She gets up.*]

MRS ELLIS: Joan. You don't understand my position here.

[JOAN *begins preparations to go out.*]

Where are you going?

JOAN: Out. [*She goes to the door leading to the hall.*]

MRS ELLIS [*alone*]: If you're hoping to go to the cinema you'll have to leave almost as soon as he comes in ... He'll be back any time now.

JOAN [*calling through*]: I won't be long. [*She enters with a coat she puts on over her pinafore.*] He's not going to find me waiting here, that's all.

MRS ELLIS: Waiting here?

JOAN: Stuck here amongst his trophies.

[MRS ELLIS *watches* JOAN *make up her face in the mirror.*]

I'll go down to the corner, or something.

MRS ELLIS: It's ridiculous.

JOAN [*turning to her*]: I'll go out the back way, then there's no chance of meeting.

MRS ELLIS: Joan. This is silly. [*Suddenly, looking at the cupboard*] You won't be long, will you, Joan?

JOAN: Don't mention *that* until I come in. [*She indicates the cupboard.*] Do you understand?

MRS ELLIS: Yes. But ...

JOAN: And for God's sake don't say I've just gone out. Say I've been gone an hour. All right? [*She leaves by the kitchen door.*]

MRS ELLIS: You won't be long, love, will you?

[MRS ELLIS *glances at the cupboard again, then goes to the table, fingers and re-arranges the various tea-things, then moves uncertainly about the room, avoiding the cupboard area completely. Finally she comes face to face with the mirror, glances at it, then becomes increasingly interested in her reflection. She begins to examine her face, its various expressions of hope and dismay, glee and uncertainty, unconsciously producing animal noises, purring and cooing. She becomes lost in herself; her body heaves for a sigh, then suddenly relaxes in a huge, vaguely grotesque smile.*

ARNIE, *a well-built man in his thirties, has appeared in the hall doorway. He watches awhile, expressionless, then comes quietly into the room until he is almost behind* MRS ELLIS. *Then he suddenly barks like a dog.*

MRS ELLIS *gives a scream of fright. Then:*]

MRS ELLIS: Oh, Arnie! Arnie!

ARNIE: Loved one!

MRS ELLIS [*recovering*]: It's just what you'd expect from a schoolmaster.

ARNIE [*Takes off his old raincoat.*]

Master, Edie. Master. Watch this, Edie. [*Using his coat as a whip he begins to beat the floor.*

MRS ELLIS *watches this with interest and pleasure, yet as though she's seen it all before. She sits down at the table to watch.*]

Take that. And that. And that – you sniffling snot-gobbling little crat. And *that*. I'll teach you to take my stick of chalk. [*He growls and roars as he drives the imaginary child into the floor. He steps on the spot and spreads the remnants thoroughly over the carpet.*] Got it! Got it! Now. How do you like that, Edie? I know how to take care of these little crats.

MRS ELLIS: I don't know. It's a wonder any of them stay alive.

ARNIE: Know? Edie! You know. You know everything.

MRS ELLIS [*pleased*]: What! Me!

ARNIE: You.

MRS ELLIS: More than a schoolteacher?

ARNIE: Yes.

MRS ELLIS: Well ... I don't know ... [*She holds her cheek with pleasure.*

   ARNIE *watches her, suddenly intent. Then:*]

ARNIE: Look ... [*His mood relaxes again.*] Did you see his face? The way he looked when I hit him the first time. He thought I didn't mean it. He thought I'd *let him off* for taking my stick of chalk. Mind you – he'd every reason to think I wouldn't beat his lousy head in. These *dwarfs* think you're frightened of being reprimanded, of being handed over to the ...

MRS ELLIS: And will you get the sack?

ARNIE: No such fortune for me. [*He sits down and begins to tug off his shoes. His mood changes again. Reflective.*] If I rape two, or perhaps it may have to be three, I might be asked if I'd mind being moved to another school. But chances of promotion like that are increasingly rare. [*He gets his last shoe off with a struggle.*] Rape apart, it's all a question of dead men's shoes, Edie.

MRS ELLIS [*concernedly*]: I wish you wouldn't use language like that, Arnie.

ARNIE [*holding up his shoes*]: Ill-will; that's the cargo these shoes carry. Along, that is, with my own personal misfortunes. [*He searches round, sees* MRS ELLIS'*s feet and, on hands and knees, crawls across to them as though they were shoes he was hunting.*] Why ... Why, these are full of hopes.

MRS ELLIS: Oh, now ...

ARNIE: Can't you feel them: growing beneath your feet? Why, Edie, your shoes are full of hope. It's sprouting through your toes ...

MRS ELLIS: All I feel is how glad I am I didn't know what teachers were like when our Joan went to school.

ARNIE: Where is SHE, by the way? Not gone off on my bike, her dress tucked into her bloomers.

MRS ELLIS: Really, Arnie ... She's just gone out. I mean, *merely* gone out.

ARNIE: Merely gone out?

MRS ELLIS: She's only gone out. That's what I mean.

ARNIE: Only gone out. Not merely gone out.

MRS ELLIS: She's ... out.

ARNIE: I see.

MRS ELLIS: Your tea's on the table.

ARNIE: We're supposed to be going to the cinema. Let me see. [*Consults his wrist-watch.*] Half an hour ago.

MRS ELLIS: She'll only be a few minutes ... [*Hurries into the kitchen.*]

ARNIE [*knowingly and quickly searching the room*]: It all seems carefully timed. What's going on?

MRS ELLIS [*calling through*]: She's so restless. She can't sit down two minutes these days without getting up again because there's something not satisfactory. I don't know ... it's just everything.

[ARNIE *turns at this and goes to the table. He sits down and begins to put some jam on the bread.*]

MRS ELLIS [*calling through*]: How's your play going at school?

[ARNIE *plays with the bread abstractedly.*

MRS ELLIS *reappears in the kitchen door with a teapot.*]

You. Can't you hear me when I talk to you?

ARNIE: What's that, chump-chops?

MRS ELLIS: None of your cheek. Haven't you been rehearsing this afternoon?

[ARNIE *breaks his mood to give a dramatic recitation.*]

ARNIE: Said Robin Hood to Friar Tuck,
      'How are you my fat fellow?'
      'I'm very well,' said the cheerful monk,
      'But I'm sorry you're looking yellow.'

      'Is that a jest or would you dare
      To challenge your captain staunch?'
      'Nay,' said the Friar, 'don't threaten me,
      Or I'll kill you with my paunch.'

MRS ELLIS [*giggles*]: Is that it?

ARNIE: A generous portion of it, Edie. On the whole, I think it will appear neither conspicuous nor insignificant on the contemporary theatrical scene.

MRS ELLIS [*pouring his tea*]: Is it going very well?

ARNIE: A minor alarm this morning when the Lionheart tripped over his scabbard. He'll appear on stage with a bandage round his leg – a wound sustained, while fighting the Turks outside Damascus.

MRS ELLIS: They're only boys. What are you calling the play?

ARNIE: I don't know. [*Thoughtfully*] 'Hands up, Sheriff, your Money or your Wife.'

MRS ELLIS: Oh, now.

ARNIE: 'The Good King Richard and the Bad King John!' Probably, 'Robin Hood and His Merry Men', Edie.

MRS ELLIS: Oh, that's nice. [MRS ELLIS *sits down opposite* ARNIE *and watches him eat his tea.*] And is it adapted from William Shakespeare, then?

ARNIE: No. Jeffrey Hanson. He's the head of the English Department. He's coming round tomorrow evening to discuss the less serious aspects of the play. So that'll be tea for two, Edie.

MRS ELLIS: Oh, I'll be out late tomorrow, getting things in. [*Silence.*] Are you looking forward to them coming? Are you listening?

ARNIE: Yes.

MRS ELLIS: What are they like?

ARNIE: Who?

MRS ELLIS: You know. Silly.

ARNIE: Oh. [*Dismisses it.*]

MRS ELLIS: Of course, I only met them that once at the wedding. Ten years. [*She broods.*] It's not often you meet decent people nowadays. [*Suddenly*] You complain that they never come to see you. Yet you've never been to see them.

ARNIE: No.

MRS ELLIS: Did you have a happy childhood, Arnie?

ARNIE: Did you?

MRS ELLIS [*laughs*]: No: I'm asking you. I bet you were a model child.

ARNIE [*pleasantly*]: I was. Facsimiles of me could be seen all over the place at one time, Edie.

[MRS ELLIS *becomes preoccupied with her thoughts, getting up and wandering round the room distractedly*.]

MRS ELLIS: You know, Arnie ...

[ARNIE *is getting out a pipe and looking round*.]

Joan. She's been in such a funny mood today.

207

ARNIE: Yes.

MRS ELLIS: You've stopped listening, haven't you?

ARNIE: I have not.

MRS ELLIS: She's been suggesting, you know ... that I wasn't much use to anyone.

ARNIE: You know, Edie, I've told you before. I'm not stepping in between your women's fights.

MRS ELLIS [*coming to the table*]: Do you want another cup?

ARNIE: Thanks.

[MRS ELLIS *pours a cup*. ARNIE *fusses with his pipe.*]

ARNIE: It would be nice to have a proper job and a decent home, wouldn't it?

MRS ELLIS: Arnie! You have a decent home. And it could be even better if you'd let me.

ARNIE: Better?

MRS ELLIS: Cleaner and neater.

ARNIE: Cleaner than this?

[*He stirs up his tea with milk and sugar*. MRS ELLIS *watches him acutely, the teapot still in her hand.*]

MRS ELLIS: In a way.

ARNIE: In a way! Why can't we ever hold a decent conversation in this house? I teach in a madhouse all day, then come home to another at night.

MRS ELLIS [*outraged*]: Arnie!

ARNIE: It's not right. You and Joan ... If you would only say what you meant. Just once.

MRS ELLIS: You don't begrudge me staying here, do you?

ARNIE: No.

MRS ELLIS: I could go away. I'm not so old ...

ARNIE: Edie. What are you talking about? [*He gets up from the table and moves about the room, apparently looking for matches.*]

MRS ELLIS: Fancy ... Do you remember that little statue I bought you once as a present? That was accidentally broken?

ARNIE: What? [*Taps out his pipe abstracted.*]

MRS ELLIS: Joan said – this afternoon – that you broke it deliberately. Because you didn't like it. And you hadn't the heart to tell me.

ARNIE: Now, look. I don't have to stand here and listen to all this,

Edie. You're a woman in your own right: you must stick up for yourself.

MRS ELLIS: I don't want to cause any bother. I don't. But Joan's always making me feel I haven't got anything at all ... nothing.

[*She's clearly upset.* ARNIE *watches her. Then crosses to her, and takes her shoulders.*]

ARNIE: I didn't break it on purpose, Edie. And it wasn't a statue. It was a piece of pottery made to look like stone. I appreciated you giving it to me. All right?

[*She looks into his eyes, then nods.*]

So there's no need to start an argument, is there?

MRS ELLIS: No.

[*The front door bangs, and* ARNIE *releases her.*]

ARNIE: Quick. Hide under the table and tickle her knees.

MRS ELLIS: Get on with you, you devil!

[*She's laughing as* JOAN *comes in: then goes to clear the table.*
ARNIE *has taken a comic from his pocket and propped it on the mantelpiece to read aloud.*
JOAN *looks at them both, then goes to the mirror and takes off her coat.*]

ARNIE: [*reading like a child*]: G .. g .. g .. gôoood ... ness g .. g .. g .. gra .. gra .. gracious! Ssss .. ssss .. ssssaid th .. th .. th .. the F .. Ffff .. Ffff ... Fairy Qu .. Qu .. Qu .. Queen ...

JOAN: That girl's followed you home from school again. I suppose you realize.

[ARNIE *goes casually to the window.*]

ARNIE: What?

JOAN: O'Connor. Isn't that her name?

ARNIE [*looking out*]: I don't know what I'd do without her. Always that faithful twenty-five yards behind ... Like a progressive following the revolution.

[MRS ELLIS *joins him to look out too.*]

JOAN: She moved smartly across the road when I came in. And no wonder.

MRS ELLIS: What does she hope to get out of it?

ARNIE: Some people do things, Edie, not for what they can get but for what they can give ...

JOAN: Oh, very nice. For two damn pins I'd go out there and give *her* something she *wouldn't* be grateful for!

[*As* ARNIE *turns from the window*]

And I thought we were going out tonight?

ARNIE: I'm ready when you are. I'll just finish this instalment then I'll be right with you.

JOAN: Is that a child's magazine?

ARNIE: It's all right. I didn't buy it. I stole it from a desk. [*He takes the comic and goes to the stairs: the sound of his feet ascending, then a door closing.*

JOAN *goes to the window.*]

JOAN: Has he seen that?

MRS ELLIS: No.

JOAN: Are you sure?

MRS ELLIS: I'm positive.

JOAN: What have you been crying about?

MRS ELLIS: I haven't been crying. [*She finishes clearing the table.*]

JOAN: It doesn't look like that.

MRS ELLIS: We were talking about his parents, if you must know.

JOAN: What about his parents?

MRS ELLIS: Nothing you would understand.

[JOAN *watches her intently. Then:*]

JOAN: I don't like this. I don't.

MRS ELLIS: What?

JOAN: This! *This!* [*She grabs and tugs at her mother's pinafore.*]

MRS ELLIS: What?

[JOAN *doesn't answer.*]

What's the matter with ...

JOAN: It's all wrong! [*She swings on the room. Neither can speak.*]

MRS ELLIS: I'll take mine off, then.

JOAN: Take *yours* off?

[MRS ELLIS *takes her apron off slowly: she lays the petite-looking thing absent-mindedly on* ARNIE's *raincoat on the chair.*]

Not there! Not there! [*She snatches it up and throws it on the floor.*]

MRS ELLIS: Joanie ...

JOAN: I don't like this. I don't.

MRS ELLIS: What is it, pet?

JOAN: Don't *pet* me.

MRS ELLIS: Joan ...

JOAN: You weren't talking about his parents. You were talking about *me*.

MRS ELLIS: Do you think we've nothing better ...

JOAN: Don't say *we*! You were talking about me. You were talking to him about me. Did you tell him ... did you say anything about that? [*She gestures at the cupboard.*]

MRS ELLIS: No.

[ARNIE's *feet are stamping down the stairs:* JOAN *goes to stand by the cupboard doors.*

ARNIE *comes in smoking a pipe. He begins to put on his shoes.*]

ARNIE: Well, ready?

JOAN: I have a surprise for you first.

ARNIE [*genially*]: Yes.

JOAN: Are you ready?

ARNIE: Yes ... Just a minute. Right.

JOAN: All right?

ARNIE: Yes.

[JOAN *swings open the cupboard doors.*]

JOAN: There.

ARNIE [*smokes on*]: Oh, that's where it is.

JOAN: How do you mean, that's where it is?

ARNIE: I couldn't imagine where you'd hidden it. It wasn't upstairs; I've just looked.

JOAN [*crying out at* MRS ELLIS]: You told him! You liar!

ARNIE: As a matter of fact, I asked the man to ring up the school and let me know when he delivered it.

JOAN: You *sneak*!

ARNIE: I'm not sneaking. I've been waiting for it to come.

JOAN: You rotten, bloody sneak. I've been walking around out there ...

ARNIE: Walking round?

JOAN: What's it doing here?

ARNIE: Walking round?

JOAN: What's it doing *here*?

ARNIE: Walking *round*?

JOAN: *What's it doing here?*

ARNIE: It looks to me as though it's standing in a cupboard. [*To armour*] Aren't you coming in, old man?

JOAN: I mean *here*! Here! At this house. You usually have all this junk thrown into your mausoleum at school.

ARNIE: But I didn't buy this with school funds.

JOAN: What?

[ARNIE *is smoking still.*]

ARNIE: It's mine. I bought it myself.

JOAN: Yours? [*Pause.*] What sort of tale is this, Arnold?

ARNIE: I've always wanted one. [*He puts his pipe in his mouth, and eases the armour out of the cupboard: he sets it upright in the room.*]

JOAN: When did you buy it?

ARNIE: What?

JOAN: When did you buy it?

ARNIE: A few days ago.

JOAN: Why? What for? Don't you think we've enough with this already?

ARNIE: You're very aggressive, Joan. Has it assaulted you or something behind my back?

JOAN: It's going back where it came from.

ARNIE: It even smokes a pipe. I told you it was respectable. I don't know. It might easily entertain political ambitions.

JOAN: I've tolerated everything else, Arnie. But not this.

[ARNIE *takes no notice: he's detaching the sword.*]

Can't you see? The place isn't built for a thing like this.

[ARNIE *leaps with a shout and swings the sword at* MRS ELLIS, *who escapes with a scream.*]

MRS ELLIS: Arnie!

[ARNIE *snorts at her.*]

JOAN: Where do you think you're going to keep it for one thing? In the garden?

MRS ELLIS [*standing behind a chair*]: Oh. We can't keep it there. [*Jumps.*] Joan! Everybody would see it.

JOAN: And I'm not having it in the kitchen, peering over my shoulder. And not in the bathroom, the bedroom, the living-room or the hall.

[ARNIE *stalks* MRS ELLIS: 'No, Arnie! No!']

ARNIE [*holding the blade to her*]: D'you think it's blood?

JOAN: It's not staying here, Arnie. It's ugly. That's enough!

ARNIE: Well. Are we ready? [*He fits the sword back into place.*]

JOAN: Ready?

ARNIE: To go out.

JOAN: Are we going out now? And leave this?

ARNIE: What do you want me to do? Hug it and give it a kiss? It won't run away. Well, Edie ... how about you then?

MRS ELLIS: Going out? I don't mind going out. Why, it's ages ...

JOAN: It's all right. [*She goes to her coat.*] Tomorrow, first thing: that's going.

ARNIE: Aren't you going to take your apron off?

JOAN: What?

ARNIE: Your how d'you do.

[*She sees she's still got on her pinafore.*]

ARNIE: Don't you want to come, Edie?

MRS ELLIS: Well ...

[JOAN *has almost wrenched off her pinafore and, watching her mother, pulls on her coat.*]

JOAN: She'll be quite all right at home.

MRS ELLIS: I wouldn't have minded going out. I don't really fancy being left alone with this, Arnie.

ARNIE: Get your coat, Granny, and away we go!

MRS ELLIS: Ay, now ...

[ARNIE *puts his arm round* JOAN *as* MRS ELLIS *gets her coat.*]

ARNIE: It's not half as bad as it seems.

JOAN: It's too much, Arnie, that's all. [*But she is appeased by his coaxing gestures.*] Stop playing around ...

ARNIE: O sing us a song, you hearty woman,
    Of all your dark crimes and your fears;
    And we'll swallow your pride and lie down by your side,
    And digest all your grief in our tears.

JOAN: Do you hear ...

[MRS ELLIS *has returned with her coat.*]

ARNIE: Ah, now, a gorgeous old lady of twenty-one ...

MRS ELLIS: Inches round the neck. I know.

213

ARNIE: Oh, now Edie. You enlargen yourself . . . [*He goes to help her with her coat.*]

MRS ELLIS: Oh, I know. Don't worry. I wasn't born yesterday.

ARNIE: If you insist.

MRS ELLIS: There you are, you see . . . And I ought to have done my face.

ARNIE: Only a disservice, my dear.

MRS ELLIS: Goodness. What's got into him?

[ARNIE *takes her hand.*]

ARNIE: Pray take advantage of my goodwill:
        Let us share it between the two;
        Take all you can and in return
        I'll do the same for you.

JOAN: Come on, we better be going out before he breaks into song.

ARNIE: A moment. [*He sidles with exaggerated caution to the window, carefully lifts the curtain, and looks out.*] The coast's clear. [*To* JOAN] Your glance spoke as eloquently as your thoughts, my dear. Her loyalty knew no bounds – and now you've presented it with several.

JOAN: At least we can go out now, without being molested.

ARNIE: You always could. It's me who is the loser. [*He puts his arm about the two women. As they go out:*]
        Gay Robin Hood to town did ride
        With maidens fair on either side:
        The evil Sheriff and the bad King John
        Ne'er recognized the gentlemon.

[JOAN *waits patiently.*]

ARNIE [*hesitates*]: . . . Yes. [*He sweeps them out of the room. A moment later, however, he dashes back in, knocks his pipe out on the armour, boxes it briefly, pats it, then hurries out.*
His voice is heard crying with pleasure, then a door crashes to, and it's silent.]

[*The room slowly darkens.*]

Scene Two

The door bursts open, there's giggling and laughter: then MRS ELLIS *and* ARNIE *enter, followed a moment later by* JOAN.

ARNIE: We should ... we should ... we should ...

MRS ELLIS: But we didn't. [*She breaks into outrageous laughter.*]

ARNIE: But we should have!

JOAN: We'd have been home a damn sight sooner if we had. Weee! [*She throws her shoes into the air and runs across the furniture.*]

ARNIE [*instructionally*]: If we had we wouldn't have had to stand all the way back. [*He belches.*]

JOAN: I'll be sick if I drink any more.

MRS ELLIS: It was your idea.

ARNIE: She doesn't have ideas, mother. Only prejudices.

    [JOAN *barks angrily like a dog at* ARNIE, *snarling then growling.*]

MRS ELLIS: Whatever anybody says, I enjoyed myself. I enjoyed myself. [*Telling herself*] How about you, Joan?

JOAN: All the time ... All the time ... asking each other if we've had a good time? All the way back [*mimicking*] 'Have you had a good time, *Arnie*? Have you had a good time, Edie?'

ARNIE: Well, have you had a good time, Edie?

JOAN: What did you call me?

    [ARNIE *has turned from her and taken* MRS ELLIS *by the shoulders, looking into her face.*]

You called me Edie!

    [ARNIE *turns from* MRS ELLIS, *one hand still holding her shoulder, and he begins to recite with a boy's mechanical, tutored gestures to an imaginary audience.*]

ARNIE: I have lived a long time, mother,
      And seen strange sights beyond the seas,
      But never a one have I seen, mother,
      To match the dimples in your knees.

    [MRS ELLIS *has burst out laughing.*]

JOAN [*calling out*]: You called me Edie, you swab.

ARNIE: There are women who shout and women who moan,
        And women who titter down the phone,
        But the only women that I ever see
        Are the ones that need hanging from the nearest tree.

JOAN [*calling*]: You're disgusting!

ARNIE: My wife Joan has a heart of stone,
        And eyes as black as charcoal,
        She wouldn't have looked bad
        If she hadn't have had
        A mouth the shape of her arsehole.

JOAN: I'll kill you!

[MRS ELLIS *attempts to drag her back:* ARNIE *has leapt with great alacrity behind the Knight who, until now, has gone unnoticed.*]

ARNIE: If you touch me I'll set him onto you.

JOAN: And tomorrow that thing's going first thing.

ARNIE: He'll tear you to pieces!

[*For a moment they stand poised, silent. Then:*]

MRS ELLIS: I think you both better get to bed.

ARNIE: Did you hear ... [*He steps cautiously from behind the Knight, reassures himself from* JOAN'S *look that he's safe.*] Did you hear, as we passed them in the street, what those ... *children* called me? Children – I might add – whom I teach and instruct in my own classroom.

MRS ELLIS: It's nothing I'd care to repeat.

ARNIE: And it's nothing, I can assure you, mother, that I've taught them. Those words are not in the curriculum. I even thought once that they liked me.

JOAN: You shouldn't go round getting plastered where they can see you.

[ARNIE *takes* MRS ELLIS'S *hand suddenly.*]

ARNIE: Here ... here darling. [*He leads her to the arm of a chair, sitting beside her to recite:*]
        There are things in your life
        Not even your wife
        Would think could pass through your brain.
        But give me a light
        And I'll show you a sight
        That would turn even Satan insane.

[MRS ELLIS *laughs, shocked, and breaks away.*]

MRS ELLIS: I think I'll be getting to bed ...

JOAN: Oh, no, mother.

MRS ELLIS: What?

JOAN: You're not going to bed till you've helped me shift this.

ARNIE: Where to?

JOAN: I'm not going to bed, I'm not. I'd never rest. Not with this wandering loose in the house.

ARNIE: What's it going to get up and do?

JOAN: It's going back in its kennel. And tomorrow ...

ARNIE: ... morning it's going out first thing. [*They finish the phrase together.*

JOAN *has begun to struggle with it back to the cupboard,* MRS ELLIS *going to help her.*

ARNIE *watches them ironically, arms folded, though he's still bleary with drink.*]

ARNIE: Rub-adub-dub, three nuts in a tub,
Who do you think they can be?

JOAN [*struggling*]: I've told you. Tomorrow morning ...

ARNIE [*together*]: ... it's going out first thing. [*He has switched on the wireless.*]

JOAN: You don't seem to believe me. But it is. The minute you've gone to school.

[*Dance music has started as the women haul the armour slowly to the cupboard.*

ARNIE *has begun to dance, taking a bottle to drink.*]

JOAN: And I don't want to see it again. Do you hear? [*She hiccups.*]

[ARNIE *dances on, oblivious to them. As* JOAN *fastens the cupboard doors* MRS ELLIS *turns to watch* ARNIE *dance, amused.*]

MRS ELLIS: That's a sight for sore eyes. He can hardly put two feet together. [*Laughs. Then claps.*

ARNIE *looks up at her with sultry affection, eyes half-closed.*]

ARNIE: Oh, I don't know ... all that there and so forth. Hup-dee. Hup-dee.

JOAN [*hiccups*]: Do you hear?

[ARNIE *takes* MRS ELLIS's *hand and they dance loosely together,* MRS ELLIS *laughing still.*]

217

ARNIE [*swaying his hips*]: That's it, Edie. That's it. Swill it all around ... Give it a good shake.

[JOAN *has picked up a bottle: she seems about to use it both on the wireless and* ARNIE, *then some instinctive coquettishness overcomes her and, bottle dangling, she puts her arm round* ARNIE, *who's spouting his own bottle to his lips.*]

JOAN: Move over, babe. [*She bumps her mother.*] Let's have a dance, honey.

[*The three of them, holding together, dance slowly and lugubriously.*]

ARNIE: Sing us a song, Joannie.

JOAN: I can't sing ... [*Hiccups.*] I can't sing. [*She makes several near-noises approximating to the music.*]

ARNIE: Oh, lovely, beautiful. [*He belches.*]

[MRS ELLIS *dances away on her own; a slow waltz, not ungraceful. She holds her skirt and dances with a slow nostalgia.*]

Oh, lovely, Edie. Lovely.

[MRS ELLIS *dances on.* JOAN *and* ARNIE *stop to watch her, intrigued.*]

JOAN: Go on, mother. Let 'em have it. [*Hiccup.*]

MRS ELLIS [*dancing*]: Do you like it?

ARNIE: Go on, Edie. Don't stop. She's good. She's good. Oh, she's good. Just look at her little old legs going!

MRS ELLIS: What's the matter with my legs?

JOAN: You should see yourself, darling.

ARNIE: Take no notice of her, Edie. They're all right. You can take my word for it.

MRS ELLIS [*stopping, looking down at her legs*]: I've got good legs ... I always have had, since I was a young woman.

JOAN: Mother!

MRS ELLIS: What's the matter? [*She lowers her skirt.*]

JOAN [*with sudden bravado*]: Those [*hiccup*] are legs, if you want them! [*Lifts her skirt discreetly and poses her legs.*]

There's no comparison ... Lift your skirt up. Lift. Come on. [*She pulls at her mother's skirt.*]

You just look. Arnie. What do you say? [*Hiccup.*

ARNIE *has already turned away.*]

Hold it up, mother. [*She turns round, for the first time aware of* ARNIE's *lack of attention.*]

Go on. What do you think? [*Pause.*] Arnie, for God's sake!
　[ARNIE *blearily turns round.*]

ARNIE: What ...

JOAN: What do you say?
　[MRS ELLIS *turns to him, holding her skirt like a child paddling, her mood a vague stupor between elation and tiredness.*]

ARNIE: What ...

JOAN: Look, damn you! [ARNIE *is overcome with weariness.*] Tell her, for God's sake. [*She has still one hand guardedly holding her mother's skirt, the other her own.*]

ARNIE: Tell her ... ?

JOAN: What you think.

ARNIE: You want me to, Edie?

MRS ELLIS: I don't mind, love. [*Giggles.*] It's getting draughty here.

JOAN: Look, look. We're walking. How's it look?
　[ARNIE *sits down, drunkenly and tired. He watches, frowning, and belches.*]

ARNIE: Like a camel. [*He finishes off the bottle, toasting the cupboard doors.*]

JOAN: Just look at her, then. Mother, you walk up and down. And keep your skirts up. [*Suddenly aware of* ARNIE's *diversion.*] You're not watching! [*Hiccup.*] For God's sake. We're walking! Here! Give me that! [*She snatches the bottle from him.*] All gone. Pig. [*She throws the bottle down, and suddenly snatches his hair.*] NOW – choose!
　[ARNIE *sinks down in the chair calling out.*]
Who's got the best legs! [*Hiccup.*]

ARNIE: Help! Let go! You're hurting ... Yarooo!

JOAN: I'm going to hurt you. Open your great mouth and tell her.

ARNIE: Edie! Tell her to let go. She's drunk. She doesn't know. OW!

MRS ELLIS: Why don't you do as she says, Arnie?

ARNIE: OW!
　[*The chair slips:* JOAN's *grip tightens:* ARNIE *falls to his knees, calling out, more helpless than he'd realized, his humour, however, still apparent.*]
For God's sake let go, Joan. I'm an historian.

JOAN: Choose. [*Hiccup.*]

ARNIE: If you don't let go I'll maim you.

JOAN: You try, then.

[MRS ELLIS *has picked up some sewing scissors from the sideboard. She's laughing, holding her skirt still with one hand as though she were paddling.*]

MRS ELLIS: If you hold him still I can cut his hair!

JOAN: Go on, then, Mam ...

MRS ELLIS: I'll cut it all off, Arnie!

ARNIE: Get off!

JOAN: Go on, Mam. Give him a cut. [*Hiccup. She pulls at his hair and* ARNIE *gives a real cry of pain, and can only bend more ineffectually to the floor.* JOAN *holds up the hair while, one-handed – her other holding up her skirt –* MRS ELLIS *cuts it off.*]

MRS ELLIS: There! ... There! He looks younger already!

JOAN: And another. Go on, Mam!

ARNIE: Let go. Or I'll kill you. Both of you.

JOAN: Go on, then. You stupid devil.

MRS ELLIS: Choose, Arnie. Then she'll let you go.

JOAN: Choose!

ARNIE: Edie! She's got the best legs. All the way.

JOAN: What? [*Hiccup.*]

ARNIE: Edie's! Edie's, all the way.

[JOAN *has released him.*]

JOAN: You prefer *her* to me!

ARNIE: Completely. [*He's still kneeling, clutching his head, still humoured, considering how best to take his revenge.*]

JOAN [*hiccup*]: You don't love *me*!

ARNIE: No!

JOAN: You've never loved me.

ARNIE: Never!

JOAN: You just wanted *that* [*hiccup*] and then it was all over.

ARNIE: Absolutely.

JOAN: You don't love me.

MRS ELLIS [*chastened*]: Let's get to bed. For goodness sake. We're not in our senses. Come on. Let's get up.

JOAN: Yes. Yes! I know ... I know ... [*implying.*]

MRS ELLIS: Joan ...

[JOAN *hiccups.*]

ARNIE: Make way! Make way! Move back!

JOAN: You've never loved me.

ARNIE: Oh! Oh! Oh!

JOAN: I know what's going on. Don't worry.

ARNIE: Why. Why. Why. All the time. Nothing but this, baby!

MRS ELLIS: Take no notice. None of you. It doesn't mean anything.
It's nothing.

JOAN [to MRS ELLIS]: Well, what are you doing here, then? [Hiccup.]
Come on. Come on. You be honest just this once.

MRS ELLIS: Joannie! Joannie!

JOAN: History or no bloody history. Don't think I haven't noticed.
[Hiccup.] And that *thing*! All the time. Stuck in there listening to
every word. [She gestures at the cupboard.]

ARNIE: I'm going up . . .

JOAN: Arnie. Tell her. Tell her to go.

  [ARNIE pauses on his way to the stairs.]
  Tell her to go. [Hiccup.]

ARNIE [pauses, then]: If your Bob doesn't pay our Bob that bob that
your Bob owes our Bob our Bob will give your Bob a bob on the
nose.

JOAN: Arnie! Tell her! Tell her!

ARNIE: Tiger, tiger, burning bright,
      In the forests of the night,
      If you see a five pound note
      Then take my tip and cut your throat.

JOAN: Tell her to go!

MRS ELLIS: No, Arnie!

ARNIE: The man in the moon has a chocolate spoon,
      And eyeballs made of custard;
      His big fat head is a loaf of bread,
      And his whiskers are peppered with mustard.

JOAN: Arnie!

  [ARNIE pauses again, bows to them with a flourish. Then:]

ARNIE: Ladies. Ladies. Ladies. [He goes.]

JOAN: Arnie!

MRS ELLIS: Arnie!

  [Lights fade.]

ACT TWO

Scene One

Late afternoon.

> JEFF HANSON *slumps in an easy chair. He's dressed in sports coat and flannels, a very long college scarf with tassels, bowler hat and yellow gloves: the eternal student. The gloves he eventually peels off, but the bowler hat remains on his head. He also retains a stout walking stick which he uses to amplify and reinforce his conversation. He is about forty, a middle-aged man with certain, perhaps obsessive desires to retain his youth.*
>
> *Standing behind him is the suit of armour.*
>
> ARNIE *himself sits at the table smoking a pipe.*
>
> JOAN *is out of sight, cleaning the stairs with a hand-brush and pan.*

HANSON [*raised voice*]: My dear Joan, I wouldn't believe a word of it.

JOAN [*heard*]: It was absolutely nothing at all.

HANSON: Absolutely.

JOAN: We were drunk.

HANSON: Of course.

JOAN [*heard*]: We'd all had too much.

HANSON: Naturally.

> [JOAN *appears in the door.*]

JOAN: So whatever he's told you ...

HANSON: My dear china, he's told me nothing. All we've heard are hints from you.

JOAN: You never know ... [*Watching* ARNIE *suspiciously.*]

HANSON: And if he had it would be of no account. Our long friendship [*indicating* ARNIE] is based on the simple precaution that I never believe a single word he says. I hate to indulge in scepticism of any sort but events have always justified my foresight.

ARNIE: He's lying as dextrously himself ...

HANSON: Arnold, I'm the last person to step between a man and his mother-in-law, as well you know. Despite all your accounts of domestic felicities I have always refrained from intruding. The only reason I don't agitate my hands about my ears is the faint hope that I may hear an explanation ... [*He is looking steadfastly at* ARNIE.]

JOAN: Of what?

HANSON: A remarkable occurrence that took place at school this morning, my dear. [*Suddenly looking up at* JOAN.] I'm astonished you're not already acquainted with it.

JOAN [*watching* ARNIE]: Well, I'm not.

ARNIE: It was nothing.

HANSON: Nothing!

ARNIE: A slight miscalculation.

HANSON: My dear Joan – hardly were we assembled in the hall – eight hundred *youthful* spirits about to make the most *hearty* obeisances to the one and only – when what should we glimpse through the door backing on to the stage but the most incredible apparition you can imagine! Beyond the Headmaster's stout and noble figure – its eyes raised, somewhat prematurely it now appears, towards the Heavens – could be discerned a man accompanied by a suit of armour, steathily creeping by under the obvious delusion that our devotions concealed him from our view. At first our benevolent autocrat mistook the huge and hideous roar that greeted this astonishing sight for one of religious fervour, his eyes travelling quickly downwards in a mixture of horror and surprise. [*Pause.*] Standing there in all his furtive glory was Arnold, smiling shyly in the arms of his new-found friend, and making unmistakable gestures with his one free hand that we should ignore his presence as best we may. God in Heaven, I said to myself, is this a manifestation – the not-unforeseen consequence of our rigorous vocation – or has Arnold, my dearest and closest friend, taken complete and utter leave of his senses?

ARNIE: She wanted to get rid of it. I had to protect it the only way I could. If I hadn't taken it to school, she'd have thrown it away.

JOAN: They must have laughed themselves sick!

HANSON: Except for the Head, my dear. Assuming it to be a comment upon his own austere régime – perhaps even on the strenuous nature of his religious practices – he ordered its immediate seizure and removal from the premises. It spent the remainder of its day, I believe, in the coal cellar, until its owner could take it home. [*He looks expectantly at* ARNIE.] Well?

  [ARNIE *puffs contentedly at his pipe.*]

Aren't you going to tell us? [*Pause.*] Is it some cheap means, Arnold, of publicizing your subject at the expense of others on the curriculum? [*Pause.*] Perhaps an indication to us of the kind of company you actually prefer.

ARNIE: I've told you why I took it to school.

JOAN: You won't get anything out of him.

HANSON: What is this, Arnold? Are we no longer sufficient for you? Your dear wife, your friends, your devoted pupils ... Or is it that you feel a sword is necessary to prompt us to a proper admiration of your extraordinary talents? Ungrateful may be the world, but, Arnold, surely not those who know you.

ARNIE: It won't be here much longer. You better take advantage of it while you can.

JOAN: Not here? [*Pause.*] Where's it going?

HANSON: Not – back to school?

ARNIE: No.

JOAN: Where, then?

ARNIE: As a matter of fact it's a present.

JOAN: A present!

HANSON: A present. Not for ... [*Gestures at himself.*]

ARNIE: No.

HANSON: Nor ... [*He gestures at* JOAN.]

  [ARNIE *moves away.*]

ARNIE: For my parents.

JOAN: Your parents!

ARNIE: That's the last I want to hear of it.

HANSON: But ... of course, I'm not acquainted with the couple ... and far be it from me to judge from preconceptions. But are they ... I mean, is it something they've always wanted? Do they have a fondness for metallic men?

JOAN: You've never said it was a present. You never said it was.

ARNIE: I take it I'm entitled to a little privacy of intention.

JOAN: Privacy of *what*?

HANSON: You mean they collect suits of armour?

JOAN: You let me shout down the house. [*Catching hold of him.*] Look
... have you just invented this?

ARNIE: That's all I want to hear of it. I've told you. Now you know.
It's a present.

JOAN: He's always inventing things when he thinks it suits him.
Why ...

ARNIE: It's over.

JOAN: My God!

HANSON: All these alarums, then, were merely to conceal the natural
benevolence of your heart. What stratagems men will go to to
disguise their proper virtues!

　　[JOAN, *however, is watching* ARNIE *with a mixture of disbelief and
condemnation.*]

JOAN: Do you expect me to believe that? What's the point of buying
them that? Of all things.

　　[ARNIE *doesn't answer.*]

　　Aren't you going to *talk*? [*Pause.*] All right. Just do as you damn well
please.

JOAN [*to* ARNIE]: And tell him to take his hat off in the house.

　　[*She goes to the kitchen: sound of cups.*]

HANSON: Have at you, man! [*He thrusts at him with his stick.*]

ARNIE: Have at you!

　　[*They fight with much groaning and exertion,* ARNIE *with his
invisible sword,* HANSON *with his stick.*]

　　Back! Back! Th ... th ... th ... i ... i ... i ... ssss ...
sssss THIS! i ... i ... i ...ssss .. IS! g .. g .. g .. gay! r ..
r .. r .. r .. ROBIN h .. h .. h .. h .. HOOD!

　　[HANSON *gives a great and ugly scream and dies writhingly in a
chair.*]

HANSON: Actually, could you lend me five pounds?

ARNIE: I haven't a cent. It all went on this.

　　[HANSON *has got up. He eyes the armour suspiciously.*]

HANSON: Oh. [*Pause.*] Actually. Why did you buy it?

ARNIE: As a present.

HANSON: For your parents?

　　[ARNIE *nods.*]

HANSON: Mmmmm! [*Watches him a moment. Then:*] The purpose of the loan was to entertain a lady. Temporarily, I'm without the wherewithal without.

ARNIE: A lady?

HANSON: A Miss Wilkinson, to be precise.

ARNIE: Not our Miss Wilkinson? From school?

HANSON: 'Fraid so. [*He talks a little in* JOAN's *direction.*] Naturally the school premises – where normally I make assignations of this nature – are the most propitious place for the dalliances I have in mind. But of late Old Thompson, despite rheumatism, a protopsic condition of the right eye, and an audibly leaking bucket, has acquired in stealth what he has so patently forfeited in spontaneity. The Park, though ample in resources, and open to all classes and creeds of men, is constant victim to the inclemency of the weather; the lady herself lives with elderly parents in a charming country cottage several miles from town; and my landlord resents frivolities of every nature.

ARNIE [*watching him cautiously*]: She's a damn fit woman, I'm told, Jeffrey.

HANSON: You were correctly informed. While we clamber daily through the portals of our plight, she is nimbly leaping over bucks, vaulting-horses and horizontal bars as lightly as ... a frog, say.

ARNIE: I had always assumed her to be the soul of integrity, Jeffrey.

HANSON: I have a curriculum to straighten out with her.

ARNIE: That would be nice.

HANSON: And her permission to examine the subject on an evening suitable to both.

ARNIE: I see.

[HANSON *finally turns from the armour just as* JOAN *re-enters carrying a tea-tray.*]

HANSON: So what's to do?

ARNIE [*perceiving* JOAN]: Entertain her here.

HANSON: In public?

ARNIE: A party. Or whatever festivities you feel she might approve.

HANSON: Tonight?

JOAN [*setting down the tray*]: Is someone coming here tonight?

ARNIE: It is a debt of honour I am endeavouring to pay with a frenzied bout of hospitality. Nothing more.

JOAN: What do you think all this is for?

ARNIE: All what?

JOAN: This! All this tidying up!

ARNIE: Any evidence of the pleasures we may have sustained will have been long removed by then.

[JOAN *stares at him in silence. Then:*]

JOAN: What *is* all this about, Arnie?

ARNIE [*to* HANSON]: You might bring a few bottles with you, Jeffrey. No reason why your pleasures should not entertain our own particular miseries.

HANSON: Oh, but of course.

JOAN: There's your tea. If you want anything else help yourselves. [*She returns to the kitchen.*]

ARNIE [*loudly*]: Talking of religious fervours, Miss O'Connor followed me home again today. The distance of twenty-five yards has increased slightly to thirty, perhaps even thirty-five. Idolatry, I fear, has given way to something verging on detachment.

HANSON: Sheila O'Connor ...

ARNIE: The one.

HANSON [*leaning on kitchen door*]: Is a girl ...

JOAN [*heard*]: I've seen enough of that.

HANSON: ... Upon whom a mischievous deity has bestowed two attributes, the largeness of which – in all humble deference – must be an embarrassment even to Himself. [*He salaams to the ceiling.*]

JOAN [*reappearing with cleaning utensils*]: Is that how you talk about the children?

HANSON: A child in the eyes of the State, my dear, but a woman in the eyes of God.

ARNIE: She actually approached me at four o'clock, just as I was entering the staff-room prior to retrieving my armour, and asked me to take her out. Tonight. [*Pause.*] Those are the first words that have passed between us.

HANSON: Oh, she's never asked me that. She never has.

JOAN: What arrangements did you come to?

ARNIE: I suggested we rendezvous at the picture palace at nine o'clock. 'Nine o'clock sharp, mind!' I said sternly, if not officiously – reminding her as casually as I could that I had a position to maintain. As it so happened, she would have followed me into the staff-room there and then if it hadn't been for the fact that old Manners was marking her arithmetic book along with several thousand others. 'Oh, Sheila,' he said, looking up obliquely from his tattered ledgers, 'I've just got to yours, my dear. Would you like to stand by me while I glance through your problems?' Wherein she vanished in the twinkle of an eye.

HANSON: There are incentives to the profession the Minister never dreamed of.

JOAN: Yes. [*She goes to the stairs but* ARNIE *takes her shoulders.*]

ARNIE: You're very contained, my little sparrow.

JOAN: I've to fly up there and finish the stairs if you don't mind, then fly back down and tidy here.

HANSON: A woman's work is never done!

JOAN: *What*!

HANSON: I ... Merely a tribute, my dear, to your ... profession.
   [JOAN *releases herself from* ARNIE.]

JOAN: God, I love you, honey. [*She blows a kiss and goes.*]
   [ARNIE *goes to the table, gets his pot, and sits down. He doesn't drink.* HANSON *watches him. Then:*]

HANSON: Say, old man. Isn't your hair somewhat oddly arranged for an historian? Or, indeed, for a man?

ARNIE: What?

HANSON: You're not short of food, I take it? It appears someone has consumed two mouthfuls of your tonsure.

ARNIE: It was a slight accident on the way to the kitchen.
   [HANSON *holds up his walking stick guardedly.*]

HANSON: Ah.

ARNIE: Mind your own business, loppy-lugs.

HANSON: Snot-nose.

ARNIE: Carpet-breath.

HANSON: That's revolting.
   [ARNIE *turns away to his tea.*]
   By such inadvertent gestures cancer is induced. Secrets go bad and affect the very flesh.

ARNIE: Cabbage knuckles.

HANSON [*with his stick*]: Have at you, Gay Robin!

ARNIE [*without gesture*]: Have at you, Big John.

[*Pause.* HANSON *taps the armour reflectively. Then he glances at* ARNIE.]

HANSON: You think, then, it's conceivable I'm mistaken about Miss Wilkinson. One grave disadvantage is that she's physically so very *fit*. It would be imprudent continually to have recourse to this stout staff while she merely relies upon the dexterity of her limbs. But my daily exercises are entirely cerebral, whereas hers, day in, day out, are designed exclusively to extend the already phenomenal resilience of her physique.

ARNIE: It could be an advantage, no doubt, in one way. And then again, in another ...

HANSON: But you do not think it strange... [*He glances round*]... that women are gradually acquiring a physical superiority to men? Do you think ... [*Goes to the stairs, listens, then returns to say slowly, putting his arm round the armour:*]

Do you think there's some sort of organization behind it?

ARNIE: A conspiracy ...

HANSON: Which we are very foolish to ignore. [*He glances quickly behind him.*] I mean, one hears so much of judo and professional equality these days.

ARNIE: Does the King know?

HANSON: The King? My dear Arnold, the very sources are corrupt. [*Moves away thoughtfully flexing his stick.*] I mean, it can't have failed to have reached your attention that we – that is men *and* women alike – emerge at some point of our lives from the body of a woman. But has it also occurred to you that whereas we are always under this obligation to them, they are never under a reciprocal obligation to us? They, as it were, *divulge* us: whereas we – we are simply *exposed*. This is an extraordinary advantage bestowed on one sex at the expense of the other.

[*As he talks he re-approaches* ARNIE *who takes* HANSON'*s stick and, as he listens, flexes it over his shoulders.* HANSON *leans over him with the confidence of a spy.*]

Have you noticed that women live longer than men? [*Pause.*] They do not fight wars, only occasionally do they murder their fellows, and they seldom, unfortunately, commit rape. Relate this to our original observation that it is *they* who breed *us*, then things like politics and finance, even philosophy and art, become like playthings bestowed on us by women merely to amuse and divert our unbreeding functions!

ARNIE: What time are you meeting her?

HANSON: What? [*Glances at his watch.*] Yes, I shall have to go.

[JOAN *has re-entered from the stairs.*]

HANSON: It is one thing to sit there and smile at present danger. It's quite another to rest there until you are *gobbled up*.

ARNIE [*quickly*]: You have caught Jeffrey in the very act of leaving.

HANSON: Ah, I did not hear you dismount, madam. [*He takes his stick from* ARNIE, *and pulls on his gloves.*] I must be about my business before it is about me. [*He suddenly turns round on* ARNIE *with his stick.*] On guard!

ARNIE: To be sure.

[HANSON *salutes with his stick.* ARNIE *has stood up and now he stands by* JOAN, *putting an arm about her shoulders.*

HANSON *glances at them a moment.*]

HANSON: I shall take my leave quickly. Imagine I am killed in the street the moment I have stepped beyond the door, and allow that poignancy to inform your farewells. [*He takes* JOAN's *hand and kisses it, salaams to* ARNIE, *then crosses to the armour. He taps it lightly with his stick.*]

That, Arnold. That I'm not altogether sure of. Well ... [*He regards it thoughtfully for a moment. Then, turning briskly:*] Remember, no fisticuffs when I introduce Miss Wilkinson to this abode. And may all our cavortings be as discreet and as anonymous as alcohol allows.

[*He ceremoniously bows and exits backwards, closing the door. A moment later there's the sound of the outer door shutting.*

ARNIE *releases her. She watches him a moment. Then:*]

JOAN [*lenient*]: You needn't be afraid.

ARNIE: Afraid?

JOAN: Of showing in private the affection you display in public. [*Pause.*] I could have told him.

ARNIE: You could?

JOAN: I heard your 'discussion' from the stairs. I could have told him how you came to lose your hair.

ARNIE: An embarrassment to both of us I would have thought.

JOAN: Doesn't *he* ever grow sick of it?

ARNIE: Of what?

JOAN [*pause*]: You despise him really.

ARNIE: I do not.

[*She watches him a moment then goes to the kitchen.*

ARNIE *sits down at the table. A moment later* JOAN *reappears.*]

JOAN: Has something sunk through all those layers at last?

ARNIE [*pause*]: Has what sunk through which layers?

JOAN: Disgust.

ARNIE: You're being boring.

JOAN: Isn't it that underneath ...

ARNIE [*calling out*]: You're being boring! I've never known anyone make such commonplace observations in so revelationary a tone!

[*They're both silent.*]

JOAN [*quietly*]: Do you have any feeling left for me at all?

ARNIE: Are you trying to be frivolous?

JOAN [*pause*]: You make me feel I don't exist. You hide away. You don't look. You show nothing but a parody of yourself. You deride even your own weakness. Isn't that self-contempt?

ARNIE: You're sickening.

JOAN: Am I ...

ARNIE: You're sickening. Your allegories are sickening, woman.

JOAN [*crying out and gesturing at the room*]: And what's this, then, but sickening! What's this!

[ARNIE *makes no response.* JOAN *watches him. Then, more quietly:*] If you'd just break up this – pretence!

ARNIE: What? What? What? What?

JOAN: Anything so long as you don't have to step up here. [*Gestures at herself.*]

ARNIE: You think that's an eminence worthy of ascent?

JOAN: You did once. [*Silence.*] Why do you stay with me, Arnie?

[ARNIE *watches her intently.*]

Go on.

ARNIE: Go knot your nose.

JOAN: Tell me. Why do you stay here?

ARNIE: Run up a flag.

JOAN: Try and answer me.

ARNIE: Leave me alone.

JOAN [*slowly*]: Why do you stay with me, Arnie?

[ARNIE *glances round at the doors.*]

Well, off you go then.

ARNIE: I can detect a piece of dust. Wait a minute, yes. It's under the near left-hand leg of the dressing-table in your mother's bedroom: a quick outflanking manoeuvre and it will be within your grasp.

[*Silence. Then*:]

JOAN: You must make yourself so *sick*.

ARNIE: Ladybird, Ladybird, fly away home:

Your house is on fire and your children have gone.

[*Silence.* JOAN *waits patiently.*

ARNIE *suddenly shouts with burlesque affectation, slamming the table.*]

Will somebody get me out of here!

Help! Help! . . . HELP!

[JOAN *watches a while. Then:*]

JOAN: It's not a game is it?

ARNIE: Leave me alone.

JOAN: No. You run away instead.

ARNIE: All right. [*He doesn't move. After a while:*] Assume I've run away.

JOAN: You insulting little *snot*!

[ARNIE *closes his eyes.*]

Come on. Get down on your knees and cry. Do something to attract some *pity*! Come on. Get down! Cry!

Come on. Cry, *baby*, cry!

[ARNIE *turns his head away.*]

Nobody's going to love you unless you show us *something*.

ARNIE: Go away.

JOAN: Let's have some rage. Isn't there anything in this world, Arnold, that you'd like to put right?

ARNIE: Go away.

JOAN: Come on, baby. Isn't there anything that offends you? Isn't there some tiny little wrong that can rouse your indignation?

ARNIE: Get out.

JOAN: Come on. Make me sickening.

ARNIE: Hop it!

[*She comes and studies his face more closely.*]

JOAN: Just look. For God's sake, Arnie.

[*They're silent. Then:*]

What are you frightened of?

[*He makes no response. Then quietly:*]

All right. All right. [*She watches him, waiting, for a response. Quietly, she goes.*

ARNIE *sits remotely at the table.*

After a while JOAN *re-enters.*

She watches him a moment, sitting exactly as she left him.]

JOAN: As a start, Arnie . . . I suggest we get rid of all these. [*Indicating the objects.*]

ARNIE: Yes.

JOAN: You agree, then?

[*Pause.* ARNIE *looks up.*]

ARNIE: Certainly.

JOAN: We get rid of all this.

ARNIE: Yes.

[*She seems about to start.*]

Not yet.

JOAN: Isn't this the best time?

ARNIE [*Pause*]: No.

JOAN: All right. When?

ARNIE: Tomorrow.

JOAN: After *they've* been?

ARNIE: Er . . . Yes.

JOAN: You promise that?

ARNIE: Yes.

JOAN: And this? [*Indicating armour.*]

[ARNIE *regards it in silence. Then:*]

ARNIE: That's going in any case.

JOAN: As a present.

[ARNIE *makes no response.*]

And if they won't have it?

ARNIE: What?

233

JOAN: I can't imagine they will. [*Pause.*] If that's what you really intend to do with it.

    [*Pause.*]

ARNIE: They'll have it because I'm giving it to them.

JOAN: Oh.

ARNIE: I like it.

JOAN: Yes.

ARNIE: And I'd like them to have it.

JOAN: Suppose they don't.

    [*Pause.*]

ARNIE: This is not a battle.

JOAN: No.

ARNIE: They'll be pleased with it because I am. And the other way round.

    [*She watches him.*]

Some people are actually like that.

JOAN: Yes.

ARNIE: All right?

JOAN: I'll believe it when I see it.

ARNIE: I doubt it.

JOAN: Well, then, while we're clearing everything away, there's one other thing. It's time my mother left and went and lived on her own.

ARNIE: What?

JOAN: In this case you'll just have to accept *my* word if you don't believe it.

ARNIE: She's harmless.

JOAN: It's time she went for all our sakes. You'll be better off for it. I will. And so will she.

ARNIE: I don't want her to go. It'd break her bloody heart.

JOAN: I'm sorry. But she'll have to.

    [*The outside door bangs.*]

That's her now.

ARNIE: Well, don't say anything to her. Not yet.

JOAN: It's my decision.

ARNIE: I've told you. Don't. [*He waits, almost threatening.*] You understand?

    [JOAN *makes no response. There are sounds outside the door, and*

ARNIE's *mood changes abruptly as* MRS ELLIS *appears. She's smartly dressed, a fur round her shoulders, and she carries a full shopping basket which she puts on the table.* ARNIE *greets her with a dashing gesture.*]

 Here comes a spy to parry at our scheme:
 I shall retire, and make it – all a dream.

MRS ELLIS [*pleased*]: Oh ...
 [ARNIE *goes with a flourish.*]

MRS ELLIS: What's got into him?
 [JOAN *doesn't answer.*]

 It's a lovely evening out. A beautiful sunset.
 [*Pause. The two women confront each other;* MRS ELLIS *with some perplexity.*]

 What's the matter?

JOAN [*goes to her*]: Let me help you off with your coat, mother.

MRS ELLIS: What?

JOAN: Your coat.
 [*Surprised, she submits.*
 The light fades.]

Scene Two

The same evening.
 ARNIE, *in shirtsleeves, tieless, lies on a couch. The suit of armour has gone.*

JOAN [*heard*]: Aren't you going to get changed?
 [*There are sounds of her working in the kitchen.* ARNIE *makes no response: his eyes are closed, apparently in sleep.*]

JOAN [*entering*]: Aren't you going to get shaved?

ARNIE [*eyes still closed*]: I thought you wanted no one here. The place kept tidy and clean.
 [JOAN *has dressed herself attractively, and her hair is tied in a ribbon.*]

JOAN [*briefly and briskly tidying the room*]: I've changed my mind ... Aren't you going to get ready at all?

235

ARNIE: Oh? [*He opens his eyes, watches her a moment.*] They might never get here.

JOAN: My mother's gone out for nothing, then.

ARNIE: She didn't have to go out.

JOAN: She didn't feel like meeting people this evening. That's all. [*Pause.*]

ARNIE: The sacrifice of one old woman ...

JOAN: She can look after herself.

[ARNIE *rouses himself, sitting up.*]

ARNIE: You can't turn people out like that, that's all. Not when they rely on you. You either do it at the beginning or not at all.

JOAN: I'm not arguing about it.

ARNIE: That's settled then. [*Sitting on the couch, slaps his thighs and looks around contentedly. Then he puts his hands together and blows between them, hooting like an owl.*

After a while:]

JOAN: You know ...

[ARNIE *hoots.*]

JOAN [*pause*]: With my mother it's my decision whether she goes or not. She's *my* mother.

ARNIE: I've told you.

JOAN: But it's my decision, Arnie. I make it!

[*The door is crashed back on its hinges and* HANSON *puts his head round.*]

HANSON: *Pray!* Hold thy hand good Robin Hood,
                And your merry men each one,
                For you'll swear this is the finest maid
                That ever your eyes fell on.

JOAN: Don't you usually knock when you come in?

HANSON [*taking her hand*]: If thou wilt forsake, housewife, thy craft,
                And wend to the greenwood with me [*kisses her hand*]
                Thou shalt have loving all the year long,
                And forty gold crowns for thy fee.

ARNIE: All right. All right.

HANSON [*to* ARNIE]: And Robin leapt up full thirty good foot,
                'Twas thirty good foot and one,
                And he cleft the rude fellow with a blow of his fist –
                And his light went out like the sun. [HANSON *disappears*

immediately through the door. His voice is heard.] Go on, dear. Straight ahead.

[SHEILA O'CONNOR, *a precociously developed girl, though by no means loutish, enters. She's dressed in slacks and a bright sweater. Her shyness tends to disappear first when she sees* ARNIE, *then the interior.*]

SHEILA: Hello, sir.

[ARNIE *is up quickly from the couch where he's been lounging.*]

ARNIE: Oh, hello, Sheila.

Didn't expect to see you here.

HANSON: Odd thing. Passing the gate just as we came in. Thought: what a coincidence! Then: why one be damned when rest sanctified by celebration!

ARNIE: Yes. [*To* JOAN] This is Sheila O'Connor, Joan.

This is my wife, Sheila.

SHEILA: Hello, Miss.

JOAN: Hello, Sheila.

[MAUREEN WILKINSON *and* HANSON *have followed* SHEILA *in. The schoolmistress is dressed tastefully: a respectable and fairly attractive woman in her late twenties.*]

ARNIE: Evening, Maureen. I don't think you know my wife. Joan – this is Maureen.

MAUREEN: It's very nice meeting you, Joan.

[*They shake hands.*]

JOAN: Let me take your coat.

ARNIE [*to* HANSON]: Well, let's sit down, and so forth.

HANSON: Look here, Arnold, would you mind awfully if Sheila and I betook ourselves to the hostelry to purchase an armful of drinks? Things came up. Distracted the intention ...

ARNIE [*to* SHEILA]: So soon arrived, so soon departed.

HANSON: You don't mind, do you, Sheila? I swear I heard you had been appointed milk monitor this term for the Lower Fifth.

SHEILA: It's not far, is it?

HANSON: Good girl! We shan't be long. Adios, caballeros.

ARNIE: Shall I ...

HANSON: Oh, we'll manage, old man.

[*They go.*

ARNIE *has got up to go with them but, rejected, returns.*]

JOAN: Does that irritate you?

MAUREEN: Oh, you get used to it.

JOAN: What is it, do you think?

MAUREEN: The school play this year is 'Robin Hood and His Merry Men'.

JOAN: No, I meant ...

ARNIE: You're being unnecessarily adventurous, aren't you, coming out with Jeffrey?

MAUREEN: He's asked me out so often it's less tedious to agree.

ARNIE: Is that all?

MAUREEN: I'm sorry.

[JOAN *watches* ARNIE'*s almost vindictive manner with* MAUREEN, *curious and intrigued*.]

There was nothing I could do about him bringing Sheila in. It's very foolish.

ARNIE: It'll give her a break from her usual sentry-go. I never know whether she's keeping me in, or keeping the others out.

JOAN: It's inviting trouble: walking through the streets with her like that, and going into pubs.

MAUREEN [*pleasantly*]: Oh, he'll take a pleasure in it.

JOAN: After all, we're partly responsible for it.

ARNIE: Of those two, the only one who can be violated is Jeffrey.

MAUREEN: You're not responsible. That's absurd.

JOAN [*indicating* ARNIE]: Oh, he has ways of encouraging her. Don't worry.

ARNIE: She asked *me* out.

JOAN [*to* MAUREEN]: Some days they say it's because they teach in a school; then on other days they say it's the world.

MAUREEN: I never knew you had a philosophy, Arnold. As well as a suit of armour. [*Stretching round*] Where is it, by the way?

ARNIE: Yes. [*He gets up and wanders uneasily about the room.*]

JOAN [*to* MAUREEN]: Are all your men staff alike?

MAUREEN: Oh, very nearly!

JOAN: Doesn't it wear you down?

MAUREEN [*laughing*]: I shouldn't worry about it, Joan!

ARNIE: Watch this. [*Does a handstand against the wall, balancing precariously.*

The women pause to watch.]

JOAN: Would you like some tea, Maureen?

MAUREEN: Love some.

JOAN: I'll just put the kettle on. I was hoping to make some sandwiches as well. Won't be a minute. [*Goes into the kitchen.*]

[MAUREEN *looks round at the objects in the room for the first time.*]

MAUREEN: Are all these yours?

ARNIE: Yes.

MAUREEN: Don't you want me here?

ARNIE: You?

MAUREEN: Us?

ARNIE: It was *my* party. Joan has appropriated it.

MAUREEN [*laughs*]: Yes.

[ARNIE *lowers himself from his handstand.*]

ARNIE: Do you know what happened to the Early Christian martyrs the moment they stopped throwing them to the lions, and loved them instead?

MAUREEN: They went off into the desert to live in caves, haunted by demons.

ARNIE: What?

[MAUREEN *waits.*]

ARNIE: I've told you before. [*Pause.*] Are you sure?

MAUREEN: Yes.

ARNIE: I see. [*Pause.*] Don't you think it's extraordinary?

MAUREEN: In what way?

ARNIE: In what way? [*Pause.*] I don't know really. It seemed extraordinary at the time ... [*Pause.*]

MAUREEN: Where is ...

JOAN [*returning*]: I'm making some sandwiches then perhaps one or two people won't get so drunk. Where are you going?

[ARNIE *has gone to the door, picking up his jacket.*]

ARNIE: Out. See if Hanson needs any help.

JOAN: I should think he'd be able to manage well enough on his own.

[ARNIE *still goes.*]

You won't be long?

ARNIE: No.

JOAN: Give us a kiss, Arnie.

ARNIE [*to* MAUREEN]: You'll notice. Always the diminutive.

239

[JOAN *waits.* ARNIE, *after a moment, comes back, takes her shoulder and kisses her on the cheek.*]

JOAN: You won't be long, Arnold?

ARNIE: No.

[*He goes. A pause.* JOAN *tentatively re-tidies the room.*]

JOAN: His parents are coming tomorrow. We haven't seen them for years.

MAUREEN: The best thing is to ride with it, isn't it? I still live with my parents: I know what a trouble they can be.

JOAN: When *we* got married and his mother came up to kiss me as we were leaving the church, she said, 'Well, you'll look after my only son, won't you, Joan?' And he said, quick as a flash, 'Your only sin, mother.' And she smiled as sweetly as anything; he laughed out loud; and God did I feel a fool! You can see just what a state I'm in. Would you like to see round the house?

MAUREEN: Yes, I'd love to.

[*They move to the stairs.*]

JOAN: I'll show you upstairs. You've seen nearly all there is to see down here. Considering how small they look from the outside it's surprising how large they are.

[*They go. Heard is* MAUREEN: *'Do you intend staying on here, then?' Then* JOAN: *'Oh, I suppose so. We've lived here since we got married. There's no point in moving into something smaller . . . This is the main bedroom . . .*

Their voices grow fainter, then disappear. After a short interval there's the sound of the back door opening in the kitchen and, a moment later, the kitchen door is cautiously opened. MRS ELLIS *enters. She's drunk. She puts a bottle on the table and stands aimlessly looking round, stifling her sobs with a handkerchief. Then she moves to the mirror and stares distractedly at herself, moaning. From above come the voices of the women as they move about: 'the bathroom there, and this is the spare room . . .' 'Well, that's convenient. . . . Goodness. Is that all Arnold's too?' 'And this my mother's room . . .'*

MRS ELLIS *swings round, hurries to the kitchen door, then across to the door leading to the hall. Then, as the women begin to descend the stairs, she remembers the bottle, hurriedly retrieves it and goes out by the hall door, leaving it open.*]

MAUREEN [*re-entering*]: His classroom's extraordinary. More like the court of King Arthur than a schoolroom. Have you see his museum?

JOAN [*re-entering*]: No.

MAUREEN: The children love it. What it has to do with history I've no idea. They seem to spend all their time building model castles, singing ballads and doing great big pictures of William the Conqueror ... It's strange we've never met at school, isn't it? You've never been to any of the plays Arnold's produced, have you? They're very good.

JOAN: He prefers me to stay away.

MAUREEN: Whatever for?

JOAN [*shrugs*]: He prefers it, that's all. He's full of prejudices, you know, Maureen.

MAUREEN: Prejudices?

JOAN: We better do the sandwiches, by the way, before they get back. The kettle should be boiling. You promise ...

> [*They go into the kitchen.*
> *After a moment* MRS ELLIS *reappears and stands hesitantly in the room, uncertain whether to go into the kitchen herself. She stifles a sob, staring at the door. Then, at the sound of a door opening and whispers from the hall, she glances wildly round and, with her bottle, departs unsteadily to the stairs.*
> *The sound of the women's laughter comes from the kitchen, and* MAUREEN's *shout of* 'Joan!' HANSON *appears in the hall door, looks left and right, then signals behind him. Giggling,* SHEILA *follows him in, a carrier bag with bottles in her arms.* HANSON *puts his finger to his lips and gestures at the kitchen.*]

HANSON [*whispers*]: Excellent. Very good, O'Connor. Next week, as a very special reward, you can be in charge of the ink *and* the chalk – and if you're extra good I'll let you clean the blackboard.

SHEILA: Oh, thank you, sir! [*Taking off her coat.*]

HANSON [*aware*]: I think for that you deserve a red star. Or is it a green one? [*He pins an imaginary medal on her chest, then kisses her on either cheek.*

> SHEILA *takes him round the neck and kisses him more directly.*
> ARNIE *has entered quietly.* HANSON *looks up in mid-kiss to see him.*]

There you are, dear fellow.

ARNIE: Saw you down the street. Thought: bound to resent my intrusion. Kept my distance.

Circumspect. All that.

HANSON: Absolutely, old boy.

ARNIE: Not at all.

JOAN [*heard*]: Arnie? [*She enters from kitchen, followed by* MAUREEN, *carrying a tray of tea and sandwiches.*] There you are.

MAUREEN: Arrived back altogether.

HANSON: Are we supposed to drink out of our hands?

JOAN: You can help yourself in the kitchen.

SHEILA: Can I find the glasses?

HANSON: You find them, love. Anything that will hold liquid. You know what liquid is, don't you?

SHEILA: Course I do, silly.

[HANSON *and* SHEILA *giggle.*]

JOAN [*to* ARNIE]: What are you doing?

[ARNIE *stands at the back of the room rubbing his hands energetically, nodding his head at everybody, his face set in a pleased grin.*]

ARNIE: Just getting it all organized. Ship-shape. Everyone on the best of terms. Pleasantries, cordialities, sparks within a fire.

JOAN: What's got *into* you?

MAUREEN [*to* HANSON]: I hope you know what you're doing with that girl.

HANSON: Oh, definitely.

JOAN: Better leave him alone, Maureen.

MAUREEN: He needs reminding.

HANSON: On whose authority, Miss Wilkinson?

MAUREEN: Those people who hire you to educate the ...

HANSON: That's their fault for serving up dishes like her. We're not sticks of chalk.

MAUREEN: I never said you were.

HANSON: So put that over your shoulder and start marching.

[*There's a cry from the kitchen and the sound of breaking glass.* JOAN *rushes out.*]

Relax, Maureen. Relax.

ARNIE [*cheerfully*]: *Relax.*

MAUREEN: I am relaxed. There's a question of behaviour, isn't there?

HANSON: My behaviour's strictly human ...

ARNIE: It's strictly human.

HANSON: Or are you against that too?

ARNIE: Are you against that too?

HANSON [*to* ARNIE]: What's the matter with you?

JOAN [*re-entering*]: One broken glass, that's all.

SHEILA [*following with tray of glasses*]: I broke a glass!

HANSON: Right, then ... [*He starts pouring out the drinks.*]

ARNIE [*to* MAUREEN]: What's got *into* you?

MAUREEN: What?

HANSON: Joan? Maureen? A little for you, Sheila?

JOAN: I'll have a glassful ...

HANSON: But certainly.

MAUREEN: I'll make do with tea.

HANSON: Naturally. [*To* JOAN] We have a little whisky here for the menfolk. If you like ...

JOAN: Oh, beer will do.

HANSON: And Arnold?

JOAN: Don't give him whisky. One glass knocks him off his feet.

HANSON: Aha!

[*He hands a glass of whisky to* ARNIE *who downs it in one swallow.*]

JOAN: I've warned you.

[HANSON *tots it up again, and* ARNIE *drinks it off.*
ARNIE *screws his face, holds his stomach, then his head, gesticulates with violent, staccatic motions, lurches erratically one way then another, goes boss-eyed, knock-kneed ...*]

JOAN: All right. All right.

[... ARNIE *stands motionless in the centre of the room.*]

HANSON [*expressionless*]: Oh dear. Oh dear, I haven't laughed so much for ages ... Are you sure you're old enough, Sheila?

SHEILA: Course I am.

HANSON: I meant for alcohol, my dear. [*He slaps his thigh.*] Oh, my!

ARNIE: My *friends*!

HANSON: *What?*

ARNIE: I would like to address you, if I may.

HANSON: Oh.

ARNIE [*swallows his next whisky. Hesitates. Then*]: This ... *celebration* ... is not an ordinary celebration. Oh, you may say, it *looks* an ordinary celebration. And I admit. It has all the signs, the characteristics, all the *moeurs*, as they say in German. Of a celebration. But the fact is ... What? ... What? [*He looks round questioningly.*]

JOAN: Is that the end?

ARNIE: I have always in my life attempted to deal ... fairly, with my fellow men.

HANSON: And women.

ARNIE: Ah. [*Holds up an admonitory finger.*] And it would, indeed, be mealy-mouthed ...

HANSON: It would.

ARNIE: Of me. Ungracious. Prevaricating. To let you assume that this is merely a celebration. This is in fact ... What is this? [*He holds up his glass.*]

[HANSON *holds up the whisky bottle to him.*]

HANSON: One of the very worst brands, old friend.

ARNIE [*wipes his hand, surprised, across his forehead*]: I'm *sweating*.

JOAN: I told you he'd fall down.

MAUREEN: Perhaps we better put on the music and calm down.

ARNIE: An event of such gigantic proportions as to be virtually invisible to the naked human eye! It is ... Do they wash up in this?

HANSON: Only one of the minor rituals of distillation. Why, I could tell you ...

JOAN: We'll have that another time.

ARNIE: I want ... *all* of you. I want all of you to be content. This evening I want you to remember ... I want you to remember. I want you.

HANSON: What?

ARNIE: What?

HANSON: Well, if not 'what' then 'why'?

ARNIE: I don't want to know why. Any damn fool can give you reasons *why*. All I'm interested in is *how*. *Why* is a kind of sentimentality I heartily eschew. I *eschew* it. Why is of no more interest to me than *when*. You can put why and when into ... wherever you'd like to put them, and blow them to smithereens, for me.

HANSON: God! A religious maniac!

ARNIE: I want an evening of ... ease, of peace, of relaxation. The ... *flow* of gentle laughter, conversation ... the natural intimacy between friends.

JOAN: I'd like to recite a poem.

ARNIE: What?

HANSON: Oh, steady, Joan.

JOAN: I think I shall.

ARNIE [*pained*]: You're being revolting ... I said the *natural* flow of conversation not a poem.

JOAN: You said the flow.

MAUREEN: Yes. You did say the flow.

[JOAN *begins to recite.*]

HANSON: Have another drink, Sheila.

SHEILA: Oh, ta.

HANSON: You are enjoying yourself?

SHEILA: Oh, super!

[JOAN *has begun to recite, at first her fingers holding her cheeks, then, as she goes on, growing more confident.*]

JOAN: I saw love passing by my window
    Early one morning on a lightsome day ...

ARNIE: Oh, no.

HANSON: Joan ...

JOAN: Its face was warm and its look so hopeful
    And pleasure and happiness in its features lay.

[ARNIE *has covered his face with embarrassment.*]

ARNIE: Oh, no. [*Groaning*] This can't go on.

HANSON: Joan: my dear, dear girl ...

SHEILA: No. Sir, it's super!

MAUREEN: No, let her go on.

[*For a moment they argue over this,* SHEILA *and* MAUREEN *attempting to quieten the other two. Meanwhile* JOAN *carries on reciting.*]

JOAN: I saw love hurrying in the meadow
    Its steps so light over the leaden clay,
    Its breath was quick and its voice beseeching,
    And I heard its cries as I fled away.

I saw love sitting in a cottage
About its feet did children play,
Their sounds were loud, their voices lusty,
And I saw love smile to see them gay.

[ARNIE *has continued to groan, gradually quietening, finally subsiding on a chair, holding his stomach and leaning forward as if in pain. The others too have quietened, turning to listen to* JOAN.]

JOAN: I saw love bending with the sickle
Though all the thorns were clustered in its way,
Its body aged and its head now shaking,
And with the wind it seemed to sway.

I saw love trudging by my window
Late one evening on a darksome day,
Its face was worn and its look despairing
And grief and sorrow on its features lay.

[ARNIE *has now looked up to watch* JOAN.]

I saw love carried to the graveside
The day was sunny and the month was May.
Across its brow was a wreath of laurel
And in its hands a clean white spray.

[*They're silent. No one moves for a moment. Then:*]

HANSON: Oh, I say. That's very good.

MAUREEN: Lovely.

SHEILA: It was super, Miss.

HANSON: No, I really do think that was very good.

[*They all seem a little awed.* ARNIE, *however, has suddenly jumped up.*]

ARNIE: There was a young woman of Leeds
Who swallowed a packet of seeds,
She grew peas on her chest,
Runner beans in her vest,
And all round her kneecaps grew weeds.

HANSON: There was a young man of Bangkok
Who swallowed a musical clock ...

ARNIE: Oh, I say ...

HANSON: ... He could play a toccata,
Chopin's Moonlight Sonata,
By simply removing his sock.

ARNIE: Oh ... This is the happiest day of my life. I want you to know that ... Revelations are simply pouring from the skies! Sheila!

[*He goes to* JOAN *and puts his arm warmly about her.*]

HANSON: Sheila: what contribution could you make, my dear?

ARNIE: A few handstands might cause a stir. Perhaps some extraordinary gymnastic feats acquired at the hands of Miss Wilkinson?

HANSON: You can commit poetry, my dear. We – we can merely recite it.

SHEILA: You've forgotten to give sir his telegram, sir.

HANSON: Telegram? Telegram?

JOAN: Telegram?

HANSON: Ah ...

ARNIE [*totally bemused, his arm still warmly about* JOAN]: I once read somewhere in a novel, perhaps ...

HANSON: Scott!

ARNIE: Scott?

HANSON: That's his name! [*Points to the door.*]

MAUREEN: Whose?

HANSON: You remember Scott? A tall, lanky boy who wore glasses and dirty teeth. Won the long jump one year, I believe, by simply falling on his head.

ARNIE: Oh, Scott! ... Wasn't he the boy ...

HANSON: Could contain himself no longer during a mathematics lesson and furtively urinated out of an upper window when he presumed no one was looking.

[JOAN *giggles.*]

MAUREEN: Now that's enough!

ARNIE: Brought on a case of Thompson's disease. An hitherto unknown medical syndrome characterized by a sudden staring of the eyes, an energetic raising of the arms, and a loud, screaming sound emitted from between the teeth.

HANSON: It was first witnessed in an elderly caretaker of that name who happened to be passing beneath the window at the time.

[JOAN *breaks out into laughter.* SHEILA *giggles.*]

JOAN: Is he *here*?

SHEILA: He was. [*Attempting to conceal her laughter.*]

ARNIE: A remarkable youth, I seem to recollect. Went through all the stages of puberty by the age of eleven. Caused endless consternation amongst the younger boys.

HANSON: As we were emerging from the house a short while ago, my young companion and I [*holds* SHEILA *firmly about the shoulders*], our course set for the hostelry, whom should we discover on the step but Scott himself attired in dark uniform and peaked cap. 'Great Heavens,' said I, 'the police.' Whereupon he indicated an insignia on his arm which suggested he was in the employ of the Post Office with special responsibility for the delivery of urgent messages. Thrusting one such into my hand he departed with an alacrity I can only assume was inspired by our past acquaintance. So intoxicated was I by the chatter of my companion that, until this moment, I'm afraid I have quite overlooked it ... [*Finally retrieving it after a search of his pockets, reads*] Greetings!

JOAN: Is that all it says?

HANSON [*tendentiously*]: That's merely the envelope. [*He tears it open.*] Ah! This is what Scott has written. Greetings again! Here we are ... Regret ... Regret. Regret mother unwell stop cutting holiday short. Stop hope to make it some other time. Stop father.

JOAN: What's that? [*She takes the telegram.*]

HANSON [*to* MAUREEN *and* SHEILA]: Another drink?

[*Having read the telegram, however,* JOAN *now giggles.* ARNIE, *his arm still about her shoulder, gazes bemusedly into the distance.*]

JOAN: I cleaned every rotten stick in this house. [*To the others.*] I've even dusted every rotten piece of dust.

HANSON: Oh! Oh, Oh ...

JOAN: There's not a mark not a sign of life anywhere and now they've decided not to come!

[JOAN *is very pleased, yet apparently, with her giggling, trying to hide her feelings from* ARNIE.]

ARNIE: Now. We are about to dance.

[ARNIE, *as if unaware of all this, goes to the gramophone.*]

JOAN: Here. Have you read this? Isn't it marvellous! That really is the best news I've had all day.

[*Music begins.*]

ARNIE: Sheila. Would you escort me about the floor? A limb here, a limb there. One or two gesticulations in unexpected places ... and there we are. Ups!

[ARNIE *is unsteady, slow and mechanical, as he manoeuvres* SHEILA *about the room.*]

HANSON: Shall we form a chorus? Surround the principal players with thrashing ...

JOAN [*to* ARNIE]: Loved one! Did you hear? Have you seen this?

[JOAN *is still giggling, despite herself; for her, now, the evening is a huge success.*]

HANSON: Arnie. Show us your armour.

JOAN: We can get rid of that too while we're at it.

HANSON: I know a secret!

MAUREEN: What?

HANSON: I know a secret!

SHEILA [*laughing*]: What is it?

HANSON: Are you ready?

JOAN: No rowdy stuff, Hanson.

HANSON: Are you ready? [*Darts to the cupboard, and with a sudden gesture:*] Woman! Behold thy ...

Oh, it's locked.

JOAN: Don't look at me.

HANSON: Arnold. What is this?

SHEILA: Oh, Arnie. Can't we see it?

ARNIE: What?

[ARNIE *has paused. He stares at* SHEILA *in consternation.*]

SHEILA [*quietly*]: Can't we see it, sir?

ARNIE: Who asked you in here?

HANSON: I did, Robin.

ARNIE [*glances at her, then moves away*]: Show her the aeroplane. There's a stuffed eagle over there.

HANSON: Aren't we going to see ...

ARNIE: And above the mantelpiece you'll observe a Lee-Enfield rifle, a weapon of historical importance to the British nation.

HANSON: Arnold, if you'll just allow ...

ARNIE: With that weapon we preserved ... [*He gestures airily about him.*]

HANSON: Look, I don't wish to get impersonal, old boy.

ARNIE: And what are we now? Gropers in the debris of our ...

HANSON: Arnold. Do I understand you are about to entertain us?

ARNIE: Tell us, Hanson. How does your mother keep her stockings up?

HANSON: Ooo! Ooo!

JOAN: I think that's enough.

MAUREEN: We better quieten down ...

SHEILA: It's good, Miss!

JOAN: If you want something to shout about there's always this. [*She thrusts the telegram into his hand.*]

ARNIE: It's Hanson. He's an historical aberration.

HANSON: Ooo!

ARNIE: A turnip!

HANSON: Ooo!

[SHEILA *has given way to giggles;* JOAN *also.*]

ARNIE: A sod.

HANSON: Ooo! Ooo! You heard him! [*Writes across a large imaginary blackboard.*] Tries hard: a willing worker, but effort frequently suffocated in pompous supposition.

[ARNIE *waves his arms about indecisively.*]

Ooo! You heard! [*Writes.*] Self-indulgent and tends to melodrama when opposed. Suffers from affectations, not least of which a pretension to reality. [*Bows to the room.*] Thus write I across all my reports. [*Vaguely facetious.*] Loved one.

JOAN: That's enough! [*Attempts to turn* ARNIE *away.*]

ARNIE: It's him. He's a propagator of untruth.

HANSON: Untruth! Why, he's a lie himself. If you measured him by any reality he'd be invisible. [*He puts his tongue out triumphantly at* ARNIE.]

ARNIE: That rifle's *loaded.*

[HANSON *pauses, then looks up. He hesitates. Then:*]

HANSON: Liar!

MAUREEN [*to* JOAN]: Is it loaded?

JOAN: I don't know. [*Giggling.*]

MAUREEN: I think we've had enough of this.

SHEILA: They're only playing, Miss!

[HANSON *lifts the rifle down.*]

ARNIE: May I? [*He puts the telegram in his pocket, first one, then the other, as* HANSON *fumbles with the rifle. Then* ARNIE *takes it from him, removes the safety catch and draws back the bolt.*] All right. A pretension to reality. [*He raises the rifle and presses it to* HANSON's *temple. He's still unsteady with drink.*] It's loaded.

HANSON [*pauses. Then calls*]: Rubbish. [*Giggles.*]

ARNIE: I'll fire it.

[HANSON *is silent.*]

Well?

HANSON: Trouble-maker, and known disseminator of bad habits.

MAUREEN: That's far enough.

ARNIE: Are you ready?

HANSON: Yes.

[ARNIE *squeezes the trigger.*]

JOAN: No!

ARNIE: It's rusty. Hold your head still.

[HANSON *stands tensely, holding the table now, assuming some dignity.* SHEILA *has covered her face up.* ARNIE *holds the rifle more awkwardly to gain further pressure on the trigger. He squeezes again. There's a click.* ARNIE *still holds the rifle there.* HANSON *laughs.*]

JOAN: Oh, God. That's enough.

HANSON: Everything you see. False all the way through. [*Takes the rifle from* ARNIE, *laughing with real pleasure. He points it at* ARNIE, *ramming back the bolt.*] Arnold: you're a falsity! [*His laughter suddenly breaks. He looks down at the rifle – examines it.*] It is loaded.

ARNIE: Yes.

HANSON [*looking up in horror*]: And you pulled the trigger?

ARNIE: Yes.

HANSON: Why ... You madman! [*He throws the rifle down.*]

ARNIE: It was a choice you made on the evidence of your own senses, Jeffrey.

HANSON: You're mad!

ARNIE: That's not true.

HANSON [*to the women*]: He could have killed me!

JOAN [*dismissive*]: Fools! You're both fools.

HANSON: What? [*He suddenly stares at her, drunkenly distracted.*] He could have killed me!

[ARNIE, *swayingly, has meanwhile picked up the rifle. He points it at* HANSON.]

ARNIE: As a matter of fact I still can.

HANSON: No!

JOAN: Arnie!

MAUREEN: No!

[SHEILA *screams.*

ARNIE *pulls the trigger, then gazes intrigued at* HANSON's *expression.*]

ARNIE: The firing pin's removed. There's no contact with the cartridge. [*He lowers the rifle.*] It can never go off.

[HANSON *grabs the rifle from him.*]

HANSON: You know what I think?

ARNIE: You take it too seriously, Big John.

[HANSON *stares at him impotently, blind with rage.* ARNIE, *slowly:*]

It really is unforgivable, isn't it?

MAUREEN: You better go, Sheila. Did you bring a coat?

HANSON: She's not going.

SHEILA: I don't want to go.

MAUREEN: I think you better, girl, and do as you're told this once.

HANSON: I said she's not going! [*He takes* SHEILA's *arm. Then, to* ARNIE:] God. What a deceiver. It was false, bogus, all the way through. He even makes a virtue of it.

ARNIE [*to* MAUREEN]: Shall we dance?

MAUREEN: You've gone too far, Arnold. I think we'd better go.

HANSON: Go! I think – with all due insolence to our host – that he should be compelled to open his bloody cupboard *door*!

ARNIE: Mockery ill-becomes you.

HANSON: I think he should ...

ARNIE: *You* think? Your thoughts, Hanson ... they're superfluous here. And your insolence undistinguished. You've been revealed as a pompous boor. Your otiose circumlocutions no longer sufficient to conceal the cringing, shivering coward within; your boldest gestures about as revelationary as a flea's. Do you really believe that I'm under any obligation to reveal *my* soul to you? My weaknesses stand higher than your greatest virtues.

MAUREEN: That's enough, for God's sake!

ARNIE: My only regret is, out of past charity, I have such weak substances on which to wreak my revenge.

HANSON [*applauding*]: Oh, bravo. Bravo.

ARNIE: I regret it all. All this. It's too puny for contempt!

JOAN: Where are you going?

[ARNIE *has gone stumbling towards the stairs.*]

ARNIE: What?

JOAN: These people: you *invited* them.

[ARNIE *comes back, takes the whisky bottle from the table and begins to go out.*]

ARNIE: Assume they aren't here. It's an easier alternative to assuming that they are.

JOAN [*casually*]: Have you read that telegram?

[*He pauses again.*]

In your pocket.

ARNIE: I heard!

[*Pause.*]

JOAN: They're not coming. As long as you realize that when you wake up. And it's just as well they aren't. You're blind drunk!

ARNIE: Do you know what you're saying? [*He snatches at his pockets, searching for then finding the telegram.*] I know what it says! I heard! [*To* HANSON:] Did you say that Scott wrote this? He wants firing! Did *he* write this? Then sack him! He's no good. Did I tell you what he did to Thompson?

JOAN: You better go to bed.

ARNIE: I am! I am! ... [*He stares round at them, full of threat.*] *I am!* [*He goes to the stairs, stumbles, regains his balance, and goes.*]

HANSON: So's friendship, if not love, repaid;

And by a graceless hand is trust betrayed.

MAUREEN Stop it! I've had enough! All this *indulgence.*

HANSON [*going to cupboard*]: Well, that comes out at least. [*He tries to wrench the cupboard door open, then kicks the thin wood open.*] Why it's empty! There's nothing here! [*He turns round, broken by his rage.*] He must have it up there with him.

JOAN: Just look what you've done ... [*Giggles.*]

SHEILA: He's jealous.

JOAN: What?

SHEILA: It's because he's jealous. That's why he's gone ...

MAUREEN: Sheila!

SHEILA: He is. He's jealous of Mr Hanson. Anybody can see.

[JOAN *is more disillusioned than annoyed.*]

JOAN [*tediously*]: Oh, for goodness sake. Get her out.

SHEILA: He is!

JOAN [*almost indifferently*]: Get out.

MAUREEN: Go on, Sheila. Go on. You better go now. [*To* HANSON:] Take her out.

SHEILA: He is! You're all jealous. All of you!

JOAN [*tediously*]: Take her out for goodness sake.

[MAUREEN *has taken* JOAN's *arm as her violence grows.*]

MAUREEN [*to* HANSON]: You'd better go.

[HANSON *has taken her arm.*]

HANSON: All right. All right. But don't blame her. That camel up there. Now you just shout at him!

[JOAN *stands tensely,* MAUREEN *holding her, until* SHEILA *and* HANSON *have gone.*

Silence. Then:]

JOAN [*quietly*]: I'll have to wait for my mother. She should have been back by now. That girl.

MAUREEN: I'll stay a little longer.

JOAN Would you? Do you mind? It's very kind of you.

MAUREEN: We might as well sit down.

[JOAN *turns out of her arms and wanders about the room. Then:*]

JOAN: That girl.

MAUREEN: I shouldn't worry.

JOAN: Isn't it quiet? It must be late. [*Pause.*] She can't be long. Everything must be shut by now.

MAUREEN: Will Arnold have gone to bed?

JOAN: Oh ... [*She listens.*] We won't see him again tonight. [*Pause.*] I've been dreading having a scene with my mother this evening while people were here. That's why I asked her to go out.

MAUREEN: Asked her?

JOAN: I told her this evening that she would have to leave. Go and live somewhere else ... It sounds hard. But there was no other way of doing it. Believe me.

MAUREEN: Is that what Arnold was in a mood about? I mean, when we came.

JOAN: No. No. He doesn't know I've told her yet.

[MAUREEN *watches* JOAN *moving listlessly about the room.*]

I had to tell her to go, you know. [*Pause.*] I've never seen her so hurt. Never. She ... I've never seen her so hurt.

MAUREEN: Where will she go when she leaves?

JOAN: She's grown so attached to Arnie. [*Sinks into a chair opposite her. They're silent. Then:*] Don't you think it's strange? The way he's always surrounded by women?

MAUREEN: Women?

JOAN: I don't know. He can't bear to be in this house alone. Can you imagine that? Don't you think it's extraordinary? [*Pause.*] You should see the look of relief on his face when I come in. Or my mother comes in. And he's sitting here alone. I don't think he's even aware of it. [*She gets up, moves around the room again, restlessly. Then:*] I was like a wild animal when we first got married. Always smashing things. I couldn't put my hand down without knocking something over. I was never still for one minute. [*She sits down again in the same seat, facing* MAUREEN.] We were always fighting. You know, fists and things. [*She laughs into her hand.*] It's awful, isn't it? But we used to stand up, bashing each other.

[MAUREEN *laughs.*]

I think this drink's beginning to have an effect on me. [*She snorts into her hand.*] Have you heard of anybody carrying on like that? I'm glad, actually. That they're not coming tomorrow. [*She looks round at the room.*] It was all prepared. All ready. Actually, they're very nice. I don't know why. Will you have something else? I'm sure you'd like them.

MAUREEN: No. I don't think I will.

JOAN: Would you like a stuffed eagle?

MAUREEN: I don't think so. No.

JOAN: A ship?

MAUREEN: No thanks.

JOAN: It's all yours if you want it. S'all going out. Sweeping changes. Actually. You mustn't tell anybody about this, will you?

MAUREEN: No ...

JOAN: You promise?

MAUREEN [*nods uncertainly*]: Yes.

JOAN: The fact is, Arnie doesn't give a damn for anybody. I'm exactly the same. Do you know anything about children?

MAUREEN: Well, I teach them.

JOAN: Ah, yes. [*She looks at* MAUREEN *freshly.*] Are you religious? You don't mind me asking?

MAUREEN [*pause*]: No. Well ...

JOAN: Do you believe in God?

MAUREEN: Well, in a sort of ...

JOAN [*lifting back her hair*]: I honestly don't know what to believe in. Is that the time? You absolutely promise?

MAUREEN: Yes.

JOAN: Well, I'll tell you. [*Looks round.*] Arnold actually ...

MAUREEN [*pause*]: Yes?

JOAN: Is God.

MAUREEN: Oh.

JOAN: He's only assumed the identity of a schoolteacher in order to remain incognito. Inconspicuous. For a God, you see, who believes in modesty and self-effacement there are severe doctrinal problems in asserting that he's God at all. Do you understand what I mean? [JOAN *watches her for a moment with some satisfaction.* MAUREEN *gives no reply at all.*] It's an enormous privilege, of course. [*Pause.*] Being married to Him at all.

[*Slow footsteps have already started on the stairs. It's only now, however, that* MAUREEN, *who is facing the stairs, actually looks up. She stands up immediately.*]

MAUREEN: Oh!

[JOAN *turns dreamily, slowly, as she sees* MAUREEN'S *reaction.* MRS ELLIS'S *appearance is dreadful: dressed in men's pyjamas, she has a bottle in her hand. Her look is compounded of many feelings: possessiveness, triumph, greed. Her matronly breasts are scarcely concealed by the jacket, and as she sways at the bottom of the stairs the vision quickly changes to that of a besotted old lady. For a moment* JOAN *fails to grasp what she sees. When she does it's with a cry of denial like a child's.*]

JOAN: Mam! [*She staggers to her feet.*] Mother!

MRS ELLIS: Do you know ...

JOAN: Mam! ... [*She glances frantically at the hall door where she'd expected her mother to appear.*]

MRS ELLIS: It's not in there. Not in there – as we all thought. [*She indicates the cupboard.*] It's not in there at all. He's hidden it – would you believe it, the cunning devil? – he's hidden it under the bed!

JOAN: No. No.

MRS ELLIS [*to* MAUREEN]: Underneath! Well! Whoever said he wasn't cunning!

JOAN: Mother.

MRS ELLIS: It's all lies. Everything. [*Violent.*] You said he wanted me to go! You did! ...

In fact. He doesn't want that at all.

JOAN: What?

MRS ELLIS: Arnie. [*She stands swaying, looking down at her daughter with something between consternation and triumph.*] You ask him.

JOAN: Oh, no ... No.

MRS ELLIS: You ... You. The things you told me.

JOAN: Oh, God. No. [*She sinks down, burying her face in her hands.*]

MRS ELLIS: Well. Well, then ... Who's sorry now? [*She collapses slowly into a chair.*] Are we having a party? Who's this, then? Another of Arnie's friends?

[*Lights fade.*]

ACT THREE

Scene One

Next morning.

The suit of armour stands to one side, around it the various 'pieces'.
JOAN *is tidying the room and preparing the table for breakfast.*
She's dressed neatly and tidily, and works briskly. Bottles from the party are stacked on the sideboard.
After a while ARNIE *appears at the foot of the stairs, tousled, genial, his shirt unbuttoned.*
He stands at the foot of the stairs, yawns, stretches, smacks his lips and looks round.
JOAN *goes on working.*

ARNIE: Well. Well. Ship-shape. Someone has been up early, I can see.
JOAN: I've made coffee. Is that all right?
ARNIE: Ah, fine. Fine. [*He comes slowly into the room, looks at the armour but makes no comment.*]
JOAN: I haven't cooked anything. I didn't think anyone would feel like eating.
ARNIE: Quite true. Quite true. [*He comes to the table, looks round at the various objects on it.*] Well, well, well. That was a very frivolous evening, Joan. All that booze. We shan't go through that again. Not for a very long time. No, we shan't. We certainly shan't. What? We shan't. [*He yawns. Snaps his mouth shut. Suddenly he shadow boxes, briefly, quickly. Then he yawns again, stretches.*] I've got to get down to weight. This is getting embarrassing. Last fight I ever had I only weighed three stone ten. No, was it four? [*He sits down at the table.*]
   [JOAN *has poured his coffee.* ARNIE *gazes across at the armour, then, after a while, begins to sing softly.*]
   Come, ye thankful people come,
   Raise the song of harvest home.
   All is safely gathered in
   Ere the winter storms begin;

258

God our Maker doth provide
For our wants to be supplied;
Come to God's own temple, come,
Raise the song of harvest home.

Where's Edie, then?

JOAN: She hasn't got up yet. [*She has rearranged the table and gone back to her cleaning.*]

ARNIE: The fact is, I feel in a very philosophic frame of mind. All my life I've looked for some positive reaction in people. Did you know that?

[*Pause.* JOAN *goes on with her tasks.*]

There are certain tribes in the Northern Province of Nigeria who use carrier bags for latrines. [*Abstracted, he now looks up at* JOAN *directly, waiting a moment, then:*] This man at school told me that. He worked out there once on famine relief. Saved thousands from starvation. His life was full of significance and meaning. [*Abstracted a moment.*] He said there's this enterprising man in Birmingham who sends them out regularly by post. To an agent. Who sells them at a fantastic profit. It cuts down the risk of malaria or dysentery or something. [*Pause.*] 'Hoyle's Supermarket' they've got printed on the side. [*Pause.*] It's amazing what human initiative will rise to once it sets itself to a particular task.

[ARNIE *has become quite abstracted.* JOAN *continues with her work.* ARNIE *gets up and goes on talking absently.*]

When I was a boy we had a milkman who came in a horse and trap. He wore a little bowler hat and a striped apron and came in each morning from the country with cans of fresh milk and ladled it all out with little ladles. Beautiful. They went up from one the size of a thimble to one as big as his hat.

[JOAN *has sat down casually on the arm of a chair, holding her face with her hand.*]

He ran over a boy one day. The wheel of his cart went over his head. It wasn't his fault. But he offered the boy's mother free milk for a year; you know, for goodwill and neighbourliness. She was very poor. She had eleven children. I don't think he knew that at the time. [*Pause.*] He went out of business in six months. Bankrupt.

[*Pause.*] You should have seen this woman's house. Milk, there was, everywhere. Nothing but milk. [*He suddenly looks round.* JOAN *gets up and resumes her tasks: taking the coffee pot to the kitchen.* ARNIE *talks through to her.*] You know, I've always had the ambition to be a writer. The things I'd write about would be fairly rhetorical in manner.

[JOAN *re-emerges.*]

Subjects ... Well, it may even have caught your attention. The extraordinary mixture of hysteria and passivity one gets in society today. I mean ...

[*While he's been talking* MRS ELLIS *has appeared from the stairs. She's carrying a small suitcase and is dressed in a coat and hat, a small fur round her shoulders.*]

MRS ELLIS: I'll send for my things when I've got an address.

JOAN: You'd better put the case down ...

ARNIE: I thought there for a moment, you know, that we were going off on holiday. God, weather like this, too. It's incomprehensible.

JOAN [*ignoring him*]: I'm heating up the coffee.

[MRS ELLIS *stands gazing irresolutely around her.*]

And do take that coat off. You'll be roasted alive. The tray's ready to fetch through. [*She busies herself now re-arranging the table.*]

MRS ELLIS: Joan ...

JOAN: All it requires is lifting.

ARNIE: This is quite extraordinary. I've forgotten his name now. But this boy fell off the school roof on ... Friday, it must have been. Over forty feet in height. No. I'm wrong there. Nearer fifty. Fell like a stone. Bang. Right on his head. By every right it should have killed him. But no. This should interest you, Edie. He's scarcely hit the ground than he stands up and says, 'Sir, I didn't fall. Somebody pushed me.' So damned anxious, in wandering near the parapet, to show he hadn't broken a rule.

[MRS ELLIS *has gone into the kitchen. She comes out again now, almost immediately, lost.*]

MRS ELLIS: I don't seem able to find it.

JOAN: Look for it, mother. Put the light on. Open the curtains.

MRS ELLIS: Yes ...

JOAN: And do take your coat off.

MRS ELLIS: Yes ... [*She starts back, falters.*] I don't know how you can just sit there.

ARNIE: Sit?

MRS ELLIS: I can hardly stand!

ARNIE: Now, then. Now, then. There's no need to get upset.

MRS ELLIS: Upset! [*She buries her face in her hands.*]

JOAN: It's all right, mother.

MRS ELLIS [*moaning*]: I don't know what to do.

JOAN: You'll stay here, mother. It's all right.

MRS ELLIS: Oh, Joan ... Joan.

JOAN: Now, you're all right. You're all right.

[MRS ELLIS *cries into her hands.*]

ARNIE [*brightly*]: How about some coffee?

[JOAN *has gone to take* MRS ELLIS *in her arms.*]

JOAN: Come on. You better come upstairs. I'll help you up.

MRS ELLIS: Oh, God, Joan. What am I going to do?

JOAN: Oh, now. You come up. Come on, now. Come on...

MRS ELLIS: I can't. I can't.

JOAN: I'll bring you something up. Now, come on. You'll be all right.
[*She leads her mother to the stairs. They go out.* ARNIE *has stood up. He walks about. Puts his hands in his pockets. Whistles.*]

ARNIE: This is quite extraordinary. [*He touches the armour confidingly.*] About two days ago the Director of Education came up to me and said, 'Bancroft,' he said – I mean it's not as if my name was Bancroft – 'Bancroft, I don't know quite how to tell you this, and I should hate it to get around. But the fact is, Bancroft, my wife has recently begun to manufacture money. The thing is, that periodically she lowers her knickers and from inside takes a miscellaneous collection of coins. The process, as far as I am aware, Bancroft, has completely taken over her excretory organs. And it's mostly silver. The coins, I mean.'
You know – would you believe it – the only comment he made after telling me all this was 'Pity it isn't gold, Bancroft. Just like that rotten bitch to produce second best.' [*He laughs.*] Anyway, I thought you'd like to know.

[JOAN *has come in as he finishes this.*]

Oh, how is the old bird?

[JOAN *begins her preparations of making a glass of warm milk.*] You know, this unnerves me. I'm looking for some sort of constructive attitude from you, Joan. Something a bit bolder. To generalize about one's misfortune is invariably a sign of moral recovery in my book. If you could work something up on those lines I'd be immensely grateful.

JOAN: Yes. [*Goes on with her task.*]

ARNIE: I think I need to feel degenerate.

JOAN: I'm taking my mother up a glass of milk.

ARNIE: You see. Those are not the sort of remarks I'm looking for, Joan.

[JOAN *has now gone into the kitchen.* ARNIE *talks through to her.*] The sort I'm looking for only you can provide. There's no one else. My only other opportunity for being punished lies immobilized, apparently, upstairs.

[JOAN *returns to collect the sugar from the table.*]

JOAN: There's an old woman up there, broken in two.

ARNIE: Well, at least she has that reassurance. What have I got? Nothing. Nothing. I don't understand it. I don't. I get no crumb of consolation from this at all. I feel I should get something. I deserve to suffer something, Joan. Even if it's only retribution.

[JOAN *hasn't answered.*]

These silences unnerve me. At any moment I'm going to suffer a relapse. I think I should warn you, Joan. You know what that might lead to.

[JOAN *still offers no answer.*]

[*Suddenly.*] I should also like it to be known that this sudden and alarming capacity to behave like a frog . . . to bespatter detachment on every side, to spawn ill humour, to sit for hours on end on a pad of disaffection . . . that all these qualities, while adding conviction to your image as a woman, *in no way*, in no way, improve your image as a man!

[JOAN *still makes no sign. Silence. Then* ARNIE *indicates the armour.*]

I don't understand. Some blame for my predicament attaches itself to you. I lie here, caught up in a million abominations, attributes, some of them fed in long before conception. And some of them, *some of them,* fed in by you! In that clammy little hand lie parts of me I don't think, in all honesty, you understand.

[ARNIE *follows* JOAN *to the kitchen door.*]

Guilt and austerity are not necessarily compatible, Joan, I mean . . . effusiveness could make your message just as clear.

JOAN: You've behaved like a dwarf. Everything in your life is like that. Dwarfish.

ARNIE: Well. Yes. That's something.

[*He talks through to her in the kitchen.*]

A dwarf. [*Pause; reflects.*] I don't like that somehow. [*Half-laughs.*] You know I object to that, Joan. I don't feel like a dwarf. [*He looks at his hands.*] I wouldn't describe them particularly, for instance, as dwarfish.

[*Silence.*]

Haven't you anything else to say?

[JOAN *re-emerges with the glass of milk.*]

JOAN: What are you going to do, Arnie?

ARNIE: I don't know. [*Pause.*] I'll do the only decent thing, I suppose.

JOAN: Yes.

ARNIE: That's all there is to do.

JOAN: Yes.

ARNIE: I'll marry her.

[*They're silent. Then:*]

JOAN: Why don't you leave, Arnie? And rid yourself of all this torment?

ARNIE [*abstracted*]: I don't know. Life has no dignity, Joan. No, I do agree with that. [*Pause.*] And death hasn't a great deal to re-commend it, either. [*Pause.*] Both of them, when you look at it: they're pretty anonymous affairs. I don't know. I feel I should be able to do something. I feel . . . the moment's come . . . it's actually arrived. [*He grasps the air.*] And yet it refuses to . . . emanate. [*Suddenly looks round at the room.*] Anyway, I couldn't leave all this. My own fireside. I've worked hard for all this. I have. It's mine. This is my situation in life.

[JOAN, *after watching him with some attention, has turned away at this towards the stairs.*]

Perhaps I could go mad. Insanity, you know, is the one refuge I've always felt I was able to afford. The insights that irrationality brings. Well, in the end, that's what we're looking for. Cleavages. Cracks. Fissures. Openings. Some little aperture of warmth and light.

[JOAN, *after some hesitation, goes with her glass of milk.*]
Look, this is a very poor arrangement. I haven't got your attention at all. [*He turns away.*] I don't know. I might as well be talking to the wall. [ARNIE *goes to the armour: examines it sadly. Then he goes to the wall. He moves from one patch to another on the wall as if carefully selecting the right one for his task, rubbing his hand over its surface, then finally choosing one spot and taking up a stance before it.*]
When I was young, my mother said to me:
'Never drown but in the sea –
Rivers, streams and other dilatory courses
Are not contingent with the elemental forces
Which govern you and me – and occasionally your father –
So remember, even if the means are insufficient, rather
Than die in pieces subside by preference as a whole,
For disintegration is inimical to the soul
Which seeks the opportunity or the chances
To die in the circumstances
Of a prince, a saviour, or a messiah –
Or something, perhaps, even a little higher –
You and me and several of your aunties,
On my side, though working class, have destinies
Scarcely commensurate with our upbringing:
I hope in you we are instilling
This sense of secret dignities and rights
– Not like your father's side, the lights
Of which, I hope, we'll never see again,
Who have, I'm afraid, wet blotting-paper for a brain!'
    [*Pause.*]
'Please, please my son,
Don't fail me like your father done.'
    [ARNIE *stands for a moment regarding the wall, expectantly, tensed. Then slowly he relaxes. His head sinks, his shoulders droop. His forehead leans against the wall.*]

Oh. Oh. Oh.
When I was young, when I was young,
There were so many things I should have done.
    [*Fade.*]

Scene Two

Evening, a few days later.
    The room has been cleared of all ARNIE'S *possessions. It's clean and immaculate. A large vase of flowers stands on the table and another on the sideboard.*
    From the hall comes the sound of voices.

HANSON [*heard*]: Arnie? [*Pause.*] Arnie? Arnie! [*Pause.*] He can't be here. [*Whistles.*]

MAUREEN [*heard*]: Arnie? [*Knocking on outer door.*] Can't hear anybody.
    [*The calling has been tentative, apprehensive. Then, finally, the door opens and* HANSON *puts his head round.*]

HANSON: No. No one here. [*Whistles.*] No.
    [*He and* MAUREEN *come in.* HANSON *carries a parcel.*]

MAUREEN: Goodness.

HANSON: I say. [*They look round at the changes.*] Drastic renovations, what?

MAUREEN: Joan?

HANSON: I say ... [*Whistles a tune to himself as he looks round, tapping furniture and empty spaces with his stick.*]

MAUREEN: Joan?
    [MAUREEN *has glanced in the kitchen.*]
    No: no one.
    [*Shrugs.*]

HANSON: Well, then ...

MAUREEN: I suppose we better wait.

HANSON [*looks at watch*]: I don't know. What? Arnie! [*Then distracted*] I say. Cupboard restored. Would you believe it?
    [*Goes to look, then, in the kitchen. Comes back. Sets parcel he is carrying on the table.*]

Ship deserted, what? Oh ...

[*Sounds of the outer door opening, etc.* HANSON *hastily composes himself, tie, etc.* MAUREEN, *who has sat down, gets up.* MRS ELLIS *comes in, carrying a basket.*]

MRS ELLIS: Oh ...

MAUREEN: Mrs Ellis ...

HANSON: We ... Oh, allow me ... [*Offers to take her basket.*]

MRS ELLIS: No ... It's all right.

MAUREEN: We found the door open. We knocked, but there was no one here.

MRS ELLIS: Oh ...

MAUREEN: Is Joan out, too?

MRS ELLIS: Yes ... I've just been ... She ... I'll just put these in the kitchen.

HANSON: Please. Allow me.

[*Offers to take basket.*]

MRS ELLIS: No. No, it's all right.

[*She goes into the kitchen.*]

HANSON: Well, well ...

[*He whistles a tune again, glances at his watch, at* MAUREEN, *wanders round the room.*

MAUREEN *goes to the kitchen door.*]

MAUREEN: How is Arnie, Mrs Ellis?

[*After a moment* MRS ELLIS *comes out.*]

MRS ELLIS: Oh, he's ... all right.

HANSON: Fine. Fine. We ... popped round. He hasn't been to school: the past few days.

MRS ELLIS: No.

HANSON: We ... ah ... thought we'd pop round.

MRS ELLIS: Yes.

HANSON: Fine. Fine.

[*She's taken off her coat and goes through to the hallway to hang it up.* HANSON *and* MAUREEN *exchange glances.* HANSON *whistles a tune.*

Outside in the hall the sound of Joan's arrival: 'Oh, it's you.' 'Visitors.' 'What?' 'Mr Hanson ... schoolteacher ...'

HANSON *re-composes himself. A moment later* JOAN *comes in.*]

JOAN: Oh, hello.

HANSON: Joan.

MAUREEN: And how are you?

JOAN: I'm well. Fine. And you?

MAUREEN: Yes. Fine.

HANSON: Fine. Fine.

JOAN: Isn't Arnie in?

MAUREEN: We knocked, and shouted.

HANSON: Found the door ajar. What? No answer.

MAUREEN: No.

JOAN [*taking off her coat*]: If the door was open he can't be far away.

HANSON: Well, then ... [*Silence.*] Everything in order, then?

JOAN: I think so. More or less.

HANSON: Well, then ... [*Glances at watch.*] I suppose we better ... be making tracks.

[MRS ELLIS *has come in and gone through to the kitchen.*]

JOAN: Stay and have some tea if you like.

HANSON: Yes. Fine. Well.

JOAN: My mother will be making some.

HANSON: Fine. Fine.

MAUREEN: How is Arnie, Joan?

JOAN: I don't know. All right. [*Shrugs.*]

HANSON: We were just remarking. Several days since he put in an appearance, what? At school.

JOAN: Yes.

HANSON: Nothing to worry about, then?

JOAN: No. I don't think so.

[ARNIE *has appeared behind them, from the stairs. His head is done up, turban-fashion, in a towel. In his hand he carries the sword.*]

HANSON: Good. Good. We were just remarking. Vast changes. What?

JOAN: What?

HANSON: The room.

JOAN: Ah, yes.

HANSON: Flowers! [*Smells them.*] Beautiful.

JOAN: Yes.

HANSON: Altogether. [*Indicates room.*] Lighter.

JOAN: Yes.

[*In glancing round they become slowly aware of* ARNIE. *Silence.
Then:*]

ARNIE: The King, though broken by his plight,
       Shall rise again to set things right!

HANSON: Oh ...

MAUREEN: Arnie ...

ARNIE: Well, well, well. How are we all? Jeff?

HANSON: I'm fine. Fine.

ARNIE: And Maureen. How are you, my dear?

MAUREEN: I'm well, Arnie.

ARNIE: Just arrived, eh?

HANSON: Yes. Yes. Just about.

ARNIE: Thought I heard sounds. Couldn't be too sure. Got both my
       damned ears fastened up.

MAUREEN: And how are you, Arnie, yourself?

ARNIE: Oh, not so bad. Not so bad. Can't grumble. Can't com-
       plain.

HANSON: The Head sends his felicitations, Arnie ...

ARNIE: Fine. Fine.

HANSON: And the staff and pupils likewise. Looking forward,
        needless to say, to your early return to duties.

ARNIE: Ah, yes.

HANSON: Brought a few essentials here, Arnie.
        [*Indicates the parcel.*]
        Keep the system mobile, mind alert.

ARNIE: Ah, yes!
       [*Silence.*]

HANSON: We were just remarking.

ARNIE: Yes.

HANSON: Vast changes since we were last here.

ARNIE: Changes.

HANSON: The room ...

ARNIE: Gave them all to the refuse-man, you know.

JOAN: I'll just see about the tea.
      [*Goes to kitchen.*]

ARNIE [*to* MAUREEN]: And how are you?

MAUREEN: I'm well, Arnie.

ARNIE: I suppose you've seen their lorry? They have a blade in the back which crushes them all up.

[*Suddenly, hugely:*]

Crush! Crush! Crush!

HANSON: What, all of them, old boy?

ARNIE: Absolutely. [*Gestures at the room.*] The lot.

[*Then, after a moment, swinging the sword:*]

'Cept this, of course.

HANSON: Yes.

ARNIE: I kept it back.

[*Whistles then between his teeth as, in demonstration, he slashes it about him.*]

HANSON: Ah, yes.

ARNIE: Bound to come in useful.

HANSON: Yes.

ARNIE: At least, so I thought.

HANSON: Ah, yes, old boy.

ARNIE: Arms, hands, feet, legs, abdomen. The lot.

[*Mimes the lorry's blade.*]

Head!

[*Gurgles, hand across his throat.*]

HANSON: We spoke to Sheila, by the way.

ARNIE: Yes?

HANSON: Had a little word in her ear.

ARNIE: Ah, yes.

MAUREEN: I think she'll show a little discretion.

ARNIE: She will?

HANSON: I think so, old man.

ARNIE: Good, good. I could do with a little bit of that myself.

[*Laughs.*] Joan?

[*Looks round. Then he gestures towards the kitchen.*]

She has a job.

MAUREEN: Oh.

ARNIE: Out to work each day.

HANSON: Yes?

ARNIE: Perhaps she mentioned it?

MAUREEN: No. [*Shakes her head.*]

269

ARNIE: She acquired her credentials, I'm glad to say, long before I married her. In a secretarial capacity, of course.

HANSON: Ah, yes.

ARNIE: Type. Type. Type. You should see her fingers. Flexing. Even in bed.

HANSON: Ah, yes, old boy.

ARNIE: On the other hand ...

HANSON: Yes, old boy?

ARNIE: Absolutely nothing to worry about.

HANSON: No, no ...

ARNIE: The doctor recommends a long sea-voyage.

MAUREEN: Sea-voyage?

ARNIE: And a complete change of air.

MAUREEN: I see.

ARNIE: I would have thought, myself, that the two of them were perfectly synonymous.

HANSON: Absolutely.

ARNIE: I'm overworked.

HANSON: My dear boy ...

ARNIE: My nerves, Jeff, are stretched beyond endurance.

[*Glances round with some exaggeration to see that he is not overheard.*]

I'm afraid I should have warned you. Joan ... [*taps his head.*] You will find her, I'm afraid, considerably changed. Her work – the contingencies of high office, the flow, the rapid, reckless inter-change of ideas which has been her lot now [*dramatically consults his bare wrist*] for the past six hours, leaves her – I'm very much afraid – *prostrate.*

HANSON: Ah, yes.

JOAN [*entering*]: My mother's bringing in the tea.

HANSON: Oh, that's very kind of you, Joan.

MAUREEN: Shouting at the devils all afternoon. Just one of those days. When you want a bit of peace you can never get it.

ARNIE: What do you really think, Jeff?

HANSON: Think?

ARNIE: Feel, if you like. What do you really feel?

HANSON: I feel we're completely out of touch with one another, if you really want to know.

ARNIE: I'm not out of touch with you. I can see, for example, that you are embarrassed at being here, anxious to conceal it, and looking forward to the moment when you leave and can tell people outside how I am looking and behaving, and what things I say. And as for Maureen – I can see how my behaviour has licensed what was previously impossible. Does that sound like someone out of touch with you?

HANSON: You take to insanity, Arnold, like other men take to drink. [*A silence. Then:*]

ARNIE: You have insufficient innocence to be a fool, Jeffrey. [ARNIE *watches him a moment. A pause, then:*]

MAUREEN: We're still struggling along, by the way, Arnie, with rehearsals ...

HANSON: Oh, yes. I'm afraid your absence, old man, has been severely felt. And, somewhat ineffectually I must confess, I have been obliged to take your place ...

ARNIE: Robin Hood!

HANSON: Ah, yes!

ARNIE: Jeff. You must have discovered it for youself.

HANSON: Yes?

ARNIE: A usurper. An outlaw!

HANSON: Ah, yes.

ARNIE: Always on the outside of things. Maureen! – cynical of the established order: disenfranchised, dispossessed. A refugee, if you like, from the proper world.

MAUREEN: Yes.

ARNIE: I hope you've kept them to it, Jeff!

HANSON: Well, as a matter of fact ...

ARNIE: *Kings.* [*A dramatic self-gesture.*]

JOAN [*to* ARNIE]: Why don't you sit down?

ARNIE: They're a sort of receptacle, if you like. Into which flow all the goodness and intentions of mankind: and out of which in turn flow benevolence – and decisions. Authority. Rule. One becomes a king, not by chance – but by right: attributes fed in long before conception. Pre-ordained.

HANSON: Well, we weren't making it that complicated. [*To* JOAN] Robin stood on his bow yesterday afternoon and nearly guillotined his ear.

ARNIE: You think kingship's something foreign to me, Jeff? Let me tell you — I've studied it all my life. It's my profession. History! ... You think I come from an age sentimental about its motives. You're wrong. My ancestry is rooted in action, in events, not causes. It's only fools who worry *why* they are. [*Pause.*] Do you know what goodness is?

HANSON: Goodness? [*Glances at the others.*]

ARNIE: Do you know what evil is? [*He looks round at them; they don't answer.*] Look. A simple arithmetical problem — set in all the schools. [*He pulls up a chair and sits facing them.*] Take what we are from everything, and what remains?

HANSON [*pause*]: I don't know.

MAUREEN [*as ARNIE looks to her*]: No.

ARNIE: Goodness and Kings. [*He studies* HANSON *a moment. Then:*] Kings rise above themselves. They become ... inanimate. Formed. [*He shapes it with his hands. Then he looks up at them; sees their looks.*] Do you know what the greatest threat to the present century is? [*Pause.*] The pygmies. [*He smiles at them.*]

HANSON: Yes.

JOAN: Arnie ...

ARNIE: So small, so inconspicuous, they infiltrate everywhere. Not only out there, but into seats of government and power. And, of course, they're disguised. Not as men. Not even as small men. But as conditions of the soul. [*Relaxes.*] You think that's a conspiracy? No. We *choose* the lesser men.

HANSON: Yes.

ARNIE: Napoleons — they have their day. Usurpers, whether for good or ill. But the king rules not by revolution but by constitution. He is *born*: he is *bred*: he is created king *inside*. [*Pause.*] His *constitution* makes *the* constitution which makes him king. Joan, I don't like you standing behind me.

JOAN: It's my mother. She's bringing in the tea.

[JOAN *has gone to hold the kitchen door:* MRS ELLIS *enters with a laden tray.*]

HANSON: Ah, grand. Lovely.

[MRS ELLIS *nods without looking up.*]

ARNIE: Isn't that a miraculous sight? A tea-tray elevated through the air entirely by its own volition.

JOAN: Arnie, I'm afraid, has taken to assuming my mother doesn't exist.

[MRS ELLIS *puts the tray on the table. She serves the tea according to instructions.*]

JOAN: Maureen. Milk and sugar?

MAUREEN: Thank you. We ought really to be leaving fairly soon. [*She looks to* HANSON.]

ARNIE: Oh, don't stay on my account, Maureen. I can perform miracles any time for your amusement. If you wish, I can make that tea-tray depart to where it came from entirely under its own resources.

JOAN: Milk and sugar, Jeff?

HANSON: No sugar. I've decided I must slim.

ARNIE: Or sugar transfer itself, unsolicited, from bowl to cup.

MAUREEN [*to* HANSON]: Ay, now . . .

HANSON: That's to say, someone has decided for me.

[ARNIE *has been overlooked.*]

ARNIE: What's that!

HANSON: My dear Arnold.

ARNIE: *What?*

HANSON: You don't have to play these games for *us*.

ARNIE: Oh?

HANSON [*taking the bull by the horns*]: We're your friends. Whatever you do, you're a friend, and we're concerned for you. [*Looks to* JOAN *and* MRS ELLIS.] Look, I don't wish to embarrass you, Joan. But you understand?

JOAN: Yes . . .

HANSON: So there's no need for this eccentricity, Arnie.

ARNIE: What are you trying to do, Jeff?

HANSON: I'm trying . . .

ARNIE: Hoping to *ingratiate* yourself with me?

HANSON: I hope there's no need for me to do that.

ARNIE: You're being very foolish. Do you know *anything*!

HANSON: It seems not.

ARNIE [*carried away*]: Scars . . . [*He holds out the palms of his hands, looking at them.*] They inhabit the skin. They grow there after a while like natural features. Deformities actually acquire that authority. [*Looks up bitterly at* HANSON.] Did you know? [*Pause.*] Remove them – and you remove life itself. Well?

HANSON: I don't know what you're talking about actually, Arnold.

ARNIE: I'm talking about ... alternatives.

HANSON: Alternatives. I see.

ARNIE: To kingship. [*Stares fixedly at* HANSON. *Then he smiles. A moment later he relaxes completely.*] Oh, Jeff. [*Laughs.*] You looked positively embarrassed. Didn't he? Pompous, if I didn't know him better.

MAUREEN: Well ...

ARNIE: Ah, come on, now, Jeff. Fair's fair. 'A friend.' You old prigster!

> I know a man with two left feet
> Who'd rather be dead than be seen in the street:
> Yet the fellow would hardly have seemed such a sight
> If he hadn't have had two more on his right.

[*He laughs, spreading out his hands.*] I shall now tell you a dirty history.

HANSON: I honestly think, Arnie, we've had enough.

ARNIE: History has always had a certain fascination for me.

MAUREEN: Joan. I really think we should go.

ARNIE: The raising of Lazarus as a permanent act of restitution. Kings, queens, emperors. Saints! Inhabited by one's own domestic soul!

[*They're silent.*]

[*Getting up*] Everything has to be defined. Yet how can you define anything except by its limitations? Why! – my limitations are limitless!

MAUREEN: I really think we ought to be going, Joan, you know. We can pop in again, later in the week – if that's convenient.

JOAN: Yes. Any time you like.

HANSON: Well ...

ARNIE: Do you remember Scott? ... Scott!

HANSON: Arnie. I'd like ...

ARNIE [*direct to* HANSON]: Certain things can't be destroyed, however much you try. Rifles rust, erode, and fall apart. They become mechanically defunct. But swords – while rusting too, preserve down to their last grain an emblem of the truth. Instruments of honour, which the world is a feebler place without! ... Dignity. [*Draws himself up.*] The past brought down to us in swords!

HANSON: Arnie, we have to be going.

ARNIE: Ah, yes.

HANSON [*to* JOAN]: If there's anything we can do, Joan ... You will let us know?

JOAN: Yes. Thank you.

MAUREEN: Bye, Arnie.

HANSON: Good-bye, Arnold.

ARNIE [*cheerfully*]: Good-bye. Good-bye. It's been very good of you to come.

MAUREEN: Good-bye Mrs Ellis.

> [MRS ELLIS *nods and, having collected the cups, etc., carries the tray out to the kitchen.*
>
> ARNIE *nods cheerfully, standing to one side as they leave. Left alone, he walks up and down a moment, then goes to the fire, gazing down. There are sounds of farewell from the hall, then* JOAN *enters.*]

JOAN: Do you want some more tea?

ARNIE: What? I don't know.

JOAN: Soon, there'll be nobody coming here at all.

ARNIE: No. No. That's quite true.

JOAN: Where did you manage to find that?

ARNIE: I extracted it.

JOAN: Yes?

ARNIE: From the dustbin.

JOAN: My father had a sword.

ARNIE: Yes?

JOAN: When I was young. [*Pause.*] He could hold it at full stretch, in one hand, without the tip even quivering, and count slowly to a hundred.

ARNIE: I look behind me, Joan.

JOAN: What?

ARNIE: I live. I go along. I look behind ... And I see ... not achievements towering in my path.

JOAN: No ...

ARNIE: Ruins. I can see ... wonderful.

> [*A vision rises before his eyes. Finally, slowly, he sits down.*]

If I raise you to the status of a queen, do you think you could be realistic?

[JOAN *takes the remainder of the things into the kitchen.*
ARNIE *sits alone, abstracted, still, the sword in his hand.*
After some little while JOAN *comes out followed by* MRS ELLIS.]

JOAN: Arnie ... ? Is there anything else you want?

ARNIE [*pause*]: What?

JOAN: My mother has something to tell you.

ARNIE: What?

MRS ELLIS: Arnie ... [*Looks concernedly at* JOAN, *then clenches her own hands.*] I ... we've ... I'll be leaving tomorrow.

ARNIE: What? What? Who said that? Who!

MRS ELLIS: Arnie. I'll be going tomorrow. I've found a room.

ARNIE: I could have sworn ...

MRS ELLIS: It's a small flat, really.

[ARNIE *looks up.*]

The place I've found.

ARNIE: It's you! It's you!

MRS ELLIS: Joan helped me to find it. And ...

ARNIE: Look. You are, or are you not, *positively speaking*?

MRS ELLIS: I ... It's already furnished.

ARNIE: Well ... at least that's clear. It would have been alarming, Joan, at this late hour, to have discovered ... of all things ... that I suffered from hallucinations.

MRS ELLIS: I think it's the best for all of us.

ARNIE: I'm sure. Yes. Yes. I'm sure. I'm sure. [*Suddenly.*] We've had a good time, Edie.

MRS ELLIS: Yes.

ARNIE [*taps side of his head*]: I had something then on the tip of my tongue. No. No. It's gone. It's gone.

MRS ELLIS: It's not so far away ... that I can't pop in from time to time.

ARNIE: No. No. I'm sure. We have, after all ... what have we? ... What? This is extraordinary. After all these years.

JOAN: Yes.

ARNIE: I'd say ...

JOAN: Yes?

ARNIE: That that was a revolution.

JOAN: Yes.

ARNIE: Or a revelation. I'm not sure which. [*Pause.*] Ahem! [*Pause.*]

I better make a speech. A moment like this ... Can scarcely go by.
Unacknowledged.

JOAN: I don't think it's necessary, Arnie.

[ARNIE *has stood up.*]

ARNIE: No? [*He puts down his sword.*] This is a very heavy sentence,
Edie.

MRS ELLIS: I'm not sure ...

ARNIE: On us. On us. I might well have to make amendments. To the
constitution. To accommodate that.

[*He holds the top of his head.*]

It had been my intention ... to leucotomize my wife.

MRS ELLIS: Yes ...

ARNIE: Amongst several other ... As it is ...

[*Gazes up at them from beneath his hands.*]

We better have a party.

MRS ELLIS: After I've gone.

ARNIE: Yes. Yes. After you've gone.

MRS ELLIS: I'll ... go up. I've still some things to finish.

ARNIE: Yes. Yes.

[*She goes.*
Silence. Then:]

Back to school. Monday!

JOAN: Yes.

ARNIE: Rest. Recuperation ... Work!

JOAN: Yes.

[*Silence. Then, suddenly:*]

ARNIE: Oh! [*Cries out.*]

JOAN: Arnie!

ARNIE: Oh! There's something coming out!

JOAN: Arnie ...

ARNIE: Oh, dear, Joan.

JOAN: Arnie ... It's all right.

ARNIE: Oh, dear, Joan. There's something here ... that's very hard
... Merciless.

JOAN: Arnie ... It's all right.

ARNIE: Oh, dear, oh!

[*He covers up his head.*]

JOAN: Arnie.

ARNIE: Oh, dear. Oh, dear. There's something. What? Oh, dear. There's something coming out.

JOAN: Arnie.

[*He looks up, still holding his head.*]

Come on, now.

ARNIE: Oh. Oh.

[*His hands are clasped to the top of his head.*]

What am I to do?

JOAN: Here.

[*She holds out her hand.*]

ARNIE: Oh. *Now.* [*Screams, hugely. Then:*]

JOAN: It's all over.

ARNIE: Oh, dear.

[*After a moment he lowers one hand.*]

Oh I'm sure ... I think.

JOAN: Yes.

ARNIE: In all sincerity.

[*He calms. He looks slowly round.*]

Nevertheless. I'm assuming that I can come out. The assumption is merely based, you understand, on a generality of feeling.

JOAN: Yes.

ARNIE: Oh.

> Oh, lovely woman ... feel no obligation;
> Beauty is its own salvation.
> The rest is meant to burn.

I can't hear a thing.

JOAN: Are you coming up?

ARNIE: Up?

JOAN: Yes.

ARNIE: Have I finished?

[*He looks around.*]

JOAN: Yes.

ARNIE: I've finished?

JOAN: I think so.

ARNIE: Are you sure?

JOAN: Yes.

[*They stand facing one another, still some distance apart.*]
ARNIE: Oh. Joan. Thank God.
[*Fade.*]

THE FARM

THE FARM

First presented at the Royal Court Theatre, London, on 26 September 1973, under the direction of Lindsay Anderson. The cast was as follows:

WENDY	Patricia Healey
JENNIFER	Meg Davies
BRENDA	Prunella Gee
SLATTERY	Bernard Lee
MRS SLATTERY	Doreen Mantle
ALBERT	Lewis Collins
ARTHUR	Frank Grimes

CHARACTERS

WENDY
JENNIFER
BRENDA
SLATTERY
MRS SLATTERY
ALBERT
ARTHUR

ACT ONE

The lounge, or living-room, of a farmhouse: amply proportioned and of some antiquity. Casement-type windows and a more recently constructed french window look out, at the rear, to the garden.

A large stone fireplace occupies the wall stage right; a door, matching the shoulder-height wood-panelling, occupies the centre of the wall stage left. The furniture is of generous proportions: a chintz-covered three-piece suite, an oak dresser with brass-work, an oak sideboard. There's a bookcase, well stocked, and a desk set against the wall, covered in papers, files, etc. The place has a spacious, easy-going atmosphere, earthy, plain, over-used: the feeling of a burrow, stained, familiar, caverned-out. One or two framed prints (old) hang on the wall.

WENDY, a young, independent, perhaps rather severe-looking woman of thirty-three is reading in one of the easy chairs. She's got a pile of books on the floor beside her, a cup of coffee on a small table, and cigarettes and a lighter. A tray with a coffee pot, milk jug, etc., stands on the sideboard.

Door closes off: low whistle.

JENNIFER comes in the door: well, not ostentatiously, dressed, she's slightly younger than WENDY. Attractive. She has on a coat with a fur collar, and a pair of gloves. She carries no bag.

JENNY [*looks round; greets her*]: Sweets . . .
WENDY: Lovey . . . [*Having looked up, resumes her reading.*]
JENNY: Freezing . . .
WENDY: How'd it go?
JENNY: Usual . . . [*Takes off her gloves: warms hands.*]
　Dad not in?
　　[WENDY *shakes head, still reading.*]
　Mum?
WENDY: Out.
　　[*Banging overhead.* JENNY *looks up, shivers from the cold, then takes off coat. Goes to coffee jug.*]
JENNY: Anything in here for me?
WENDY: Might be.

285

JENNY: Hardly ...

WENDY: Oh, dear. [*Still reading.*]

JENNY: Hardly any.

WENDY: See what you've been missing, love.

[JENNY *picks up* WENDY's *cup: pours a drop of coffee. Banging overhead: hammer blows.*]

JENNY: What you been doing, Sweets?

WENDY: Nothing.

JENNY: Why do you use lipstick in the house?

WENDY: What? [*Looks up: first look of interest.*]

[JENNY *holds up the cup.*]

JENNY: Can't you get that stuff that doesn't come off?

WENDY: Dunno.

JENNY: Expecting anybody, are you?

WENDY: No.

JENNY [*having tasted it, puts cup down*]: Don't think I'll drink it after all.

WENDY: Sick?

JENNY [*groans, murmurs in affirmative*]: You in a rotten mood as well?

[WENDY *reading: hums assent, singsong.*

Banging comes from overhead.]

JENNY [*looks up.*]: What's she up to?

WENDY: Placards.

JENNY: Placards?

WENDY: Notices.

JENNY: Who for?

WENDY: Exhorting herself to rise and shine. (*Looks up at* JENNY.) See the one she put on the old man's table? ... 'The shortest distance between two people is a smile.'

[*They laugh.*

Pause.]

JENNY: Mother and the old man out together?

WENDY: On her own. [*Looks up at clock, above fireplace.*]

JENNY [*picks up book from pile*]: How many of these do you get through in a week?

WENDY: Dunno.

JENNY: On average. .

WENDY: No idea.

JENNY [*picks up another*]: Why do you never read books by men?

WENDY: Dunno.

JENNY [*examines book. Directly, since* WENDY *goes on reading*]: Brenda's been writing one for years ... I hate to think what she's putting down ... Do you think it's got anything to do with us?

WENDY: Doubt it. [*Still reads.*]

JENNY: Got a light?

> [*She takes a cigarette from* WENDY's *packet.* WENDY *flicks the lighter.*]

Have you seen this restaurant they've got? Top of an office block or something... 'Poulet aux Galette de Mais'. Everything they've got is chicken ... 'Chaudfroid de Poulet Yorkshire' sounded rather good.

WENDY: What's his name?

JENNY: Harold.

WENDY: Do you call him that?

JENNY: Why not?

WENDY: Dunno ...

> [JENNY *wanders round the room. Then:*]

JENNY: I read a book the other day by a woman who'd been married fourteen times.

> [WENDY *goes on reading.*]

You get married again, then, Wendy?

WENDY: Think I might?

JENNY: Only one round here who's tried.

WENDY: Alus Mother.

JENNY: Alus Mam.

WENDY: Hear her extra-mural course is leading her into very deep waters.

JENNY: What?

WENDY: Lecturer in sociology, I hear, is a disenchanted man ... Divorced his wife two years ago... An era of disillusionment has been lightened by our ma.

JENNY: Good grief.

WENDY: Introduced, I fear, an element of hope.

JENNY: Who told you?

WENDY: Last night. Came into my room ... asked me if I'd mind ...
Hearing all about this man, I mean ... Apparently he's only forty-four ...

JENNY: Good God.

[WENDY *reads.*]

Would you marry a man who's forty-four?

WENDY: Dunno.

JENNY: How old was Bryan?

WENDY: Twenty-two.

JENNY: How old is he now?

WENDY [*still reading*]: Dunno ...

JENNY: Forty-four's quite old, I reckon ... [*Considers it.*] Would
Bryan have suited me, you think?

WENDY [*reading*]: Had his eye on you, you know.

JENNY: Really! ... Never told me!

WENDY: We'd only been married about six months.

JENNY: Perseverance.

[JENNY, *having sat down during this dialogue, gets up: wanders off
towards the window.*]

[*Gazing out*] He's not this man with a black moustache?

WENDY [*reading*]: That's right.

JENNY: Saw her with him in town, the other day ... Thought he was a
salesman ... looked innocuous to me.

WENDY: Not up to the psychologist, you think?

JENNY: Rather fancied him, I think, meself. Mother went off him
when I asked her what colour ties he wore.

WENDY: Always resented growing old ... I think she feels we're
catching up ... would like to share our effervescence ... [*Bangs
overhead.*] A little longer ... [*Looks up.*] I think she's coming down.

[WENDY *goes back to her book, intently.*

JENNY *hastily picks one up: crashing on stairs, off.*

BRENDA *comes in: fierce girl of twenty-three, in jeans and sweater.*]

BRENDA: Have you seen a box of screws ... S'got a yellow label on one
end ... You're back.

JENNY: Been back for hours.

BRENDA: I saw you in the drive. Mauling that man from the plastics
factory.

JENNY: Not true.

BRENDA: I've got two eyes ... Half-strangled him, she did. Be glad to get back to his plastic pots.

JENNY: At least I kiss the man good night ... I don't shake hands and slap him on the back.

BRENDA: I've been meaning to tell you this for some considerable time. You're nothing but a whore.

JENNY: I am.

BRENDA: She's another. God help me if I ever turn out like one of you.

WENDY: What're you screwing up, then, Brenda?

BRENDA: What?

WENDY: Bedroom. [*Gestures up.*]

BRENDA: I'm fastening a bookshelf to my wall.

WENDY: Why don't you buy one?

BRENDA: I don't buy one, because I'm quite capable of making one myself ... It's as simple ... [*To* JENNY] and as reasonable ... as that.

WENDY [*puts down her book*]: Do you remember when Brenda here was a little girl?

JENNY: Fastened Father in the lavatory, she did.

BRENDA: I did not.

JENNY: Oooh!

BRENDA: *Arthur* locked the door – but hadn't the courage to admit it ... As a result I took the blame myself.

WENDY: Poor old Arthur.

BRENDA: Poor old Arthur! ... Poor old Arthur got out of it – I thought – rather well. Poor old Arthur gets out of everything, in my view, rather well.

WENDY: You'd never think she was the youngest sister.

JENNY: You wouldn't.

WENDY: You'd imagine all that militancy to come out of someone who'd been exposed – prematurely – to all the perverse vicissitudes of life which we – Jenny and myself – have encountered virtually alone ...

JENNY: Unaided.

BRENDA: I've never been protected.

JENNY: Too gracious to admit it ...

WENDY: Always has been.

BRENDA: Have you seen my screws?

[*They laugh.*]

WENDY: Looked in Mother's bedroom. Always picking something up . . .

BRENDA: If you're trying to draw me into that, I better warn you . . . For one day, I've had enough. [*Starts searching round the room.*]

[WENDY *returns to her book.*

JENNY *lights another cigarette.*]

WENDY: I can't see why you can't use a nail instead.

BRENDA: If you ever acquired any *useful* information – you would realize that a nail breaks up the plaster. It also, after a while – *drops out.*

[*Outer door bangs: gruff coughs, clearing of throat, etc.*]

WENDY: Specialist's here. Ask him . . . Bound to tell you. [*To* JENNY] Put your cigarette out, girl. Look out.

[BRENDA *goes on searching.*

JENNY *composes herself, stubbing cigarette.*

WENDY *stubs hers; sets herself more firmly in her chair, still reading.*

SLATTERY *comes in. He's a stocky, well-built man, sixty-five.*]

SLATTERY: Evening. [*Looks round: suspicious, wary.*]

WENDY *and* JENNY [*together*]: Evening, Father.

SLATTERY: Thought some of you would have been in bed.

JENNY: Here, you mean, or somewhere else?

SLATTERY [*examines* JENNY *for a while. Then*]: Your mother in, then, is she?

WENDY: Out.

SLATTERY: Find me slippers for meself, 'spect.

BRENDA: I'll get them for you.

SLATTERY: Give ought for a cup of tea . . .

WENDY: That's coffee.

SLATTERY: Oh, well . . . Do without as soon as ought . . . Where you been tonight, then, Jenny?

JENNY: Out, Father. Looking for a feller.

SLATTERY: Aye. Well . . . [*Eyes her for a moment. Sits.*] Been up at top end, meself . . . Bloody stack's blown down . . . Blown down! Not a drop of bloody wind. Shoved it up any old bloody fashion. Don't go

up meself you'll get nowt done ... Bloody labour force ... I ne'er
see much bloody labour ... As for bloody force ... [*Looks from one
to the other: they take no notice.*] Been bloody smoking. Don't worry,
I can tell ... Be dead afore you're fifty. I'm telling you. Won't listen.
Bloody cancer. [*Coughs.*]

    [BRENDA *brings his slippers.*]

Mother's out at college, is she?

BRENDA: Yep.

SLATTERY: O'der I get, less I understand. Fathered three and
married one: I know less now than when I started.

WENDY: Could be said of all of us, I think.

SLATTERY: Thy's only one life ... Make best on it while thy's got the
chance ... If they were all like you, where would you get to, then?
Eh? Nowt living as us call a human kind ... nowt but bloody
animals and trees ... Can tell you your trouble for a bloody start.

WENDY: I'm listening ... [*Looks up from book.*]

SLATTERY: Thinks I'm bloody daft ... [*To* BRENDA] Prick up
their bloody ears one day. Mark my words.

JENNY [*sits on the arm beside him*]: Nay. Come on. Out with it ...
What's our trouble, Dad?

SLATTERY: Nay ... [*Mollified*] I think if I married again I'd bring up
half a dozen bloody goats ... Bloody hosses ... Damn sight more
rewarding ... Still ...

    [*They wait, all turned towards him.*]

I've seen nowt as daft as your bloody mother ... trying to learn at
night-school all she's known for fifty bloody years ... and from men
half her bloody age at that ... learnt nowt but what they've read
inside a book ... God Christ! ... Nay. I've said enough ...

WENDY: Maybe we should've all been sons.

SLATTERY: Aye ... Well, example thy's had, I shouldn't think you'd
get very much from that.

    [*They're silent.*]

Nay, well. I just hate to see something going to rot.

JENNY: *What's* going to rot?

SLATTERY: When your mother was your age she'd had all four of you.

WENDY: You think if we all had children you'd feel a bit easier about
us, Dad?

SLATTERY: I'm saying nowt ... If a woman can't have babbies when she's young, I don't know what else she can have. I don't ... Comes naturally as bloody breathing ... Your own nature's enough to tell you that.

JENNY: You've lived on a farm too long, old lad.

SLATTERY: I've lived next to God's good earth. That's where I've lived ... Still ... Aye.

BRENDA: In any case, I'm leaving. I thought I'd mentioned that.

SLATTERY: You've mentioned it. You've mentioned it two or three times, as I reckon it, afore ... No doubt you'll mention it again.

WENDY: Bed for me ... [*Yawns. Gets up.*]

SLATTERY: You want to think on what I've bloody said.

WENDY: Don't worry. Bear it all in mind. [*Kisses his forehead.*]

SLATTERY: Off to work tomorrow?

WENDY: I am ...

SLATTERY: Your mother's told you, has she? ... Your brother's coming.

WENDY: Well, *I've* been told ... Don't know about the others.

JENNY [*shakes her head*]: I didn't know.

BRENDA: Neither did I.

JENNY: What's he coming for?

SLATTERY: Nay. Don't ask me ought. You better ask your mother ... Cadging round her, I shouldn't be surprised ...

JENNY: Doesn't usually forewarn us. [*To* WENDY] Usually collapses on the doorstep, unannounced.

SLATTERY: Going to give us one more of his surprises, then. Can't bloody wait for it meself ... [*To* JENNY] You off to bed as well, then, are you?

JENNY: Think I might ... Had a rotten night. Feel sick.

SLATTERY: Don't worry. It'll all go bad ... It rots away inside ... And bloody smoking doesn't help.

JENNY: Aye. Well. Too late to worry now. [*Kisses his cheek.*] See you in the morning, love.

SLATTERY: 'Spect so. If you're up in time.

JENNY: What time's he coming, then?

SLATTERY: Don't ask me. His own time as usual, I expect ... God's *great* bloody gift ... Be grateful whatever time it happens.

WENDY: Aye. Well.

SLATTERY: Drops like bloody manna ... The usual arrangement, I expect.

BRENDA: There's no need to be bitter.

SLATTERY: Nay, I'm not bloody bitter ... I've had every damn reason enough to *feel* embittered ... But I'm bloody not. I can tell you that.

JENNY: Well, up to bed-for-cheers, for me ... [*Collects her coat and gloves. She goes.*]

WENDY [*to* SLATTERY]: I'll make you a pot of tea, if you like, before I go.

SLATTERY: S'all right. I'll wait up for your mother ...

WENDY: Ah, well ... Brenda ...

BRENDA: Yeh ... Good night.

[WENDY *picks up her books, her cigarettes and lighter: goes.* SLATTERY, *after a pause, gets up. He goes to the oak dresser.*]

SLATTERY: Aye. Well ... Reckon a drop of this won't go astray.

[*Gets out whisky: pours an ample measure.*]

BRENDA: I thought you'd been rationed, Dad.

SLATTERY: Had half a drop this morning, love ... Means I can have t'other half on it right now ... [*Drinks.*] By go ... What the bloody doctor ordered ... Don't split, now. Don't let on.

BRENDA: You know why you drink so much now, don't you?

SLATTERY: Aye. Well. A've a bloody good idea.

BRENDA: Don't want to hear about it, I suppose.

SLATTERY: I don't give a damn. Not one road nor another.

[BRENDA *doesn't respond.*

SLATTERY *looks across.*]

Sithee ... know where I was when I was half your bloody age? [*Holds up two hands.*] On my knees, twelve hours of the day, scrattin' bloody 'taties.

BRENDA: Ah, well. You haven't done so bad.

SLATTERY: I haven't ... Sat down on me backside half the bloody day – like somebody I could mention – you'd hear some bloody complaints. You would.

BRENDA: Everything we have here ... [*Gestures round, looking*] ... has been gained at the expense of other people.

SLATTERY: Aye. [*Pours another ample one.*]

BRENDA: That's your answer, I think, to everything.

SLATTERY: Aye. Almost. [*Drinks.*] Like your bloody mother, you ...
  Two of a kind ... One good thing about your mother: she got it late
  in life, and not afore.

BRENDA: Not afore she was disillusioned, then.

SLATTERY: Your mother's not disillusioned ... She's just not got
  much bloody common sense ... No great failing, that, in my book
  ... She's got a heart as big as that bloody door ... It'll alus see her
  through.

BRENDA: It'll not see her through all that whisky, I can tell you.

SLATTERY: It'll see her through the next ten years or more ... As for
  me. Like petrol to an engine, this: I couldn't run a day wi'out.

  [BRENDA *watches him for a while.*]

BRENDA: Your trouble is ... You see me ... and Jenny. And our
  Wendy ... Like some sort of primeval cattle. Cows.

SLATTERY: Nay, coos know what they're bloody after ... I don't
  think any one of you know one end of a man from bloody t'other ...
  Look at Wendy. Married sixteen months ... Then leaves ... A
  bloody doctor. God Christ: I'd almost marry the man meself ... As
  for bloody Jenny. By God: I've heard of flitting from flower to
  flower ... she never even stops to rest. [*Drinks.*]

BRENDA: I pity you more than anything else.

SLATTERY: A thought thy bloody would ... [*To himself*] Have
  another ... Aye. All right. I will.

BRENDA: You're nothing but an animal yourself ... All these years ...
  We've tried to think of you as something else.

SLATTERY: Aye ... [*Drinks up.*] By go. Man that invented this
  goes very high. In my bloody book ... He does. Knew summat
  about human nature ... Didn't get his notion from reading bloody
  books ...

  [MRS SLATTERY *comes in: a pleasant, cheery woman, com-
  panionable, not easily overwhelmed. She's dressed in a warm coat
  and has a practical woollen hat and gloves.*]

MRS SLATTERY: What's this? I can hear it down the drive.

SLATTERY: Thy bloody lasses. Don't blame me. Swallowed a gramophone needle at some time i' their lives: I don't know when.

MRS SLATTERY: Them or you? [*Smiles at* BRENDA.] Just look at this

...[*Goes to the bottle.*] You've not had more than you're supposed to have?

SLATTERY: Nay, what does a man who's never had a drop know about how much you're supposed to have? God Christ.

MRS SLATTERY: I should think the doctor's had a drop or two ... *In his time.*

SLATTERY: He's bloody tee-total. Told me so himself ... 'Come off it, Joe,' he said, 'and I can promise you another ten years at least.' 'Ten years without?' I said. 'I mun drop down deard now if I thought thy meant it.'

MRS SLATTERY [*to* BRENDA]: I shall have to give up these evenings ... He's like a child ... Can't be left alone for two minutes.

SLATTERY [*finishes his glass*]: No need to worry ... Our Brenda's been setting me to rights ... Have me out i' the cowsheds if she had the chance, not tucked up warm in bed ... Where's thy been all this time, then? ... Woman thy age ...

MRS SLATTERY: A woman my age, surely, doesn't have to account for where she's been?

SLATTERY: A woman thy age ought to have more bloody common sense ... Gallivanting out ... All right. I'll say nowt else. I know my bloody place. Should do. All these years.

BRENDA: Self-pity ... It's the one commodity he's never short of.

[SLATTERY *looks to* MRS SLATTERY *to intervene.*]

MRS SLATTERY: Nay, I don't want to intrude, love ... You argue all you want ... I can tell you: I've had quite a few hours of it down there ... I used to think I'd got *some* things *half*-worked out ... as it is, the more I listen, the less I seem to know ...

SLATTERY: You know a damn sight more than half those silly sods down there ... I'm surprised you give 'em two minutes of your bloody time ... Psychiatry? ... By bloody hell ... Gi'e me ten bloody minutes wi' 'em in top end and I'll psychiatrize the bloody lot.

MRS SLATTERY [*to* BRENDA]: Look ... hand's shaking ... I've got a splitting head ... Has Wendy gone to bed?

SLATTERY: She has ... Be up there all bloody day if she got half a chance ... Surprised she troubles to get out at all ... Up at bloody half-past four meself ... seven days a week, fifty-two weeks i' the year ... fo'ty-five bloody years .. [*To* BRENDA] How's that for a bloody life?

BRENDA: Can't beat it.

MRS SLATTERY: Is Jenny in, then, love, as well?

BRENDA: She is.

MRS SLATTERY: Can lock up, then ...

SLATTERY: Been telling her ... and *them* ... it's not men they've gotten wrong ... It's *hers'en* that never comes up to scratch.

MRS SLATTERY: Oh, well. I think I've had enough ... I'm too tired to listen to any more tonight ... [*To* BRENDA] All goes past me. [*To* SLATTERY] They seem to know what they're on about.

SLATTERY: If they do, they keep it to their bloody s'ens ... Mek a bloody secret of it, I can tell you ... And we'll have another bloody load tomorrow. [*Toasts.*] God's bloody gift to the bone bloody idle. [*Finds his glass empty, puts it down.*] Eat me bloody food ... sleep i' me bloody beds ... Seen nowt like it ... Get a job, she will, one day ... Freeten us all to bloody death ... [*To* BRENDA] Gi'e us all a bloody shock.

MRS SLATTERY: Time he was in bed.

SLATTERY: I'm going. Don't worry. Another hour down here and I'm going to have nowt left ... Are you coming up?

MRS SLATTERY: I'll be up in a couple of minutes ... I'll just lock up.

SLATTERY: Lock up? There's nowt to lock up here ... You ask her ... Gi'e it all away, if she had a chance ... [*To* BRENDA] Gi'e it all away, you know, and they'd still come back for more ... [*Sees* MRS SLATTERY's *look*.] Aye ... Well ... [*Shakes his head and goes.*]

MRS SLATTERY: Ah, well ... Another day over, love ... At times you think it'll never end. [*Goes to put bottle away:* BRENDA *picks up glass*.] What've you been up to, then?

BRENDA: Nothing.

MRS SLATTERY: Here. I'll cope with these ...

SLATTERY [*reappearing*]: Forgot to say good night.

BRENDA: Oh ... Good night.

SLATTERY [*looks over at* MRS SLATTERY]: See you in a minute, then?

MRS SLATTERY: Don't worry ... I shan't be long.

SLATTERY: Aye ... [*Looks over at* BRENDA, *looks at* MRS SLATTERY.] Good night. [*He goes.*]

BRENDA: I don't know how you put up with it.

MRS SLATTERY: I think he'll be all right.

BRENDA: All these years ... [*Waits.*] Didn't you ever run away?

MRS SLATTERY: Run away?

BRENDA: Before you had our Wendy ...

MRS SLATTERY: Run away from what?

BRENDA: Nay, if you don't know ... I don't think I could begin to tell you.

MRS SLATTERY: Nay, love ... [*Brushes back* BRENDA's *hair.*] Your father's not as bad as that.

BRENDA: He's contemptible.

MRS SLATTERY: Nay, love ... He's your father ... I can't change how you feel ... But I wish you wouldn't say it ... Not here ... Not to me.

BRENDA: I just feel so bloody sorry for you, Mam.

MRS SLATTERY: You're making something out of nothing, girl ... Just because he drinks ...

BRENDA: Drinks ... Do you think if he didn't drink he'd be any better? If anything he'd be a damn sight worse.

MRS SLATTERY: Nay, well I don't want to hear it, love ...

BRENDA: Did you love him when you married him?

MRS SLATTERY: I suppose I must have done ... It's not something you care to talk about. Not really.

BRENDA: Why not?

MRS SLATTERY: Well ... I never think of it like that.

BRENDA: How do you think of it, then?

MRS SLATTERY: I don't know ... I was only twenty when I married him ... He was very much the sort of man, you know, who, if he saw a thing, went out and got it ... There don't seem to be many people like that nowadays ...

BRENDA: Nowadays?

MRS SLATTERY: Well, I don't know ... Everybody seems so uncertain ... The ones who do seem confident ... you'd dismiss as stupid, I expect.

BRENDA: I don't know. It depends what they're confident about.

MRS SLATTERY: Yes ... Well. [*Pause.*] I better get to bed.

BRENDA: I'll lock up for you, if you like.

MRS SLATTERY: Yes. All right, then, love ... [*Kisses her.*] Good night.

BRENDA: 'Night.

[MRS SLATTERY *goes.*

BRENDA *looks round, aimlessly, at the room. Then she goes to the dresser and pours a drink herself. Takes a deep drink: swallows; savours it, closing eyes.*

Tapping at window.]

What ...

[*Startled, goes across: pulls back curtain on french window; peers out.*]

Albert? [*Listens to someone talking the other side.*] Go round ... No ... Round ... *Round* ... Oh. All right. [*Unlocks the french window.*]

[ALBERT *comes in, a young workman, dressed in jeans and zip jacket.*]

ALBERT: Freezing ... Been out there half an hour.

BRENDA: Why didn't you come in?

ALBERT: Saw your father ... Then your mother came ... Have your sisters gone to bed?

BRENDA: Here ... Have a drop of that. [*Hands him her glass.*]

ALBERT [*sips it*]: Crumbs ... You drink that a lot?

BRENDA: Sometimes ... [*Takes it back.*] Feel any better?

ALBERT: Nearly gave up ... walked up and down for half an hour ... set off back ... Do you think they'll come back down?

BRENDA: Don't think so.

ALBERT: Better leave the window open.

BRENDA: Not likely. Freeze to death. [*Closes it.*]

ALBERT: Can't stay long ... Thought I'd just pop up. [*Prowls around, uncertain.*]

BRENDA: Here ... If anybody comes I'll leave it on the latch ... You'll hear them. Anybody moves in this house half the woodwork creaks ... Here. Sit down.

ALBERT: Must think I'm mad.

BRENDA: What?

ALBERT: Coming here like this.

BRENDA: Not really ... [*Watching him.*] How did you get here, then?

ALBERT: Bike ... [*Looks to the window.*] I left it by that hedge.

BRENDA: Lights on: pedals ready ...

ALBERT: No ... [*Laughs.*] Not as bad as that.

BRENDA: What've you been doing, then, tonight?

ALBERT: Got home from work ... Mucked around ... I rang you up, as a matter of fact.

BRENDA: Tonight?

ALBERT: Earlier on ...

BRENDA: They never told me.

ALBERT: Well, it was your sister answered.

BRENDA: What d'you say?

ALBERT: Nothing ... I put it down ... [*Laughs.*] Don't know why.

BRENDA: Without telling her you wanted me?

ALBERT: I didn't say anything, as a matter of fact ... When I heard her voice ... I don't know why ... Heard her say the number ... [*Looks up.*] Put the phone down.

BRENDA [*studies him. Then*]: Are you the same with other people as you are with me?

ALBERT: Dunno ... Never been in a house like this before.

BRENDA: What's the matter with the house?

ALBERT: Dunno ... So old ...

BRENDA: I come down to your house, don't I?

ALBERT: Yeh.

BRENDA: What's the difference, then? People live in here: people live in your house.

ALBERT: You can walk right through ours and not notice it's even there.

BRENDA: I'd have thought you'd have despised it ... Not been afraid of it ... Not run away.

ALBERT: I haven't run away.

BRENDA: No.

ALBERT: I'm here, then, aren't I?

BRENDA: How many times have you been up here before?

ALBERT: Once or twice.

BRENDA: How many?

ALBERT: Half a dozen.

BRENDA: And never knocked?

[ALBERT *doesn't answer.*]

You can't be frightened of the house. I don't believe it ... Have another drink.

ALBERT: I better not.

BRENDA: Not if you're riding back, you mean?

[*Pause.*]

ALBERT: You're always laughing, you know.

BRENDA: Laughing?

ALBERT: Scoffing.

BRENDA: Scoffing?

ALBERT: I've cycled up here, haven't I?

BRENDA: Why are you so frightened, then, of Wendy?

ALBERT: I'm not frightened ... Well. All right.

BRENDA: And Jenny? ... Are you frightened, then, of her?

ALBERT: Why don't you women ever get married?

BRENDA: Wendy has been married.

ALBERT: About two years, by what I reckon.

BRENDA: Who've you been talking to?

ALBERT: Nobody ... Just asked around.

BRENDA: I'll tell you anything you want to know ... Or are you frightened of me as well?

[*Pause.*]

ALBERT: Don't think so.

BRENDA: Why not?

ALBERT: Dunno ... Still a bit of hope, I 'spect.

BRENDA: They're only just over thirty. For goodness sake. How old are you?

ALBERT: Twenty ... Twenty-one ... Nearly ... What's that? [*Leaps up.*]

BRENDA: Nothing ... S'always creaking ... At night you can almost hear it breathe ... Like being inside a person ... I'm only two years older. It can't be age.

ALBERT: What do your sisters do?

BRENDA: They teach ...

[ALBERT *moves round, uneasy.*]

ALBERT: I came up here – one day last summer ... Just after I'd met you ... It wa'n half hot. It took me over an hour to cycle up ... I went by along that road down yonder ... I don't know whether I meant to stop ... I looked over the hedge and saw them sitting on the lawn ... One of them was smoking ... Had her hair cut short.

BRENDA: Wendy ...

ALBERT: The other one was reading something from a book ... Couldn't hear what it was ... just the voice ... Wendy started laughing. Leaning back ...

BRENDA: Must have put you off.

ALBERT: I just felt she'd laugh at ought ... anything that took her fancy ... Must have settled it right then ... Couldn't understand it ...

BRENDA: What?

ALBERT: Dunno ... I came back about ten minutes later ... Your mother – must have been your mother ... She'd come out and joined them ... All three of them were laughing ... Don't know what it was.

BRENDA: You make it sound like a bloody harem.

ALBERT: My sister got married when she was seventeen ... Got three kiddies now ... She's not much o'der than you ... hasn't been back home since the day she wed ... not for long enough you'd notice ...

BRENDA: Well?

ALBERT: 'Tisn't as if your dad's an invalid or ought ... or your mother needs looking after.

BRENDA: It seems unnatural?

ALBERT: Unnatural ...

BRENDA: Not quite right?

ALBERT: Dunno ... I've never heard of it afore.

BRENDA: Lots of things, I imagine, you've never heard about before.

ALBERT: What's your brother do?

BRENDA: Nothing.

ALBERT: Hasn't he got a job?

BRENDA: He's had a job ... What he's got at present I haven't a clue.

ALBERT: How's he earn his living?

BRENDA: No idea.

ALBERT: Does your dad pay him something, then?

BRENDA: Shouldn't think so.

[ALBERT *looks around the room again, mystified*.]

ALBERT: My father's lost his job ... Don't think I told you.

BRENDA: No.

ALBERT: Don't think he's bothered ... Not while *I'm* working ... My mother's the one who frets ... They've taken a liking, you know, to you ... My father's never got over you coming down to see him.

BRENDA: That's not why he lost his job?

ALBERT: No ... No ... Two or three hundred been set off ... They're closing down an entire shop ... My turn next. Then we'll be all right ... Nobody's ever come down to see somebody at work. Not while they're wukking ... Not unless their wife was taken bad ... or they had a child knocked down, or summat ... Here. Gave me this book to give you back. Said he'd read it. Couldn't understand a word. Thanked you for lending it to him, that is ...

[*Takes the book out of his windcheater.* BRENDA *takes it.*]

BRENDA: What's he doing about being out of work?

ALBERT: Doing?

BRENDA: Haven't they gone on strike?

ALBERT [*laughs*]: Nay. It's more of a godsend, really. He gets the same money for doing nowt ... I'm hoping they'll close down all on t'rest. Be all of us on unemployment pay ... Can race me pigeons.

BRENDA: God.

ALBERT: Ever wukked in a factory, have you?

BRENDA: No. I never have.

ALBERT: Till you have I'd mek no comment ... I mean that ... Remember when you first met me?

BRENDA: Don't think I do. Beginning to doubt if I ever did.

ALBERT: Couldn't make head nor tail of it ... Not for weeks ... When I told the lads at work they wouldn't believe it. Not till you came down that day ... Remember that?

BRENDA: Why shouldn't I talk to somebody?

ALBERT: In the street?

BRENDA: Where else? If I hadn't have come up to you we'd never have met ... You wouldn't be here ... We wouldn't have known anything about each other.

ALBERT: Nay ... a young woman ... coming up to a man she's never known ... Only tarts do that ... Cloud-cuckoo-land, if you ask me.

[BRENDA *laughs.*]

You'll see. One of these days you'll be going up to somebody ... as'll not respect ...

302

BRENDA: What?

ALBERT: Your intentions.

BRENDA: You're just telling me you don't know what my intentions are.

ALBERT: You'll find out. Don't worry. It'll not always be somebody who takes ... an interest.

BRENDA: Interest! [*Laughs again.*] Your entire life – do you know what it's based on?

ALBERT: What?

BRENDA: On fear.

ALBERT: Fear. [*Laughs himself.*]

BRENDA: It's a wonder you get out of bed on a morning ... Every single man I've ever met down there ... They couldn't be more accommodating if they'd been manufactured in that bloody factory ... They even go on strike like a flock of bloody sheep ... Strike ... strike ... strike ... to show they're as mean-minded as everybody else: small, mean, bigoted, cheap, materialistic. When they've got something to strike about, like now ... nothing. Not a whimper.

ALBERT: I'm surprised you've let me in the house.

BRENDA: I'm surprised myself ... I'm surprised, too, that I come to yours. So small ... In everything you'd think worthwhile ... Even those bloody pigeons ... I can see their fascination now ... Let them go ... free them from those horrible little pens ... Up they go ... Then what do they do? ... The silly little sods come back.

ALBERT: They know they're on to a good thing, that's why. Regular food ... shelter ...

BRENDA: I can just see why you get upset if one of them flies off.

ALBERT: That's five quid ... ten or twelve quid sometimes ... And don't worry ... Other people pick them up.

BRENDA: I think the fact that one of them flies off undermines your entire existence ... Contravenes your philosophy of life: *nothing ventured, nothing lost.* All of you: you're about as mean-minded as the people who exploit you. Between the two of you – I couldn't make a choice.

ALBERT: Didn't have to open that window, you know. If you'd have shaken your head – I might as well tell you – I'd have probably gone straight off.

BRENDA: I can just imagine.

ALBERT: No wonder your sisters are like they are.

BRENDA: That's right.

ALBERT: I mean, I've never heard of anything so bloody daft ... This book you gave my dad ...

BRENDA: You better read it.

ALBERT: Psychology. Crikey. What's a 55-year-old workman got to do with that? Do you think he's going off his nut, or something?

BRENDA: I think he's already off his nut. So are you. Immobilized. Reconciled to that.

ALBERT: People in glass-houses, you ask me.

BRENDA: Why did you come up here tonight?

ALBERT: Brought that book.

BRENDA: Anything else?

ALBERT: Dunno ... Thought I might see you.

BRENDA: Then what?

ALBERT: Dunno ...

BRENDA: Have it off, then, somewhere? Back porch ... Greenhouse. Got a couple of barns out back.

ALBERT: See I shouldn't have come.

BRENDA: Better get your bike.

ALBERT: Perhaps I better.

BRENDA: On to a good thing, then? ... Your mates: think you're on to a good thing, do they?

ALBERT: How do you undo this catch?

BRENDA: A workman. Should manage a simple thing like that.

[ALBERT *does so, releasing french window: looks back.*]

ALBERT: Well, then ... Better say good night.

BRENDA: Yes. Good night.

ALBERT: I'm sorry you have to be like that.

BRENDA: Yeh ... Sorry.

ALBERT: Well, then.

BRENDA: Thanks for the book. Should have kept it. Told him he could.

ALBERT: Yeh. Well ...

BRENDA: Not beholden. Understand exactly. Well, then, love. Good night.

ALBERT: Aye. Well ... Good night.

[*Gazes at her.* BRENDA *has already turned away.*]

BRENDA: I should go. There's a terrible draught.

ALBERT: Yeh ... Well ... Good night.

[*Gazes at her hopelessly: goes.*

BRENDA *searches round: gets a cigarette from mantelpiece. Lights it. Goes to the dresser. Pours another drink.*

WENDY *comes in. She's dressed in a housecoat.*]

WENDY: Pour one out for me, then, lovey?

BRENDA: What ... [*Swings round, startled.*]

WENDY: Touch of soda ... Not used to it without.

BRENDA: I thought you'd gone to bed.

WENDY: Heard voices ... Didn't intrude. [*Gets her own drink.*]

BRENDA: Listened at the keyhole.

WENDY: Heard a few of the last refrains ... Why not give up the revolution? See exactly how it is.

BRENDA: Why don't you go to bed? [*Flounces across room: sits down.*]

WENDY: What's his name?

BRENDA: Mind your own bloody business.

[WENDY *makes herself comfortable in a chair near the fire.*]

WENDY: Have you ever met anyone you didn't despise?

BRENDA: Not round here: don't think I have. [*She waits.*] Why do you stay here, Wendy?

WENDY: Stay?

BRENDA: Why don't you go away? Get off. Do anything ... Clear out.

WENDY: Don't know ... Used to worry about it, a bit, myself ... Doesn't seem a problem any more.

BRENDA: You ought to be a nun.

WENDY: Could almost say I am.

BRENDA: Why has Jenny never married?

WENDY: Don't know.

BRENDA: I'm beginning to feel the same. Don't think I ever will.

WENDY: No?

BRENDA [*commenting*]: Don't sound surprised.

WENDY: Surprised at nothing, love, in this house. [*Gets out a cigarette and lights it.*] Rail all night at the old man drinking ... come midnight, and down she comes herself.

BRENDA: I feel at times we already are.

WENDY: What?

BRENDA: Married.

    [*Pauses: gazes at her.*]

  I think I'll go to bed.

WENDY: That's right ... I'll lock up for you ... [*Stubs out her half-smoked cigarette.*] Leave it to the eldest.

BRENDA: Thanks.

WENDY: I suppose you're more like me than Jenny.

BRENDA: I don't think I'm like anyone. Not anyone here, at least ... Want the light? [*Has gone to the door.*]

WENDY: No thanks.

BRENDA: 'Night ... [*Looks over at the dresser; turns off the light: goes.*]

    [WENDY *sits in the firelight. She lights another cigarette. Smokes. Drinks. Abstracted.*

    Pause.

    Click of the window.

    WENDY *swings round in the chair.*

    Moment later french window is pushed quietly back. Figure comes inside.]

WENDY: What ...?

    [*She gets up: switches on the light.*]

ARTHUR: Good grief! Jumped out of me bloody skin ... Light went off. Thought you'd gone to bed.

WENDY: What are you doing coming in like this?

    [ARTHUR *is a young man of twenty-one or -two, pale, slender-featured: he's somewhat roughly dressed.*]

ARTHUR: Got here earlier than expected ... Didn't want to wake the family ... Been out there half an hour ... Did you know our Brenda's been consorting with a feller? Tripped over his bloody bike ... Half frightened him to bloody death ... Won't come back. Not for a long time ... Here. [*Goes to the dresser: gets a drink.*] Life-saver. By God. Needed that ... [*Coughs: shakes his head.*] Well, then ... [*Looks round.*] How's our eldest?

WENDY: Surviving.

ARTHUR: Not got wedded yet?

WENDY: Not yet.

ARTHUR: Won't have you? Or can't afford it?

WENDY: Bit o' both, I should imagine.

ARTHUR [*looks around him, holding glass*]: Nowt changed in here, then, has it?

WENDY: Not much.

ARTHUR: Thought I'd trip in ... Postpone the usual felicitations ... Could see the old man's face ... woken up at midnight.

WENDY: As a matter of fact the front door's still open.

ARTHUR: Well, I'll be damned ...

WENDY: I thought you might be coming this evening.

ARTHUR: What?

WENDY: The phone rang earlier on ... Picked it up. No answer ... Thought it might be you.

ARTHUR: Not me.

WENDY: Run out of coppers ... or whatever it is they use.

ARTHUR: Not me ... Thought if I couldn't break in, I'd use the barn ...

WENDY: Slept there many a time before.

ARTHUR: I have.

[*Pause. Sudden tension between them. Then:*]

Exploited all me native craft for nothing.

WENDY: That's right.

ARTHUR: Fancy one of these? Or are we rationed?

WENDY: Help yourself. [*Turns away: lights cigarette.*]

[ARTHUR *pours another drink:* WENDY *turns towards him: finds him gazing at her.*]

Oh ... Sorry.

ARTHUR: Ta ... Run out.

[*Takes cigarette from her.* WENDY *holds lighter for him.*]

Lovely ... [*Blows out cloud of smoke.*]

WENDY: Well, then ... [*Waits: watches him.*]

ARTHUR: Damn freezing out there ...

WENDY: I can imagine.

[*Pause.*]

ARTHUR: Jenny here as well, then?

WENDY: That's right.

ARTHUR: Home from home ... [*Pause. He looks up, overhead.*] Can sense any foreign element in this house ... I remember him lying sozzled there one night ... been comatose for about twelve hours ...

Came creeping in ... Heard him call out ... '*Don't worry: I can hear you.*' Dead to the bloody world apart from that ... There's a kind of seismograph inside his brain ... implanted there, I should think, from birth ... its sole function is to measure the proximity, or otherwise, of his only son ... [*Pours from the bottle: nearly empty.*] It can't be the only one he's got.

WENDY: That's his showpiece.

ARTHUR: Showpiece?

WENDY: Doctor's orders ... He came over funny in the fields ... About a month back ...

ARTHUR: Stinking bloody drunk.

WENDY: I think *he* thought the same, at first ... Had a stroke, as a matter of fact ... Has bottles, I should imagine, all around the fields ... Secreted in the roots of trees ... gateposts ... potato pies ... hedge bottoms ... That one's to show he's sticking to his ration. [*She watches him.*]

ARTHUR: Poor old sod.
    [*They're silent. Then:*]

WENDY: What've you come back for, then, Arthur?

ARTHUR: Didn't mention it in me letter ... Thought I'd deliver it by hand.

WENDY: Going to prison?

ARTHUR: No. [*Laughs: shakes his head.*]
    [*Pause.*]

WENDY: Finish him off, then, will it? ... Or just another jab?

ARTHUR: Neither, really ... Uplift, I'd imagine ...

WENDY: Well, then.

ARTHUR: Getting married. [*Pours last of the bottle into his glass.*]

WENDY: Good God.

ARTHUR: What I said.

WENDY: Who is she?

ARTHUR: Might like her.

WENDY: Hope so.

ARTHUR: An actress.

WENDY: Actress.

ARTHUR: Well ... [*Looks at his glass.*]

WENDY: Go on.

ARTHUR: She was at one time.

WENDY: Older than you?

ARTHUR: A bit.

WENDY: Older than me?

ARTHUR: Bit.

WENDY: Not ... older than Mother?

ARTHUR: Not that bad yet.

WENDY: How old is she? ... [*Shakes her head.*] Not that it makes any difference ... Seem to have age on the brain in this house. [*Turns away.*]

ARTHUR: She's over forty.

WENDY: Forty ... [*Watches him. Then:*] Don't know why you bothered ... Coming to tell them here, I mean ... A letter might have been ... as good.

ARTHUR: She's come up with me, as a matter of fact.

WENDY: What?

ARTHUR: Not out here. [*Laughs.*] In town ... Booked her in ... I thought ... Introduce her in the morning ...

WENDY: Why didn't you stay with her, then?

ARTHUR: No money.

WENDY: I see.

ARTHUR: I'm paying ... For this hotel ... It was the condition I made when she asked to come ... Would have had to come at some time, anyway ... I'd enough for the train fare ... And for one night, you see, at this hotel.

WENDY: Why didn't you bring her straight up here?

ARTHUR: I thought I ought to tell them first.

WENDY: Mad.

ARTHUR: Any more of this, then, is there? [*Indicates empty bottle.*]

WENDY: Ought to celebrate, I suppose. Bit late ... [*Opens cupboard in dresser.*] Doesn't know he has this one, you see. Me mother's been keeping it, in reserve ... I suppose, if she's over forty, she's been married once or twice before.

ARTHUR: Yeh.

[WENDY *waits.* ARTHUR *looks up.*]

Once ... She's got two kiddies.

WENDY: A father quicker than you thought.

ARTHUR: Yeh ...

WENDY: Not much younger than you ... her children?

ARTHUR: Not really. No.

WENDY: Funny having children ... what? ... almost older than yourself.

ARTHUR: Yeh.

WENDY: Could probably give you some advice.

ARTHUR: Yeh ...

[*Having got the bottle and opened it* WENDY *pours a drop into his glass.*]

WENDY: I shouldn't have any more ...

ARTHUR: No.

WENDY: If you want to present it all, that is, tomorrow ... [*Waits.*] Is she divorced: or a widow, then?

ARTHUR: Divorced ... Her ... husband was an actor.

WENDY: Oh.

ARTHUR: Quite ... Well. I've seen him in a film or two.

WENDY: Famous.

ARTHUR: Not really.

WENDY: Who's going to do the supporting, Arthur?

ARTHUR: I thought I'd get a job.

WENDY: Good God. [*Gestures up.*] Going to cheer him up no end ...

ARTHUR: Yeh.

WENDY: Does she work as well?

ARTHUR: Yeh ... sort of.

[*Pause.*

WENDY *watches him.*]

WENDY: Do you want another cigarette?

ARTHUR: Wouldn't mind.

[*He takes one: she lights it.*]

WENDY: Three people to support, and until now you haven't been able to support yourself.

ARTHUR: Quite an adventure.

WENDY: Do you still write poetry, then?

ARTHUR: Yeh ... [*Shrugs.*]

[WENDY *gazes at him.*

They're silent.]

WENDY: How long ... [*Gestures at his hands.*]

ARTHUR: What?

WENDY: Have your hands been shaking?

ARTHUR [*looks at them: shakes his head*]: Shock of being back, I reckon.

WENDY: Do you feel all right?

ARTHUR: Yeh.

WENDY: If you really wanted to do all this why didn't you write a letter ... Send a postcard. Anything ...

ARTHUR: Dunno.

　　　[*Pause.*]

WENDY [*watching him*]: What sort of woman is she?

ARTHUR: All right ... [*Shakes his head, unable to describe her.*]

WENDY: Are you ill or something?

ARTHUR: I think I'll sleep down here.

WENDY: He gets up before any of us here, you know ... [*Looks at clock.*] Four hours' time ... You'll be safer, I should have thought, up there.

ARTHUR: Perhaps if we creep up to bed together.

WENDY: Yes.

ARTHUR: Do you mind?

WENDY: No.

ARTHUR: Camouflage ... Calls out: 'Don't worry: I can hear you.' Might call: 'All right, Dad. It's only me.'

WENDY: Yes ... [*Watches him.*] Well, then ... Bit late ... To shut the stable door ... I'll just lock up ... Shan't be a second. [*Goes.*]

　　　[ARTHUR *looks round. Touches the furniture, edge of chairs, dresser. Stands by a chair, worn out, exhausted.*

　　　WENDY *reappears.*]

　　You all right?

ARTHUR: Sure ...

WENDY: Should have had an early night.

ARTHUR: Yeh.

WENDY: Anything you need down here?

ARTHUR: Don't think so ...

WENDY: Another fag?

ARTHUR: Yeh ...

WENDY: Have the packet.

ARTHUR: Thanks. I'll get you one tomorrow

WENDY: No bother.

ARTHUR: Well, then ...
WENDY: Welcome home, then, Arthur ... Don't look now. [*Looks overhead.*] I think we'll be all right.
[WENDY *turns light off.*
They go.
Silence.
Last light slowly fades.]

ACT TWO

The same. Morning.

MRS SLATTERY, *wearing glasses, is working at the desk.*

MRS SLATTERY: Damn! ... [*Crosses out. Works.*]
    [JENNY *has come in.*]

JENNY: You ought to have someone else to come in and do all that.

MRS SLATTERY: Can't concentrate these last few days ... Did you have a nice time, then, last night?

JENNY: All right.

MRS SLATTERY: Is Wendy giving you a lift to town?

JENNY: She'll have to hurry ... Walk down to the stop otherwise. The speed she drives, the bus is sometimes quicker.

MRS SLATTERY: I think even this ready-reckoner gets it wrong at times.

JENNY: Ought to have a digital computer.

MRS SLATTERY: That's what I said – He says something different ... What's twenty seven-and-a-half p's?

JENNY: One pound fifty.

MRS SLATTERY [*writing*]: Honestly ... It's amazing ...

JENNY: Brenda's where, then?

MRS SLATTERY: Went out ... Heard her up this morning, before your father ... Must have been up half the night.

JENNY: What's the old man doing, in any case, in bed?

MRS SLATTERY [*laughs, still writing*]: Bed, love? He's not in bed. He's out. Working.

JENNY: I heard him in his room. Just now. Thought he'd choke to death. Coughing. Called out ... Said he'd be all right.

MRS SLATTERY: Well ... [*Pausing, looking up.*] His breakfast's been waiting half an hour ...

JENNY: Must have come in through the back.

MRS SLATTERY: I suppose I better go up ... [*Looks up, uncertain.*]

JENNY: Sounded sober.

MRS SLATTERY: Got up this morning ... I thought I heard him going out ... Well ...

JENNY: That's Wendy now ... Want one of us to go up with you?

MRS SLATTERY: It's all right, love ... [*Looks up at her suddenly, sees her concern, then laughs.*] For goodness' sake, I'll be all right.

[WENDY *comes in.*]

WENDY: 'Morning, Mother.

MRS SLATTERY: 'Morning, love.

JENNY: Just discovered the old man's still up yonder.

WENDY: So I heard.

MRS SLATTERY: Is he all right, then? ... We've had his breakfast waiting here for hours.

WENDY: Didn't look in ... Going to be late this morning.

MRS SLATTERY: Who else is up there, then? [*Listens, looking up.*] That's not your father.

WENDY [*glances at* JENNY. *Then*]: Arthur came back, Mother. Late last night.

MRS SLATTERY: Oh.

WENDY: Didn't want to disturb you ... Coming down. Shouldn't be a second.

[*Pause.*]

MRS SLATTERY: Why didn't you wake me? Let me know.

WENDY: Would have done. Normally. As it is ... preferred to do it this way, love. [*To* JENNY] Always been eccentric. Make allowances, you know.

MRS SLATTERY: Well ... [*Gazes up.*] How late was it?

WENDY: Quite late.

MRS SLATTERY: Does your father know?

WENDY: He might.

[*Sounds of someone descending stairs.*]

Seems in very good spirits ... [*To* JENNY] Arthur.

JENNY: Explains all the preparations, then, last night.

WENDY: Last night?

JENNY: Thought you'd been expecting someone.

WENDY: Lovey ... Since when have preparations of that sort been necessary to welcome Art?

JENNY: What I thought ... Suspected, even, you'd been having someone in.

WENDY: Good God. [*Turns away.*]

[*Door opens:* ARTHUR *comes in: gazes at each of them in turn.*]

MRS SLATTERY: Hello, love ...

ARTHUR: Hello, Mother.

MRS SLATTERY: This is a bit of a surprise, then, love.

ARTHUR: Yes.

MRS SLATTERY: Give us a kiss, then ... Not expecting you for a few hours yet! [*Laughs.*]

> [*They embrace:* JENNY *and* WENDY *move away.*]

Got here last night, then, Wendy says?

ARTHUR: Didn't want to wake you.

MRS SLATTERY: I don't mind being woken, love, for that!

ARTHUR: No ...

> [*They laugh, uncertain,* MRS SLATTERY *still holding him.*]

MRS SLATTERY: Did you sleep well, then ... ? I was going to air your bed this morning.

ARTHUR: No ... No ... Slept very well. [*Coughs.*] Could do with a cigarette ... Got through all those last night ...

MRS SLATTERY: Here, love ... I keep some in this cupboard. [*Goes immediately to dresser.*]

ARTHUR [*to* JENNY]: Jenny ... How are you?

JENNY: Very well ... You're looking ... better.

ARTHUR: Yep ... [*To* WENDY] Brenda looked in a few minutes ago ... scooted out ... [*To* JENNY] Seen a ghost or something ...

MRS SLATTERY: Brenda's been in a strange mood these past few months ... Made her mind up to go off somewhere ... doesn't quite know where ...

ARTHUR: Yeh ...

MRS SLATTERY: Well ... [*Having given him the cigarettes she stands gazing at him, pleased, excited.*]

ARTHUR: Hope it's not inconvenient, me coming.

MRS SLATTERY: No. No, love. Not at all ...

ARTHUR: Meant to ... present myself this morning ... Wendy here ... discovered me last night.

> [*They gaze at him: he doesn't finish. He suddenly looks about the room.*]

Well, nothing's changed here, to any great extent.

MRS SLATTERY: Very little ... Can I get you something to eat, then, love?

ARTHUR: Yes ... I'll ... If there's anything going.

MRS SLATTERY: Have anything you like ... You stay here. I'll fetch it through ... It's warmer in here than in the kitchen ... I don't know why ... that great big stove ... I shan't be a minute, love ... [*Gazes at him, watching, before she goes.*]

ARTHUR: Work today, then? ... [*Gestures*] All dolled up.

JENNY: Wendy is always dolled up these days, Arthur ... As for myself: it's true ... We're on our way.

ARTHUR: Don't hang around on my account.

JENNY: No ... No hurry. Let the dust settle in here, I think, before either of us can relax ... depart.

WENDY: Have you spoken to the old man, yet?

ARTHUR: No. I ... Thought I'd leave it ... Usually finds an occasion to make his presence felt.

WENDY: Sulking in his room, you think.

ARTHUR: I heard him sort of ... wandering about.
   [*Pause.*]
   Is Brenda all right, then?

JENNY: Didn't she say anything at all?

ARTHUR: Sort of ... 'You're back, then? Break in, or gain legal entrance?' so forth, etcetera ...

WENDY: She and the old man, I think, are very much alike ... despite their frenzied attempts to point out all their differences ...

ARTHUR: Well, she was quite friendly when I was last here ... [*Laughs, scratches his head.*] Forget now when that was.

JENNY: Two years.

ARTHUR: Two years? ... As long as that?

JENNY: Then there was that occasion when my mother met you on that station ... Forgotten where it was ... We never did hear how that meeting went ...

ARTHUR: It went all right.

JENNY: Passed over the necessary, did she, Arthur?

ARTHUR [*looks out*]: Window was all frozen up when I woke this morning.

JENNY: Been trying to persuade the old man to put in central heating ... Even offered to pay for it ourselves ... 'Who's ever heard of a farm wi' central heating? The whole thing's a bloody paradox o' terms.'

WENDY: Be wishing he had it now, this morning ... Not often he spends his time upstairs.

ARTHUR: I heard him getting up, you know ... I don't know what time it was exactly ... Opened the door ... put the light on ... Must have stood there for a couple of minutes ... I don't know what made him look inside ... Like a damn great bear ... In fact, for a while, I thought I must be dreaming ... Wasn't until he put the light off and closed the door ... and went off down the stairs, that I knew I wasn't.

JENNY: Why didn't *you* say something to him, then?

ARTHUR: I couldn't think of anything to say ... Don't know ... Usual situation ... I thought he was going to speak instead.

JENNY [*to* WENDY]: The proprieties observed in this house, at times, astonish me ... Can't understand it when, normally, you'd expect us to be at one another's throats.

WENDY: Not as bad as that, then, surely?

JENNY: It's like one, huge, corporeal mass ... I often dream of it at night ... a sort of animal with seven heads ...

WENDY: Seven?

JENNY: Don't know why. Only six of us at present.

[*Sounds of* MRS SLATTERY *returning. Carries on a tray.*]

MRS SLATTERY: You can have your father's ... it's been waiting half an hour ... still fresh ... I'll cook him something else ... Here, love. Pull up a chair.

ARTHUR: Thanks ...

MRS SLATTERY: Look as though you could do with a good meal, love.

ARTHUR: Don't know ... Been eating pretty well these last few weeks.

MRS SLATTERY: Doesn't seem to make much difference. What do you think, Wendy?

WENDY: Don't know ... Very hard to tell.

MRS SLATTERY: Used to fill him up when he was little. Never changed his shape.

WENDY: Congenital defect.

MRS SLATTERY: Well ... I wouldn't say that.

WENDY: Anything for me?

MRS SLATTERY: Oh ... love! I thought you'd had it.

WENDY: Don't worry. Get something ... [*Glances at* ARTHUR.] Shan't be long. [*Goes.*]

MRS SLATTERY: Jenny: you're sure, then, are you?

JENNY: Get me coat ... Need me boots on, I think, this morning. [*Goes.*]

MRS SLATTERY: Well, then ... Like old times ...

ARTHUR: Yes. [*He looks up.*]

MRS SLATTERY: Do you remember? We used to eat here when the girls had gone to school.

ARTHUR: Yes.

MRS SLATTERY: Have you ... done much, since we last saw you?

ARTHUR: Not much ... Worked on a farm, as a matter of fact.

MRS SLATTERY: A farm!

ARTHUR: Last summer ... Had a job in a hotel before that ... Then a chap I know got me a job ... sort of teaching.

MRS SLATTERY: Teaching? Are you qualified for that?

ARTHUR: It was a sort of private school ... Sweated labour, really.

MRS SLATTERY: How long were you there, then, love?

ARTHUR: Oh ... Not long.

MRS SLATTERY: Have you got anything ... Have you got any job at present, then?

ARTHUR: No ... I'm ... I had a poem published.

MRS SLATTERY: Oh ... love!

ARTHUR: A few months since.

MRS SLATTERY: Can we get it? I mean ... buy it anywhere?

ARTHUR: I've brought you a copy ... I left my luggage in town, as a matter of fact ... Thought I'd go back and get it, perhaps, this morning.

MRS SLATTERY: The girls ... or your father ... can give you a lift.

ARTHUR: Yeh. I'll ... sort it out.

MRS SLATTERY: Well ... [*Gazes at him with a kind of animal affection.*]

ARTHUR: I thought ... while I was up here ... we might go out.

MRS SLATTERY: Out?

ARTHUR: My dad and yourself ... sort of ...

MRS SLATTERY: Together?

ARTHUR: Yep.

MRS SLATTERY: Well ... That'll be very nice.

ARTHUR: Hadn't you better go up ... [*Gestures up.*] See how he is.

MRS SLATTERY: Yes ... I suppose I better ... I found his bottle empty when I came down this morning.

ARTHUR: That's me, I'm afraid ... Last night ... Came in. Wendy was here. We had a drink.

MRS SLATTERY: Oh well, then ... That's a relief.

ARTHUR: Yes.

MRS SLATTERY: Don't you want any more, then, love?

ARTHUR: No ... I'll ... That's fine. I think my dad's appetite's a bit bigger than mine.

MRS SLATTERY: Yes ...

JENNY [*returning with coat and suede boots*]: Well, then ... Nearly ready.

MRS SLATTERY: Are you sure you don't want anything, love?

JENNY: Positive. [*Sits down to pull on boots.*] What I want at present, I'm afraid, couldn't – without a great deal of difficulty – be brought in on a breakfast plate. [*Looks up: winks at* ARTHUR.] Wendy's buttering her toast ... eating up her yoghurt.

MRS SLATTERY: The amount that these two eat wouldn't nourish a mouse. I'm quite sure of that.

JENNY: Love, love is what we need: more love!

MRS SLATTERY: Well, I'm sure that's your affair. Can't do anything about that. [*Looks to* ARTHUR *and laughs.*]

ARTHUR: Aye ... Well ... I'll carry it back, if you like. It was very nice.

MRS SLATTERY: No, love. You sit down ... I'll take it ... Better get your father something ... Go up and see him. I shan't be long. Is there anything else I can get you, love?

ARTHUR: No. No. That's fine.

MRS SLATTERY: Well, then ... [*Takes tray and goes.*]

JENNY: Home for good, then, Arthur?

ARTHUR: Shouldn't think so.

JENNY: Did our Wendy know you were coming, or didn't she?

ARTHUR: Last night? [*He shakes his head.*]

JENNY: Storm brewing, I should imagine ... [*Looks up.*] Collecting his weaponry ... Don't seem bothered.

ARTHUR: Get used to it, I expect.

JENNY: Yes.

ARTHUR: I thought I'd stay a couple of days. See how things went.

JENNY: Want a forecast, do you?

ARTHUR: No. [*Laughs: shakes his head.*]

JENNY: Heard about his heart?

ARTHUR: Yes.

JENNY: Might quieten down. Grown more morose, if anything, since it happened . . . Oddly absent-minded too, at times.

ARTHUR: Surprised to find you still here, as a matter of fact.

JENNY: Me personally, or all three of us in general?

ARTHUR: You . . . [*Shrugs.*] Wendy . . . well. Think she'll die here if she gets the chance.

JENNY: Put up the shutters.

ARTHUR: Don't know. She seems content . . .

JENNY: Disenchanted . . .

ARTHUR: Quiescent.

JENNY: Might use that, perhaps, in one of your poems . . .
> [ARTHUR *doesn't answer.*
> *Pause. Then:*]

ARTHUR: I remember working here with you.

JENNY: Working?

ARTHUR: Stooking . . . Harvesting . . . Days of yore.

JENNY: Yes . . .

ARTHUR: Remember Herbert? . . . Blond hair . . . moustache . . . fat . . . had you in the haystack a couple of times.

JENNY: *Wendy!* . . . More than twice. Though she wouldn't admit it.

ARTHUR: I remember that thin chap better . . . Gordon. Always fighting: squabbling over who should work with what. Do you remember them fighting about who should drive the tractor . . . ?

JENNY: You laughed so much you were rolling on the floor.

ARTHUR: Never seen anything as funny as that. Never . . . Saddest day of my life, I think, when those two left . . . Never been the same since then.

JENNY: Bone idle: both of them . . . Met Herbert, as a matter of fact, not long ago . . . so fat he could hardly move about . . . married: seven children.

ARTHUR: Sounds just like him. Used to get me dad drunk in the back of the barn, then they'd sleep it off together ... Remember the time they ran away? The old man running round the cow-shed saying, 'What? ... *What?* ... They've *never!*'

[*They laugh together.*]

God ... I enjoyed those bloody days ... Never seemed to rain ... Can scarcely remember any frost ... [*Quietens.*]

[WENDY *comes in.*]

WENDY: You ready, then, our lass?

JENNY: Shall be. Shan't be a second.

[WENDY *watches* ARTHUR.]

WENDY: Told her your good news, then, have you?

ARTHUR: No ...

JENNY: News? What good news is that?

WENDY: Thought he had.

JENNY: No ... nothing.

ARTHUR: I was telling Wendy ... last night ... I might be getting married.

JENNY: Good God.

WENDY: Sounded more definite than that – last night.

ARTHUR: Yes ... Well ... [*Looks up at* JENNY.] I shall be getting married.

JENNY: Well, then, love ... I'm glad.

WENDY: Not told Mother yet, then, Arthur?

ARTHUR: Not yet.

JENNY: Not anyone we know, then, Arthur?

[ARTHUR *shakes his head.*]

Well ... [*Looks at* WENDY: *shrugs.*] Nothing more than that?

WENDY: Brought her with him.

JENNY: Here?

WENDY: In town ... Aren't you going to tell her, Arthur?

ARTHUR: I thought I'd bring her up – this evening ... Introduce her.

WENDY: It was going to be this morning.

ARTHUR: Evening, I thought ... it might be better.

JENNY: Well, then, love. Look forward to meeting her ... Young and pretty?

WENDY: Divorced.

JENNY: Divorced? ... Well, she can still be divorced and young and pretty ... Look at our Wendy here, herself.

WENDY: A little older than me.

JENNY: Older?

WENDY: Two children.

JENNY: Arthur! ... You've not done anything daft?

ARTHUR: Don't think so.

JENNY: Honestly, love ... How old is she?

ARTHUR: I don't know ... Forty ... one or two.

JENNY: Good God.

ARTHUR: I don't know. It's not as bad as that.

JENNY: Laddy! You're barmy! Have you told the old man yet?

ARTHUR: No.

JENNY: Go through the roof ... can just imagine.

WENDY: An actress.

JENNY: Actress!

ARTHUR: I said she *was*.

JENNY: She's retired now, you mean. [*To* WENDY] In expectation.

ARTHUR: She's got another sort of job.

JENNY: Well, love, if it'll make you happy ... [*Kisses him.*] Congratulations, love.

  [MRS SLATTERY *comes in.*]

MRS SLATTERY: What's that, then, love? ... Congratulations.

JENNY: He's been telling us ...

ARTHUR: About my poem.

JENNY: Poem.

MRS SLATTERY: He's brought us a copy. In his luggage ... By the way, love. Do you want them to give you a lift to town?

ARTHUR: No. I'll ... go in, later.

MRS SLATTERY: Your father's coming down.

WENDY: Ill, is he? Or recuperating, rather?

MRS SLATTERY: No ... He hasn't felt so well.

WENDY: Since when?

MRS SLATTERY: Since when he got up this morning.

WENDY: I see.

MRS SLATTERY [*to* ARTHUR]: You've heard about his heart ...

ARTHUR: Yes.

MRS SLATTERY: I wanted to write and tell you ... I didn't have any address.

ARTHUR: No ... I was ... sorry to hear about it.

MRS SLATTERY: It's only to be expected, I suppose ... He takes no notice ... He has one bottle, but I've a feeling he's got one or two hidden somewhere else ... He wouldn't admit it ... He'd lie himself black in the face rather than admit it ... [*Looks up.*]

   [*Sounds of* SLATTERY *coming down.*]

[*To* WENDY] Hadn't you two better be off.

WENDY: We'll give it another couple of minutes ... See the prodigal's welcome.

JENNY: Wouldn't miss it.

WENDY: 'Morning, Father.

SLATTERY: 'Morning.

JENNY: 'Morning, Dad ...

   [SLATTERY *has appeared at the door in shirt-sleeves and braces.*]

MRS SLATTERY: Do you want to come over by the fire, love?

SLATTERY: No. No ... It's all right ... I'm all right over here. [*Gets out a cigarette: begins to light it.*] How are you, lad? ... We met afore: earlier this morning. Put me head in his room ... Didn't disturb him.

ARTHUR: I hope you're feeling a bit better, Dad.

SLATTERY: Better?

ARTHUR: I heard about your accident ...

SLATTERY: Accident? ... Oh ... that ... Doctors mek up half o't' stuff they find: be out of a bloody job if they didn't ... Well, then ... [*Crosses uncertainly: puts out his hand.*]

   [*They shake.*

   BRENDA *comes in the room; she's dressed in a jacket, unzipped: stands watching at the back.*]

'Spect you find it a bit cold up here.

ARTHUR: Cold?

SLATTERY: Been travelling round the south, and so on, your mother tells me.

ARTHUR: Oh ... Yes.

SLATTERY: Got here after I got to bed, I expect.

ARTHUR: Yes.

SLATTERY: Never told me ... Your mother.

MRS SLATTERY: I didn't know myself.

SLATTERY: Tell me nowt in this house ... Run by women. Better warn you. [*Turns away to cough and laugh.*] Here's another ... [*Indicating* BRENDA.] Came up with a drop of whisky half an hour back ... Asked me if I'd need it ... Must keep a bloody stock herself ... [*To* MRS SLATTERY] Didn't know you'd been sabotaged, did you, love? Tell'd me last night I was nothing but a sot ... Comes up with a tumblerful this morning.

ARTHUR: Hello, Brenda ... Missed you earlier on.

BRENDA: Yes.

MRS SLATTERY: Aren't you going to give him a kiss, then, love?

BRENDA: Yes ... [*Kisses him formally.*] Glad to see you back.

ARTHUR: Yeh.

BRENDA: Going to stay for long?

ARTHUR: Dunno ...

WENDY: Well, then, Jenny ... off to work ... Anything crops up – know where to find us ... Well, then. Best be off.

MRS SLATTERY: Drive carefully, won't you? These roads ... That lane'll be covered in ice.

JENNY: A hearse overtook us the other day... I don't think, until then, she'd appreciated the timidity of her driving.

WENDY: Back-seat exponent ... Never learnt, herself.

MRS SLATTERY: Well, then, love ... Take care ...

WENDY: See you all then, later ... 'Bye, Arthur.

ARTHUR: 'Bye.

JENNY: 'Bye, Arthur ... Think on.

[ARTHUR *nods: they go.*]

MRS SLATTERY: Well, then ... [*To* BRENDA] Where did you get to, love, this morning?

BRENDA: Went for a walk.

MRS SLATTERY: Walk? [*To* ARTHUR] Strange hours they keep in this house.

BRENDA: No stranger than before.

MRS SLATTERY: No ... I suppose it's always been a little odd ... [*To* SLATTERY] I'll go and get your breakfast, love ... I let Arthur have what I'd cooked already.

SLATTERY: No breakfast, love, for me.

MRS SLATTERY: Nay, you'll have something, love, I'm sure.

SLATTERY: Nowt ... Don't want ought ...

MRS SLATTERY: Think I ought to ring the doctor ...

SLATTERY: You'll do no such bloody thing.

BRENDA: I wouldn't mind having something, Ma.

MRS SLATTERY: What? [*Hesitates.*] Well, then ... I'll get you some-thing, love.

BRENDA: S'all right ... No trouble ... Done it often enough before. [*Goes.*]

MRS SLATTERY: She gets more wrapped up in herself, I think, each day ... [*To* ARTHUR] Got a job in an office about a year ago ... The manager came to see us. Didn't want to sack her, but he said she'd been going round encouraging the employees to strike ... not for more money, or anything. Wanted them to take over the manage-ment ... [*To* SLATTERY] I think he was quite attracted by her – apart from that ... I think if she'd be less dictatorial she'd attract all sorts of interesting people. As it is ... Well, that's *her* problem, I expect ... Spends nearly all her time now writing ... I read a bit of it once when I was cleaning out her room ... Don't ever tell her I told you ... I've never read anything, well ... so lewd. Not just the language ... Well, anyway ... Good job your father didn't see it.

SLATTERY: Meks no difference to me. Gone their own bloody ways ... Gi'en no bloody attention to me ... Never ... Puts me down with the bloody cows ... telling me that last night, she was. Aye. Well. I better get out ... Mechanization ... get just like the bloody machines out theer ... if you don't tell 'em, direct 'em, switch 'em on, tell 'em when to stop and start, reckon they can't do it by the'selves ... By God: had nothing but hosses here when we first came ... I'nt that right? Bloody 'osses know more about bloody farming than any man you can hire today ... Aye ... Well ... I'll go on out ... Back o' yon bloody barn they'll be – brewing up, I reckon ... [*Going.*]

MRS SLATTERY: Get your clothes on, love, you know.

SLATTERY: Don't worry ... Ne'er gone out i' me bloody undies yet. [*Goes.*]

MRS SLATTERY: He takes some looking after ... Ten years older ...

At times it feels more like fifty ... Is there anything you want to do, specially, while you're here?

ARTHUR: No – I thought I'd just ... look around.

MRS SLATTERY: Past haunts.

ARTHUR: Yes.

MRS SLATTERY: What was your poem about ... The one you published?

ARTHUR: Oh ... [*Shakes his head.*]

MRS SLATTERY: Did it have a title?

ARTHUR: 'Evening.'

MRS SLATTERY: Evening.

[*Pauses.*]

Can you remember any of it, then?

ARTHUR: Not really.

MRS SLATTERY: Some of it, then. [*Laughs.*]

ARTHUR: It wasn't very long ...

MRS SLATTERY: Go on.

[*Pause. Then:*]

ARTHUR [*Uncertain*]:

We sat by the window talking, I thought, of love;
The light fell on your face:
A frown.
Mine sat in shadow:
'A simple division,'
You said.
'If you move to my side the sun, too,
Will fall on yours.'
'Darkness,' I said, 'like light,
Moves only up or down.'

The sun set;
The light crept up the pane.
'Blackness,' I said, 'comes always from below.'
'Warmth rises,' *you* said, 'I know.'
[*They're silent. Then:*]

MRS SLATTERY: That's lovely, love ... [*Waits.*] Did it sell well, then, the poem?

ARTHUR: There are only two or three hundred people buy the magazine.

MRS SLATTERY: Well, that's something ... At least, *they*'ll have read it.

ARTHUR: Yes ...

MRS SLATTERY: It's not the quantity ...

ARTHUR: No.

[*They're silent. Then:*]

I came to tell you, Mother, that I'll be getting married, probably, quite soon.

MRS SLATTERY: What ... ?

ARTHUR [*joking*]: Can't you ever think of me as being married?

MRS SLATTERY: Well, yes ... Of course I can.

ARTHUR: Well, then ... Not as bad as I thought.

MRS SLATTERY: Goodness ... Well, I've never thought ... I mean, I thought you'd take much longer, settling down.

ARTHUR: Struck lucky, I expect.

MRS SLATTERY: Yes ...

ARTHUR: I suppose we're engaged, in a way, already ... I've brought her up ...

MRS SLATTERY: Here?

ARTHUR: I thought I'd come ahead ... I booked her in at a hotel in town.

MRS SLATTERY: What she must think.

ARTHUR: No ... No. I preferred to see how people felt ... rather than sort of springing her on you ...

MRS SLATTERY: Yes.

ARTHUR: I'll ... Well, I hope you'll like her.

MRS SLATTERY: Yes.

ARTHUR: Her name's Alison.

MRS SLATTERY: Alison ...

ARTHUR: Not very fond of it myself ... But then I've never been fond of Arthur, really ... You see: two A's ...

MRS SLATTERY: Oh ... Yes.

ARTHUR: She's much older than me ... She's been married once already.

MRS SLATTERY: Oh.

ARTHUR: Certain similarities, I suppose, between her and Wendy.

MRS SLATTERY: Yes.

ARTHUR: Well ... I ... hope, you know, you'll feel quite pleased.

MRS SLATTERY: Yes ... Goodness. I feel a bit dazed, I think ... I never ... Well, then ... Do Wendy and Jenny know?

ARTHUR: Yes. I told them.

MRS SLATTERY: When do you want to bring her up?

ARTHUR: This evening ... I thought it might be best.

MRS SLATTERY: Yes ... Well, we'll have ... [*Looks round.*]

ARTHUR: Oh, there's no need to do anything special.

MRS SLATTERY: We can't have her just coming in ... unprepared.

ARTHUR: Oh, she's very ordinary ... I mean, she won't expect anything special.

MRS SLATTERY: You'll have to tell your father.

ARTHUR: I suppose he'll be relieved.

MRS SLATTERY: Relieved?

ARTHUR: Well, I imagined that he would.

SLATTERY [*off*]: God damn it ... Brenda? Is that you?

BRENDA [*off*]: Yes!

SLATTERY [*off*]: Got that back door wide open? There's a bloody gale through here.

BRENDA [*off*]: Yes ...

SLATTERY [*off*]: Well, shut it, for God's sake ... [*Comes in rubbing hands.*] Gonna snow. This time of the year an' all. Thought we might've got through without ... Muffled up to the bloody ears. Wonder they can move at all ... Know when they're bloody well off, they do ... Think it's time, tha knows, I had a drop ... [*Has gone to the dresser.*] By God, then. Look at that ... Hope you don't think I've been at it, missis.

MRS SLATTERY: No. No ... Arthur had a drop last night.

SLATTERY: A drop? Half a bloody bottle ... God Christ: I don't sup as much as that myself.

MRS SLATTERY: I thought you'd had a drop already.

SLATTERY: A drop? A drop? ... God Christ: diluted it, she had. Teaspoon to one bloody pint o' watter ... [*To* ARTHUR] Our Brenda ... don't know where she fund it ... Here, then. Was that all we had?

MRS SLATTERY: No ... There's a bottle in reserve. [*Going to the cupboard.*]

SLATTERY: God Christ ... See what it is, then, lad? See what A've come to ... ? Tek me as an example. Don't come any clearer ... a shining bloody light to them that have the eyes to see ... Here. Somebody's been at this, an' all.

ARTHUR: That's me again, I'm afraid.

SLATTERY: Well. I'll be damned ... Sup more than me. I could have told you ... Not in the house five bloody minutes: one bottle gone, another started ... Bloody good job A came down when I did ... By go ... Been overtaken, love: that's me.

ARTHUR: There wasn't much in the bottle when I had it.

SLATTERY: Much? Half on it, that's all ... Mek me into the bloody black sheep and they're supping it when I'm not even theer.

MRS SLATTERY: All right. Now just get a drop and put it back ... There couldn't have been much in, I know Arthur.

SLATTERY: And I know bloody Arthur ... I know Arthur, don't you forget it ... I know Arthur, now, of old ...

MRS SLATTERY: All right, now. I think we've heard it ...

SLATTERY: Heard it? We've bloody heard it. We've done nowt else but hear it ... all my bloody life ... What's he going to do about it? That's what I bloody want to know.

ARTHUR: Do about what?

MRS SLATTERY: Now that's enough. He's not come home for us to start all that.

SLATTERY: Don't know what he bloody well has come home for. If it's not to borrow one thing it'll be to see if he can borrow summat else ... Never done a day's bloody work. Not all his life.

ARTHUR: I have.

SLATTERY: Not that I give a damn. I don't. I want you to know that, lad. I mean that sincerely. It teks all sorts to mek a world ... I might work like a bloody animal meself ... no reason why you or anybody should do the same ... T'only trouble is ... them that do the bloody work get no attention ... them that do damn all get nowt but bloody praise ... Not blaming you. S'human nature.

MRS SLATTERY: Arthur's had jobs, if you want to know.

SLATTERY: Jobs? What jobs?

MRS SLATTERY: He's worked on a farm, as a matter of fact.

SLATTERY: On a farm! [*Laughs.*] How long for? ... Go on. Go on.
I'm listening.

MRS SLATTERY: He's worked in hotels ... He's even taught.

SLATTERY: Taught? Couldn't teach my bloody flat cap, I'm telling
you ... And that's nothing personal, mind. It's just a statement of
bloody fact ... Thy sisters teach. Bloody woman's job is that ...
Good God. They spend more time on bloody holiday than they
do in front o' their bloody class ... God Christ: I could teach as
much as they do and still run this entire bloody farm meself.
Single-handed ... no bloody half-baked buggers mooching
round those bloody sheds ...

MRS SLATTERY: Yes. Well, love. We've heard all that before.

SLATTERY: Thinks I'm drunk, but I'm bloody not.

MRS SLATTERY: I don't think that at all.

SLATTERY: Thinks I've got one hidden away.

MRS SLATTERY: I don't.

SLATTERY: Well, you must think I'm bloody funny if I haven't.

MRS SLATTERY: I think, if anything, you're pleasanter when you're
drunk.

SLATTERY: What? [*Gazes at her, uncertain.*]

MRS SLATTERY: There, now ... We've said enough.

SLATTERY: Thy's said enough. *I've* said hardly owt.

MRS SLATTERY: Well, hardly owt is enough for one day, love.

SLATTERY [*pauses. Then to* ARTHUR]: Spends all her spare time in
town ... Evening classes ... Sociology ... Psychiatry ... *Anthropology* ... Trying to find out what went wrong, lad.

ARTHUR: Wrong?

SLATTERY: What went wrong. In here. This house.

MRS SLATTERY: That's not the reason.

SLATTERY: Thinks I'm bloody stupid. Never read a bloody book
in my entire life ... I'm wrong theer. The Bible ... That's t'ony
book that's any use.

MRS SLATTERY: You wouldn't think so, to hear you speak.

SLATTERY: Didn't know the meaning of Anthropology when she
started ... When she got married she was as ignorant as me.

330

MRS SLATTERY: Well, at least one of us has made some progress.

SLATTERY: Ne'er see this side of her when you're not here, you know ... When you're not here butter wouldn't melt inside her mouth ... Done sod all in your life ... Whereas me ... worked every bleeding minute ... Never loved me ... It's true. She'll tell you ... Never has ... Idolized you, lad. Been your bloody ruin ... Been my son you'd never have turned out like that ...

MRS SLATTERY: That's not true. You know it.

SLATTERY: Nay, if you don't know when you're not bloody loved, then you'll never know bloody owt. As for him ... God Christ.

MRS SLATTERY: Don't listen to him, love ... As he gets older he gets more like a baby ... You do. I mean that. Every day.

SLATTERY: Aye ... Brought four up. I ought to bloody know ... [To ARTHUR] I ought to know about bloody babbies. Brought four into this bloody world.

MRS SLATTERY: Brought four in. But who's brought four up? You've brought up nothing but cows and horses ...

SLATTERY: Aye ... Kept you from bloody starvation a time or two ... Ask Him ... Ask *Him* ... *He*'ll tell you ... [*Looks up beseechingly, raising his hands.*] He knows ... He knows everything I've been through. He's been my one true witness all these years.

[BRENDA *has come in.*]

BRENDA: Is anything the matter?

MRS SLATTERY: Nothing's the matter ... It's just that your father I'm afraid's been out again.

BRENDA: Out?

MRS SLATTERY: Wherever he keeps it ... I don't know. He seems determined to spite himself ... All the care we take. [*To* SLATTERY] Arthur's brought us some news which I thought would have made him very happy.

SLATTERY: News? What news? Theer: that's me ration. [*Has held up the bottle after pouring a second drink.*] What bloody news is that, then, Arthur? Good news, I hope. Something that'll gi'e us all a bit of cheer.

ARTHUR: I'm getting married. I wanted you to know.

SLATTERY: Good God. [*Stands gazing at him, stupefied, glass half-raised to his mouth.*]

ARTHUR: I thought I might bring her up this evening ...

SLATTERY: Don't believe it ... [*Bangs his head.*] Summat matter wi' me bloody ear ... That's better ... Hear nowt straight off, you know, these days ... Getting old ... Ask your mother ... Doctor told her: older than me bloody years ... Life I lead: no bloody wonder. Work I bloody get through.

ARTHUR: Her name's Alison ... I'd like to bring her here, if that's all right.

SLATTERY: What?

MRS SLATTERY: He's heard you right enough.

SLATTERY: How old is she? I hope she's got her mother's permission ... I hope you're not shoving her up here, lad, inside a bloody pram.

ARTHUR: No.

SLATTERY: By go ... I've no great opinion of women much, meself ... what wi' the examples I have around me here ... but this ... She's either been bloody locked up and they've let her out – against their bloody better judgment – or she's run away from bloody home.

ARTHUR: She's much older than I am, as a matter of fact.

SLATTERY: *Much* older? How much older? She can't be so much older, I can tell you that.

ARTHUR: She's over forty.

SLATTERY [*bangs his head again*]: I'm sure ... [*Bangs his head again.*] I'm not hearing this correctly ... [*To* MRS SLATTERY] That doctor's bloody right, you know ... A'm fading ... Can't hear ought ... A'm fading bloody fast ... [*To* ARTHUR] If I disappear while you're talking, I shouldn't be surprised ... If you suddenly find yourself looking at nowt but that bloody wall behind me ... don't worry ... Natural processes. [*To* MRS SLATTERY] That's what he told me. It is. That's what he bloody said.

MRS SLATTERY [*to* ARTHUR]: Is she quite as old as that, love?

ARTHUR: I can't see that it makes any difference.

MRS SLATTERY: No ...

SLATTERY [*to* BRENDA]: Could've sworn he said this woman was over forty ... Good God. As o'd as your bloody mother, here, is that.

MRS SLATTERY: Nay, I'm a little bit over that. [*Moves aside.*]

SLATTERY [*to* ARTHUR]: *Over* forty ... ? What's that mean, then? Fifty? ... *Sixty?* ... She's not a bloody octogenarian, is she? ... By go ... Be wheeling her in i' a bloody bath-chair next ... [*Laughs. To* MRS SLATTERY] I alus said he was off his bloody rocker ... That he hadn't two penn'orth o' bloody common sense ... By God. Of all his bloody schemes, that one takes the bloody can. [*To* BRENDA] Going to end up wi' a bloody daughter-in-law o'der than mesen! [*Laughs. To* MRS SLATTERY] Better get your books out ... Anthropology. Psychiatry ... See what you can mek on that ... By go: set them bloody lecturers by their bloody ears, will that. Have to write new bloody text-books ... sithee ... mu'n marry somebody o'der than his mother, then.

[MRS SLATTERY *has turned away.*]

[*To* BRENDA] Well: aren't you going to shake his hand or summat? ... *To* ARTHUR] What's her name? Alison? ... Welcome thy new sister ... T'only new un, now, thy'll ever have.

BRENDA: Congratulations, Arthur.

ARTHUR: Thanks ...

SLATTERY: Aye ... Congratulations, lad. If you've done nowt else you've proved me bloody right ... through all these bloody years. He has.

MRS SLATTERY: That's a cruel and a wicked thing to say.

SLATTERY: Nay ... I've suffered enough for it, haven't I? Bloody immortalized that lad afore he was even born ... that's been your trouble all along ... Set him up ... Good God ... Thought he was bloody Shakespeare before he'd even opened his bloody mouth ... sit him in his pram ... waiting for him to bloody speak ... God Christ ... Thought we had a new Messiah ... Believed half on it me bloody se'n ... When he failed every examination that'd ever been invented I still thought ... '*Bloody genius is that* ... Can't go t'same road as everybody else.' [*To* BRENDA] Sweating i' the bloody fields ... looked over the bloody hedge one day ... lying on his back ... composing bloody sonnets ... God Christ. Never twigged it. Not till then ... Slave me bloody gut out and there he was, twiddling his bloody thumbs and rhyming bloody moon with June ... Seen nothing like it. Never have ... Here. Better have another ... Shocks like that don't come every day, you know. [*Pours another.*] Nowt else to tell us, then? Better get it over. Let us have it all at once ... No *compulsion* about it, is there? ... I mean ... no kiddies on the way ... Nothing that's going to prostrate us any further?

ARTHUR: No ... [*Shakes his head.*]

MRS SLATTERY: All right ... I think we've had enough.

SLATTERY: Enough? ... The fireworks haven't even bloody started yet ... Brenda. Better fill a glass thase'n.

BRENDA: No thanks.

SLATTERY: What do you think about it, then?

BRENDA: It's very good news. I'm very glad.

SLATTERY: Can see that ... Bringing a light to her bloody eyes ... Just look. Going to cheer her up, is that, no end ... Me likewise. 'Have another' ... 'Don't mind' ... 'Deserve it' ... 'Know that' ... 'Not at all' ... 'Cheers' ... 'Cheers' ... 'Here's to it' ... 'To it' ... 'Well done' ... 'Well done' ... 'Congratulations' ... ''lations.'

MRS SLATTERY: Come on, love. Leave him to it.

SLATTERY: S'all right ... I'm off out meself ... Need me out yonder ... Indispensable in some parts, if not in others ... See it through ... always have done ... Shan't turn back ... Never have done ... By God. Last of the bloody line is that.

MRS SLATTERY: Will you be in tonight, or not?

SLATTERY: In? I'll be bloody in ... Damn it all. Wouldn't miss it. Not for ought ... Is that when she's coming, Arthur? Give her my regards ... Look forward to it. Shall ... Don't worry. Shan't let you down. Sit here. Shan't move ... If you think she'll make you happy ... s'all I want to hear ... Theer ... Glass down ... Shan't have another ... Summat in to toast tonight ... Best wishes ... Congratulations ... Sithee ... not drawing her old age pension yet? [*Rams his hand in his pocket.*]

ARTHUR: Don't think so ...

SLATTERY: Could have helped you out a bit ... Know how much it is? Damn all to live on, I can tell you that ... What're you going to live on, if you don't mind me asking?

ARTHUR: I'll get a job.

SLATTERY: Heard all. No ... Really ... I bloody have ... Not been divorced, then, has she?

334

ARTHUR: Yes.

SLATTERY: Good God ... [*Waits.*] She's not got any children, has she?

ARTHUR: Two.

SLATTERY: Jesus in his holy heaven ... [*Looks up.*] I hope He's bloody listening. I hope to God that He can hear ... Have I ever done ought to deserve a family ... the likes of the bloody one I've got? ... Have I *transgressed*? ... Have I *overlooked* ...? Have I *condoned* ...? Have I sinned? Have I done *ought* ... at any time ... in any place ... Said all this before ... I know ... Maybe when I bloody get theer ... He'll tell me what it was all about ... Won't be long ... Blood pounding ... Fit to bloody burst ... Feel that ... Go on. Like a bloody engine ... Get to bloody work ... Hand to the plough: never look back. Truest words He ever spoke ... 'Dead bury the bloody dead ...' He's right ... All I've looked for ... *always* ... all I've ever looked for ... all my bloody life ... [*Goes.*]

[*Silence. Then:*]

BRENDA: I'll go up to ... One or two things to see to.

ARTHUR: Yes ...

[*She goes.*]

MRS SLATTERY: I ... better get these seen to, then ...

ARTHUR: Yes ... Here ...

[*Goes to the desk with her.*]

Sit with you ... Give a hand.

MRS SLATTERY: Yes ... Got to get them off this morning ... Never troubles to do them ... Well ... [*Starts on the bills.*]

ARTHUR: Here, come on ... What's this, then? ... Get them sorted out.

[ARTHUR *sits.*

MRS SLATTERY *cries.*

ARTHUR *holds her.*

Light fades.]

ACT THREE

Scene One

The same. Evening.

BRENDA [*off*]: Have you got it?

JENNY [*off*]: No. I've not.

BRENDA [*off*]: It's somewhere ... It was in your room.

JENNY [*off*]: Well damn well go and look ... I'm not following you around, looking for everything you've dropped. [*Comes in.*] God ...

[*Goes to framed picture: examines herself in the glass: looks for comb: dressed smartly: trousers, blouse.*

WENDY *wanders in: book, paper, tosses them down: smoking: dressed in slacks, cardigan; no special effort made.*]

WENDY: Not seen my fags, then, have you?

JENNY [*in picture*]: Honestly ... what a house ... Brenda's looking for a ribbon: swears she's left it in my room ...

WENDY: What she doing in your room?

JENNY: I let her go there ... to write ... Sun shines in, she says. Finds it warmer.

WENDY: Wouldn't let that nosey-parker anywhere near my things, unattended ... bet she's got my cigarettes ... Pretends not to smoke, keeping herself clean for the revolution ... and all the time, like a bloody furnace ... not to mention all that bloody booze ... A real subversionist is Brenda ...

JENNY: Acquired it from her dad.

WENDY: What?

JENNY: He's a natural burrower ... underminer ... Quite secretive, in fact ... Beneath all that bluster lurks a very mischievous, furtive heart.

WENDY: Don't believe it.

JENNY: Don't want to. That's your trouble.

WENDY: You mean the bottles he's got hidden around ... ? Pathe-

336

tic ... If you call him a natural subversionist I don't know what you'd call our Brenda ... I've never seen idealism confused with so much self-regard before ... or perhaps that's an essential part of it ... I mean, all idealism, at some point, presupposes a certain degree of paranoia.

JENNY: Weren't they supposed to be here, then, by now?

WENDY: So he said.

JENNY: Not looking forward to it, really, are you?

WENDY: Not really, no, as a matter of fact.

JENNY: Why not?

WENDY: I think he's mad.

JENNY [*lightly, regarding herself again in picture*]: I think you're quite envious, really.

WENDY: Think I am.

JENNY: Green about the gills.

WENDY: That's right.

JENNY: He's done a very courageous thing, as a matter of fact.

WENDY: Really.

JENNY: He must feel a great deal for her, or he wouldn't have gone this far. Not Arthur.

WENDY: Depends how much he's getting, love.

JENNY: ?

WENDY: How much she's giving him, girl.

JENNY: That's your answer to everything, I think.

WENDY: That's right.

JENNY: Like living in a shop. Give ... take.

WENDY: Never thought of that before ...

JENNY: If it doesn't come across to your advantage – nothing ... I'd say that was another Slattery trait.

WENDY: Really.

JENNY: You're like a miser ... Store it up ... Accuse Brenda. My God ... What supreme charitable act are you going to endow, Wendy, with all your worldly, intellectual charms?

WENDY: You been at the Scotch as well?

JENNY: Don't need to. Got it all in here ...

WENDY: Indifferent as to who gets a share of it, an' all.

JENNY: Not really ... Pick and choose ...

337

WENDY: Pick some *I* would never choose ... I've never seen so many men immobilized by one woman in my life before ...

[JENNY *laughs.*]

I've seen them waiting for you here ... How many, over the years, I couldn't recall ... All of them: one thing in common ... *constipation.* [*Grabs at her stomach and doubles up.*]

[JENNY *doesn't answer: gets a cigarette: lights it.*]

You're as incapable of making a moral decision as I am.

JENNY: What?

WENDY: Of committing yourself to anything.

[JENNY *doesn't answer: puffs away, unaffected.*]

Accuse me of an acquisitive instinct where people are concerned, but you ... you never even make a purchase. You'll end up in some bloody flat ... house ... tenement ... inviolate ... At least, when I got rid of Bryan, I got rid of someone who was only asking to be used ... There was some common decency, I would have thought, in that ... Are those my cigarettes? I bloody well knew you'd had them.

JENNY: Found them lying around.

WENDY: Where you find everything in your life, girl. [*Takes one: drops the packet down.*]

JENNY: Child of nature: what I am.

WENDY: Get here when the old man's gone to bed, 'spect ... might be the best, at that. [*Moves away, lighting cigarette.*]

JENNY: You're not making it any easier.

WENDY: Easier?

JENNY: Saying that.

WENDY: The woman's over forty ... Good God. Either she's a raving bloody lunatic, or so insatiable that she'll take anything she can grab.

JENNY: I wouldn't say Arthur was anything.

WENDY: That's more or less how I would sum him up.

JENNY: You don't always talk about him in those terms ... If anything, I always thought if there was one person in the place to whom you are, in reality, quite vulnerable ... that that person might very well be Arthur ... Used to talk glowingly of his literary gifts, I recollect ... Remember? Typing out his poems

338

and sending them to some magazine ... who sent them back and
said most of them were a parody of Yeats ...

WENDY: Think I'll start early, as a matter of fact ...

[*Goes to drink: pours one, holds up glass.*]

JENNY: No thanks.

WENDY: Got it all inside. Forgot.

MRS SLATTERY [*off*]: Wendy ... ?

WENDY [*goes to door, calls*]: Ma?

MRS SLATTERY [*off*]: Is your father down there, love?

JENNY: No ...

MRS SLATTERY [*off*]: S'all right, love ... He'll be in his room.

WENDY: More likely in Ten Acre ... Totting up.

JENNY: On the whole, I think he'll behave quite well.

WENDY: Really.

JENNY: You know how circumspect he is with strangers.

WENDY: Not with this one, love, I think. [*Looks up at* JENNY, *who doesn't answer.*] Be my guess, for what it's worth.

JENNY: Think he'll surprise you, then. Give you quite a shock.

WENDY: Give me quite a shock, I think: give himself an even bigger one. [*Drinks.*]

BRENDA [*entering*]: Told you. Found it in your room ... [*She's dressed smartly, in a short skirt and a blouse.*]

JENNY: Know where to look, then, next time.

WENDY: No Rosa Luxemburg we're entertaining, Brenda. Just Arthur's forty-year-old whore.

JENNY: Shut up.

WENDY: Do you think she cited him, or what?

BRENDA: So bloody funny. So bloody snide.

JENNY: Look quite excited, Brenda ...

BRENDA: Yes ... I think I am. That's right.

WENDY: I'd love to see Brenda with a gun ... Do you remember when the old man used to go out shooting ... ? Brought back those bloody pigeons ... I thought Brenda here would die of fright ... Shock ... Paralysis. Seen nothing like it. '*Just look at their eyes!*' [*To* BRENDA] Remember saying that? ... If she behaves like that with a parasitic wood-pigeon what's she going to be like when she gets the plutocratic bastards up against a wall?

[BRENDA *turns away*.]

I think you look quite beautiful ... Really, I think both of you look terrific ... It's astonishing what Arthur's done for us. I can feel the vibrancy running through the building ... tremor ... tremor ... tremor ... even the house, you see, is beginning to feel excited ... And I know this house as well, I think, as I know anything at all.

MRS SLATTERY [*entering*]: There you all are ... Your father's struggling into his suit.

WENDY: Suit.

JENNY: Good God.

MRS SLATTERY: When he tries he can make a very good impression.

WENDY: On whom? On whom?

MRS SLATTERY: On whoever he wants to ... now don't go stirring trouble up. We've enough on with keeping one of us quiet.

WENDY: Shan't say a word. Lips are sealed. Condolence: commiseration: sisterly affection.

MRS SLATTERY: One of us is in a good mood, then, at least ... Is that the time? I thought he said he'd be here by now.

JENNY: Post a look-out ... [*At window*] See the lights ... could blow a bugle. What d'you think?

WENDY: I offered to drive them up but he wouldn't have it. Independence. Wanted to carry in his bride ... cross the threshold ...

MRS SLATTERY: It's not got that far yet.

WENDY: That's what we're all here for, isn't it? ... First family reunion for ... How many years?

MRS SLATTERY: I don't think I'll bother to count ... Brenda, you're looking very nice ... Jenny, too.

[*They look at* WENDY.]

WENDY: I made a special effort ... shook out all the dust ... Even put on some lipstick. [*Looks in picture.*] Wore it last night but nobody noticed ... 'cept Jenny. Jumped entirely to the wrong conclusion.

JENNY: Why did you put it on, as a matter of fact?

WENDY [*looks again in picture*]: Don't know ... narcissistic ... instinctive ... a bloody-minded reversion, I suppose. Some common or garden impulse, you can be sure of that.

JENNY: Been battling with her femininity all these years ... Quite suddenly, you see, given in ... Makes quite a change. A vast improvement.

WENDY: Brenda battles with her social ideals ... entirely unrealistic ... I battle with my sense of inferiority in being a woman ... Jenny battles with ... I don't know what she battles with ... lasciviousness ... indolence ... sexuality ... acquisitiveness ... What battle would you choose, Ma? What secret is it that you nurture, down there, at the Workers' Educational Institute? Does a rudimentary knowledge of anthropology, psychiatry, sociology, actually enhance your existence, Ma ... does it take it on a step? Or is it a means of protecting yourself against all your lurking fears and fancies that otherwise might pop out ... in bed ... at night?

MRS SLATTERY: Well, I'm sure I don't go down for that ... And I'm sure we're not going to have a discussion at this time of the night ... Brenda: we ought to have a kettle on ... I don't know if Alison drinks ...

WENDY: Bound to ... Woman her age, dispositon ... Can imagine her, in fact, quite clearly.

JENNY: Give a year or two, of course: yourself.

WENDY: That's right ...

BRENDA: I've put the kettle on already, Ma.

MRS SLATTERY: Good girl. You see. Not as helpless as you think.

WENDY: Never thought of her as helpless ... ingenuous ... naïve ... She could do a great deal, could Brenda, if she really tried ... Like shooting somebody ... or blowing something up.

BRENDA: Might take a bit of your own advice.

WENDY: I might ... Not sure what tonight is going to inspire me to.

MRS SLATTERY: Brought out a strange streak in you, I think!

WENDY: Bring out a strange streak in all of us, Ma ... Ay up ...

[*Sounds on stairs:* SLATTERY *enters.*]

SLATTERY [*entering*]: Ay up. Ay up, then. Are we here? [*He's dressed in a suit, fresh-faced, hair combed.*]

WENDY: Good God.

JENNY: Amazing.

BRENDA: Super, Dad.

SLATTERY: That's right. Look a picture: nobody here, then, is there?

JENNY: We're here, I'm afraid, but no one else.

SLATTERY: Come early: give us all a bloody shock. [*Goes straight to the drink.*]

MRS SLATTERY: Should you start on that right now?

SLATTERY: Won't do any harm. Oil the wheels ... You're looking very smart ... Not seen a turn-out like this for bloody years ... By God ... you're at it, then, as well?

WENDY: Lubrication.

SLATTERY: Lubrication! [*Raises his glass to toast, and drinks.*] Eldest daughter! [*Toasts. Then:*] Smoking: don't think so bloody much o' that.

JENNY: Drinking, I gather's, just as bad.

SLATTERY: Do as I say, not as I do. Don't take me as an example – told you that afore.

JENNY: I don't think we ever have, you know.

SLATTERY: Is that a fact? Hear that? Bloody daughter. Live inside your bloody back pocket ... any time you ask for ought: 'No thank you. Manage by meself.' ... Look very nice, my dear. [*To* BRENDA] Look like a bloody lass, at last. Almost given up bloody hope ... As for these ... God Christ ... What's matter with a bloody skirt or dress ... ? Look at your mother: couldn't look lovelier than that.

MRS SLATTERY: I think they look very nice ... [*To* JENNY] I think it suits you very well.

SLATTERY: Bloody suits, all right ... Here. One more. Then I'll give it a rest ... S'only food. Quite natural. Meat and drink. Me meats in theer ... [*Gestures off*] ... and me drink's in this. [*Pours.*] Not have another?

WENDY: No thanks.

SLATTERY: Moderation. What I believe in ... Sithee, thy'll not be content, then, till men start having babbies and thy can strut around with thy hands inside thy pockets.

JENNY: Might be a good idea.

SLATTERY: Tell thee thy trouble in a bloody flash.

MRS SLATTERY: We've heard all we want to hear of that ... Is that a car?

[*They pause: listen.*]

BRENDA: Gone past.

SLATTERY: Here ... S'not often, you know, we see a sight like this ... By God. Better get the cards out. Have a hand or two at bridge ... [*To* MRS SLATTERY, *giving hug*] Remember that, then, eh? Gin rummy ... Used to lake that, you know, in winter. Too young, these lot, to remember ... Jefferson came across from Shepherd's Nook and old Morrisey from Temple Bank: took some bloody money off 'em, didn't we? Kept thee alive some weeks on what we won at whist ... By God ... some years it cost us more to keep this bloody place running than we ever bloody well got out of it ... All gone now ... motor-car factory, Temple Bank. Used to be a lovely bloody farm did that. Could pot rabbits theer any day of the bloody week ... go over ... have us a dinner for the cost of a bloody cartridge ... Shepherd's Nook ... municipal bloody housing. Had some lovely bloody fields, had that. Woods ... Did our courting there, remember?

MRS SLATTERY: I remember.

SLATTERY: S'likely not forget. [*Laughs.*] Be our turn bloody next ... where we're sitting ... two years' time: six-lane bloody highway.

BRENDA: Probably be worth it.

SLATTERY: I reckon to you it would.

MRS SLATTERY: If the water's on, I better go and turn it off. [*Goes.*]

SLATTERY: Be dead and buried afore then; I shan't have to worry. [*To* BRENDA] Be your heritage: see what sort of job *thy* makes ... with your computerized, mechanized, de-humanized, antiseptic bloody lot.

BRENDA: It'll be all right ... if it's not uséd to disadvantage.

SLATTERY: Disadvantage?

BRENDA: To give power to some and not to others.

SLATTERY: Power! Want everything in bloody brackets yon: everything has a bloody label ... think we all ought to run down bloody rails ... S' not worth bloody living ... Mek people in bloody factories next. You see. Bloody laugh. They will. Get rid o' bloody ones like me. Old. Out of bloody date. No good ...

BRENDA: I think it's you who runs on rails. Blinkers: never see anything you don't really want.

SLATTERY: I believe in nowt, don't worry ... I want everything ... to be absolutely different ... That's what I bloody well want ... an endless chain of possibilities ... Look at thy two sisters. They're emblem-atic of the modern age ... Free and easy. Responsible to bloody nowt ... Thy brother's another ...

JENNY: We ought to have invited you to school.

SLATTERY: Aye.

JENNY: They'd be entranced. Could give a lecture.

SLATTERY: Ten minutes in that school and you wouldn't have any pupils theer.

WENDY: Where would you send them, Dad?

SLATTERY: Work. Work's the only bloody thing that's real.

JENNY: I think he means it.

BRENDA: I think he does. I don't see any reason why he shouldn't.

JENNY: Good God. I can see now where she gets it from.

SLATTERY: Gets it – anything that's any bloody good, that is – gets it bloody well from me.

BRENDA: That's right. I do.

[*They laugh.*]

MRS SLATTERY [*entering*]: It's almost an hour ... just look.

WENDY: Do you want me to go and fetch them?

MRS SLATTERY: I don't know ... [*To* SLATTERY] Do you think she should?

SLATTERY: Nay, don't bloody well ask me. [*Turns away.*] Know bloody nowt.

WENDY: I'll drive down. If I see them coming up I can always follow them back ... They might not be able to get a taxi, and the bus isn't due for ages yet. [*To* JENNY] Is that all right?

JENNY: All right by me.

WENDY [*to* MRS SLATTERY]: Do you know which hotel she's staying in?

MRS SLATTERY: No, love ... I've no idea.

SLATTERY: There's on'y two ... Tha mu'n ask at each.

WENDY: Right ... Well. If nobody's any objection, then. [*Looks round.*] I'll see you. [*Goes.*]

344

MRS SLATTERY: She's a good lass ... Always hides her feelings.

JENNY: Where? Where, though? That's what I would like to ask.

MRS SLATTERY: I'm sure I don't know, love. And why: that's another mystery to me.

SLATTERY: I think it's time I had another. [*Getting one.*]

MRS SLATTERY: You've just had another.

SLATTERY: That was the one afore; this is the one that comes just after.

MRS SLATTERY: I'm putting this away. [*Takes the bottle after* SLATTERY *has poured his drink.*] And don't come following me — or I'll put it where you'll never find it. [*Goes.*]

SLATTERY [*calls*]: And I've fund it in *that* damn place afore! [*Laughs. Then, to* JENNY] Means the dustbin. Been rooting in there, I have, a time or two. Pour it down the sink, 'cept she's too appreciative of the cost ... If she thought the tractors could use it she'd pour it all in theer instead.

JENNY: You're in a very cheerful mood.

SLATTERY: I am.

JENNY: What have you been up to, then?

SLATTERY: Up to?

JENNY: This ... euphoria: it can't spring up from nothing.

SLATTERY: It springs up from a hard day's bloody work: that's what it bloody well springs up from ... If you did a bit yourself, you'd know.

JENNY: Brenda?

    [BRENDA *shakes her head.*]

Moods change in here so quickly: can never follow them. What're you so glum about?

BRENDA: Nothing ... [*Moves away.*]

    [JENNY *looks after her: takes out another cigarette. Then* WENDY *comes in, in coat: collar up, headscarf: brisk.*]

WENDY: Is my mother here?

BRENDA: No.

JENNY: She's hiding the old man's bottle, as a matter of fact.

WENDY: Right.

JENNY: Anything the matter?

WENDY: No. [*Goes.*]

345

JENNY: Well ... as long as we know ... [*To* BRENDA] ... we'll be all right.

> [*A door is slammed off: feet run down stairs.*
> JENNY *looks at* BRENDA.
> SLATTERY *has gone over to the fire: bends down, pokes it. Door opens.*
> WENDY *comes in: casual, coat unbuttoned, headscarf off.*]

WENDY: Got one of those?

> [*Takes a cigarette from a curious* JENNY.]

JENNY: What's going on, then? I thought you were off.

WENDY: The prodigal's arrived.

BRENDA: Arthur?

WENDY: I shouldn't go out ...

> [BRENDA *has gone to the door.*]

I shouldn't go ...

> [BRENDA *goes.*]

JENNY: Extraordinary ... [*Then:*] And where are you off to, then, old lad?

SLATTERY: Up ...

JENNY: Aren't you going to wait?

SLATTERY: What?

WENDY: I should keep it on, you know ... for a little longer.

SLATTERY: Aye ... All right ... All right. I bloody will. [*Turns back towards the fire.*]

JENNY [*to* WENDY]: Has he come alone?

WENDY: That's right.

JENNY: Good God.

> [*Door opens:* MRS SLATTERY *comes in: tense, suppressing. They watch her. Then:*]

Well, then ... Ma?

> [MRS SLATTERY *wanders, aimless, straightening cushions, etc.*]

Is Arthur back?

MRS SLATTERY: Yes.

JENNY: With or without?

MRS SLATTERY: He's come alone. [*Wipes her eyes.*]

JENNY: Here we are ... Dressed up ... Queen of Sheba. [*Gestures at herself. Laughs.*] What's his excuse then, this time, Ma?

MRS SLATTERY: Better ask him ... He's hanging up his coat.

JENNY [*to* WENDY]: No one ever tells us anything, you know ... treat us like bloody yokels ... even the kids at school put on a bloody accent ... 'Art 'a barn up o' moor, Miss Slatt'ry? Wearst t'a keepin' sheep?'

　　[ARTHUR *comes in.*
　　Pause. Then:]

ARTHUR: Hi ... [*Moves round a moment, restless.*]

　　[BRENDA *comes back in.*
　　Pause.]

JENNY: What's it all about, then, Arthur?

ARTHUR: She decided not to come.

JENNY: Why not?

ARTHUR: Don't know. [*Still wanders round the room, fingering various things, putting them down.*]

WENDY: Has she left already?

ARTHUR: Yep.

JENNY: You mean: she *won't* be coming?

ARTHUR: No.

　　[*Pause. They look at one another. Then:*]

SLATTERY: Well ... coo-shed time, I think, for me.

WENDY: Oh, no. [*Backs up to door.*] Nobody's going until we've sorted this thing out.

SLATTERY: Nay, there's nowt that I mun add. I've said all I've to say, tha knows, afore.

　　[*Pause.*]

WENDY [*watches him*]: You don't seem very concerned about it, Art?

ARTHUR: No.

JENNY: Did you see her earlier in the day?

ARTHUR: I might.

JENNY [*to* MRS SLATTERY]: Did he go into town this afternoon?

MRS SLATTERY [*looks to* ARTHUR. *Then*]: I don't know, love. I've no idea.

SLATTERY: We've gone through all this, tha means, for nowt?

ARTHUR: All what?

SLATTERY: Nay, tha mun look around ... Thy sisters dressed up like they've never been dressed afore ... thy mother dressed up like a bloody bride ... I've even put on a bloody suit mesen.

ARTHUR: Then you'd better take it off, it seems.

SLATTERY: Tha'd welcome bloody that, I know ... The invisible event: the story of his life ... Great bloody things he's been and gone and done ... on'y when you bloody well get theer: nothing but a puff o' smoke.

ARTHUR: Do you think it'd do any good, then ... me bringing her up here?

SLATTERY: Thy invited her ... That's what we're all bloody well waiting for ... That's why we're all collected ... that's why we're all on bloody tenterhooks, you know.

ARTHUR: I changed my mind.

SLATTERY: You changed your mind. *You* changed your mind?

MRS SLATTERY: Nay, well ... [*She's about to speak: she turns away.*]

SLATTERY: Nay, bloody hell. Let's have it out ... I've got on me bloody best suit, tha knows. If I can't hear ought in this, I never shall. It's t'best bit o' cloth inside this house ... it mun hear summat for all its bloody pains ... it's been wrapped up in that cupboard long enough ... [*To* BRENDA] Just smell at that. Preservatives. God Christ: I smell like a bloody moth mesen ... What is it? Some clandestine meeting has t'a had? With your mother and your sisters behind my back?

JENNY: Nay, it's not with me.

WENDY: Nor me ... [*She lights a cigarette.*]

[*Looks to* BRENDA.]

SLATTERY: D'ost thy know ought about it, Brenda, lass?

BRENDA: No. [*She turns away.*]

SLATTERY [*to* MRS SLATTERY]: Thy's seen her, missis, h'ast'a then?

MRS SLATTERY: No. [*She shakes her head, bowed.*]

SLATTERY: Nay, sithee. [*To* ARTHUR] Tha mun let it out. If we can't celebrate her bloody coming, we can bloody well celebrate her going back.

ARTHUR: I thought it better she didn't come, that's all.

SLATTERY: And when did you decide on that, then, lad?

ARTHUR: This afternoon.

SLATTERY: And you got in touch by telepathy, like?

ARTHUR: I rang her up.

SLATTERY [*to* MRS SLATTERY]: I hope he paid for the bloody call. Though if he explained it as quickly to her as he has to us it'd cost him hardly anything at all.

[MRS SLATTERY *has turned aside: she cries.*]

Thy advised her, then, she shouldn't come.

ARTHUR: I left it up to her.

SLATTERY: And you let us bloody well get dressed up for nowt.

ARTHUR: I've got dressed up, you see, as well.

SLATTERY: Nay, bloody pigs dress up as well as that – to have their dinners in the bloody yard.

MRS SLATTERY: Joe ...

SLATTERY: Nay, bloody hell ... I've said enough. God damn it! If in just one thing in his life he kept to what he said.

ARTHUR: I brought her here ... hoping that time might have changed, if not your character, at least your manner ... It seems nothing's got better ... if anything, it's got far worse. I don't know why I troubled even to think of coming back.

SLATTERY: I know why you bloody troubled, lad, all right ... A soft touch ... Me one foot in the grave, soft-headed ... your mother – as always – as silly as a bloody brush ... your sisters more interested in themselves than anything that bloody matters ... One shove, tha thought, and I'll be o'ver the bloody edge ... an apoplectic bloody seizure when you bring this octogenarian in the house ... and the rest is easy ... Well, I'm stronger than thy bloody thinks ... It'll take more than thee, old as I am, to get me down. [*Sits down.*]

MRS SLATTERY: Oh, now. We've said enough.

WENDY: Aye ... I think we better take the war-paint off ... Brenda: have you any useful commentary to add?

BRENDA: Not really. No.

WENDY: Usually loquacious on occasions such as this.

BRENDA: I think Arthur did quite right. He'd be very foolish to bring someone – or something – he values, into this.

SLATTERY: That's thy opinion, is it?

BRENDA: For what it's worth.

SLATTERY: That's not so bloody much, I can tell you that. Minus fifteen quid a week, as near as ought. That's what it costs to keep her opinions on all and sundry coming out. A back-pocket orator, our Brenda is. And it's my bloody back-pocket she does it from ... [*He coughs.*] God Christ ... He'll get me yet.

[MRS SLATTERY *has brought* SLATTERY *a drink.*
He swallows it down: gasps, coughs.]

MRS SLATTERY: Now that's enough. If anything, I think, you ought to go to bed.

SLATTERY: My God. Can't you see it, lass? Like all his bloody poems is that ... God Christ. [*Chokes.*] Tha mun keep away in future, lad ... Tha mun do it as a favour to mesen ... I haven't got long to go: I can tell you that. But I mun go my own road: not with thy pushing from behind.

MRS SLATTERY: Now that's enough ... *Enough.*

SLATTERY: D'ost think I don't see through all his scheming, then? D'ost think I'm as simple as he makes out? I may be finished ... I may be half-way o'ver the edge already ... but, by God, I'll go in my own good time ... I bloody shall ... [*Gasps, holds his chest.*]

WENDY: Here, Mother, then: I'll give you a hand.

SLATTERY: You'll do no such bloody thing! I'll stand mesen ... [*He rises.*] D'ost think I've lost me faculties, then? [*To* MRS SLATTERY] D'ost see them running the house already? I've gone o'ver the bloody top, then, have I?

MRS SLATTERY: He's over the top in one thing, that's for sure. His allowance for the day. You've been drinking in your room.

SLATTERY: I have ... [*To others.*] Mun think I run on nowt. Been married fo'ty years: it scarcely shows. Young as when I first met her, I mun grant her that ... just as pretty and twice as daft ... I reckon I've done all on t'ageing that's gone on inside this house ... there mun be all on't years shoved on me back ... whereas thee, tha knows ... there's not one of you any o'der than when I first clapped eyes ... [*To* ARTHUR] Thy did quite right. If thy'd brought her back I'd have probably been reconciled. You realize that? When it comes face to face – with her, or you, or you ... with whoever they bring in here – I soon step back ... I don't have a bite. You realize that? All bark ... [*Coughs. Chokes.*] I think you're right ... [*Goes.*]

[*Allows himself to be led out by* MRS SLATTERY.
WENDY *sees them to the door: stays behind.*
Pause.]

WENDY [*pours herself a drink*]: Brenda?

    [BRENDA *shakes her head.*]

JENNY: I'll have one ... Art?

ARTHUR: No thanks. [*He shakes his head.*]

JENNY: Perhaps it was a mistake ... Inviting her, I mean, like that.

ARTHUR: Yeh.

    [*Pause.*]

BRENDA: I'll go up to my room, I think. [*She goes.*]

    [WENDY *offers* ARTHUR *a cigarette: he hesitates, then takes one.*]

WENDY: She's been making placards the last few days.

ARTHUR: ?

WENDY: Notices.

JENNY: 'Promises are contracts that you never keep.'

WENDY: 'Two stones may often weigh as much as one.'

JENNY: 'A sorrow shared is a trouble doubled.'

WENDY: 'It's cynicism that makes the world go round.'

    [WENDY *and* JENNY *laugh.*]

JENNY: I even wondered ... whether this woman of yours, Arthur ... actually exists.

ARTHUR: That's right.

WENDY: We'll have to take your word for it.

ARTHUR [*hesitates*]: You will.

JENNY: We could ask at this hotel.

ARTHUR: I suppose you might.

JENNY: Did you tell her not to come?

ARTHUR: I left it up to her.

WENDY: Do you know where she's gone to?

ARTHUR: I've a good idea.

WENDY: Do you feel like following?

ARTHUR: I suppose I might.

    [MRS SLATTERY *comes in.*]

MRS SLATTERY: Your father's asleep ...

JENNY: That's quick.

MRS SLATTERY: I found a bottle half-empty beneath his bed ... He had that while he was getting dressed ... Where's Brenda, love?

JENNY: She's gone upstairs.

MRS SLATTERY: I was wondering whether I should call the doctor.

WENDY: He's been as bad as this before.

MRS SLATTERY: Once ... There was only once, you know, that's all ... He went out like a light when he reached the bed. I've left him in his clothes.

ARTHUR: I thought, Mother, I'd probably leave tonight.

MRS SLATTERY: Love ... where would you go as late as this?

ARTHUR: There's a train tonight ... I've got a ticket.

MRS SLATTERY: Stay till tomorrow, love. I'd hate to see you leave like this.

[ARTHUR *looks round him: sees the others.*]

ARTHUR: I ought to go ... We were going, in any case .. after we'd been up here.

MRS SLATTERY: Look, love ... if you like, you could stay at this hotel ... If you went tonight ... [*Looks overhead.*] I wouldn't like you to leave him when he's been like this.

ARTHUR: I think I ought to go, then, Mother ... I've arranged to go ... I think I should.

SLATTERY [*off*]: Missis! Are ye there?

WENDY: Oh, God.

SLATTERY [*off*]: *Mother!* Where is she? ... Where's she gone?
   [*A great crash, as of someone falling down a stair.*]

MRS SLATTERY: Oh ... No! [*Goes to the door.*]

SLATTERY [*off*]: God damn and blast ... what's happened to these bloody stairs? ... Who's shifted these bloody steps out here?

MRS SLATTERY [*off*]: I thought you were asleep ... In bed.

SLATTERY [*off*]: At this time of the bloody night? Has Arthur gone?
   [SLATTERY *appears at door: gazes in, dazed.*]
   I thought he'd left ... I thought you'd left ... Apologies. Spoke out of turn.

MRS SLATTERY [*having followed him in*]: Joe ... you better go to bed.

SLATTERY: Bed's for the dead ... [*Calls up*] Can write that on thy board! ... [*To others*] Painting notices, tha knows, is Bren ... 'The longest distance between two people is a frown.' Pinned it up outside me door. 'Sin is the sum you can never add up.' 'Don't cross the road afore you know it's there ...' I've worked like an animal all my life ... she'll tell you ... He'll tell you.

[*Looks up.*] Lived like a bloody animal, an' all ... can't keep up ... did I ever tell you that ... seen nothing like it ... stuck here like a Brontosaurus ... detritus from the past: that's us.

WENDY: Do you want another drink, then, Dad?

MRS SLATTERY: For God's sake, love, don't give him any more.

WENDY: How else are you going to knock him out?

SLATTERY: He wouldn't say no ... he wouldn't say yes ... Just pass him the glass ... he'll do all the rest ... [*Sways as if dancing.*] Take my photograph if you like ... Which side do you fancy, lad? Back view's the best ... good for sticking daggers in ... She thinks I'm gone ... One or two loose nuts inside his head ... she could be right ... He's seen it all. I have. He has. D'ost think a Brontosaurus never dies? I've seen animals at night stand on their heads ... horns stick in the mud ... that's right ... pull at the plough ... pull at the cart ... Like a dung-heap is this house ... ever so high ... grow cows and bullocks and geese and hens ... Be-asts ... be-asts ... be-asts for meat, and milk ... and bread ... That's very kind. [*Takes glass. Drinks.*] I think our children, you know, should be in bed ... long past their beddy, beddy, beddy-times ... want my advice ... She's hardly watered this, tha knows. [*To* MRS SLATTERY] Take more than this to put me down ... I'll have another. [*Holds out empty glass.*]

[BRENDA *has entered.*]

BRENDA: It's like acid, or alcohol ... Remorse. It eats him out. [*Has gone to help him.*]

WENDY: I thought you were on Arthur's side.

BRENDA: I am.

SLATTERY: Been imbibing on her own, has Bren. Sits in front of her manuscript, pen raised ... her glass in hand ... a race, at times, to see which gets there first ... ink to paper, or glass to mouth.

WENDY: I'll bring you one up ... a big one ... if you go to bed ... Go to bed and stay there, then?

SLATTERY: How big is a big one, then?

WENDY: As big as you like ...

SLATTERY: I'll give it a try.

WENDY: And no more getting out again.

BRENDA: Come on. Come on, then, Dad ... I'll take you up.

[SLATTERY *is helped out by* BRENDA.

WENDY *gets a drink.*

JENNY *goes to the door: helps* BRENDA *get* SLATTERY *through.*

WENDY, *having got drink, follows.*

ARTHUR *and* MRS SLATTERY *are left alone.*]

MRS SLATTERY [*regards him for a while. Then*]: Would you stay the night, then, love?

[*Pause.*]

ARTHUR [*looks over, helpless. Shrugs*]: Yes ... All right.

[MRS SLATTERY *goes.*

ARTHUR *is left alone. He goes to the drink: pours one. Looks around at the room.*

Light slowly fades.]

Scene Two

The same. Night. The room is faintly lit.

ARTHUR *sits alone in a wooden chair, facing the fire: abstracted, still. Pause.*

The door's pushed slowly open: MRS SLATTERY *comes in. She wears a housecoat.*

MRS SLATTERY: Arthur ... ? [*She comes in.*] Arthur ... [*She switches on the light. She sees his mood.*]

I couldn't sleep either, love ... I heard you coming down ... [*Watches him.*] Is there anything I can get you, love?

ARTHUR: No. [*He shakes his head.*]

MRS SLATTERY: There's not much heat in that. [*She pokes the fire.*] Are you sure you wouldn't like something, love?

ARTHUR: No thanks.

MRS SLATTERY [*watches him: looks up*]: He's sleeping like a child ... You'd never believe it, after all that noise.

ARTHUR: No.

MRS SLATTERY: He doesn't mean half the things he says, you realize that?

ARTHUR: Yes. [*Nods.*]

354

MRS SLATTERY: And as he gets older he gets more intransigent.

ARTHUR: Yes.

MRS SLATTERY: I suppose . . . it hasn't changed your mind – all this?

ARTHUR: No.

MRS SLATTERY: Well ... [*Waits. Looks up. Goes to window.*] I suppose it's cold enough to snow tonight ... [*Looks back at him.*] You never brought that poem.

> [ARTHUR *looks up.*]

The magazine.

ARTHUR: I'll send it, if you like.

MRS SLATTERY: I'd like that, love. [*Waits.*] I suppose it's difficult, really.

ARTHUR: Yes.

MRS SLATTERY: Getting them accepted.

ARTHUR: Yes ... [*Waits.*]

MRS SLATTERY: I found one in your room ...

ARTHUR: What?

MRS SLATTERY: I ... didn't want to read it, love ... [*Takes a piece of paper from her pocket.*] I couldn't make it out, in any case ... I was going to keep it, love ... If you didn't mind ...

ARTHUR: That's all right ...

MRS SLATTERY: It doesn't have a title ...

ARTHUR: No ...

MRS SLATTERY [*blinks: examines it*]: I still can't make it out ... [*Shakes her head. Looks up.*] In pencil, you see ... it's half rubbed out ...

> [ARTHUR *after a while takes it from her. Gazes at it. Reads:*]

ARTHUR:

'What will be left? ... A line of bone
and of the brain
little else but dust and stone ...
the frame
of one thought leading to another ...'

> [*Waits: studies paper:*]

'And of all the things he played –
a father, and the game of lover ...
nothing; except the spot where one limb has stayed

the dust, held back a space
and in the earth a gesture
maybe measures out the trace
of flesh, of blood – a creature
still to those who can
recognize in this the emblem of a man.'
　　[*Pause.*
　　They're silent.
　　ARTHUR *puts the paper down. He gets up.*]
I think I'll go on up.
MRS SLATTERY [*watches him. Then*]: All right, then, love.
　　[*He stoops: kisses her.*]
ARTHUR: Good night ...
MRS SLATTERY: Good night, then, love.
　　[*He goes.*
　　Silence.
　　MRS SLATTERY *covers her face: silent.*
　　Light slowly fades.]

Scene Three

A simple wooden table has been set in the centre of the room, the other furniture pushed back.
　　Shouts, calls off.

WENDY [*off*]: Are you in there?
JENNY [*off*]: I shan't be long.
WENDY [*off*]: For God's sake hurry up, then.
JENNY [*off*]: Has anybody seen my boots?
　　[*Banging on stairs and of doors.*
　　BRENDA *has come in, brisk, carrying a tray: plates, cups, spoons, etc. Begins to set them out.*
　　MRS SLATTERY *comes in: headscarf, coat, gloves.*]
BRENDA: I thought we'd have it in here this morning ... It's freezing in that kitchen, Ma.
MRS SLATTERY: I've just been out to the sheds ... your father's not

356

got up, and the men have come in late ...

BRENDA: He's up and about. I've heard him stamping. [*Gestures up: having set the tray down she goes to the door.*]

MRS SLATTERY: Are the girls up yet?

BRENDA: They're coming down. [*Goes. Calling off*] Jenny! ... Wendy!

JENNY [*calls off*]: Have you seen my boots?

[MRS SLATTERY, *having taken off her coat, goes to the door.*]

MRS SLATTERY: Didn't you leave them in the hall, then, love?

JENNY [*off*]: Could you have a look?

[*Pause. Then:*]

MRS SLATTERY: All right ... I'll see.

WENDY [*entering*]: I should tell her to come down and find them herself ... *Cow!* ... Lolls around all day like a bloody queen in bed ... God Christ: but it's bloody cold. [*Goes to fire.*]

MRS SLATTERY [*off*]: They're here, love. Shall I bring them up?

WENDY [*calling*]: Leave them down here, for God's sake, then.

JENNY [*off*]: It's all right ... I'm coming.

WENDY: Just look at the time! ... [*Calls*] Jenny! For God's sake!

JENNY [*off*]: I'm coming ... [*Call: shriek, off*]

MRS SLATTERY: Bare foot: you see. [*Coming in.*]

WENDY: Serves her right. Has Arthur gone?

BRENDA [*coming in*]: That's right.

WENDY: And never said good-bye ...

BRENDA [*entering*]: Don't look at me. [*She is carrying in a tray: steam rises from a tureen of porridge.*]

JENNY [*bursting in*]: The only reason they were down here ... is because somebody used them to go out last night ...

MRS SLATTERY: That was me, I'm afraid, this morning, love ... Your father wasn't well enough to go out to the sheds.

JENNY: He's well enough now. He's stomping about upstairs ... Is that for me? Oh, jolly d! [*Sits at table.*]

[BRENDA *is serving porridge into bowls.*]

Coffee? Tea?

BRENDA: Both.

JENNY: Oh, I say, then. Jolly good ... Is that my bowl or Mother's, love?

357

MRS SLATTERY: I won't have any, love ... I'll have some later.

SLATTERY [*entering*]: Hello, hello, hello, what's this? Bloody bre'kfast over, is it? afore the maister of the house has had a chance to eat.

BRENDA: Yours is here. It's out and ready.

SLATTERY: By God. Smells bloody good does that ... [*To* MRS SLATTERY] Aren't' a sitting down, then, lass?

[*Waits.*] Nay, I'll not sit down till thy has, love.

MRS SLATTERY: Oh ... Well.

[SLATTERY *holds her chair: she sits.*]

SLATTERY: Arthur's not come down, then, has he?

MRS SLATTERY: He's gone already ...

SLATTERY: Aye, well ... A journey before midday, tha knows, is best.

WENDY: What does that mean?

SLATTERY: Tha mun ask Brenda ... Like 'Sleep before midnight gives deepest rest ...' Wrote that on me bedroom wall ...

[*They laugh.*]

Thy not eating, Mother, then?

[MRS SLATTERY *waits, seated.*]

I'll not bloody start, tha knows, till thy starts, love.

[*They wait.*

MRS SLATTERY *draws a bowl towards her.*

Finally BRENDA *herself sits down.*]

Right, then ... a drop for your mother, Brenda ... let's mek a start ...

[*There's a tap at the room door.*

ALBERT *puts his head round.*]

ALBERT: Hello ...

SLATTERY: Good God.

ALBERT: I've been knocking at the door ... the front door, you see ... I found it open ... I couldn't get an answer at the back.

SLATTERY: Nay, come in, then, lad. Come in ... I've never seen you before, then, have I? ... that doesn't matter much in this house, I can tell you ... Come in. Come in. Tek off your coat.

ALBERT [*to* BRENDA, *who has risen*]: I thought I'd just come up, you see.

BRENDA: This is Albert, Dad ... Albert ... this is my father ... my mother ... Wendy. Jenny.

SLATTERY: 'Ow do, lad. Have a bowl. Come on. Sithee. Pull up a chair ... Brenda: get us a bloody cup, then, lass ... Don't freeten him to bloody death ...

[MRS SLATTERY, *however, has got up.*]

MRS SLATTERY: I'll get one. [*Goes.*]

SLATTERY: What's his name again?

BRENDA: Albert.

SLATTERY: Albert ... Thy's a friend of Brenda's, then?

ALBERT: Sort of ... Well. Yes.

SLATTERY: Thy work round here, then, d'ost'a?

ALBERT: Yes ...

BRENDA: In town.

SLATTERY: In town ... By God. A bloody big place is that ... Tea?

ALBERT: Well, then ... Thanks. [*Sits on chair pulled out for him by* BRENDA.]

[MRS SLATTERY *comes back, with an extra bowl and cup.*]

SLATTERY: Sithee, then. Here's bowl o' bloody porridge ... e't it up ... Put a bit o' bloody muscle on will that ... these bloody town lads ... don't know what a spot o' work is till they come out here ... Art'a set, then, lad? ... [*To others*] All ready? ... 'For what we are about to receive may the good Lord make us truly thankful ... for Jesus Christ's sake ...'

WENDY: Amen.

SLATTERY: Amen ... when I say three ... nay, bloody hell ... they've bloody well begun already ... Reet ... one, two, three, then, lad ... we're off!

[*Laughter: they start eating.*
Steam rises from the table.
Light slowly fades.]

MORE ABOUT PENGUINS
AND PELICANS

DAVID STOREY IN PENGUIN PLAYS

Home/The Changing Room/Mother's Day

Home

'As a view of crippled lives and wintry tenderness between them, the play is beautifully spare and sustained in tone' – Ronald Bryden in the *Observer*

The Changing Room

'Behind the ribbing, and the swearing, and the showing off, the piece is permeated by a Wordsworthian spirit. You can, if you listen, hear through it "the still, sad music of humanity"' – Harold Hobson in the *Sunday Times*

Mother's Day

'Mr Storey's farcical invention is tireless, and has the advantage of unlimited permissiveness' – *Financial Times*

Early Days/Sisters/Life Class

Early Days

'It has the insidious simplicity of a piano piece by Satie or a Wordsworth lyrical ballad . . . it touches deep chords' – Michael Billington in the *Guardian*

Sisters

'Deals in betrayal, love and finally, madness . . . A remarkable, stimulating, and unsettling gem of a play' – Gerard Dempsey in the *Daily Express*

Life Class

'Art itself may have moved into happenings some years ago; but, to my knowledge, this is the stage's first tribute of that event, and we are not likely to see it bettered' – Irving Wardle in *The Times*

DAVID STOREY IN PENGUINS

This Sporting Life
Winner of the Macmillan Fiction Award and the
United States Fiction Award

Players, backers, Saturday crowds, bloody noses and broken teeth, communal baths and landladies – here is the world of professional Rugby Football in a tough, northern industrial city. And as Arthur Machin discovers, it is a physical life, fouled by grime, sweat, intrigue and naked ambition, allowing for little sentimentality.

Internationally acclaimed, the subject of a powerful film by Lindsay Anderson, David Storey's brilliant first novel is the work of 'one of the finest English writers of his generation' – *The Times*

Flight into Camden
David Storey was awarded the John Llewelyn Rhys Memorial Prize, and the Somerset Maugham Award for his second novel, *Flight into Camden*.

This moving story is recounted by Margaret, the daughter of a Yorkshire miner, who falls in love with a married teacher and goes to live with him in a room in Camden Town, London.

'A love story written with seriousness, sensibility, and intensity' – *Observer*

Radcliffe
The story of a passionate relationship between two men and its tragic and terrible consequences.

'It tears viciously at you one moment and sets you shivering the next', commented the *Observer*. 'A brainstorm of a book; it boils in the mind long after it is done', wrote the *Sunday Times*. 'Comparable with another classic rooted in Yorkshire, *Wuthering Heights*', said *The Times Higher Educational Supplement*, whilst the *Daily Telegraph* paid tribute to 'an astonishing achievement', adding that *Radcliffe* established David Storey as 'the leading novelist of his generation'.

DAVID STOREY IN PENGUINS

Pasmore

A young university lecturer is in the grip of a nervous breakdown, struggling to resolve a disintegrating marriage in a chaotic and meaningless world.

'Swift clean and painful ... as good as anything he has done' – Michael Ratcliffe in *The Times*

A Temporary Life

Colin Freestone, ex-professional boxer, has forsaken the Noble Art to teach Fine Art in a provincial town. Remote at first from the threatening atmosphere of greed and pretension, he later becomes drawn into violent confrontation, battling against the forces of modern evil like a legendary knight, but without the shining armour.

'Brilliant, always intelligent and absorbing. Storey's command both of pathos and of comedy is increasingly sure ... Few novelists now writing see so vividly, think so intelligently, command so much sheer understanding of people and society' – *The Times Literary Supplement*

Saville
Winner of the 1976 Booker Prize

'One of the finest and truest novelists of his generation' – *The Times*

The passionate conviction and almost physical impact of *Saville* confirm David Storey as the outstanding writer of his time. The novel is an overwhelming and evocative saga of a Yorkshire mining family – at its centre, Saville, a boy whose growing-up in the forties and fifties forges a powerful conflict in his nature and a destructive resistance to his environment.

MICHAEL HASTINGS IN PENGUIN PLAYS

Three Plays

Gloo Joo
Winner of the *Evening Standard* Best Comedy Award

'Michael Hastings has produced two giant dramatic creations: the unspeakable Idi Amin in *For the West* (*Uganda*), and now in *Gloo Joo* a satisfying comic counterpart – Meadowlark Rachel Warner. Man, did it satisfy ma soul!' – *Time Out*

Full Frontal

'Full of measured innocence, sarcasm and spleen – funny and moving' – *Gay News*

For the West (*Uganda*)

'Tough, gripping, puzzling ... I have a sneaking suspicion that it's a great play' – *Punch*

Carnival War/Midnite at the Starlite

Carnival War

Set at the Notting Hill Carnival, this unnerving and savage farce has been acclaimed as 'the best English costume farce since Joe Orton's *What the Butler Saw* ... Hastings has written a comedy more complex than his successful *Gloo Joo* and, in its stunningly evocative and physical climax, much more daring' – Michael Coveney in the *Financial Times*

Midnite at the Starlite

'Has something of the tempo of the quick-quick-slow rhythm of the foxtrot. It is an exhilarating spin through the tinsel and tears of competitive ballroom dancing' – *Daily Express*

HUGH LEONARD IN PENGUIN PLAYS

Da/A Life/Time Was

Da

'A beguiling play about a son's need to come to terms with his father and himself ... in a class with the best of Sean O'Casey' – *The New York Times*

A Life

'Even better than its famous predecessor (*Da*): as human and funny, but richer in texture and even more cannily aware of the sad complexity of life' – *Daily Telegraph*

Time Was

'Proves once again that he's Ireland's funniest playwright ... snappy, witty, polished ... Leonard's observations on Dublin suburbia are acidly accurate' – *Sunday Press* (Dublin)

Also by Hugh Leonard in Penguins

Home Before Night

A delightful evocation of his Dublin childhood in the thirties and forties, Hugh Leonard's autobiography is like an Irish *Cider With Rosie* – crammed with people and conversations, rich in poetry, full of love, laughter and rare pleasures.

'Entrancing ... the playwright author's gift of language and apparently total recall make his account of growing up in the thirties and forties absolutely irresistible' – *Sunday Telegraph*

'Impossible to put down ... a brilliant, multi-faceted gem' – *Hibernia*

'An unqualified delight ... (he has) a marvellous eye for character, the ability to weave show-stopping funny stories into larger narrative, and to recreate the past with the sensuous immediacy of childhood' – Irving Wardle in *Books and Bookmen*

'Superb ... moving and very funny' – William Trevor

PETER SHAFFER IN PENGUIN PLAYS

Amadeus

Winner of the *Evening Standard* Drama Award as best play of 1979, and of the *Plays and Players'* London Theatre Critics Award

'*Amadeus* may be a play inspired by music and death, but it fills the theatre with that mocking, heavenly silence that is the overwhelming terror of life' – *The New York Times*

'A marvellously engrossing and often amusing comic thriller, a feast for the eye and the ear ...' – Steve Grant in the *Observer*

The Royal Hunt of the Sun

'One writer who manages to get right to the edge of experience ... He manages to evoke the gods' – Colin Blakely

'This tremendous, this admirable, this profound, this enduring play' – Bernard Levin

Three Plays

Equus

'Sensationally good' – Michael Billington in the *Guardian*

Shrivings

'A brilliant and deeply significant modern play' – *The Times*

Five Finger Exercise

'Peter Shaffer is one of our major playwrights, of a kind we need badly' – Eric Keown

Four Plays

The Private Ear/The Public Eye

'Pure comedy that is fresh and delightful ... suddenly and immensely touching' – *Punch*

White Liars

Proves him 'a master of his art' – Harold Hobson

Black Comedy

'An uproarious farce ... being written by Mr Shaffer it also has, over and above the demands of farce, wit and sophistication' – Bernard Levin